THE
AMERICAN
WOMAN

2001–2002

D0879700

Edited by Cynthia B. Costello and Anne J. Stone

for the Women's Research & Education Institute

With an introduction by Jean Stapleton

W. W. NORTON & COMPANY

NEW YORK / LONDON

THE
AMERICAN
WOMAN

2001–2002

GETTING TO THE TOP

The text of this book is composed in Bembo with the display set in Centaur
Composition by Allentown Digital Services Division of R.R. Donnelley & Sons Company
Manufacturing by Haddon Craftsmen, Inc.

ISBN 0-393-32142-8 (pbk.)

W. W. Norton & Company, Inc. 500 Fifth Avenue, New York, N.Y. 10110
www.wwnorton.com

W. W. Norton & Company Ltd., 10 Coptic Street, London WC1A 1PU

1 2 3 4 5 6 7 8 9 0

The editors dedicate this book
to Betty Parsons Dooley
without whom
The American Woman *would not exist*

CONTENTS

WOMEN IN CONGRESS

LIST OF TABLES AND FIGURES

American Women Today: A Statistical Portrait

SECTION 1   Demographics

ACKNOWLEDGMENTS

THIS EIGHTH EDITION of *The American Woman*, like the first seven, has been made possible by the Ford Foundation and many others who have provided generous financial or in-kind support to the Women's Research and Education Institute (WREI) and its work.

We are deeply grateful to the Ford Foundation for its substantial assistance to the *American Woman* project since its inception in 1986 and to the individuals at the Foundation whose confidence in WREI and the book has supported and inspired our efforts. Helen Neuborne, Janice Petrovich, and Barbara Phillips Sullivan, in particular, have earned our gratitude for their help and good counsel. Alison Bernstein, too, deserves special thanks for her encouragement over the years.

The Revson Foundation has helped fund several editions of *The American Woman*, including this one, and we are grateful to Eli Evans and Lisa Goldberg for their interest and generosity.

We wish also to express our gratitude to the scores of other individuals, companies, labor unions, and foundations without whose generosity WREI would not have been in a position to prepare *Getting to the Top*. They include Aeltus Investment Management; Akin, Gump, Strauss, Hauer & Feld; Amalgamated Bank; American Express Company; American Income Life Insurance; American Management Systems; the American Postal Workers Union; Associated Actors & Artistes of America; the Association of Flight Attendants; AT&T; Avon Products, Inc.; The Boeing Company; Chemical Manufacturers Association; Chlorine Chemistry Council; Citicorp Foundation; The Communications Workers of America; DC Comics; Esther Coopersmith; the DaimlerChrysler Corporation Fund; Elisebeth Driscoll; Evy Dubrow/UNITE!; Elizabeth and Robert Ehrenfeld; Fannie Mae;

Denise Gwyn Ferguson; the Geon Company; Greenberg Traurig; Hoechst Marion Roussel; IBM; the International Association of Machinists and Aerospace Workers; Johnson & Johnson; Juanita Kreps; the Lear Family Foundation; Lockheed Martin; Merck & Company; Philip Morris Companies, Inc.; Motorola; Northeast Utilities Services Company; Pfizer, Inc.; J.C. Penney Company, Inc.; Ryder System, Inc.; Sara Lee Corporation; Schroder Capital Management; Jean Stapleton; Time Warner, Inc.; the United Auto Workers; and United Technologies.

Many of the individual donors to WREI are members of WREI's board of directors and, indeed, the board has offered extensive practical help as well as continuing encouragement for *The American Woman*. Board chair Jean Stapleton has found opportunities to plug every edition in the series from platforms in cities and towns across this country. JoAnn Heffernan Heisen and Barbara Easterling have promoted *The American Woman* enthusiastically in the corporate and labor communities. WREI's staff is grateful to the entire board for its enthusiastic support of our efforts.

My hat is off to Brigid O'Farrell, Cynthia Harrison, Lesley Primmer Persily, and Sara Rix of our *American Woman* advisory committee. They were generous and creative with ideas as well as wisdom and expertise, as was Shari Miles, then WREI's executive director, who played a key role in helping us settle on the focus of this edition. Thanks, too, to Marjorie Lightman for her good counsel.

Many people at the Bureau of Labor Statistics, the Bureau of the Census, and other government agencies helped us track down key statistics. Howard Hayghe, who has assisted with every edition of *The American Woman,* and Steven Hipple, both of the Bureau of Labor Statistics, deserve our particular thanks for providing, or guiding us to, a wide range of useful data on women in the workforce.

Gilda Morales of the Center for American Women and Politics and Marjorie Connelly of the *New York Times* furnished invaluable information for the section on elections and officials. Cynthia Hall and Mary Ann Leary of Women's Policy Inc. were generous with information and expertise. Sarah Orrick's writing and editorial assistance have been indispensable. Our editors at W. W. Norton, most recently Patricia Chui, have shepherded us down publishing's pathways.

Every member of WREI's staff played a role in realizing WREI's latest volume. The editorial team, consisting of Cynthia Costello (formerly WREI's research director) and Anne Stone with Vanessa Wight, devoted most of its time for many months to the planning, shaping, and physical preparation of the eighth edition. Jennifer Griffith (now on Senator Olympia Snowe's legislative staff) laid the groundwork for the statistical section. Lory

Manning compiled and analyzed the statistics on military women. Brigid O'Farrell provided expert advice and analysis in connection with statistics about women in nontraditional jobs. Adrienne Starr, working with intern Hope Wedderburn, proofread many statistics. Anne Kuh saw to it that WREI's financial obligations for the book were handled expeditiously.

Ensuring that WREI remained in a position to meet those financial obligations was the responsibility of Betty Dooley, my predecessor as WREI's president. There would be no *American Woman* series without Betty's unwavering confidence in WREI's ability to produce it, her steadfast determination to raise the funds to support it, and her continued success in that endeavor.

I want to stress that our funders, board members, and advisors are not responsible for any errors or misstatements that may be contained herein. Nor should the opinions expressed in any part of the book be ascribed to anyone other than the person who wrote them.

WREI and I acknowledge with warm regard these individuals and organizations who helped us in *Getting to the Top*.

SUSAN SCANLAN
President
Women's Research & Education Institute

THE AMERICAN WOMAN: GETTING TO THE TOP

INTRODUCTION

Jean Stapleton

TODAY, FEMALE EXECUTIVES and leaders may be found in a wide range of industries and institutions—including those that traditionally have been closed to women. Twenty-five years ago, who would have thought that a woman—Madeleine Albright—would be appointed to serve as Secretary of State? Or that Carleton Fiorina, also a woman, would rise to the position of CEO at the giant Hewlett-Packard Company?

As we begin a new century, we can proudly point to the many prominent women who are exercising their leadership at the helm of America's public and private institutions. Indeed, these leaders are showing us that women can—and will—crack the glass ceiling and make their way to "the top."

And yet, women have by no means achieved leadership parity with men. When we look at the numbers, it is clear that women still make up only a small percentage of America's leaders. Women who do make it to the top are often keenly aware of their outsider status in a world that is still led primarily by men—and white men at that. This is especially true for women of color, who are woefully underrepresented in leadership positions.

For the women who do make it to the top, what explains their success? What barriers do they encounter along the way? Do women of color have different experiences from white women as they strive to obtain positions of leadership? Do successful women primarily "fit in" to the organizations they lead—or do they bring a unique perspective that makes a difference in their leadership style and priorities? And finally, can we expect continued progress so that sometime in the first century of the new millennium, women and men leaders will be found in equal numbers? Or will some of the same barriers remain, limiting women's options?

This eighth edition of *The American Woman* explores these questions by taking a look at women's leadership in politics, higher education, business, trade unions, and the military. Our book begins with an interview with JoAnn Heffernan Heisen, Worldwide Vice President and Chief Information Officer of Johnson & Johnson and the highest-ranking woman in that company. A member of the board of the Women's Research and Education Institute (WREI), Ms. Heisen exemplifies the success stories we celebrate here.

Following this interview are five chapters by prominent women who guide us through the complex story of women's leadership in American society. A detailed statistical portrait of American women comes next, providing the hard numbers that describe women's status with respect to education, health, employment, income, and the like. Our book concludes with a section on women in Congress—including an essay by Lesley Primmer Persily, former president of Women's Policy Inc.—on the accomplishments of the Congressional Caucus for Women's Issues in the 105th Congress, and brief biographies prepared by WREI of all the women in the 106th Congress.

WOMEN IN LEADERSHIP

In our first chapter, Ruth Mandel, executive director of the Eagleton Center for Politics at Rutgers University, documents the remarkable progress women made during the late twentieth century in moving into political leadership.

Since 1979, women's representation in elective office in Congress has increased fourfold, from three to 12 percent. In the 106th Congress—the last of the twentieth century and the first of the twenty-first—56 women serve in the House of Representatives; eighteen are women of color. At the state level, women's representation in statewide elective offices has more than doubled—from 11 to 27 percent since 1979.

Despite women's breakthroughs, we still have a long way to go. The fact remains that the higher the office, the smaller the number of women. In 1999, there were still only nine women among the 100 members of the U.S. Senate and three women among the 50 governors. At the municipal level, there were only 16 women among the mayors of the 100 largest cities and only two were women of color.

In our second chapter, Mariam Chamberlain, founding president of the National Council for Research on Women, explores women's progress in achieving leadership positions in higher education. Over the last several decades, women have made significant gains in academic leadership. In 1999, there were 480 women college and university presidents in the United States, 16 percent of whom were women of color. Several of the women head institutions that are among the most prestigious in the nation. Still, women make up only 16 percent of college and university presidents.

Why so few? Candidates drawn from the senior faculty usually fill academic leadership positions. Although many more women earn doctoral degrees than was the case 25 years ago, fewer than one in five full professors today is a woman. This limits the pipeline of female candidates for executive academic jobs.

Our third chapter documents women's significant inroads into executive suites and corporate boardrooms in recent years—and the obstacles that remain. The chapter is written by two top executives at Catalyst, a New York–based organization that tracks women's leadership in business: Sheila Wellington, president, and Katherine Giscombe, director of research and advisory services.

As the chapter explains, women now hold about 12 percent of corporate officer positions—up from less than nine percent in 1995. And for the first time, over half of Fortune 500 companies have more than one woman officer. Still, women have not come as far as one would expect in corporate America, given their work experience and academic achievements. The fact that there are only four female CEOs of Fortune 500 companies underscores how far women have yet to go.

The authors tell us that women of color face many of the same barriers to corporate advancement as white women do. But minority women experience the double stigma of being both female and nonwhite in a corporate world dominated by white men. The overwhelming majority of women who hold management or administrative positions in business are white. And women of color are promoted more slowly than white women are, prolonging their climb up the corporate ladder.

In our fourth chapter, Lois Gray, professor emeritus of labor-management relations at the New York State School of Industrial and Labor Relations, explores women's leadership in organized labor. Not surprisingly, more women labor leaders are found in unions representing workers in occupations where women predominate—such as nursing, education, and public-sector clerical and administrative work. Still, women hold the top leadership positions in only three national unions: the American Federation of Teachers, the American Nurses Association, and the Association of Flight Attendants. The number of women at this level has not changed in the past twenty years.

The good news is that, overall, women's leadership in national unions affiliated with the AFL-CIO has been on an upward trend. President John Sweeney's appointment of Linda Chávez-Thompson as executive vice president of the AFL-CIO was an important breakthrough—the first time that a woman, and a Latina, had risen to the highest levels of leadership in the labor movement.

In recent years, there has been an increase in the number of women serving as national union vice presidents, secretary-treasurers, and executive board members. And the number of women assuming leadership roles in local unions and federations is increasing, a positive development since this is the pool from which national leaders are drawn.

The final chapter, written by Judith Youngman, an associate professor of political science at the U.S. Coast Guard Academy, examines women's leadership experience in probably the most tradition-laden sector of our society—the military. The replacement of the draft with an all-volunteer force in 1973 brought many more women into the armed services. Since 1972, the percentage of enlisted women has grown almost ninefold, and the percentage of women officers has more than tripled.

As women have gained experience and longevity in new career fields, they have assumed new leadership positions in all the services. For example, women officers in the Air Force have commanded the space shuttle and served as fighter pilots and fighter test pilots. Women aviators in the Navy flew combat missions in Operation Desert Fox. And in 1996 Vice Admiral Patricia Tracey was appointed Assistant Secretary of Defense for Military Personnel Policy and became the first woman to achieve three-star rank in any of the armed forces.

Women leaders in the military today, both commissioned and noncommissioned officers, are often more visible and assume greater responsibility for people and assets than their civilian counterparts—and at a younger age. But they still face constraints on their leadership not experienced by women in other sectors. Government policies restrict women's access to combat positions. This bars women from the central functions of the military and impedes their advancement.

WHAT ACCOUNTS FOR WOMEN'S SUCCESS?

Women who make it to the top are, in many respects, no different from the men who succeed: they work hard, perform beyond expectations, make themselves visible to top management, and show a willingness to take risks and act boldly.

And yet, our authors tell us, women must often do more than their male counterparts to gain recognition. One way women get noticed is by taking on "stretch" assignments—difficult tasks that others may shy away from. In a corporation or labor union, this may take the form of volunteering for a challenging project that is important to top management, but that no one else wants to do. In the military, this may mean accepting an assignment for a hardship tour in a remote location that others try to avoid.

Many women leaders attribute their success, in part, to having learned to play the "male game." To make it in a male world, a woman must "fit in." This is as true in the halls of Congress as it is in the executive boardroom, the leadership circles of organized labor, the ivory towers of academia, and the officer ranks of the armed services. Across these varied sectors, ambitious women strive to keep their personal lives separate from work, to demonstrate their organizational loyalty, and to make sure that they do not rock the boat.

Acquiring unique skills and expertise is also a plus for women aspiring to top positions. In the world of politics, skills are typically learned on the job: women politicians, like their male counterparts, often start out in local elected positions, where they hone their skills in campaigning, issue management, and political brokering.

In business, an MBA can be just the ticket a woman needs to increase her credibility with top management as well as colleagues. An advanced degree typically is a prerequisite for promotion in higher education. In the armed services, women's selection for advanced military training programs can enhance their careers. And for trade union women, attendance at labor summer schools can provide important skills that boost their leadership prospects.

Networks can be crucial to women's success. As JoAnn Heffernan Heisen points out in her interview, men have access to natural networks in organizations. A promising male employee is likely to be integrated into the network of powerful men. This is not necessarily so with women. For women to succeed, they often must *create* their own networks, either within the workplace or outside of it in associations or coalitions of like-minded women.

Finding a mentor is one of the keys to moving up in any organization. Many women leaders have relied on male mentors to provide them with advice and encouragement. Still, in the male-dominated environments described here, women often have difficulty finding mentors and gaining the inside knowledge that mentors can provide.

Developing a relationship with a mentor can be an even greater challenge for women of color. When a CEO or vice president is grooming a manager for promotion, he (and it is usually he) will often choose someone who is not only of the same gender but also of the same race or ethnic background.

He does this not because he is trying to exclude women and minorities, but because most of us—to some degree—gravitate toward those who are "like us."

A strong commitment from top management can make the difference between a culture that encourages women's advancement and one that does not. The proactive approach taken by Lewis E. Platt when he headed Hewlett-Packard demonstrates just how effective support from the top can be. Having found himself abruptly thrust into the role of single parent by the death of his first wife, Mr. Platt—then a general manager at Hewlett-Packard—developed a sharp appreciation for the difficulties faced by working women. When he later became CEO of the company, Platt made work-family policies a priority. This paid off in dramatically increased retention rates for management women.

Another example is found in the labor movement: the election of John Sweeney to the helm of the AFL-CIO brought positive changes as women were appointed to head half of all the departments at AFL-CIO headquarters. When the head of an organization demonstrates a real and visible commitment to advancing able women and minorities, others in the organization can have no doubt that doing so will be looked on with approval—and women and minorities can see that they have a serious chance to climb the leadership ladder.

POLITICAL AND PUBLIC-POLICY DEVELOPMENTS

A number of political changes have occurred in the last thirty years that have enhanced women's leadership prospects. In the world of politics, it is women's voting power that has made a difference. Since 1980, women have outvoted men in every national election. Supporting female candidates is one of the ways that women have used their power at the ballot box.

Public policy has also played an important role in expanding women's leadership prospects. Today, it is hard to believe that, before 1963, it was entirely legal to discriminate against women in employment. This all began to change with the Equal Pay Act of 1963 (guaranteeing equal pay for equal work) and Title VII of the Civil Rights Act of 1964 (prohibiting discrimination on the basis of race, color, religion, or sex). Federal statutes followed requiring that federal contractors establish affirmative action plans to ensure equal treatment of all employees, including women.

Of course, the civil rights movement and the women's movement played an important role in the policy changes that took place over the decades of the sixties and seventies. Without the push from advocates, it is unlikely that equal opportunity and affirmative action laws would have been passed.

We think that our authors would agree that government policy has made a difference, opening doors formerly closed to women and persons of color and supporting their career advancement. Yet it is not clear whether affirmative action has been as effective as it could have been.

One reason, according to the women of color interviewed by Catalyst, is that many corporations have not put much muscle behind their affirmative action programs. Another problem is that affirmative action and equal opportunity laws have sparked a backlash. A stigma has been associated with women and minorities—so that too often it is assumed that an individual achieved his or her position because of "government interference" rather than merit or talent.

One promising development in recent years has been the introduction of diversity programs designed to identify and groom women and minority employees with high potential. Initially, employers instituted these programs to aid compliance with government requirements. The strongest programs have set numerical targets for the representation of women and minorities—and held managers accountable for achieving them. Yet some women question the success of diversity programs and wonder how serious companies have been about career advancement for women and minorities.

One reason for the limited success of diversity initiatives may be timing. Most large companies—even the growing number that now provide structured career development programs to promote diversity—did not offer these opportunities 10, 20, or 30 years ago. Many of the women in leadership positions today got there without the benefit of corporate support.

Many of the legal and policy changes affecting women's advancement occurred in the sixties and seventies. Perhaps a good part of the progress we see today is the result of the passage of time and increased educational opportunities and career possibilities for able women. The women who entered law and business schools in the 1970s and early 1980s, for example, are now in their forties and fifties—the age when the career rewards for talent and hard work are likely to be greatest.

In the military, too, it takes 20 to 25 years to reach the senior ranks, whether officer or enlisted, and we are now seeing generals' stars and sergeant majors' stripes on women who entered the military after the early 1970s when career opportunities for women in the services increased. Clearly, at least some of the talented women who get in the pipeline and stay in it are likely to be rewarded.

WHAT BARRIERS REMAIN?

Yes, women's success to date is certainly partly the result of the passage of time. However, the authors in this volume remind us that barriers to women's leadership are not simply a relic of the past—they are still with us. Some of the obstacles women face stem from their family responsibilities. Others are cultural and, in the case of military women, the result of government restrictions.

For the most part, the care of children and the running of households remain in women's hands. Like women in lower-level positions, most women in leadership positions must juggle work and family—although the salaries that come with high positions certainly help. For the most part, executive women do not believe that family-friendly policies—such as flextime, parental leave, telecommuting, and part-time work—are for them. In fact, women with leadership ambition recognize that their success depends upon keeping family and work commitments separate.

It is difficult to read these chapters and not conclude that culture—the assumptions and stereotypes about women and men—continues to play a pernicious role in holding women back. For example, our Catalyst authors tell us that stereotyping of women's abilities excludes them from consideration for important "line" management jobs. This has serious consequences. To reach the upper echelons of the corporation, an individual must manage products, services, clients, or customers—in short, the "business of the business."

Women are still found predominantly on the "soft" side of the corporation as directors of human resources, communications, and government affairs departments. It can be quite difficult for women to move into the central operations of the company, partly because upper management assumes that men are better suited for these jobs. This has to change if more women are going to find their way to the executive suite.

It is perhaps in the armed services that women face the greatest constraints on their leadership. As Dr. Youngman reminds us, the ideal military leader is defined as masculine, not just male. Masculine strengths are valued; feminine strengths are devalued.

These cultural ideals underlie the Department of Defense policies that prohibit women from serving in units whose primary mission is direct ground combat. Since the combat mission is the military equivalent of "the business of the business," serving in such units is fundamental in the career tracks most likely to lead to key leadership positions in the Army and Marine Corps.

As a result, women's opportunities to reach the top in these services are severely limited.

Are we to conclude that our authors see evidence of a glass ceiling at work? Yes, they do. The term *glass ceiling* was coined some years ago to describe the experience of women who found that their advancement ceased at the middle management level, beyond which opportunities were limited or nonexistent. Certainly the progress women have made into leadership positions suggests a softening of the barriers that held them back in the past. But my reading of the chapters suggests that a ceiling still exists—perhaps not as impenetrable as before, but formidable nonetheless.

ARE WOMEN LEADERS DIFFERENT FROM MEN?

Many books and articles have examined whether women lead differently from men. Some argue that to succeed as executives, women must emulate the style of men. Others maintain that women bring a more open, democratic, and "people-centered" approach to their leadership positions.

The picture of women's leadership styles presented here is mixed. In the political, business, and trade union arenas, our authors see evidence that women do bring a more inclusive and participatory approach to leadership. This does not appear to be the case in the military and academia, according to our authors.

Perhaps it is too soon to draw conclusions about women's leadership styles. We are a long way from seeing women leaders in equal numbers to men. When women do reach a critical mass at the top, then it may be possible to identify a distinctive leadership approach.

But it is important not to make broad generalizations about how women lead. As with men, women leaders are a varied group. Women can be authoritarian and men can be democratic. And if the institution is a rigidly hierarchical one, such as the U.S. military, large numbers of women in positions of power might not make much difference in the culture.

However, the chapters in this volume do show that women leaders can have somewhat different priorities from men. It is not uncommon for elected women to develop a shared agenda, sometimes across party lines, on issues arising from their roles as caregivers. In trade unions, women leaders have helped to broaden organized labor's priorities to include child care, family leave, and pay equity—issues of great importance to working women. In academia, too, female trustees have demonstrated a greater concern for diversity and quality-of-life issues than their male counterparts. As the number of women in leadership positions increases, we may see a more profound shift toward quality-of-life issues in American institutions—to everyone's advantage!

There is little question in my mind that the increasing presence of women in leadership has the potential to strengthen our nation's democracy. Certainly a cornerstone of our democracy is equality of opportunity for girls and boys, women and men, and individuals of different racial and ethnic backgrounds. The presence of women leaders can inspire girls and young women to pursue their dreams. It is also important that boys grow accustomed to both male and female leaders—and that they grow into men who are comfortable working side by side with women in high positions.

WHAT DOES THE FUTURE HOLD?

The authors of this volume are, for the most part, optimistic about the future. I share Ruth Mandel's belief that it is only a matter of time before this country will elect a woman vice president and president. I also believe that the new millennium will bring many more women to top posts in business, academia, the labor movement—and yes, even the military.

Of course, women's continued progress to the top will not happen automatically. Preservation of the laws that have encouraged women's leadership must be a priority. In the military, removal of the remaining government restrictions on women's service would pave the way for women's advancement. In addition, organizations must be willing to nurture women leaders—grooming them for the same leadership positions as men. For their part, women must be willing to go beyond their "comfort zone"—to take risks and act boldly. On this last point, I have no doubt that women will continue—as they always have—to rise to the challenge!

At the Top: A Profile of JoAnn Heffernan Heisen

Cynthia B. Costello

JoAnn Heffernan Heisen is one of 10 officers who run Johnson & Johnson, one of the world's largest health care corporations with over 97,000 employees, approximately 190 operating companies in 51 countries, and worldwide sales of $27.5 billion in 1999. The highest-ranking woman at Johnson & Johnson, Ms. Heisen serves on the company's executive committee and as the Worldwide Vice President and Chief Information Officer (CIO).

Ms. Heisen joined Johnson & Johnson in 1989 as Assistant Treasurer and the company's first investor-relations officer. Over the last decade, she has steadily moved up the corporate ladder. She was named Vice President, Corporate Staff, in 1990, Treasurer in 1991, and Corporate Controller in 1995. She rose to the CIO and executive committee positions in January 1997.

Ms. Heisen has oversight responsibility for 2,500 information-management professionals working for the company's approximately 190 operating companies worldwide. She also provides guidance and strategy for $900 million in the information-management budget annually.

Several years back, Ms. Heisen started the Women's Leadership Initiative to accelerate career development opportunities, networking, and mentoring for women throughout the company. In 1996, Johnson & Johnson's Affirmative Action/Equal Opportunity Award went to Ms. Heisen.

Ms. Heisen is married and the mother of four, including twins: two sons, age eleven and fifteen, and two daughters, age ten and eleven. In addition to her roles at home and at Johnson & Johnson, she serves on the board of directors of the Vanguard Group and on the board of each of Vanguard's mutual funds. She is also on the boards of the Princeton Medical Center, the Maxwell School of Public Affairs at Syracuse University, and the Women's Research and Education Institute (WREI).

I interviewed Ms. Heisen in the fall of 1999.

JoAnn, what would you say are the major factors that have contributed to your success?

First of all, I acknowledge that I am a risk-taker. I'm willing to move outside my comfort zone and to find new challenges. I can look back at my experience at Chase Manhattan Bank, which I joined after college and assumed that I would one day retire from. One company, one career. But after five years with Chase, I had the opportunity to join a much smaller company as CFO [chief financial officer]. I decided to take the job because I had confidence in my ability to take on new tasks and to move outside my comfort zone.

Second, I am not afraid to work hard—I work extremely long hours. I am always conscious that I need to put in the time and effort to create the deliverable.

Third, I am thick-skinned. Women oftentimes want to be liked. Our style of management is such that we want to keep everybody happy. One of the things I have been able to do is develop a thick skin so that I don't go down with the first arrow that is slung at me. In any job, disagreement is part of a healthy exercise to get options out on the table. Women have to learn not to take dissenting views personally but rather to see them as other options to be considered. I try not to walk out of meetings with hurt feelings.

I often give the example of how girls and boys choose teammates. When girls choose members for their team, first they choose their best friend, then they choose the prettiest girl in the class, and then they choose the most popular girl—hoping that they will become best friends. Boys choose the biggest, strongest, meanest team members, and their decisions have little to do with friendship. When there is a job to do at the office, women need to choose individuals who can get the job done, not their friends. This is what men do and what women need to learn to do.

What would you say are the major barriers faced by women in corporate America?

One of the major barriers has been the old boys network. Men simply do not recognize that women often are excluded from the network. The mentoring that takes place through networking is critically important to the development of any leader. Along the way, people need senior managers and executives to provide advice and guidance. I feel lucky because I have had mentors along the way—and they have all been men.

The fact that women tend to work in staff positions rather than line positions is another barrier. As women entered the workplace in significant numbers during the 1960s and 1970s, most of them were hired into staff positions in departments such as human resources, public relations, and community affairs. They were not hired into the central line functions of sales, marketing, and operations.

Today, there is a huge bulge in the pipeline of women who are now in their forties and fifties and have spent their entire careers in staff positions. It is at this point that natural leaders become the president of a division or the chairman of the company. For the most part, women are not candidates for these positions because they have not been in line positions. There are, of course, many exceptions to the rule, but certainly it is true for the most part that women have been channeled into staff functions. But in the recent past, women have made terrific strides in moving into sales and marketing.

And finally, women's family responsibilities pose a major barrier. It is very difficult to be a working mother. Many women, particularly as they climb the corporate ladder, try to deny the difficulties, but I think it's important for the men we work with to understand that we really do have two major roles to play.

When I was in a junior position, I felt that I had no other choice but to downplay my family responsibilities. There was a time when I had babies who kept me up at night and threw up on my suit at 7:30 A.M. as I was walking out the door to work. The senior men did not want to hear these concerns. They wanted to know, "Did you get your report written last night?" Men who have small children themselves are painfully aware of the work-family issues, but they are fighting for their own careers. There is no question, however, that many women have a terribly difficult time balancing work and family.

I frequently address women's groups. I try to convey that it's okay to make different life choices. It's okay to stay home with your children for all or part of their growing-up years. It's okay to have a career. And it's okay to change your mind. The important thing for corporate America to remember is that we shouldn't exclude good women just because they made the decision to take a different path for a while.

What else do you tell women's groups?

First of all, no matter what job you do, do it well. You have to be successful at what you are currently doing before you can ask to move on to another job.

Second, you need to learn something about the business itself. All of us start out in entry-level positions, and most of us start out in departments rather than in corporate management. But it is very important for women to understand the big picture—where their corporation fits into the industry. Learn the company's products and understand the competitors.

Third, I would say, take risks. Women tend to think that if they are "good girls" and do their jobs extremely well, someone will recognize and promote them. The point is, women need to get outside their comfort zone and ask for their next job.

Men tend to say, "I have been in this job a year, where is my next job?" Women need to do the same. Women can get stuck by doing well in a function and spend many years in one job. Instead, they need to think, "Could I take these skills and transfer them into another job category? My people skills are terrific, could I go into sales?"

Fourth, women need to embrace change. The pace of change in technology and the corporate environment is accelerating. Companies are buying companies. Acquisitions are being made. Product lines are being spun off. The corporate life we know today may not be the same tomorrow. Corporations are downsizing, "right sizing," and restructuring. Women need to acknowledge that the corporate environment is changing and they need to be part of the change and part of the solution.

Fifth, women need to understand that they have a shared responsibility with their corporations for continued career growth and opportunities. They need to take responsibility for their own development, including keeping their skills current and getting the credentials they need. It is a shared responsibility and women need to be proactive participants. That's where networking is important.

The last point I would make is that you need to enjoy what you are doing. If you have a passion about what you are doing, you will willingly put in the time and effort. If you do not like what you are doing, move to another field or another company.

Could you describe the Women's Leadership Initiative at Johnson & Johnson?

When I first came to Johnson & Johnson in a corporate role, I looked around and did not see a lot of other women in senior positions at corporate headquarters. But I knew that there were a lot of women at Johnson & Johnson because of the nature of the business. I decided to organize networking dinners for women at the company. I had the opportunity in my position as treasurer to be able to reach out and invite very senior women from the company to speak at these dinners. These were women who were on the management boards of the different operating companies of Johnson & Johnson.

Many of the most senior women at Johnson & Johnson were like me.

They had come into the company in mid-career positions. Johnson & Johnson is a wonderful company, and one of the company's hallmarks is that it grows its own talent. The senior men had a natural network because they had been around for decades. Most of the women who had joined the company at mid-career were not a part of that network.

It was important for the women at Johnson & Johnson to have an opportunity to exchange ideas and to learn about the business. For these dinners, I brought in women speakers to talk about the company's newest acquisitions or newest product lines. The fact that the speakers were women reinforced the significant contribution that women were making to the company.

In 1994 I realized that, as a senior woman, I had a responsibility to continue to make women's leadership a "visible issue." Some of the women in the company conceived the idea of putting on a women's leadership conference. I thought this was a terrific idea. It was clear to me that the future of Johnson & Johnson, just as is the case with all companies, depended on good leadership. If there was a possibility that women's leadership might be overlooked, it was crucial to highlight what women could bring to the table.

In March 1995, we held a one-day conference to demonstrate that Johnson & Johnson valued women's leadership and women's leadership development. This conference, which brought together women from Johnson & Johnson's divisions around the country, was a tremendous success. This was the start of the Women's Leadership Initiative.

Through this initiative, we have continued to highlight the importance of developing women's leadership. As is the case at most companies, over the years, we have had a significant number of women at Johnson & Johnson in human resources, safety, and government relations—but not in line positions. There is now a greater openness about putting more women in sales, operations, etc. The men now acknowledge that we need to move women into line positions. In fact, we now have a significant number of women in line positions.

Johnson & Johnson has always been a terrific place for women to work. In the last several years, we have made tremendous progress. We now have women presidents leading six of the 25 operating companies in the United States. We have a half dozen women who are managing directors of our international operating companies. And we have one woman who is a company group chairman—this title is given to an individual who has many companies in a similar franchise or product line reporting to him or her.

Building on the success of the first conference, we recognized that Johnson & Johnson's many different operating companies could start their own women's leadership programs. We now have a dozen operating companies with ongoing programs to develop women's leadership through networking, communications, and other educational programs.

We are planning to have a series of women's leadership conferences in 2000. We have grown so significantly that there are now many more women in senior-level positions at Johnson & Johnson. We will therefore have three meetings organized by our group of operating companies, instead of one national conference.

What can companies do to encourage women's success?

Corporations should acknowledge that women need a network. Companies need to encourage women through leadership initiatives. Providing women with networking opportunities is good for women—and it is good for business. It sends a positive message to women who currently are working for a company, and it sends a positive message to women who might want to work for that company in the future.

What do you expect the future to look like for women in corporate America?

It is inevitable that in the next ten to fifteen years, senior management in major corporations will be evenly balanced between men and women. Women exhibit the leadership qualities that corporations will need in the new millennium. Women have a collaborative style. They have an inclusive style. Women naturally know how to multitask. Women can handle more than one program at a time and keep them in balance. Men tend to be more single-minded and single-focused.

My disappointment is that it probably will take another ten to fifteen years for this change to occur. However, each and every year we are making more progress. There is recognition that the U.S. economy is moving toward a knowledge and information economy—where women have an advantage because of their style of leadership.

Another element that bodes well for women leaders is the acknowledgement that women make the majority of consumer purchases. Women are the major purchasers of autos, home appliances, and other consumer goods—and they make most of the health care decisions in a family. Companies are recognizing that having women in leadership positions can improve their profitability.

I also think that as more and more women attain senior positions, and also have family responsibilities to deal with, they will serve as change agents in the culture of their corporations. Corporations increasingly will recognize that employees need support to balance their work and family responsibilities. Now, it is true that most family-friendly policies are not geared toward executive women but rather toward the average employee. Executive women must still work long hours to succeed—and for the most part they cannot take full advantage of family-friendly programs and policies.

When I entered the workforce in the early 1970s, I thought that corporate America would change in the next ten to fifteen years. But today, I am more realistic and recognize that radical changes do not take place in a short period of time. However, I do think that we will continue to make steady progress. Women will achieve parity with men, and this is going to happen soon. In just the last year, a woman was named CEO of a Fortune 50 company and there are dozens, if not hundreds, of women who now lead smaller corporations as well. Before we know it, women will be competing with other women for the very top positions—and that will be good!

Let's face it. We have to recognize that the changing demographics are changing the face of America and the face of corporate leadership. This is going to make our senior management much more diverse in terms of gender, race, and ethnicity—and that is definitely good for business!

ONE

WOMEN'S LEADERSHIP IN AMERICAN POLITICS: THE LEGACY AND THE PROMISE

Ruth B. Mandel

HIGHLIGHTS

SINCE OBTAINING THE RIGHT to vote in 1920, American women have slowly and incrementally made their way into the halls of government and elective office. In the past, their routes into politics were often through marriage or as an extension of their civic activities. In the late twentieth century, women have made remarkable progress, coming from many directions, in forcing open the gates of the American political system. In doing so, they have used their gender strengths to promote the causes they believe in and to forge a more collaborative, inclusive approach to debating issues and solving problems. Their legacy is the promise of a "regendered" public world, characterized by more diverse representation and shared political leadership.

- Over the last several decades, women have broken through the barriers to political office, increasing their representation overall from less than five percent in the early 1970s to over 20 percent at all but the federal level.
- By 1999, every state legislature in the country included at least a few women, with women representing 11 percent of leadership positions in state legislatures nationwide. In New Hampshire, they held the three top positions of governor, senate presidency, and house speakership. Yet there were only three women governors, and only sixteen women among the mayors of the country's 100 largest cities.
- In the 106th Congress, the last of the twentieth century, there were still only nine women among the 100 senators and 56 women among the 235 members of the House.
- While political women's ideological stances vary widely, their policy agendas and priorities often have come from their direct experience with do-

mestic concerns and the central role that children, family, and community play in their daily lives.

- In general, women's political leadership styles differ from those of men, with women favoring more participatory, collaborative modes of management and decisionmaking.

- When a man seeks office, gender is not an issue; but when women run for election, gender often *is* an issue. Political women have adopted different ways of coping with this reality—from attempting to separate themselves entirely from a gendered identity to making it central to their self-image and the policies they support.

- In the late 1970s and early 1980s, many political women sought to distance themselves from traditional "women's issues" (usually domestic social policy concerns) and to gain credibility in areas more often associated with male leadership, such as appropriations and finance. That was no longer necessary by the late 1990s. In the era when Madeleine Albright was appointed Secretary of State under President Clinton, women had achieved acceptance as leaders on a broad spectrum of issues, and social welfare concerns had become "winning issues" at the top of government and campaign agendas.

- It was not until 1964 (44 years after winning the vote) that women voted in equal numbers with men in national elections. Yet by the time another sixteen years had gone by, women's voting rates were exceeding those of men, and since 1980 women have outvoted men in every national election.

- Two remarkable twentieth-century first ladies, Eleanor Roosevelt and Hillary Rodham Clinton, broke the molds for political wives and women everywhere by using their positions as first ladies to establish their own legitimacy as leaders.

INTRODUCTION

Children born in the United States in the year 2000 will vote for women presidents. They will witness the celebration inaugurating the first woman popularly elected chief executive of the most powerful nation on earth. In their lifetimes, they will come to think it odd that it took their country— idealistically conceived as a land of freedom and equality, and brilliantly established to function as a democracy of checks and balances—well over two centuries to welcome the majority of its population to top political leadership positions. This injustice will appear as outlandish to future generations as denying women the right to vote at the turn of the last century seems to us today.

Twenty-first-century Americans will grow up accustomed to the idea of women in roles of public power. In this new world, women will hold government office at every level and in every branch of government—from city councilperson to member of Congress, from school board member to federal cabinet secretary, and from justice of the peace to chief justice of the U.S. Supreme Court. While decades will pass before gender parity is fully achieved in elected and appointed offices, women's steady, incremental progress in politics witnessed in the last quarter of the twentieth century will continue.

Since 1979, women's representation in elective office in Congress has increased from three to 12 percent—and at the state level, women's representation in statewide elective offices has increased from 11 to 27 percent, although there were wide variations among the states. By 1999, every state legislature in the nation included at least a few women, with Washington State, where women occupied 41 percent of legislative seats, holding first place. Also in 1999, Arizona made news by becoming the first state to elect women to its top five statewide constitutional offices, including governor.

In addition to building a presence in sheer numbers, elected women began to acquire formal leadership positions within governmental institutions. Although men kept a lock on the top positions in both houses of Congress (see Table I-1), by 1999, women had acquired 11 percent of leadership positions in state legislatures nationwide, including six senate presidencies and four state house speakerships, as well as a number of majority and minority party leadership positions (see Table I-2). In New Hampshire, by late 1999, women held the governorship, the senate presidency, and the house speakership—the state's top three leadership positions.

Notwithstanding historic breakthroughs for political women in virtually all positions (save the nation's top two elective spots and several federal cabinet posts), the pattern of growing empowerment reveals that the higher the office, the smaller the number of women. As telling evidence, in 1999 there were still only nine women among the 100 members of the U.S. Senate (although in two states, California and Maine, both senators were women) and only three women among the 50 governors. At the municipal level, a mere 16 of the country's 100 largest cities had women mayors and only two were women of color (see Table I-3). (It bears nothing that in the 106th Congress, the last of the century, the 56 female representatives included 12 African Americans, five Hispanics, and one Asian American.)

It seems fair to say that while late-twentieth-century women made remarkable progress in forcing open the gates of the American political system and winning positions of governmental power, a widely inclusive political world—characterized by full representation and shared leadership—remained a worthy, distant goal to be achieved by the children of the new millennium.

Table I-1 • Women in the 105th and 106th Congresses in Leadership Positions

	Congress	
	105th	*106th*
U.S. Senate		
Republicans		
Majority Leader	0	0
Assistant Majority Leader	0	0
Chief Deputy Whip	0	0
Conference Chair	0	0
Conference Secretary	0	0
Republican Policy Committee	0	0
National Republican Senatorial Committee	0	0
President Pro Tempore	0	0
Deputy Majority Whip	1	1
Secretary of Senate Conference	1	1
Democrats		
Minority Leader	0	0
Minority Whip	0	0
Deputy Minority Whip	0	0
Conference Secretary	1	1
Assistant Minority Floor Leader	0	0
Democratic Senatorial Campaign Committee	0	0
Deputy Minority Whip	0	1
U.S. House of Representatives		
Republicans		
Speaker	0	0
Majority Leader	0	0
Majority Whip	0	0
Conference Chair	0	0
Republican National Congressional Committee	0	0
Deputy Majority Whip	2	1
Vice Chair of Republican Conference	1	1
Assistant Majority Whip	1	1
Republican Conference Secretary	0	1

(continued)

Table I-1 (continued)

	Congress	
	105th	*106th*
Democrats		
Minority Leader	0	0
Minority Whip	0	0
Caucus Chair	0	0
Democratic Congressional Campaign Committee	0	0
Chief Deputy Minority Whip	2	0
Vice Chair of Democratic Caucus	1	0
Assistant to Democratic Leader	0	1
Deputy Minority Whip	0	2
Minority Whip at Large	0	2

Source: Center for American Women and Politics (CAWP), *Women in Congressional Leadership Roles*, March 1999.

Beyond a history of breakthroughs and the attendant slowly rising numbers, what legacy will twentieth-century political women have bequeathed to the future? Qualitatively as well as quantitatively, has a course been set that could alter the substance and manner of public leadership?

Coming from a centuries-old patriarchal culture, sex-role divisions in society, and gendered experiences in childhood and adult families, school, and work, women have entered the public world with perspectives, values, and priorities influenced by their life histories as females. In one way or another, gender has colored their experience of leadership or influenced its content or style. The real question is not so much why a leader's gender should mat-

Table I-2 • Women State Legislators in Leadership Positions, 1999

	Leadership Positions		
		Women	
	Total	*Number*	*Percentage*
In state senates	155	13	8.4
In state houses	183	24	13.1
Total	338	37	10.9

Source: Center for American Women and Politics (CAWP), *Women State Legislators: Leadership Positions and Committee Chairs 1999*, 1999.

Table I-3 • Women Mayors of 100 Largest Cities, 1999

City	Population	Rank (by size)	Mayor
San Diego, CA	1,171,121	7	Susan Golding
Portland, OR	480,824	26	Vera Katz
Kansas City, MO	441,259	31	Kay Barnes
Virginia Beach, VA	430,385	32	Meyera Oberndorf
Long Beach, CA	421,904	34	Beverly O'Neill
Tulsa, OK	378,491	38	Susan Savage
Minneapolis, MN	358,785	45	Sharon Sayles Belton
Cincinnati, OH	345,818	48	Roxanne Qualls
Colorado Springs, CO	345,127	49	Mary Lou Makepeace
Lexington, KY	237,612	65	Pam Miller
Durham, NC	195,428	78	Carolyn Allen
Lubbock, TX	193,565	79	Windy Sitton
Glendale, CA	184,321	90	Ginger Bremberg
San Bernardino, CA	183,474	91	Judith Valles
Orlando, FL	173,902	92	Glenda Hood
Huntsville, AL	170,424	93	Loretta Spencer

Source: Center for American Women and Politics (CAWP), *Women in Elective Office 1999*, August 1999.

ter as why it should not matter. In addition to other bedrock conditions of their personal histories (at a minimum, their ethnic, racial, class, and religious backgrounds), people's experiences as males or females are simply too fundamental and far-reaching not to affect who they are, what they think, how they behave, or how they are viewed by others. With only a few women scattered here and there in public office, this gender coloration would be insignificant, but with the increase in numbers over time, the potential is enormous for eventually "regendering" the public world.

At a bare minimum, a regendered public arena would contain a fairly even mix of women and men at all levels of politics and government, thus projecting an image of equal opportunity in public service and shared leadership in society. Such a picture would be even more salubrious for the evolving democracy if removing the barriers to women in power also helped clear the way for a colorful mix of new leaders from diverse communities and social backgrounds. Regendering the public world would thus play a part in progressively reconstituting the democracy well beyond changing demographics. The new leaders would be those who collaborated constructively, practicing politics with respect and rewards for all in a nation of differences.

In the meantime, what has been the early impact and significance of women's leadership in politics? Reflecting their roles in a workforce that is pervasively segregated by sex and, most centrally, their experiences as nurturers and caregivers in the family and society, women's policy agendas and priorities often have come from their deep knowledge of daily home life, domestic responsibilities, and the central role that children, families, and community issues play in their consciousness (Dodson and Carroll 1991; Carroll, Dodson, and Mandel 1991; Mandel and Dodson 1992).

Common issue areas on women's legislative agendas have included child care and education; domestic violence; women's health care; insurance coverage for mammograms, pap smears, and contraceptives; protection for victims of rape, sexual assault, and harassment; and equity in pay, pensions, insurance, and credit. In Washington State, for example, during the 1999 legislative session, women lawmakers took the lead on such issues as Medicaid payment for contraceptives for low-income women, increased day-care funding for mothers in college, and new privacy protections for domestic violence victims.

At the federal level, groups of congresswomen also have collaborated, sometimes across party lines, on equity issues and other matters of special concern to women (Dodson et al. 1995; Gertzog 1995). Needless to say, political women's partisan and ideological stances have varied widely, affecting their individual positions on policy issues. As with all public officials, women's behavior in office has also been influenced by the political culture of the institutions in which they serve, their positions and tenure inside those institutions, and the constituents to whom they pay heed. On the whole, however, women leaders have expressed shared interests in areas formerly ignored by male leaders and, in so doing, have already made a distinctive impact on agenda setting and decisionmaking in government.

It is generally believed that men and women favor different management and leadership styles. Studies suggest that women incline toward participatory, consensus-building, interactive modes of leadership (Rosener 1990). Early research specifically focused on women in politics found that women favor open deliberations, reach out to include the views of previously excluded constituencies, and engage in collaborative problem-solving and decisionmaking (Carroll, Dodson, and Mandel 1991; Rosenthal 1998). In her study of state legislative leaders, Cindy Simon Rosenthal (1998) concluded that because women exhibit a different, "integrative" style of leadership, government will be transformed by their growing representation in public office.

GENDER FOCUS IN POLITICS: HOW WOMEN COPE WITH THE NOVELTY FACTOR

A core difference a woman brings to political leadership is herself—her identity as a woman. By definition and experience, women are different from the norm. Political processes, practices, and institutions in the United States were created by and for men—especially those of a particular class, race, and religion. The history of politics and government is one of stories about men. At the beginning of the new century, the average citizen watching television news finds men dominating political leadership as presidents, members of Congress, governors, candidates for high office, party leaders, advisors, and government spokespersons. Some men still see women leaders as interlopers in their territory—or at the least as participants whose presence requires a special adjustment.

Almost everywhere in public leadership, women experience what it is like to be part of a small minority by virtue of gender. If a man seeks office, gender is taken for granted and goes unremarked upon. Yet it remains unimaginable for gender to go completely unnoticed for women. The public, the parties, opponents, colleagues, and the media all take note—and often use the tag "the woman" to describe the candidate or officeholder. Remarks about a politician's gender are rarely hostile; on the contrary, women are often welcomed as promising alternatives to business as usual. Yet women in politics are still considered to be different—not as the norm, but as "the other"—whether the observation is positive, negative, neutral, or simply curious.

If the candidate is a woman—and especially if she is vying for an office that has only been held by men—the media are likely to focus on her gender. Common gender questions asked by reporters include: "Has the time come for a woman president (secretary of state, secretary of defense, governor, senator, mayor)?" "Is it more difficult for a woman to raise the money for this race?" "Will the political party (establishment) support a woman for this position?" "Are voters ready to elect a woman to this office?" "Will women vote for this candidate because she is a woman?" "Will men have a hard time voting for her?" "What special problems will a woman face in seeking or holding this office?" "Will it make a difference to have a woman in this job?" In 1999, Elizabeth Dole's campaign for the Republican presidential nomination aroused this kind of interest.

The question of how political women define themselves in relation to their gender has long been a subject of considerable interest to the media and students of women in politics (Mandel 1983; Carroll 1985; Witt, Paget, and Matthews 1993; Norris 1997). Based on surveys, media coverage, and observation over the past several decades, it seems fair to say that most women entering public office, especially at the state and federal levels, should expect their gender to be an issue. A late-twentieth-century political woman is challenged to confront the twin questions of what it means to her to be a leader who is a woman and what is expected of her because she is a woman political leader.

Here again, women have not responded monolithically. Although former Congresswoman Patricia Schroeder's oft-quoted response to the reporter's question of whether she was running as a woman—"Do I have a choice?"—seems patently unarguable, women have chosen a variety of ways to cope, or not cope, with their identities as women. At one extreme is the woman who separates herself from her gender identity entirely, taking offense when someone so much as notices that she is a woman and returning a researcher's questionnaire with an angry comment about any study comparing men and women being a waste of time and, especially, money.

Somewhat less defensive is the woman officeholder who maintains that gender does not matter. This woman, found quite often in legislative bodies, accepts the culture and mores of the institution she has worked hard to enter. She is proud to serve there and eager to fit in and excel according to time-honored traditions; she wants to be called "Mr. Chairman," the title accorded the majority of her legislative colleagues in leadership positions. After all the time and effort she has given to "mastering" the system, she wants to make it work for her. The last advice she wants is that she should stand apart and change the system. Now is her time to reap rewards, not shoulder a special burden to remake the world. If she can succeed, she believes, so can other women.

Next comes a woman leader who also knows the ropes and has won both status and respect in the political world. This woman believes that gender is a relevant issue that makes a difference in some, but not all, public matters. Seeing herself as someone who can help others, she makes a special effort to work for policies that aid women and to encourage women with political aspirations. She knows how to compartmentalize. Her success illustrates that a woman can have a gender agenda and still be supported by men. Women leaders of this type have risen to major leadership positions in institutions where the overwhelming majority of officeholders are men. They have done so with the support of many male colleagues who felt comfortable with the women's agendas and their styles of leadership.

Farther down the gender road is the elected official who is admired as effective and successful inside the male political world, but whose leadership as a woman is central to her self-image and the policies she supports. She works very well with her fellow officeholders and on many issues important to the state and her diverse constituency, but she also has a gender agenda and is sensitive to the special needs of women. Issues with special gender content may not come up every week or every month, but when they do, she can be counted on to pay attention. A feminist consciousness colors her perception of daily politics, legislative issues, and institutional interactions in the same way that any heightened aspect of someone's experience would contribute a special perspective or awareness. Should this feature of her personality make her colleagues slightly uncomfortable, she is ready to draw on humor, collegiality, and political savvy to finesse the situation.

In theory, at the opposite end of the spectrum from the woman who is hostile to her gender being noticed at all is the political woman for whom gender is all that matters. Because promoting gender issues is her mission, she would not think of compartmentalizing her agenda or behavior. While such a leader can be imagined, in reality, she is more likely to be found as an activist in the advocacy community outside traditional politics, since mainstream political parties shy away from nominating single-issue candidates, and voters tend not to elect them.

Except for the last example, each of the above sketches is based on a real woman leader holding legislative office in 1999. Elected and appointed women across the country loosely mirror these models, encountering expectations and questions regarding their gender and often embracing and resisting them at the same time. On the one hand, many women in politics still enjoy the advantages of celebrity status and accept the roles and extra burdens they carry as pioneers; on the other, they look forward to a day when women leaders are not a novelty, when their presence in public life is so common that gender, no longer a handicap, loses its status as a special category of identity. Presumably at such a time, women leaders will no longer have to shoulder responsibilities for the diverse unrepresented interests of more than half the population.

THE GENDER ISSUE OVER TIME

It bears noting that after three decades of progress for women in politics, the gender issue has grown more, not less, complicated and intriguing. In the early days of the women's political movement, the main challenge was to recruit and find ways to support female candidates. By appealing to the principles of fairness and equity, and arguing the social economy of using the neglected talents of half the population, the women's political movement of the 1970s sought to change attitudes, break down traditional barriers, and build a base of women in public office.

In the early 1970s, it was common to hear elected women reject the term *politician*. They believed themselves to be public servants outside of politics and power. This attitude was expressed by elected women attending a landmark national conference for women state legislators—sponsored by the Center for American Women and Politics (CAWP)—in the spring of 1972.[1] Among these early women officeholders—many of them well educated, economically comfortable suburban wives, mothers, and civic volunteers— more than a few were motivated primarily by humanitarian goals, and saw their positions as extensions of their civic-minded community voluntarism.

During the late 1970s and into the 1980s, many political women believed they should distance themselves from subjects with which they might be most familiar personally and professionally (such as health, education, and welfare issues) and gain credibility in areas traditionally associated with male leaders (such as budget and finance, appropriations, economic development, business and industry, and transportation). They believed that to be seen as effective they had to become "one of the boys"—a view expressed by the late Barbara Jordan in CAWP's documentary film *Not One of the Boys* (1984) and described in a biography recounting her years in the Texas Senate and the U.S. Congress (Rogers 1998).

Later in the 1980s, and especially in the early 1990s, political women came out of the gender closet, with many openly acknowledging that who they were was inseparable from what they had to offer their constituents. Feeling less pressured to conform than their predecessors, they campaigned for office as women seeking a place in the halls of power and bringing something new to politics (Witt, Paget, and Matthews 1993). More than ever before, women running for high office believed in the political viability of a gendered campaign message and sounded confident that the public would benefit from electing individuals whose leadership reflected what was authentic and special from their own personal backgrounds and communities.

In one of the most widely reported examples, Patty Murray, a state legislator in Washington State, won her U.S. Senate race in 1992 by appealing to voters as just "a mom in tennis shoes"—an image she has continued to emphasize during her Senate years. Sometimes candidates have worked

---

[1] The Center for American Women and Politics (CAWP) was established in 1971 as a research, education, and public-service unit of the Eagleton Institute of Politics at Rutgers— the State University of New Jersey. Its mission is to promote greater understanding and knowledge about women's relationship to politics and government and to enhance women's influence and leadership in public life.

to create a double-gendered message, associating themselves with both classic male and classic female strengths. For example, in gubernatorial races in Texas and New Jersey in the 1990s, Ann Richards, a Democrat, and Christine Todd Whitman, a Republican, projected themselves as outdoor enthusiasts who enjoyed hunting, fishing, and mountain bike riding. Both campaigns also emphasized that the candidates' sensibilities and ability to empathize with voters' interests were related to their experiences as mothers.

During the post-Soviet, post–cold war 1990s, it helped that the United States's international preeminence and strong economy made it possible for the government to give priority to a domestic policy agenda that emphasized social welfare issues compatible with many women's traditional interests and expertise. Women could lead unapologetically from their strengths, calling attention to a wide range of education, health care, Social Security, child welfare, juvenile justice, gun control, and environmental issues. Soon men seeking public office, including the presidency, were building campaign platforms with planks from a classic women's agenda. By the mid-1990s, what had once been considered "soft" women's concerns had turned into hard, winning issues.

To become a leader, a woman no longer needed to abandon her putative gendered strengths. At the same time, with women like Secretary of State Madeleine Albright, Attorney General Janet Reno, and U.S. Trade Representative Charlene Barshefsky exercising leadership on issues long considered part of an all-male preserve and even alien to women, it became easier for women to serve the public in all areas that interested them. Furthermore, they could bring a different perspective to traditional male territory.

For example, while Secretary of State Albright has pursued familiar, conventional foreign policy strategies, promoting the use of tough measures and even military force in solving international problems, she has also acted from her perspective as a woman. Thomas Lippman (1997) reported in the *Washington Post* that, shortly after Secretary Albright was sworn in, she "instructed U.S. diplomats around the world to make the furtherance of women's rights a central priority of American foreign policy." From her earliest days as head of the U.S. Department of Justice, Janet Reno identified support for children's programs as one of her priorities—saying that the best crime prevention is the care, feeding, and education of children. During the 103rd Congress (1993–95), California Senator Dianne Feinstein was instrumental in the enactment of major new crime legislation pushing for a ban on assault weapons (Dodson et al. 1995).

During the 106th Congress, the Democratic leadership designated three female House members as spokespersons for gun control. In the wake of the

April 1999 shootings at Columbine High School in Colorado, Congress-woman Carolyn McCarthy and Nita Lowey of New York and Rosa DeLauro of Connecticut gained wide media coverage promoting the Democratic position on restricting sales of firearms (Bruni 1999). The congresswomen were seen as representing the most compelling image for progressive change on matters of guns and violence, an issue area that is expected to hold a key place in state and national politics into the early twenty-first century.

With such women exercising leadership in the legislative and executive branches, it becomes easier to imagine not only a less rigidly traditional sex-stereotyped world, but also to pick up intimations of how a "regendered politics" might look. In the long run, we can expect women's growing representation in positions of power to have an enormous impact on the content and style of public decisionmaking.

THE GENDER GAP: VOTING POWER AND THE INEVITABILITY OF A WOMAN PRESIDENT

Although women won the vote in 1920 with passage of the Nineteenth Amendment to the Constitution, they did not vote in large numbers immediately. It wasn't until 1964 that women and men voted in equal numbers in national elections. By the time another sixteen years had gone by, however, women's voting rates were beginning to exceed those of men. Ever since 1980, women have outvoted men in every national election. Since women outnumber men in the population at large, when they vote in greater proportions than men the numbers add up to a difference of millions (for example, in the 1996 national elections, over seven million more women than men voted).

Women had been increasing their voting strength for decades before they collectively took on the issue of increasing their numbers in public office. Enfranchisement happened first, gaining force incrementally; later, the push for empowerment followed the same pattern. By the end of the century, women's enfranchisement and empowerment together had become a potentially formidable force for regendering American politics.

The issue of gender has become more politically complex and intriguing largely because of women's voting patterns. How women vote influences attitudes, strategies, and opportunities regarding women's leadership in politics. As women continue to outvote men, and as women and men continue to make different voting choices—creating an identifiable "gender gap" in many races in all national elections since 1980—women have accrued formidable ballot box power. Their interests and policy preferences count as never before.

Campaign experts spend a good deal of money trying to find out what women want. No longer is it assumed that women will just vote as their husbands do. In fact, large numbers of female voters do not have husbands. Nowadays women are polled, studied in focus groups, and analyzed according to many variables (e.g., age, education, marital and parental status, race, religion, occupation, domicile, partisan affiliation, and so forth) by campaigns determined to capture their votes. Political commercials are directed toward women; candidates hire consultants and sometimes special staff to reach out to women; the media vie to find the right gender sobriquet for the season ("year of the woman," "year of the angry white male," "year of the soccer mom," "year of the waitress mom").

As a consequence of their voting power, women have leverage in politics. Recruiting, electing, and appointing women to office have in themselves become politically relevant actions. It looks bad if a party or an administration can count no visible women in its ranks. It is easier for a male leader to convince women voters of his respect for their concerns if he can show evidence of working with women colleagues and gaining the support of women leaders. A party proves its sincerity by nominating women; an official proves his sincerity by appointing and promoting women. Political parties parade their women leaders in front of television cameras at peak viewing time. Presidents and governors issue statements tallying the number of women appointed to their administrations, when possible contrasting themselves favorably with the appointment records of preceding administrations or political rivals.

Heightened awareness of women as political leaders has led to speculation about how long it will be before a woman is on the presidential ballot. Interest in the subject was fueled when Elizabeth Dole—a woman with a history of holding high public office and a credible record of public leadership—launched a serious candidacy for the Republican presidential nomination. In addition, a well-publicized, public-education initiative called the White House Project, begun in 1998 by a group of women activists and led by Marie Wilson of the Ms. Foundation for Women, called attention to the absence of women at the top and urged the public to ponder the question "Why not a woman for president?" Well over a year before the 2000 elections, political insiders and observers, and even the proverbial person on the street, expressed the opinion that presidential candidates, presumably male, should nominate female running mates. On the Republican side, Christine Todd Whitman and Elizabeth Dole were most frequently mentioned, the assumption in Dole's case being she would not be the presidential nominee but would be a logical vice presidential candidate. On the Democratic side, several senators and cabinet officials were mentioned, with Senator Dianne Feinstein leading the list.

Whether or not a woman becomes vice president or president in 2001, 2005, or 2009, the first woman elected on a national ticket will have won that distinction in part because of her gender. If she becomes president, more likely than not the race will have excited and energized women to help her win. During the early months of Elizabeth Dole's quest for the Republican presidential nomination, it was women (especially young women) who came out for her campaign stops, volunteered for her in Iowa, and raised money to keep her candidacy alive (Ayres 1999). Gender will also be a factor when the next woman is selected as a running mate for a male presidential candidate. As Geraldine Ferraro, the first female vice presidential candidate, acknowledged during an interview in 1984 for the documentary film *Not One of the Boys,* "I must say, in all honesty . . . take a look at the discussion about the Vice President—would they be discussing Geraldine Ferraro, a third-term member of Congress, if I were not a woman? No. This is probably one of those nice times to be in the right place at the right time, be the right sex. And I think that's positive" (CAWP 1984).

In 1999, one heard a very different kind of commentary than in 1984, when it was mostly women who were advocating for a female vice presidential candidate. In 1984 a public relations effort and a strong delegation of feminist advocates had to organize and argue to convince men of the idea's merits. Fifteen years later, the situation is completely different. Early in the presidential season, more than one political commentator expressed the opinion that naming a woman to the national tickets would be advisable. The emphasis has shifted from "whether" a woman should be on the ticket to "which" woman, and from "why a woman?" to "why not a woman?" (the slogan of the White House Project's effort). The new visibility of women in politics and government has added to the new awareness of women in the voting booth—forming a powerful combination that points inevitably to the top of the ticket.

TWO FIRST LADIES: PORTRAITS OF LEADERSHIP

ELEANOR ROOSEVELT

In mid-twentieth-century America, one remarkable woman rose above all others in the public world. Her name was Eleanor Roosevelt. Although her contribution to American history and her importance as a standard for women in leadership are still undervalued, her influence and stature have yet to be matched by any other woman in the United States.

Shy, dependent, and self-deprecating as a young adult, she spent the first decade of her marriage to Franklin Roosevelt pregnant or taking care of infants. Not very interested in women's issues, she seems to have projected her own self-image onto her sex. When her husband, newly elected to the New York legislature in 1910, supported women's suffrage, she described herself as "shocked," never having "given the question serious thought." She commented that she "took it for granted that men were superior creatures and knew more about politics than women did" (Roosevelt 1978, 68). By virtue of her marriage to an ambitious, uniquely successful political man, whose personal character and physical handicap led her to become more and more involved in the issues of the day—and because of her proximity to all phases of politics and public life over many years—Eleanor Roosevelt spent the next half-century growing into a consummate politician and world leader.

She also became an "ardent citizen and feminist," recognizing the value of suffrage: "I had learned that if you wanted to institute any kind of reform you could get far more attention if you had a vote than if you lacked one" (ibid., 103). She came to see that in national party politics women "stood outside the door of all important meetings" (ibid., 125). She worked with such women's organizations as the Women's Trade Union League, the League of Women Voters, and the women's Division of the Democratic State Committee in New York. She urged FDR to insist that his cabinet members seek out women for federal appointments. She held regular press conferences for women reporters in a conscious effort to help protect their jobs. She came to believe that it was important for women to play a much greater role in public life.

Eleanor Roosevelt took on such a role in her own right in 1945 when, by then a widow, she accepted an appointive position in President Harry Truman's administration. As a member of the United States' delegation to the United Nations General Assembly, she attended its first meeting in London and a subsequent session in Lake Success, New York. She continued to serve for several years as both a U.N. delegate and the U.S. representative to the Human Rights Commission. She was aware at the outset of the double burden she bore: ". . . I walked on eggs. I knew that as the only woman on the delegation I was not very welcome. Moreover, if I failed to be a useful member, it would not be considered merely that I as an individual had failed but that all women had failed, and there would be little chance for others to serve in the near future" (ibid., 305). In fact, she did so well in the face of extraordinarily difficult challenges that two of her fellow delegates, John Foster Dulles and Senator Arthur Vandenberg, said at the close of the first session that they were pleased to have worked with her and would gladly do so in the future—but admitted that they originally had begged President Truman not to appoint her to the delegation (ibid.).

In her work as chairperson of the Human Rights Commission, Eleanor Roosevelt was responsible for the creation of the Universal Declaration of Human Rights. Accepted by the United Nations General Assembly in December 1948, the declaration formulates a universal standard for human conduct left by Eleanor Roosevelt to all future generations. Informed by her humanitarian values and feminist sensibilities, she took the lead in an area where she foresaw the potential for transforming life on a global scale.

Eleanor Roosevelt is admired for her caring and compassion, her sensitivity to the plight of those in pain, her efforts to create world standards for human rights, and her innumerable trips, speeches, and magazine columns championing displaced persons, hungry children, civil rights, disarmament, universal education, and many other causes. She is listed in dictionaries, encyclopedias of history, and other references as a "humanitarian," a term that aptly describes her public career.

To that well-deserved title, the appellation "leader" should be added, especially in the context of women's political history. Although she grew up in a world of privilege and benefited from unique educational, social, and economic advantages, Eleanor Roosevelt may have had more in common with other women in all walks of life than she did with her own social class. Like the women who entered public life in the second half of the nineteenth century, Eleanor Roosevelt's public biography is a record of issue activism, much of it linked to reform efforts on behalf of the forgotten or powerless segments of the population. Like politically active women before and after her, she was particularly concerned about women's rights and opportunities and about ways to encourage women to take on public roles. The historian William Chafe calls Eleanor Roosevelt's "dynamic leadership" the most important cause of the "increased political role of women during the 1930's . . ." and also notes that "throughout the administrations [women] looked upon her as a personal friend and as a 'resident lobbyist' for their point of view. Her presence in the White House ensured that the voice of female reformers would not be ignored . . . (Chafe 1972, 42–43)."

Eleanor Roosevelt's last political position was a symbolically appropriate one. In 1961, President John F. Kennedy appointed her to serve as chair of the President's Commission on the Status of Women, a position she held until her death in 1962. Like many in the early generations of women political leaders, Eleanor Roosevelt's initial path to politics was through marriage. And like many women who spoke out strongly in public, she was criticized and mocked for not behaving in expected ways. Coming into prominence through affiliation with her husband's career offered Eleanor Roosevelt unusual opportunities but also limited her activities. In effect, she reformed the position of first lady, leaving it a more flexible "job" than she had found it, and one with significant potential power.

Eleanor Roosevelt's life journey from comfortable domestic preoccupations to a public life of committed advocacy was solidly in the tradition of women leaders in American public life. From Abigail Adams to Elizabeth Cady Stanton to Eleanor Roosevelt, American women—motivated often by their outrage at some injustice close to home—have been drawn from the confines of an exclusively private or domestic role to the role of advocate. Whether with the pen or speaking from the podium or microphone—sometimes on the campaign trail itself—they have claimed the right to be heard on matters of gender and justice. Eleanor Roosevelt is a symbol of the legacy of American women's political leadership, a legacy with deep gender roots.

HILLARY RODHAM CLINTON

At the close of the twentieth century, another remarkable first lady made a claim on public leadership in her own right. Hillary Rodham Clinton cracked the mold for political wives and, by extension, for many other women. Throughout an extraordinarily difficult eight years in the White House, and under the most complex circumstances, she performed simultaneously as a mother, wife, and first lady as well as a colleague, policy and political adviser, and legal counselor to the President. At the same time, she became an acclaimed international advocate and spokesperson for programs and policies to ameliorate the lives of children and women.

Throughout her tenure as first lady, Hillary Rodham Clinton has been outspoken on behalf of women's rights and status. As head of the United States delegation to the 1995 United Nations Fourth World Conference on Women in Beijing, China, she used the occasion and her global platform to make a forceful statement defining women's rights as human rights. Through a project entitled Vital Voices, she encouraged and supported the development of women's political leadership in developing democracies in Eastern Europe and elsewhere. She traveled often and extensively, both at home and abroad, to address women's organizations on the challenges and opportunities facing their members and constituents. She spoke for the Administration in asserting, "What this Administration believes is that if half the world's citizens are undervalued, underpaid, undereducated, underrepresented, fed less, fed worse, not heard, put down, we cannot sustain the democratic values and way of life we have come to cherish" (Lippman 1997, A9).

Hillary Rodham Clinton attracted a worldwide political following and eventually, while still serving as first lady, began to explore building an independent career in electoral politics. The unique phenomenon of a sitting first lady hosting White House social events, working as she does in partnership with the President on a wide variety of cultural and societal issues, while simultaneously hiring staff and planning her own campaign for high elective office breaks old molds, presenting an image of dynamic choices and new ways to live as a woman. In effect, Hillary Rodham Clinton has sought determinedly to be herself, an almost impossibly difficult posture to sustain given her situation. In her circumstances, knowing herself and acting with integrity on that knowledge must involve considerable struggle, discipline, and strength. The example of Hillary Rodham Clinton shaping her life has sent messages to millions of women about autonomy, options, personal decisionmaking, and self-determination. While her impact has already been significant, the future is still before her, and so is her promise as a major figure in women's political leadership.

It is premature to define and judge Hillary Rodham Clinton's leadership in terms of specific legacies. However, it is not too early to take note of her outspoken interest in a range of issues familiar to observers of women in politics—health care, education, and national and global policies sensitive to the needs of women, children, and families. With the announcement of her interest in becoming a candidate for a New York seat in the U.S. Senate, Hillary Rodham Clinton stepped beyond the boundaries accepted by every previous first lady. As a widow and former first lady, Eleanor Roosevelt continued her career in public life by agreeing to accept a high-level appointment; Hillary Rodham Clinton did not wait to be appointed before acting on her ambitions to build her own political career. Even before winning nomination for any office, she had become, by 1999, arguably the best known and most influential woman in the world—and a woman with perhaps more potential for future power than any woman of her time.

Notwithstanding their qualifications and records of public service, Hillary Rodham Clinton, Elizabeth Dole—who seriously explored becoming the first female presidential candidate of the next century—and Eleanor Roosevelt in her time—all three—attracted public attention largely because they were wives of powerful political men. Yet they went far beyond their identities as wives to achieve their own standing as public leaders. With remarkable determination, discipline, strength, and even defiance, they transformed a traditional female role—the wife—into an opportunity for their own leadership. Without abandoning or abjuring the role, they reshaped it into a useful foundation from which to build a platform for leadership.

Like other women of their time, these women emerged as leaders from backgrounds and circumstances that suggested other expectations for their life choices and behavior. Rejecting the conventional restrictions of the sex-stereotyped roles they were playing, they forged new opportunities for service and leadership. Their examples illustrate that women can make pathways from where they are situated, requiring neither a blueprint for becoming surrogate men nor basic training in political men's ways.

These women exemplify the legacy and promise of women's political leadership in the United States. Some view first ladies primarily as women of privilege, projecting their public voices from the luxurious advantage of an office in the White House, if not the Oval Office itself. Others perceive them as women confined by highly traditional expectations in a position that allows them little freedom to achieve independent status and political power. From this vantage point, first ladies and other women married to powerful political men face different but nonetheless formidable barriers if they wish to establish their own legitimacy as leaders. In overcoming traditional obstacles and bending restrictive situations to their own purposes while standing for concerns typical of women in politics, the lives of Eleanor Roosevelt and Hillary Rodham Clinton exemplify central aspects of women's public leadership in the second half of the twentieth century.

CONCLUSION

The legacy of American women's political leadership is change. A journey began in 1848 with what was then considered the outrageous request for a vote for women in the Seneca Falls declaration. The journey continues today with women's arrival, over 150 years later, at the doorstep of real political power. Along the way, the path was forged by the thousands of women who broke down barriers to make their values, voices, and votes count in the halls of public power, as well as by women who entered the political arena as wives of public men and stayed on to become leaders in their own right. All have contributed to the future promise of women's political leadership in a regendered, and consequently renewed, public world. Such a world is not unrecognizable; it is simply imbued with a fuller, and thus richer, representation of humanity.

TWO

★

WOMEN AND LEADERSHIP IN HIGHER EDUCATION

Mariam Chamberlain

HIGHLIGHTS

OVER THE LAST SEVERAL DECADES, women have made significant gains in higher education leadership. Many more women now earn doctoral degrees, and women are now approaching parity with men in faculty positions at the assistant professor level. However, women still lag behind their male peers in advancement from assistant professor to tenured status as associate and full professor. This limits women's opportunities because senior faculty make up the major source of candidates for academic leadership positions.

- Women first gained entry into higher education in the United States when Oberlin College admitted female students in 1837. That was more than 200 years after Harvard College was founded in 1636 for the education of young men. In colonial America, as in Europe at the time, there was no precedent for the higher education of women.
- During the second half of the nineteenth century, women's colleges were established and enrollment accelerated rapidly; meanwhile, the founding of state universities and land grant colleges under the Morrill Act of 1862 expanded coeducational opportunities.
- In 1979, the number of women students in higher education surpassed that of men; by 1996, women accounted for 56 percent of student bodies.
- Women earned 55 percent of bachelor's degrees and 56 percent of master's degrees in 1995/96.
- Although women have made dramatic gains in attaining doctoral degrees, they have not reached overall parity with men in this area. Women earned

12,557—46.5 percent—of the 27,668 doctorates awarded to U.S. citizens in 1996/97 (between July 1, 1996, and June 30, 1997).

- More women than men earn Ph.D.'s in some fields, particularly education and certain areas of the social sciences and humanities; however, women earn only 22.1 percent of the doctorates awarded in the physical sciences.
- Women have expanded their presence substantially in the professorial ranks. They constituted 22 percent of full-time faculty members in 1972 and 33 percent in 1998. Minority women represented 11 percent of female full-time faculty members in 1972 and 14 percent in 1995 (the most recent year for which data providing racial/ethnic information were available at the time of this writing).
- The proportion of women holding the rank of full professor increased from 9.5 percent in 1972 to 18.7 percent in 1998.
- Since the 1970s, women's gains in the academic profession have been aided by federal statutes. In 1972, Congress expanded Title VII of the Civil Rights Act of 1964, which prohibited discrimination in employment, to include all educational institutions; amended the Equal Pay Act of 1963 to cover executive, administrative, and professional employment; and enacted Title IX of the Education Amendments to prohibit sex discrimination in all federally assisted education programs.
- Also in 1972, the federal government issued guidelines for implementing Executive Orders 11246 and 11375, requiring institutions of higher education to institute affirmative action plans to ensure equal treatment of all employees. Prior to 1972 these executive orders, which cover all federal contractors, were not applied to higher education institutions.
- Another factor contributing to the advancement of academic women was the formation of women's caucuses and committees in professional associations. These groups served as both support networks and pressure groups, and were instrumental in the development of women's studies, which created new faculty positions.
- Academic leadership positions are usually filled by candidates drawn from the senior faculty ranks. Since the 1970s, women have entered these leadership positions in increasing numbers. In the mid-1970s, women held 23 percent of executive, administrative, and managerial positions in higher education—and minority women held 2.8 percent of these positions. By 1995, the proportion of women in these positions had increased to 45 percent. Seven percent were held by minority women.
- In 1975, only five percent of college and university presidents were women. By 1999, there were 480 women college and university presidents in the United States, or 16 percent of the total. Several of the

women are CEOs of institutions that are among the most prestigious in
the nation.

• Women also have made substantial gains as trustees of higher education
  institutions. In 1977, they represented 15 percent of all trustees. In 1997,
  they made up 26 percent of the boards of independent colleges and universities and 30 percent of the boards of public institutions.

BACKGROUND

The progress of women in leadership positions in higher education can best
be examined in the context of historic conditions and changes. Women first
gained entry into higher education in the United States when Oberlin College admitted female students in 1837. That was more than 200 years after
Harvard College was founded in 1636 for the education of young men. In
colonial America, as in Europe at that time, there was no precedent for higher
education for women (Chamberlain 1988).

Notwithstanding the emergent women's movement in the 1840s, opportunities for women in higher education remained limited until mid-
century. During the latter part of the nineteenth century, however, women's
higher education enrollment accelerated rapidly. While elite men's institutions were closed to women, liberal arts colleges for women offering comparable curricula opened their doors to women during this period, notably
Vassar College in 1861 followed by Smith and Wellesley in 1875 and Bryn
Mawr and Mount Holyoke in the 1880s. Meanwhile, the establishment of
state universities and land grant colleges under the Morrill Act of 1862 advanced coeducational opportunities. In the aftermath of the Civil War, institutions of higher education for southern black youth also were established.

By the turn of the century, women made up 30 percent of the student
bodies in higher education. The rapid expansion of public school systems,
and the resulting need for teachers, fueled the growth in women's enrollment during that period. Women's enrollment in higher education has continued to increase since then; however, the percentage of women's relative
to men's enrollment peaked in 1940, then declined sharply after World War
II, when returning veterans dominated the campuses. Women's enrollment
did not regain its prewar rate until 1970, when it resumed its climb. Women
students continued to gain in number until 1979, when their proportion in
higher education surpassed that of men. Women's enrollment reached 56
percent in 1999 and was projected to approach 57 percent by the year 2000
(Koerner 1999).

In degree attainment, women are now awarded 55 percent of bachelor's degrees and 56 percent of master's degrees; however, they have not yet reached parity with men at the doctoral and professional level. Nor is women's representation in the student body matched by their presence in the faculty and administrative ranks in institutions of higher education.

THE DOCTORATE AND ENTRY INTO FACULTY POSITIONS

The usual prerequisite for faculty positions in higher education is the doctoral degree, and women have made substantial—indeed, dramatic—gains in degree attainment at that level, particularly since the 1960s.

American universities began awarding doctorates in the 1870s. The first woman to receive that degree was Helen Magill, who received a doctorate in the classics from Boston University in 1877 (James 1971). At the turn of the twentieth century, the number of doctorates awarded to both men and women was quite small. By 1920, however, it had increased significantly. That year, institutions of higher education awarded a total of 615 Ph.D.'s, 15 percent of them to women. This percentage declined somewhat during the Great Depression and in the aftermath of World War II, when it fell below 10 percent. Although the number of doctorates earned by women increased throughout this period, the proportion relative to doctorates earned by men did not regain the 1920 level until 1972. From then on, however, the rise was rapid in both numbers and percentages.

In 1996/97, 27,668 doctorates were awarded by U.S. institutions to U.S. citizens.[1] Of these, 12,557 (46.5 percent) were earned by women. Of the women awarded doctorates, 1,973 (15.7 percent) were minority women— 808 black, 508 Hispanic, 569 Asian, and 88 American Indian women (Sanderson and Dugoni 1999).

More women than men earn Ph.D.'s in some fields, notably education and certain areas of the social sciences and humanities. In 1997, women earned 63 percent of the doctorates awarded in education, 67 percent of those in psychology, 56 percent of those in anthropology, and 55 percent of those in sociology. However, despite steady gains, women have not yet achieved parity with men in other fields, particularly the physical sciences, where they received 22 percent of the doctorates awarded in 1997. The disparity is almost as wide in the field of economics within the social sci-

[1]Another 15,037 doctorates went to foreign students, who accounted for more than one-third of all doctorates awarded in 1996/97 by U.S. institutions. About 32 percent of the foreign recipients were women.

ences, where the proportion of doctorates earned by women was 23 percent (ibid.).

Since 1958, the National Research Council has conducted annual surveys of earned doctorates in U.S. universities as part of a program of the Office of Scientific and Engineering Personnel. Survey participants are asked about postgraduate plans, including definite commitments for employment or for postdoctoral study at the time the doctorate is awarded. In 1976, 66 percent of the women doctoral recipients surveyed had definite commitments for employment or postdoctoral study, compared with 74 percent of male doctoral recipients. By 1991, however, the percentage was 70 for both sexes (Ries and Thurgood 1993).

In 1997, the most recent year for which data were available at the time of this writing, parity was maintained. The overall figure for both men and women who had definite plans for employment or postdoctoral study was 86 percent. Among those with employment commitments, more women than men planned employment in educational institutions, while more men than women were headed for employment in industry (Sanderson and Dugoni 1999).

In the 1991 summary report of doctoral recipients, the National Research Council devoted a special section to female doctoral recipients, including an in-depth analysis by racial groups. The data indicated that, in comparison to white women, a higher proportion of black and Hispanic women and a lower proportion of Asian and Native American women were headed for careers in academe (Reis and Thurgood 1993).

In summary, the number of women with doctorates has increased dramatically, particularly in recent decades. Women's share of the doctorates awarded annually to U.S. citizens has reached 46 percent, with minority women earning 16 percent of all doctorates awarded to women. In addition, the proportion of women with doctorates headed for academic careers is higher than that of men. Presumably, then, at least 46 percent of the pool of qualified candidates for entry-level faculty positions in higher education are women.

THE STRUCTURE OF COLLEGE AND UNIVERSITY ADMINISTRATION

The governing structure of institutions of higher education consists mainly of three categories of administrators. First and foremost are those in academic leadership positions, including provosts, academic vice presidents, and deans. Second are those who work in admissions, financial aid, student affairs, counseling, placement, and registration. The third group includes business and financial officers, personnel managers, and directors of external affairs, such as development, public relations, and alumni affairs. Overall responsibility resides, of course, with the president or chancellor, and he or she in turn is ultimately accountable to the board of trustees.

Candidates drawn from faculty ranks usually fill academic leadership positions, and the first step in academic administration is often department chair. The next step is deanship, which may lead to the top ranks of academic administration and possibly to the presidency (Mitchell 1993). There is no similar ladder for the other categories of college and university administrators. The individuals who fill those positions are more frequently recruited from outside and have more varied academic experience. They may have degrees in physical education, counseling, information systems, or accounting. They may rise to such senior positions as chief business officer, general counsel, or director of personnel and affirmative action, but usually not to the top executive rank.

WOMEN IN FACULTY POSITIONS

The normal entry-level faculty position for those with Ph.D.'s is assistant professor. This is usually a renewable term appointment, initially lasting perhaps two years. The assistant professorship is a tenure-track appointment in that, based on performance and the availability of vacancies, it is expected to lead to advancement to senior-level positions with tenure. Most institutions confer tenure at the associate professor level, a few at the full professor level only.

In the normal course of events, an assistant professor is expected to attain tenure within a period of seven years, contingent upon a positive evaluation of teaching effectiveness and research productivity. The prevailing policy on tenure is based on the 1940 Statement of Principles of Academic Freedom and Tenure, jointly formulated by the American Association of University Professors (AAUP) and the Association of American Colleges and endorsed by educational associations and learned societies. (The 1940 Statement was updated in 1989–1990 to remove gender-specific language.) On the basis of these principles, institutions of higher education that continue to employ full-time faculty for longer than the probationary seven-year period without conferring tenure are subject to censure by AAUP.

Institutions of higher education employ many faculty members besides those in tenure-track positions. These include instructors, usually individuals who have not yet earned Ph.D.'s, lecturers, adjunct professors, other part-time faculty members who may hold professional positions outside the university, and visiting faculty members. Those holding these positions do not have the same AAUP protections as the full-time faculty on tenure track, nor do they have influential roles in university administration.

Prior to the 1970s, women faculty members were disproportionately relegated to non–tenure-track positions. Since then, however, they have substantially expanded their representation in the professorial ranks, moving into tenure-track positions in proportion to their increasing attainment of the doctorate. In 1998, according to the AAUP, women constituted 43 percent of those holding probationary tenure-track appointments. They represented 26 percent of tenured faculty members and 33 percent of full-time faculty members, as compared with 22 percent of full-time faculty members in 1972 (Benjamin 1999).

The latest data available on minority women, as reported by the U.S. Office of Education, applied to 1995. At that time, minority women—including black, Hispanic, Asian/Pacific Islander, and American Indian women—represented 14 percent of female full-time faculty members who were U.S. citizens, compared with 11 percent in 1972 (National Center for Education Statistics 1998).

In spite of the gains that women have made in the academic profession, significant gender disparities persist in salary, rank, and tenure. Discrimination against academic women, particularly with regard to salary, is regularly monitored by the AAUP Committee W on the Status of Women in the Academic Profession. According to the committee's 1998 report, salary disparities remain substantial. This is attributed in part to the fact that more women than men are new entrants into the profession and thus, on average, have less seniority. But the committee also found that women remained longer within rank before promotion. Moreover, women continue to be more likely than men to hold appointments in lower-paying institutions and disciplines.

One reason women remain longer in the rank of assistant professor is because many institutions "stop the clock" on the seven-year rule for up to two years to permit women to take time out for childbearing or rearing. The extended time in rank is most troublesome, however, at the associate professor level, suggesting the possibility of the glass ceiling at work. In any case, the proportion of women among faculty of full professor rank was only 18.7 percent in 1998—admittedly an improvement over 1972, when it was 9.5 percent.

THE FORCE OF LAW AND THE ADVANCEMENT OF ACADEMIC WOMEN

Women's gains in the academic profession were not achieved without support from federal statutes and academic women's groups. Until 1972, it was entirely legal to discriminate against women in higher education. At that time, the federal government established several laws and regulations to equalize opportunities for women in higher education. Since the 1970s, federal statutes have aided women's gains in the academic profession.

In 1972, Congress expanded Title VII of the Civil Rights Act of 1964, which prohibited discrimination in employment, to include all educational institutions; amended the Equal Pay Act of 1963 to cover executive, administrative, and professional employment; and enacted Title IX of the Education Amendments to prohibit sex discrimination in all federally assisted education programs. Also in 1972, the federal government issued guidelines for implementing Executive Orders 11246 and 11375, requiring institutions of higher education to establish affirmative action plans to ensure equal treatment of all employees. Before 1972 these executive orders, which cover all federal contractors, were not applied to education. The federal government was spurred to enforce the executive orders against colleges and universities after Bernice Sandler of the Women's Equity Action League (WEAL) filed the first charges of sex discrimination in education in 1970. Other charges against academic institutions by other women's organizations soon followed.

Under the 1972 guidelines, all contractors with at least fifty employees and a contract of $50,000 or more were required to develop a written plan of affirmative action. The plan had to include an analysis of the institution's employment of minority and women workers. If these workers were found to be "underutilized," the contractor was required to establish specific numerical goals and timetables for correcting the discrimination. Virtually all institutions of higher education were covered by the order and filed affirmative action plans accordingly. The Office of Civil Rights of the then Department of Health, Education and Welfare was responsible for enforcing the affirmative action guidelines as they applied to colleges and universities. The office carried out contract compliance reviews and investigated complaints. Later, this responsibility was assigned to the Department of Education.

These federal requirements, and the threat of losing lucrative government contracts, appear to have been effective in addressing discrimination in entry-level positions. As noted, women are now entering tenure-track positions in proportion to their attainment of the Ph.D. Moreover, they are not relegated, as in former times, to less prestigious institutions but have established their presence in institutions of all kinds. Discrimination most frequently becomes a salient issue at the point of tenure.

The tenure decision is essentially a process of peer review. The faculty member's departmental peers make the initial evaluation and recommendation, sometimes soliciting the views of those outside the institution who are familiar with the candidate's scholarship. Once the department reaches a decision, the chair passes it on for review by such higher administrative authorities as the dean or academic vice president. The process is highly subjective and, because of the confidentiality element, not particularly open. At the same time, there is a great deal at stake for both the faculty member and the institution, since the decision involves a lifetime commitment.

Before the 1970s, faculty litigation over sex discrimination was virtually unknown. With the new legislation, however, faculty women who were denied tenure under circumstances that they viewed as discriminatory were empowered to bring suit—and they did. Their efforts were supported in part by such organizations as the National Women's Law Center, the National Organization for Women (NOW), the Legal Advocacy Fund of the American Association of University Women, and the American Association of University Professors.

Academics in Court, published in 1987, reviews the outcomes of the body of faculty discrimination litigation. It is based on a three-year study by George R. LaNoue of the University of Maryland and Barbara A. Lee of Rutgers University. LaNoue and Lee (1987) report that, during the 1970s, the federal courts decided a total of 145 academic discrimination cases. In the 1980s, there was an average of 34 such cases a year.

Although a few of the suits brought by women faculty members have been successful, notably *Lamphere* v. *Brown University* (1977) and *Rajendar* v. *University of Minnesota* (1980), most decisions have gone against the plaintiff. Class action suits have been somewhat more successful than individual suits, but by and large the courts have made it clear that they are reluctant to intervene in the academic peer review process. In view of the significant time and money spent on these cases, as well as the preponderance of negative results for the plaintiffs, women faculty members have relied less over time on litigation as a remedy for discrimination. At the same time, the litigation process, regardless of the eventual outcome, has led to improvements in university procedures and greater accountability in faculty decisionmaking.

OTHER STRATEGIES

In addition to litigation, with all the difficulties that entails, academic women have used other career advancement strategies. Foremost among these is the formation of women's caucuses and committees within professional associations. These structures function as pressure groups to improve the status of women in the profession. Women's caucuses and committees emerged in the late 1960s in the fields of sociology, history, political science, and psychology, and rapidly spread to other disciplines. There are currently well over 100 such groups, ranging across the academic disciplines and professional fields. The groups can be found within such educational associations as the American Association of University Professors and the American Association for Higher Education. The AAUP Committee W on the Status of Women, first established in 1918 but disbanded after ten years, was reactivated in 1970.

In addition to the women's committees or groups within professional associations, there are independent women's organizations in many fields. For example, in addition to the Committee on the Status of Women of the American Mathematical Society, there is a separate Association of Women Mathematicians. In some fields, there are also groups for minority women, such as the Association of Black Women Historians. The independent groups work in collaboration with the committees in the association to provide greater freedom for activist agendas.

The initial purpose of the committees and caucuses was to conduct baseline surveys of the status of women in the profession, and they have continued to monitor ongoing changes and trends. At the same time, the groups have sought to enhance women's roles within the association and their visibility in the broader profession. Specifically, the groups have pressed for better representation among the association's officers, greater participation in the annual meeting program, and a more significant role in the editorial policies of the association journals. They also have argued for the provision of child-care facilities at annual meetings. In all these efforts, they have been largely successful. Women have perceptibly increased their influence in the professional associations and their presence in the programs of the annual meetings.

To assist women further in their professions, caucuses and commissions have sponsored career advancement workshops, coaching women on résumé writing, interviewing techniques, getting papers published, and strategies for achieving tenure. Some have established mentoring programs. At the campus level, these groups have monitored and assisted in the implementation of affirmative action programs in their respective disciplines. All in all, the caucuses and commissions of professional associations have been and continue to be an important part of the support structure for faculty women in academic life.

While pursuing affirmative action efforts, the caucuses and commissions have also been concerned with the omission of women from research agendas in their respective fields. They have encouraged scholarly research on women and have lobbied for sessions on women at their associations' annual meetings. Such sessions, once rare, are now quite common. The professional women's groups also have been instrumental in the development of women's studies courses, which form the basis for interdisciplinary degree programs. Women's studies courses are now widely available on college and university campuses, and over 600 institutions have organized degree or certificate programs. These programs have led to new faculty positions, most of them held by women. Usually such appointments are made jointly with traditional departments. Overall, the programs are a significant factor in expanding opportunities for women in higher education faculties.

Recently a new strategy for the advancement of academic women was devised by a group called the Committee for the Equality of Women at Harvard, organized by Harvard and Radcliffe alumnae. Not satisfied with the progress that Harvard was making toward gender equality, the group urged graduates to divert contributions to the university into an escrow account, to be withheld until a more significant increase in the number of tenured faculty women was achieved. The campaign was launched in 1995, and within the first year the fund, designated the Harvard Women Faculty Fund, received gifts and bequests approaching $500,000. While this sum is not large by Harvard standards, the idea captured much attention from the press, as well as at Harvard (Rimer 1997).

In the fall of 1998, the committee organized a conference on women in research universities. The purpose of the conference was to identify and share information on policies and practices that have been initiated in other institutions to expand the number of women faculty members, promote their research, and improve the academic environment. A volume on the proceedings is planned so that information about effective strategies can be more widely disseminated.

A different strategy for the advancement of faculty women was followed at the Massachusetts Institute of Technology (MIT), again with much attention from the press. Clearly, particular attention was given to this group because of MIT's importance and prestige in science and engineering. In 1994, a group of tenured faculty women met to discuss the quality of their professional lives and the extent to which their careers differed from those of their male colleagues. They found a pattern of gender-related discrimination—inequities not only in salaries but also in allocation of resources for research, teaching assignments, and other matters, including laboratory space. The group proposed that MIT establish a committee to study the problem.

A committee was duly constituted in 1995 to analyze the status of women in six departments in the School of Science. The committee submitted an initial report of its findings in 1996, followed by amendments in 1997 and 1998. Among other things, it found that the percentage of faculty women in the School of Science, eight percent, had not changed in at least 10 years. They recommended specific steps to address the inequities identified and to increase the number of women faculty members through affirmative action efforts.

In 1999, the report was made public by MIT with what was seen as an extraordinary admission by the president, Charles M. Vest, that pervasive, though unintentional, discrimination existed. At the same time, MIT reported that steps had already been taken and were being taken to improve conditions for women, and that between 1995, when the initial report was submitted, and 1999, the proportion of women in the science faculty had climbed to 12 percent (Goldberg 1999). The candor and cooperation on both sides was unprecedented. It remains to be seen what the impact might be, if any, on policies and practices at other institutions.

Although black women have a long history as faculty members and administrators in higher education, until the 1970s they were largely confined to predominantly black institutions. During the 1980s, they achieved a significant presence in white institutions, including the most prestigious ones, for the first time. Their numbers, however, were thinly spread throughout university departments and administrative structures. In an effort to offset conditions of isolation, to provide a forum for exchange of experiences, and to facilitate internal communication, a national conference on black women in higher education was held in 1994 on the campus of MIT. Two thousand scholars and academic administrators from across the country attended this landmark conference. A comprehensive volume emanating from the conference, entitled *Black Women in the Academy: Promises and Perils,* was published three years later. It comprises essays on a wide range of topics relating to the dynamics of academic life (Benjamin 1997). A follow-up conference, entitled "Black Women in the Academy II: Service and Leadership," was held in June 1999 on the campus of Howard University, a leading black institution.

WOMEN FACULTY AND ENTRY INTO ACADEMIC ADMINISTRATION

As noted above, those in academic and leadership positions in colleges and universities are usually recruited from the ranks of faculty members. The transition from faculty to administration, however, is not clearly established. The first step is often department chair. The chair, normally a senior member of the department, may be appointed by the academic dean or provost or may be elected by members of the department. He or she may serve for one or more terms as chair and then return to teaching or research or continue as chair for an indefinite period.

The chair can be a position of considerable power in the department, with influence over appointments, salaries, and teaching assignments. Yet there are no specific prerequisites or credentials for the position, and the selection process seems highly subjective, based on little more than a perception of potential leadership capabilities.

For those in the position, various resources are available for enhancing managerial skills. For example, the American Council on Education conducts workshops for department chairs and deans to support their development as academic leaders within their departments and the institution as a whole. There is also a newsletter for academic administrators entitled *The Department Chair,* published by Anker Publishing Company. Anker Publishing, which specializes in resources for professional development in higher education, also publishes guides and reference manuals for department chairs on academic leadership. Within specific disciplines, there is usually a chairman's group of some kind that provides opportunities to discuss common problems and share recruiting information.

At the national level, there is very little information about department chairs in institutions of higher education. The National Center for Education Statistics conducts surveys of faculty and staff of postsecondary institutions, but department chairs are reported in the broader category of executive, administrative, and managerial staff. The College Mailing Group (CMG), an academic marketing firm that serves publishers and other organizations that produce scholarly material, compiles the only data available about the overall number of chairs and the breakdown by discipline.

For 1998/99, the CMG database lists a total of 37,573 department chairs in colleges and universities. Of these, 10,567, or 28 percent, are women. This represents a sizable pool of potential candidates for higher education administration, but much depends on what fields the candidates represent.

Senior-level administrators are more likely to be drawn from liberal arts disciplines, particularly those in which men predominate, than from education or other fields where women are more numerous.

Although the position of department chair is the principal entry point to higher levels of academic administration and leadership, it is not the only one. Faculty members may come to the attention of higher authorities by serving effectively on university-wide committees.

Women who are not department chairs in traditional disciplines can gain administrative experience as directors of women's studies programs. There are currently over 600 interdepartmental women's studies programs and several formal women's studies departments in colleges and universities, all headed by women. Women's studies program administrators are represented as a standing committee within the National Women's Studies Association, forming a network similar to those of the department chairs in the traditional disciplines.

Colleges and universities may sometimes recruit chairs from outside the institution, seeking individuals with experience in administering a department. In view of the critical role of the department chairmanship as a gateway to leadership in higher education, it is clear that we need more information than is currently available about the selection process, as well as about the number and distribution of women and minorities in such positions.

WOMEN IN HIGHER EDUCATION ADMINISTRATION

Since the 1970s, women have entered positions in higher education administration in ever increasing numbers. In the mid-1970s, the total number of individuals employed in executive, administrative, and managerial positions was 102,465. Of these, 23.1 percent were women, including 2.8 percent minority women. By 1981, the total had increased to 116,557, of whom 30.2 percent were women, including 3.4 percent minority women. In 1995, the latest year for which data were available at the time of this writing, the total had increased to 147,445. Of these, 65,318, or 45 percent, were women and 10,623, or 7.1 percent, were minority women.

The above figures are from the National Center for Education Statistics (NCES) of the U.S. Department of Education, which conducts biennial staff surveys of higher education institutions. These surveys include, within the category of executive, administrative, and managerial staff, the positions of president, vice president, deans or directors, and positions subordinate to these such as associate deans, assistant deans, and department heads.

The NCES surveys also provide information on other professional positions in higher education administration. These include such support and service positions as librarians, accountants, affirmative action officers, student counselors, and public relations officers. In 1995, women held 60 percent of these positions. While these are not leadership positions, and normally do not lead to leadership positions, they are perceived as part of the professional staff of higher education and as such offer important career opportunities for women.

Surveys conducted by the College and University Personnel Association (CUPA) provide a closer look at the position of women in the hierarchy of higher education administration. CUPA conducts annual administrative compensation surveys covering 174 administrative positions. Unlike the NCES staff surveys that cover all 3,716 institutions of higher education in the United States, the CUPA surveys cover approximately 1,500 institutions. Although the CUPA surveys are not all-inclusive, they do cover the major universities, liberal arts colleges, and two-year institutions, and are indicative of employment patterns and trends that are necessary to the analysis of compensation.

CUPA reports provide data on employment of college and university administrators in five principal categories: executive, academic, administrative, external affairs, and student services. The executive category consists of chief executive officers, their assistants, and executive vice presidents. The academic category includes chief academic officers, deans, and directors of library and information services and institutional research. The administrative category includes business officers, personnel directors, staff attorneys, affirmative action officers, and other nonacademic personnel. External affairs encompasses a variety of functions, such as development, public relations, and alumni affairs. The student services classification includes such positions as admissions officer, registrar, director of financial aid, director of housing, director of athletics, and director of counseling.

The 1998/99 CUPA survey reported a total of 53,580 incumbents, of whom 42.3 percent were women. Table II-1 shows the breakdown by category. Within the academic category, the top position is chief academic officer. The CUPA survey for 1998/99 reported that 1,085 incumbents held this position; 302 of these, or 27.8 percent, were women.

An earlier analysis of CUPA surveys was carried out in 1985 under the auspices of the Russell Sage Foundation Task Force on Women in Higher Education and reported in the volume *Women in Academe* (Chamberlain 1988). Table II-2 shows the gains made by women between 1985/86 and 1998/99.

The executive and academic categories comprise leadership positions in higher education. At the executive level, the increase in the proportion of

Table II-1 • Women Employed as College and University Administrators by Selected Categories, 1998/99

| | Total | Women | |
Category	Number	Number	Percentage
Executive	2,242	574	26.0
Academic	12,673	5,425	43.0
Administrative	17,577	6,441	37.0
External affairs	6,046	3,067	51.0
Student services	15,042	7,483	49.0

Source: College and University Personnel Association (CUPA), *Administrative Compensation Survey. 1998–99,* 1999.

Table II-2 • Women Employed as College and University Administrators by Selected Categories, 1985/86 and 1998/99

| | Percentage Female | |
Category	1985/86	1998/99
Executive	9.0	26.0
Academic	28.0	43.0
Administrative	22.0	37.0
External affairs	39.0	51.0
Student services	36.0	49.0

Source: Chamberlain, Mariam K., ed., *Women in Academe: Progress and Prospects,* 1988; and College and University Personnel Association (CUPA), *Administrative Compensation Survey. 1998–99,* 1999.

women from nine percent to more than 26 percent is impressive, although, of course, still considerably short of parity. At the academic level, women are well represented but tend to be concentrated in less influential positions, such as dean of nursing or education. Be that as it may, the overall picture is one of remarkable progress in higher education leadership on the part of women.

This progress may be traced on the one hand to changes in institutional attitudes and practices relating to women and on the other to the increase in the pool of qualified women. It is unlikely, however, that so much progress would have been made without special programs to promote the capacity of women to benefit from new opportunities. Many such programs were launched during the 1970s to identify women with a potential for and interest in higher education administration, to facilitate their entry into administrative careers, and to promote their advancement to senior positions.

Foremost among these programs was the Summer Institute for Women in Higher Education Administration, cosponsored by Bryn Mawr College and Higher Education Resource Services (HERS). HERS was established by a group of women administrators in 1972 with support from the Ford Foundation. Its purpose was to develop programs for the career advancement of women in higher education.

Initially, HERS served as a talent bank and referral service; later it expanded to offer career advising and professional development programs. The Summer Institute at Bryn Mawr has been the centerpiece of the HERS program since its initiation in 1976. It is a four-week residential program, open to women administrators and faculty members from institutions in the United States and abroad. Approximately 20 percent of the participants are minority women. The curriculum includes sessions on the academic environment, academic governance, finance, budgeting, employee relations, information technology, and management skills.

The national HERS office is based at the University of Denver and is directed by Cynthia Secor, one of the co-founders of HERS. In addition to the Summer Institute, HERS maintains a network of women administrators for mutual support and offers a mentoring program in which those with experience give guidance and advice to those who are newer in the field. HERS also conducts a management institute in New England on the campus of Wellesley College. This program consists of a series of technical skills seminars presented over five weekends spread throughout the academic year. The subjects are similar to those covered in the Summer Institute (Tinsley, Secor, and Kaplan 1984).

The HERS program is not intended to bring women into careers in higher education but rather to help those who are already in administration advance to upper-level positions. Many women who are now presidents, vice presidents, and deans have benefited from the Summer Institute and other HERS programs. The institute, originally supported by foundations, is now self-supporting from tuition revenues, usually paid on behalf of participants by the higher education institutions with which they are affiliated.

WOMEN IN LEADERSHIP POSITIONS: THE PRESIDENCY

In 1971, Alan Pifer, then president of the Carnegie Corporation, gave a speech on women in higher education before the Southern Association of Colleges and Schools. He noted: "In the top ranks of college and university administration, if one excepts the Catholic women's colleges, one has to look far and wide to find a woman. There are currently virtually no four-year coeducational institutions headed by a woman" (Chamberlain 1988).

Women Presidents in U.S. Colleges and Universities, a report issued by the American Council on Education (ACE), presented data showing that as of 1995, 453 women (or 16 percent of all presidents), including 72 minority women, served as heads of educational institutions of all types and sizes (ACE 1995). This figure represented a startling change over a period of approximately 25 years. What is more, there is every indication that the trend is continuing.

ACE is the umbrella organization for the nation's colleges and universities. Its membership also includes other education and education-related organizations. ACE's annual meetings and other activities provide forums for the discussion of major issues related to higher education. ACE also serves as an advocate on higher education issues to policymakers. Its main constituency is college and university presidents.

In 1973 ACE established the Office of Women in Higher Education (OWHE) and a Commission on Women in Higher Education to advise it. Because of ACE's involvement with senior administrators, the OWHE focused on increasing the number of women in higher education administration, with special emphasis on presidencies, vice presidencies, and deanships. Following deliberations by staff and commissioners, as well as investigations into the barriers to women's advancement, OWHE concluded that qualified women were available but overlooked in the promotion process. Accordingly, in 1977, OWHE launched the National Identification Program for the Advancement of Women in Higher Education, known as ACE/NIP. The program was funded by a grant from the Carnegie Corporation and institutional support from ACE.

The objective of NIP was to identify talented women and enhance their visibility as leaders by creating networks of women (including minority women) and men who were in a position to recommend and sponsor women for advancement. This was achieved by holding national forums on higher education topics for senior-level women and selected men, and state and regional forums for "emerging women leaders." The group also created state and city networks throughout the country that organized their own events. Some of the issues addressed at these NIP gatherings were: financing higher education, ethics in education, the role of trustees, and the importance of diversity to the educational mission.

In 1975, OWHE began to compile data on women CEOs in colleges and universities in the United States. They found that there were 148 women in CEO positions at 2,500 accredited institutions. Two out of three women

CEOs were members of religious orders. Surprisingly, women headed fewer than half of all women's colleges. No data were available on women of color. Twenty years later, as noted above, OWHE reported that the number of women CEOs in colleges and universities had increased to 453, representing 16 percent of the total. Of these, 72 (16 percent), were women of color—including 39 African Americans, 24 Hispanics, seven American Indians, and two Asian Americans. In addition, women headed 16 percent of all higher-education system offices, state commissions, and state departments of higher education (ACE 1995).

In 1985, OWHE conducted an in-depth survey of women in college and university presidencies, including size and type of institution, race/ethnicity, marital status, educational background, career path to the presidency, and perceptions of women and minority issues. OWHE found that women presidents were represented in significant numbers in all sizes and types of institutions—public and independent, two-year and four-year, coeducational and women's colleges, and comprehensive and research as well as liberal arts institutions. Women CEOs who were members of religious orders remained an important group, although they represented a declining proportion of women CEOs overall. The survey also found that women presidents collectively were becoming more racially and ethnically diverse (Touchton, Shavlik, and Davis 1993).

With regard to marital status, 32 percent of the women CEOs in 1985 were married, 18 percent were separated, divorced, or widowed, and 50 percent (including members of religious orders) had never married. Overall, 54 percent of the lay presidents and 38 percent of all respondents reported having one or more children. In marital status, women CEOs differed from men by a wide margin. A 1986 study of all college presidents, both male and female, conducted by ACE's Center for Leadership Development, showed that 93 percent of male lay presidents were married (Touchton, Shavlik, and Davis 1993).

In terms of educational background, 81 percent of women CEOs reported holding an earned doctorate or professional degree. A preponderance of women CEOs had their highest degrees in education (40 percent), humanities or fine arts (29 percent), or the social sciences (12 percent). Those with Ph.D.'s in education were predominantly CEOs of two-year rather than four-year institutions. The degree attainment of women CEOs did not differ markedly from that of male CEOs.

The survey found that women's career paths to the presidency were similar to those of men. Over 70 percent served as chief academic officer, vice president, or president of another institution before assuming the presidency. The rest served as dean, department chair, faculty member, or in one of a variety of other positions not typically associated with the career path to the presidency.

Of the women CEOs surveyed by ACE in 1995, 37 percent had participated in ACE/NIP and two percent had participated in the HERS/Bryn Mawr Summer Institute for Women in Higher Education Administration. In addition to these two programs, which focus specifically on women, there are other programs that are designed to promote career advancement in higher education for both men and women by providing training in academic administration. The most prestigious and influential of these are the ACE Fellows Program and the Institute for Educational Management (IEM) at Harvard University.

The ACE Fellows Program consists of a year-long internship combined with seminars on basic administration skills, public-policy issues, and career planning. The Institute for Educational Management is a six-week summer program for senior-level administrators. Its curriculum covers such topics as budgeting, information systems, fund-raising, endowment management, and government relations. Women were all but invisible in these programs at the beginning of the 1970s. Since then, their presence has increased significantly. Of the women CEOs surveyed in 1995, 15 percent reported that they had attended the IEM program; nine percent had held ACE Fellowships.

The co-founder of the ACE National Identification Program and director of the Office of Women in Higher Education from 1982 through 1995 was Donna Shavlik. In 1998, the National Association for Women in Education (NAWE) awarded her a Lifetime Achievement Award for her work on behalf of women in higher administration, particularly women presidents. In the previous year, NAWA presented a similar award to Cynthia Secor, co-founder and director of the HERS/Bryn Mawr Summer Institute, for her contribution to the career advancement of women administrators.

As of 1999, there are 480 women college and university presidents in the United States. Several women are—or were—CEOs of institutions that are among the most prestigious in the nation. The first to break into these ranks was Hanna Holborn Gray, who was appointed president of the University of Chicago in 1978 (and held that position until 1993). Before that she had been a professor of history, provost, and acting president at Yale University. She remains at the University of Chicago as a professor of history, a field in which she has a long and distinguished record.

Donna E. Shalala was appointed chancellor of the University of Wisconsin, Madison, in 1988 after serving as president of Hunter College of the City University of New York from 1980 to 1988. A political scientist by training, she began her academic career as an assistant professor of political science at the City University of New York. Her next move was to Teachers College at Columbia University as associate professor of politics and administration. During this period she became prominent as a specialist in state and local school finance and educational policy issues. At the University of Wisconsin, she held the position of chancellor until 1993, when she was appointed Secretary of Health and Human Services in the Clinton Administration.

Nannerl O. Keohane, also a political scientist, was appointed president of Duke University in 1993, after serving as president of Wellesley College from 1981 to 1993. Before that she was a professor of political science at Stanford University.

Judith Seitz Rodin was appointed president of the University of Pennsylvania in 1994. After receiving a Ph.D. in psychology from Columbia University, she began her academic career in 1970 as an assistant professor of psychology at New York University. She next moved to Yale University and rose through the ranks as associate and full professor. While at Yale, she held a number of academic administration posts, including chair of the department of psychology, director of graduate studies, dean of the graduate school, and finally provost.

In 1999, Shirley Ann Jackson was appointed president of Rensselaer Polytechnic Institute. She had earned a doctorate in physics from MIT in 1973, the first black woman to earn a doctorate in any field from that institution. Ms. Jackson began her career in industry, conducting research at the AT&T Bell Laboratories in New Jersey, where she remained until 1991. She then spent four years as a professor of physics at Rutgers University and, in 1995, was appointed chairwoman of the U.S. Nuclear Regulatory Commission. It was from there that she was recruited to Rensselaer (Rolnick 1999).

Clearly, a number of women have broken through the glass ceiling in higher education. However, we still have a long way to go to achieve parity between women and men in college and university presidencies.

WOMEN TRUSTEES

In the governing structure of American colleges and universities, the ultimate source of authority is the board of trustees. Although the faculty and administration exercise day-to-day power over financial and academic matters and campus life in general, the board constitutes the legal body or corporate presence of the institution. As such, the board is vested with power and authority over setting institutional policies and priorities, long-range planning, approving and monitoring budgets, and—possibly most important—selecting and evaluating the president. In practice, boards exercise oversight, rather than direct control, over such matters, except in times of crisis.

In view of the role and potential power of trustees, it is surprising that relatively little attention has been paid to their demographic characteristics. By the same token, there has been limited information about women on boards. This situation began to change during the 1960s when concerns were raised about diversity among board members, and some initial studies were carried out to identify the trustee population.

Beginning in the 1970s, more comprehensive surveys were conducted under the auspices of the Association of Governing Boards of Universities and Colleges (AGB), the national organization representing trustees of institutions of higher education. A 1977 survey, entitled *Composition of College and University Governing Boards,* covered more than 47,000 trustees and regents serving 2,314 governing boards responsible for 3,036 colleges and universities. Of all trustees at that time, 15 percent were women and seven percent were members of minority groups. A subsequent study in 1985 showed an increase in the proportion of women to 20 percent and of minority groups to 10 percent (AGB 1986).

The most recent AGB survey was conducted in 1997 and published in 1998 in two separate reports, one on independent colleges and universities and one on public institutions. From the viewpoint of trustees, the distinction between independent and public institutions is particularly important because of the different ways their board members are chosen. Nearly half of all public board members are selected by gubernatorial appointment, 29 percent by public election, and 22 percent by other methods, such as appointment by state legislatures. By comparison, boards of independent institutions are self-governing. More than 60 percent have policies that set renewable three-year terms for trustees, while others have six-year terms or longer. Many institutions require representation of particular constituencies, such as faculty, students, and alumni, and 55 percent provide for the chief executive officer to serve as a voting member of the board (Madsden 1998).

As of 1997, 30 percent of all public board members were women, an increase of seven percent since 1985. Twenty-six percent of the members of boards of independent higher education institutions were women, compared with 20 percent in 1985. The racial and ethnic composition of boards, public or independent, has not changed significantly since 1985. With regard to age distribution, the largest group of trustees for both public and private boards is between 50 and 59 years old (38 percent in each case). In terms of primary occupations, 37 percent of public board members and 42 percent of independent board members are business executives. Professionals in various fields represent 18 percent of public board members and 14 percent of independent board members.

There have been a few studies of the individual characteristics of board members, their backgrounds, their roles as trustees, and their views on higher education issues. One of the earliest of these was carried out by Rodney Harnett in 1968 and reported in *College and University Trustees: Their Background, Roles and Educational Attitudes,* published by the Educational Testing Service (Harnett 1969). After comparing the attitudes of male and female trustees on a range of educational issues, Harnett concluded that women contribute a more liberal viewpoint to most governing boards. For example, he found that women trustees were more supportive than their male colleagues of free faculty expression of opinions and were more opposed to administrative control of the content of the student newspaper. Later studies confirm these findings. In general, women trustees are found to be more concerned with diversity and quality-of-life issues than their male counterparts.

CONCLUSION

Women have made significant gains in higher education leadership over the last twenty-five years. They have increased doctoral attainment dramatically and are now entering faculty positions at the assistant professor level in numbers approaching parity with men. However, their advancement from assistant professor to tenured status as associate and full professor lags behind that of their male peers, and it may be that the need to make decisions about childbearing and rearing, at least in some cases, is one of the factors involved. The proportion of women among full professors, while nearly twice as high as in 1972, is still only 18.7 percent, and this remains a matter of concern.

Women frequently make the transition from faculty positions to careers in academic administration and leadership positions in higher education through appointment or election as department chair. Yet very little is known about incumbents in this position, male or female—who they are, the criteria by which they are selected, or the qualifications required. More information about department chairs should be high on the agenda for future research in higher education.

The advancement of women into positions of academic leadership has been aided by federal laws and regulations prohibiting discrimination and by special networks and training programs such as ACE/NIP and the HERS/Bryn Mawr Summer Institute. The proportion of women in posi-

tions of academic administration now exceeds 42 percent, an impressive figure. Less impressive is the proportion of women presidents and CEOs—16
percent—although this is an improvement over the mere five percent in
1975.

What does the future hold for women in academic leadership? The trends
described in this chapter may be expected to continue as long as the pool
of qualified women continues to grow. In general, women have been more
successful in reaching leadership positions in education than they have been
in the corporate world.

Beyond the numbers, and the issue of equality of opportunity for women,
the increasing presence of women in academic leadership positions has implications for the environment of higher education. There is no conclusive
evidence that women have a different managerial style from men. They may,
however, have somewhat different priorities, giving more attention to
quality-of-life issues in particular, as indicated by the study of women
trustees. Moreover, the presence of women in faculty and leadership positions can inspire women students to choose careers in academic life. And
finally, it is important for male students to grow accustomed to seeing
women faculty in the classroom and for male administrators to grow accustomed to working with women as colleagues.

THREE

WOMEN AND LEADERSHIP IN CORPORATE AMERICA

Sheila Wellington and Katherine Giscombe

HIGHLIGHTS

IN THE LAST QUARTER-CENTURY, American women have made significant gains in achieving positions of corporate leadership. However, old attitudes and misconceptions about their abilities, as well as lack of opportunities, still hold women back. As a result, they have needed to develop creative strategies for proving themselves and gaining recognition. For women of color, the ascent to the upper echelons of the corporate world is particularly challenging. Despite increased opportunities for advancement, women of color still must contend with issues of race and culture as well as gender.

- While women today make up 39 percent of the business workforce, they hold less than 12 percent of Fortune 500 corporate officer positions and only about 11 percent of Fortune 500 positions on corporate boards.
- Women represent less than seven percent of all corporate officers in line positions—that is, in positions with revenue-generating or profit-and-loss responsibility.
- Only 63 women were among the five highest-paid officers in Fortune 500 companies in 1998. Still, this is more than double the comparable number in 1995.
- The number of Fortune 500 companies with three or more women directors has increased from 19 to 45.
- While women have made significant gains, they must still struggle for recognition. Many women say their success has depended upon consistently exceeding expectations, developing a style with which male managers are comfortable, seeking out difficult assignments, having an influential mentor, and networking with influential colleagues.

- Women report that they are most hindered in their pursuit of top management positions by stereotyping by male colleagues, exclusion from informal networks of communication, and lack of significant general management and line experience.
- According to CEOs, the major factors limiting women's advancement are lack of general management and line experience, not having enough time in the pipeline, and lack of mentoring opportunities.
- The overwhelming majority of women who hold management or administrative positions in the private sector are white. Of the 2.9 million women Catalyst found holding these positions in the mid-1990s, 86 percent were white, seven percent were African American, five percent were Hispanic, and three percent were Asian or other ethnic minorities.
- Corporate women of color, like corporate women in general, most frequently cite these major factors as contributing to their success: handling high-visibility projects; exceeding performance expectations; having access to an influential mentor or sponsor; and having opportunities for informal networking with influential colleagues. Women of color also cite having an acceptable communication style.
- Barriers to advancement for women of color include such factors as the absence of an influential mentor or sponsor; the lack of informal networking with influential colleagues; and the lack of company role models of the same race or ethnic group.
- Although three out of four women of color are aware of diversity training in their companies, slightly more than half (53 percent) say that diversity efforts fail to address subtle racism. Comparatively few believe that managers receive adequate training in managing a diverse workforce, and only 18 percent say that managers are rewarded for achieving diversity goals.
- While half of women of color say that their company appreciates cultural differences, over 79 percent of those who strongly intend to leave their company say they must make many adjustments to "fit in."

INTRODUCTION

This chapter explores the experiences of American women in achieving positions in corporate leadership—their progress, the barriers they have encountered, and the prospects for change. It is based on recent research by Catalyst, a New York–based nonprofit research and advisory organization that works with business and the professions to advance women. Catalyst has conducted surveys, interviews, and public forums on women and corporate leadership, including studies focusing on the challenges faced by women of color in corporate management.[1]

Over the last 25 years, women have demonstrated that they are committed to and prepared for careers in business. Today, women make up nearly half the U.S. workforce, more than half of students earning bachelor's and master's degrees, and nearly 44 percent of law school graduates (see Table 2-6 in the "Statistical Portrait"). Yet they represent only about 29 percent of student enrollment in MBA programs at the top ten business schools—even though an MBA often gives women a distinct advantage in their pursuit of corporate leadership positions (Byrne, Leonhardt, Bongiorno, and Jespersen 1996).

Women have made significant inroads into corporate leadership positions in recent years. They now hold almost 39 percent of the positions as executives, administrators, and managers in the business sector and almost 12 percent of corporate officer positions (up from 8.7 percent in 1995) (see Table III-1). For the first time, over half of Fortune 500 companies have more than one female corporate officer.

Executive women surveyed in 1996 earned an average of $248,000 a year when both salary and bonuses were taken into account. In 1998, some 63 women, compared with 2,257 men, were among the five most highly paid officers at Fortune 500 companies. Although this is a small number, it is more than double what it was in 1995.

Women also have made notable gains as board directors. The number of Fortune 500 boards with women directors has increased by 24 percent since 1993, and the number of women serving on those boards has grown by 34 percent since 1994. The biggest strides have come in the number of companies with three or more women directors: since 1994, that number has grown from 19 percent to 34 percent.

While these numbers represent real progress, women have not come as far as one would expect, considering their work experience and academic achievements. Today, there are only four female CEOs of Fortune 500 companies.

Women's success is tied, in part, to the industries that employ them. Diversified financial companies have better than average representation of women at all levels of management. Industries with no women corporate

[1]Unless another source is given, Catalyst is the source of the information in this chapter: Catalyst, *Census of Women Board Directors of the Fortune 1000, 1999; Census of Women Corporate Officers and Top Earners, 1999; Creating Women's Networks, 1999; Women of Color in Corporate Management: A Statistical Picture, 1998; Women of Color in Corporate Management: Dynamics of Career Advancement, 1998; Women of Color in Corporate Management: Opportunities and Barriers, 1999; Women in Corporate Leadership: Progress and Prospects, 1996.*

Table III-1 • Women's Representation in American Business, 1999

	Percentage Female
Business workforce (estimate[1])	39.3
Executives, administrators, and managers employed by business (estimate[2])	39.8
Corporate officers in Fortune 500 companies	11.9
Directors of Fortune 500 companies	11.2
Highest titles at Fortune 500 companies[3]	5.1
Top earners at Fortune 500 companies[4]	3.3
CEOs of Fortune 500 companies	[5]

[1]The estimate was arrived at by subtracting women and men employed in hospitals, health services, educational services, social services, and public administration from the total numbers of women and men employed in 1998, and calculating the female percentage of the result.

[2]The estimate was arrived at by subtracting women and men employed in executive, administrative, or managerial occupations in "professional and related services" and "public administration" from the total numbers of women and men employed as executives, administrators, and managers in 1998, and calculating the female percentage of the result.

[3]Chairman, vice chairman, chief executive officer (CEO), president, chief operating officer (COO), senior vice president, and executive vice president.

[4]The five most highly compensated officers in a company.

[5]Less than one-tenth of one percent (four women).

Source: Bureau of Labor Statistics, unpublished data from the 1999 Current Population Survey (annual averages); and Catalyst, *Census of Women Board Directors of the Fortune 1000*, 1999a, and *Census of Women Corporate Officers and Top Earners*, 1999b.

officers include trucking and textiles; others with low representation include electronics, semiconductors, and waste management.

Being a woman of color in corporate America is particularly challenging. Although Catalyst studies show that a clear majority of executives who are women of color like their jobs, few are satisfied with their advancement opportunities. According to a study by Cornell University (1994), women of color are promoted more slowly, experiencing an average of 3.6 years between promotions compared with 2.6 years for white women.

CHALLENGES AND BARRIERS

Corporate women believe that they must overcome challenges not faced by their male counterparts. Women's central challenge is to break through the glass walls that prevent them from moving into line jobs. To reach the upper echelons of the corporate world, women must manage products, services, clients, or customers—in short, the "business of the business." If a woman is not making money for the organization, she is not likely to become a CEO. Consequently, until more women become plant managers, heads of sales and marketing, vice presidents for operations, and the like—until they are in charge of business divisions with substantial profit-and-loss responsibilities—the pipeline to corporate leadership will continue to lack a critical mass of women.

By and large, the glass walls are there because of the myths that women will not take risks, that women go home and stay home after having children, and that customers and clients will not accept women. While women's achievements have dispelled such myths to some extent at corporate headquarters, these views persist in field operations. Some CEOs attribute women's relative scarcity in line management functions to women's own choices, or to their lack of understanding of the importance of these experiences. Others fault company practices. Said one CEO interviewed by Catalyst, "I think that, without question, some women have chosen not to pursue certain tracks that might be more attractive to men. I think the larger reason is probably that we, the men of the organization, have built in credentials that we measure people against and that, for one reason or another, probably are biased against women."

Other CEOs maintain that women have not risen to line positions because they have not spent enough time in the pipeline. "My class from business school had seven women in it out of 650," reported one CEO. "It wasn't until the early seventies that there were large numbers of women entering the managerial ranks with the academic background to put them on a par with men. So there is a pipeline issue. And it'll take another five to eight years before the number of 45-year-old women ready for senior management jobs is balanced with the number of men. I see lots of women in the step just below senior management, indicative of their numbers in the workplace."

Executive women are far less likely than male CEOs to support the pipeline theory. Many women also dispute the view that it is only a matter of time before they will catch up with men. Women point instead to the inhospitable work environment, contending that the major factors hindering their advancement are stereotyping and preconceptions on the part of male colleagues as well as the exclusion of women from informal networks of communication.

One successful female executive at a consumer products company described how the environment operates to exclude women: "I went to our chairman and I said, 'You know you have lots of good women. The only problem is when you're starting to look for senior management, you tend to hire and promote the person that you know. And you guys get to play golf [together]. . . . You know each other for twenty or thirty years, so that when you have a slate of candidates for a job, you know these men. And if you have a slate of candidates and one woman, 'Oh, that woman has been here only three years, does anyone know her?' "

Catalyst research found that men, unlike women, tend to discount the importance of the corporate culture, possibly because they have the luxury of taking it for granted. After all, the expectations, values, and norms of the male majority heavily influence corporate environments. The movement of women into management positions has disturbed the values and norms that underlie corporate culture. Some male managers are intimidated by the idea of supervising women. Others have difficulty reporting to a woman manager. One female executive vice president at an insurance company described her experience: "Probably the most difficult part was when I was in Human Resources and a number of my [male] peers were very resentful of me and said they wouldn't work for me, which really created a problem for me. . . . They did as much as they could to kind of impede me."

As women have gained ground in corporate America, some men believe that women's progress has come at their expense. According to Catalyst's findings, some 40 percent of women executives and 20 percent of CEOs believe that men are concerned about reverse discrimination. Unfortunately, beliefs about reverse discrimination can undermine corporate efforts to promote greater diversity in leadership.

Women must also confront the challenges that come with breaking new ground. Performance expectations of women in management positions can be high while support can sometimes be tepid. One senior vice president for a health care organization described her experience: "With 13 men on the management committee and I'm the only woman . . . it was very awkward at first. But it's been over two years now, and what I have found is that they are never truly comfortable because it's not a hundred percent men. And that's not because they don't like me, or they don't like the fact that a woman's there. It's that there's always that certain guard that what they might say in a roomful of men will be taken wrong when a woman is there."

Family responsibilities can present another obstacle for women executives. Seventy-two percent of women executives who participated in the Catalyst study (1996), *Women in Corporate Leadership: Progress and Prospects,* were married. Another 17 percent had been married, and 64 percent had children. Although family-friendly policies like flextime, parental leave, telecommuting, and part-time work options are now common in many corporations, women executives are reluctant to use them.

In fact, women executives often go to great lengths to avoid the impression that family responsibilities might interfere with their career commitments. Said one female bank vice president, "One of my friends . . . advised me when I went to work [that] if my kids were ever sick, I should stay out and say I'm sick. Not to call in and say my kids are sick because . . . the message is, 'When her kids are sick, she's not going to be here.' So I did."

The concerns of women executives are well founded. Catalyst studies show that many companies still are not supportive of employees who opt for flexible work arrangements. Even a decision to take advantage of a temporary alternative arrangement, such as a reduced schedule, can be mistaken for a sign that an employee is less committed to her career. Most executive women readily acknowledge making many trade-offs—from greatly curtailing their social lives and postponing vacations to being resigned to messy houses and putting up with a long commute in order to live closer to their husband's job (so that husbands can share household responsibilities).

OVERCOMING CHALLENGES AND OBSTACLES

Despite challenges and obstacles, increasing numbers of women are ascending the corporate ladder. Women surveyed by Catalyst reported that a number of factors were responsible for their success: consistently exceeding performance expectations (77 percent), developing a style that men were comfortable with (61 percent), seeking difficult or high-visibility assignments (50 percent), having an influential mentor (37 percent), and networking with influential colleagues (28 percent) (Catalyst 1996).

Corporate America looks for superior results from all its executives—male and female—but women report that more is expected from them. Essentially, they must always excel, even when no one is paying attention. For women, building a track record counts for a lot.

"I was always true to my word. I got things done. People knew they could count on me. And they knew that I would either produce a quality product myself or that I would insist that a quality product be produced by my staff," stated a successful insurance company executive.

A female airline vice president agreed: "I'd say the most important thing was consistently delivering quality products so that people came back to you over and over again and you developed a reputation."

Taking on "stretch" assignments—difficult tasks that others might shy away from—has proven to be an effective way for women to gain the attention of top management. Tackling such jobs can be of pivotal importance for women. Not only do they benefit from the professional growth and learning challenges inherent in such assignments, but women also gain exposure to key decisionmakers who can become valuable contacts and career boosters.

PROFILE OF KAREN BATENIC, EXECUTIVE DIRECTOR
OF HUMAN RESOURCES AT SARA LEE CORPORATION

When I came to Sara Lee thirteen years ago, with braces on my teeth and one child, there weren't many women in the organization and most of the meetings tended to be all men. And you felt a little funny, and you didn't know if they sensed it or not . . . when you are the only woman in the room, will you be heard, will you be taken seriously? And what I found at Sara Lee was that as long as you worked hard and produced quality work, that's all that mattered. They didn't care if you were a man or a woman, black or white, yellow, red, anything, as long as you could produce the work, they would just give you more. But they would reward you for that work, which was positive too.

As I went through my career, with child one and then they saw me with child two, or pregnant . . . "Are you coming back to work?" and "Yes, definitely, I'm coming back . . ." That question was still asked. By the time I was pregnant with the third one, nobody asked anymore. They figured, "She's just coming back to work." And I did.

But there were some great strides that I felt personally. I was eight months pregnant with my third child when I was promoted to a director. And, it was one of those things that another company could've said, "We can wait till she comes back. We can wait and see if she comes back." But it was quite a surprise for me. It was something that made me feel really good. And there were other women in the organization that the same things happened to. And probably the men in the organization didn't even realize what a significant thing that was for us, as we talked among ourselves. Being recognized at that point in your life, instead of being dismissed, was a very strong point for the company.

Then there were men in our organization that I thought were very insightful but a lot of them didn't understand. "Did you realize someone drives thirty minutes to drop their child off before they come to work?" "No, I didn't." Or, "What do you do when your child's sick?" The answer I heard was, "I don't know. My wife takes care of it." So, I helped to educate them.

Also, I had a very supportive boss. One time, we had to come up to an issue where our A, B, and C players, the highest level in the company, were eligible for a bonus plan. The plan document was written from who knows where or when, or how long ago, that when anyone was on short-term disability, those earnings would not count towards [a] bonus. Well, I pointed out to him that most of the people who would go on short-term disability were probably women with pregnancies, and that was hurting their earning potential. There wasn't red tape. There wasn't discussion. The first thing he said was, "Well go ahead and change it." And that's how [quickly] things happen at Sara Lee. When you find the right answer, they just go ahead and do it.

Acquiring unique skills and expertise is also a plus. Women who do so are likely to be viewed as indispensable. Almost half of women surveyed by Catalyst said that upgrading their educational credentials was important for two reasons: It helped lay the foundation for their careers by providing them with problem-solving skills and/or technical expertise, and it gave them credibility with male colleagues.

These findings make women's stagnant enrollment in MBA programs all the more troubling. "Had I not had the MBA, I clearly wouldn't be in this position. . . . Certainly, I could have acquired a fair amount of the knowledge base and financial skills on my own, but it really helped in having the staff respect you because you have the same ticket to entry that they did," reported one female executive in the airline industry.

Although superior performance may be essential, business results alone do not assure promotability. In many work environments, factors not related to performance—such as personal style, visibility, influential mentors, and political astuteness—also play a pivotal role.

Female executives often struggle to fit into the upper ranks of a corporation without losing their identity. Yet some Fortune 1000 CEOs interviewed by Catalyst praised women's uniqueness. "I think a woman definitely understands much better, intuitively, how teams work, how to lead by recognition and encouragement, mentoring, more so than men. Rather than a command-and-control approach, there's a desire to get consensus—to empower others, to teach others. I think the great companies of the twenty-first century really understand what we're talking about here and already have begun to move in that direction. It's something that comes more easily to a woman than a man," reported one CEO.

PROFILE OF ANAT BIRD, EXECUTIVE VICE PRESIDENT OF WELLS FARGO BANK AND REGIONAL PRESIDENT FOR THE NORTHERN CALIFORNIA REGION

John Simpson did wonders for my career. The first thing that he did was send me home to get properly dressed my first day at work. I was working in Washington, D.C., and it was 100 percent humidity and they expected me to wear pantyhose. Where I come from they don't wear panty hose in that temperature. So, it was a learning experience for me. But John taught me about the variables that really made a difference in the business world at that time. I always felt that it was my job to fit myself into the environment so that we can create change from within. It's very difficult to change things from the outside. John got me started by taking me to Brooks Brothers to get properly dressed.

You can absolutely be who you are. I would say that is my number one advice. Be who you are. It doesn't mean that we have to make other people uncomfortable and make a statement by doing something that is so dramatically different that it would just make the other team members uncomfortable. But realize that who you are is what they pay for—that's what you're there for. And that's what your talent is. But it doesn't mean you have to be as thorny as possible.

John also advised me about how to get my next job. I was very fortunate to have an incredible mentor who told me that one day he woke up and his kids were 21 and he had no idea who they were. So I figured that I had to reach a reasonable balance between work and my family and that was something that served me extremely well throughout my career.

Nevertheless, many successful female executives report that they have needed to learn to play the game as men play it. And by that they mean playing golf, keeping their personal lives out of the office, vigorously demonstrating company loyalty, and not "rocking the boat" or "making waves."

Said one senior vice president in retailing, "I'm really into sports and can talk sports with the best of them . . . and I think that's how I disarm them. . . . As soon as I turn the subject to sports, they think, 'Oh, she's not that different, I can relate to her.' So that's a little tool I have in my toolbox that I use sometimes."

Corporate America rewards managers who show initiative. Often, women must signal explicitly their willingness to take on unusual assignments. Otherwise, managers may assume women are not interested or available and decide not to offer them the opportunity. A majority of human resources officers in a recent Catalyst study acknowledged that many managers in their companies regarded assigning women to line management responsibilities as risky. The message here is that women cannot wait for potentially career-enhancing opportunities to come to them; they must be proactive in identifying such opportunities and letting their managers know that they are interested in them.

Several CEOs underscored the importance for women of taking the initiative. One CEO interviewed by Catalyst summed it up this way: "I think a woman has got to indicate that she'd like to do something different. There's been an assumption on the part of men that opportunities everywhere are open to them, whereas there might be a perception that a woman may not want to move because of personal interests of one kind or another [and] 'move' can mean from one function to general management, to different kinds of disciplines as well as geographic moves. . . . Managers are reluctant to talk about these things today, for whatever reason. . . . I think it's more incumbent on a woman to come forward and say how free she is to do things."

Then, too, there is strength in women's networks. Working with other women within their companies to bring about change is an effective strategy some female executives and CEOs recommend as a means both to enhance women's own careers and to improve institutional practices for the benefit of all women.

One need only look at the investment firm Dain Rauscher for proof of how women's networks can be effective. According to *Creating Women's Networks* (Catalyst 1999c), the Women's Brokers Association at Dain Rauscher promised the CEO that if the company supported their network—with mentoring programs, career-development opportunities, and the like—they would become better brokers. As a result, sales from women's network members increased by 19.2 percent—five percent more than was the case for the rest of the firm.

Increasingly, corporate America regards its workforce as a strategic resource to be managed and developed like any essential resource. As a result, large corporations are addressing diversity in a variety of ways. Companies are creating recruitment and developmental programs designed to identify and groom high-potential women and minority employees, setting numerical targets for the representation of women and people of color at particular levels, and holding managers accountable for developing diverse talent.

How helpful have such strategies been? According to a study conducted by Catalyst in 1996, not very helpful as yet. When women were asked to rate the importance of 11 possible company-initiated strategies—including giving women visible assignments, developing high-potential employees, using cross-functional job rotation, implementing external executive development programs, and requiring management accountability for women's advancement—no more than 22 percent of respondents said that any of these corporate strategies had been critical to their success. Taking initiative, it seems, is far more effective than waiting for corporate assistance. Said one female executive, "The companies talk the talk, but at a certain level [above entry level] they don't walk the walk! You have to do it yourself."

Probably the most significant reason for the limited success of corporate initiatives to date is timing. Catalyst found that many Fortune 1000 companies—even the growing number that now offer structured career-development opportunities to promote diversity—did not offer strategies for advancement in the earlier phases of many women's careers, anywhere from a decade to 30 years ago. Some 40 percent of executive women surveyed reported that their companies did not offer such strategies when they were starting out.

CHALLENGES FACED BY WOMEN OF COLOR

Catalyst studies show that white women report greater progress up the corporate ladder than women of color do. According to unpublished data from Catalyst's 1996 study, *Women in Corporate Leadership: Progress and Prospects,* 60 percent of senior white women, compared with 47 percent of senior women of color, reported that their opportunities for advancement had improved either "somewhat" or "greatly" over the last five years.

The overwhelming majority of women who hold management or administrative positions in the private sector are white. Of the 2.9 million women Catalyst (1999d) found holding these positions in the mid-1990s, 86 percent were white, seven percent were African American, five percent were Hispanic, and three percent were Asian or other ethnic minorities. Although African American women have joined the managerial ranks, they are more likely than Asian, Hispanic, and white women to work in lower-paying industries and occupations. Sixty percent of the managers who are women of color work in just three industries—retail trade, professional and related services, or finance, insurance, and real estate.

Catalyst's analysis revealed a yawning wage gap between different groups of managers in the private, for-profit sector of the economy. For every dollar earned by white male managers, male managers of color earn 73 cents, while white female managers earn 59 cents and female managers of color earn 57 cents. Each group of female managers earns less than her male counterpart.

Corporate women of color certainly understand what it takes to succeed. Those participating in Catalyst studies reported that success depends upon obtaining high-visibility projects, performing over and above expectations, having an acceptable communication style, having access to an influential mentor or sponsor, and having opportunities for informal networking with influential colleagues. But for now, such opportunities often elude women of color. Not only do they face some of the same obstacles to corporate advancement that white women do—that is, they often lack access to influential mentors or sponsors, to opportunities for informal networking with influential colleagues, or to high-visibility assignments—but women of color often face additional barriers, such as the absence of role models of the same race or ethnic background (see Figure III-1). They express concerns about what they term the "concrete ceiling."

In the 1990s, race and culture continue to shape the opportunities for women of color, who face more difficulty than white women in finding mentors. "It's easier for management to mentor those who are like them, so you get the same people rising through the organization and you don't see change," said one Hispanic woman manager.

An African American woman manager interviewed by Catalyst pointed out another difference: "Access to opportunities is easier for white women because they share informal experiences with the power structure—[they] live next door to each other, [their] kids go to the same schools, [and their] husbands [or] brothers are head of something . . ."

Cultural differences can be a factor for many women of color. Fifty percent of women of color interviewed by Catalyst reported that their company appreciated cultural differences, but 79.4 percent of those who strongly intended to leave their company said that they must make many adjustments to "fit in."

Many Asian American women are foreign-born and did not come to America until they were adults. For these women, communication style can be a stumbling block in their career path. One Asian American manager stated, "Opportunities are difficult because it's assumed that you lack communication skills. I have to work harder to prove myself because I don't speak English as well, but I can get my questions across" (Catalyst 1998b).

For Hispanic women, the challenge of balancing work and family can be a significant barrier to advancement. In one Catalyst study (1998b), 21 percent of Hispanic women (compared with 17 percent of Asian American women and nine percent of African American women) reported that their culture emphasized traditional gender roles.

As costs of recruitment increase, corporations cannot afford the turnover

PROFILE OF EMMA BATTLE, VICE PRESIDENT OF
MARKETING OF WOMEN'S WEAR, A DIVISION OF
SARA LEE SPORTSWEAR:

The first employees that I was assigned to manage didn't understand me, didn't know why I was there or what the management
team was doing in bringing in someone like me. I was fortunate
enough to get an offer from the Quaker Oats Company's management trainee program. I was the first hire at the age of 22 for
the Jackson, Tennessee, manufacturing facility.

Many employees couldn't understand an African American
woman at 22 years old coming in to be their boss. Many of the employees had been there quite a few years and had worked their way
up from the bottom, and I came in not knowing a thing about making waffles, pancakes, or French toast, but they were supposed to
listen to me, so I had to learn very quickly and gain their respect.
In order to do this, I spent a lot of time with them on the floor,
but that still didn't seem to do it. They thought of me like a baby.
Many of them had kids older than me.

How I was able to succeed was through a wonderful mentor, Bob
Hefling, a gruff old man who had come out of maintenance. He
was a mechanic and he was a maintenance supervisor and now he
was a department manager. And, he was very skeptical. But he said,
"Okay, corporate is making me take you. We'll see what you're
made of." So he threw me to the wolves and he said, "I want you
to get out there and supervise." I went out and tried to supervise
and I tried to do what I thought was supervising and most of that
was trying to figure out what instructions to give the employees.

And he saw that I was trying to do a good job. I was making
headway. So he pulled me aside one day and said, "I think 'ya' got
it. You're tough. You look like you want to do a good job. I'm
going to give you my philosophy. You go out there, you gotta be
fair, you gotta be firm, and you gotta be consistent. If you remember
those things when you're doing your job, you gonna do well." I
adopted that as my personal philosophy and in the meantime I had
some really smart employees who said, "And you gotta listen to us."
I had wonderful mentors who helped me succeed in my first assignment and there were many of them along the way.

Figure III-1 • Barriers to Advancement for Women of Color, November 1997–January 1998 (in percentages)

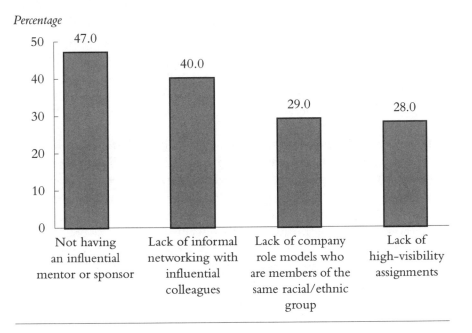

Source: Catalyst, *Women of Color in Corporate Management: Opportunities and Barriers*, 1999d.

that results from losing qualified women of color, yet companies risk losing them at all levels of their organizations. One study conducted by Catalyst (1998b) found that nearly 22 percent of the women of color surveyed intended to leave their current companies. *Women of Color in Corporate Management: Opportunities and Barriers* (Catalyst 1999d) found that several factors influenced the decisions by women of color to remain with a company: the behavior of management, the corporate climate, and effective diversity practices. If managers do not provide opportunities for visibility, if they do not explain organizational policies, and if they do not map out clear developmental goals, women of color are likely to move on.

AFFIRMATIVE ACTION AND EQUAL OPPORTUNITY

Executive women report that affirmative action and equal opportunity policies have had mixed consequences for their careers, but women of color are more likely than women in general to believe that these policies have facilitated their advancement. Overall, one in three executive women reports that affirmative action and equal opportunity policies have had a positive impact on her career, while slightly more than one in five (22 percent) reports that the impact of these policies on her advancement has been both positive and negative. By contrast, almost half (46 percent) of women of color say that affirmative action and equal opportunity policies have opened corporate doors for them, and 31 percent say it has played a role in their promotions. "I have benefited from being at the right place at the right time. I have excelled in my field, but affirmative action has made companies seek me out," stated one Hispanic woman.

However, another woman of color described how affirmative action and equal opportunity policies have been a mixed blessing: "Though I was qualified, consideration for being female probably gave me the edge over qualified males. It has, however, kept the spotlight on me and created extra scrutiny with zero mistakes [possible]."

Without question, affirmative action and equal opportunity policies have heightened companies' awareness, forcing them to focus on ability rather than gender, and making management rethink the status quo. Government policies have opened doors for women and minorities, and put external legal and social pressure on employers to change. One executive who is a woman of color summed up the impact this way: "Without requiring employers to consider talented women, I believe many employers would have continued to believe that women are not suited for many nontraditional roles. I would have been a casualty of that thinking."

Unfortunately, affirmative action and equal opportunity policies have also sparked a backlash. Many individuals assume that employers have given minorities and women special treatment, hiring or promoting less-competent individuals because of sex and race considerations. Resentments have festered, sometimes creating a hostile work environment.

HOW WOMEN OF COLOR VIEW DIVERSITY POLICIES

In many workplaces, diversity policies have not succeeded in eliminating entrenched biases against women and minorities. Many CEOs are trying to make changes. Most CEOs interviewed by Catalyst expressed a deep commitment to implementing corporate diversity strategies. All CEOs cited the importance of diversity as a business imperative and the majority of companies studied have a wide range of initiatives focused on workforce representation, senior leadership management, career development and planning, and education and awareness.

The trouble is that most of the women of color surveyed by Catalyst (1999d) say those efforts are not as effective as they could be or were intended to be. Fifty-three percent say that their company's diversity efforts have failed to address subtle racism in the work environment, and only 22 percent believe that managers at their companies receive adequate training in managing a diverse workforce. Even fewer women of color report that managers at their company are held accountable (17 percent) or are rewarded (18 percent) for achieving diversity goals. Furthermore, only about one in four women of color (26 percent) agrees that career development is an important part of her company's diversity program. Similarly, only one in four saw a connection between her company's diversity efforts and her own career advancement.

Many women of color believe that part of the problem stems from the fact that many corporations have not put much muscle behind affirmative action programs. In order for women to achieve significant gains, there needs to be a greater commitment to equity from the top.

Businesses have compelling reasons to pay increasing attention to women of color. The demographic diversity of the labor pool will continue to increase, and women of color will represent a growing pool of talent for corporations. The Bureau of Labor Statistics (BLS) has projected that by 2008 women will make up nearly half (47.5 percent) of the U.S. workforce and that women of color will represent a larger share of the total than they do today. If the BLS projections are on the mark, between 1998 and 2008 the African American women's share will grow to 6.6 percent, the Hispanic women's to 5.5 percent, and the Asian women's share to 2.7 percent. Altogether, women of color will account for close to 15 percent of the total labor force in 2008, up from a little over 12 percent in 1998. At the same time, non-Hispanic white women's share will decline by about one percentage point (to 33.3 percent), and non-Hispanic white men's share will drop by more than two percentage points (to 37.4 percent) (Fullerton 1999).

Corporations also need to consider the buying power of women of color and their growing numbers as business owners. The Selig Center for Economic Growth at the University of Georgia predicts that African American buying power will have grown from $250 billion in 1990 to $506 billion in 1999 (Catalyst 1999d). And the increasing importance of Hispanics as a consumer group cannot be overstated, given that by 2005 they will be the nation's largest minority group.

PROSPECTS FOR CHANGE

What does the future hold for women in corporate leadership? Women and CEOs surveyed by Catalyst were positive about the recent progress of women in management. Eighty-five percent of women and 97 percent of CEOs believe that opportunities for women to advance to senior leadership in their own companies have improved in the last five years.

Many women executives are optimistic about the prospects for continued momentum in rising through the ranks of senior management. The fact that women have for the first time attained the most senior positions in corporate legal, communications, and human resources departments is a major milestone. This accomplishment alone is evidence that barriers can be broken.

Women's continued progress into corporate leadership positions is a shared responsibility between corporations and women themselves. For their part, corporations must make a commitment to lifting roadblocks to women's achievement—and they must pay particular attention to the barriers faced by women of color. One CEO interviewed by Catalyst described how senior-level support for diversity can affect the entire organizational culture: "We have a formal values statement, which we look at periodically to make sure it's in line with the times we operate in. It's very important. We also have ongoing talks about diversity in our quarterly operating review meetings. . . . It doesn't just pop up once a year. It's something that's continuously out in front of people."

Companies must be willing to take risks on women. Both CEOs and women executives agree that to expand opportunities for talented women, companies must be willing to assign them to nontraditional positions and offer them "stretch" assignments, just as they have typically prepared high-potential men for executive leadership. "In the case of women, we use the lack of specific training for a job as a reason not to open the jobs to them, when we are more ready to bring men into jobs for which they are not specifically trained," admitted one CEO.

Women must also be prepared to take initiative and responsibility for their careers. They must understand the choices involved and decide if they are willing to make the trade-offs that executive success requires. "They've got to do a lot of the background stuff that a lot of us have done—acquire skills, acquire credibility, take chances, do the same things that men do," stated one company executive.

To ascend the corporate ladder, a woman must know the company she works for, assess what it wants, and deliver it. As one CEO put it: "I think that anybody, male or female, black or white, has to recognize . . . what the corporation wants. Although you don't particularly like it, it's important enough that you improve your career [that] you're going to go along with it. That's very definitely necessary. . . . You'd better conform with the form of the organization. . . . Basically, I think that women are far more adaptable than men."

There are certainly good reasons to be positive about the future. Companies in the 1990s have increasingly developed and expanded initiatives to address workforce diversity issues. A 1992 Conference Board study noted growing attention to these issues, including support for formal diversity management programs, and predicted that the scope of these efforts would broaden: "As business environments become more global and labor markets become more heterogeneous, diversity will play an increasingly prominent role in the way companies manage their resources" (Catalyst 1996).

There is another motivation for companies to promote the advancement of women: it makes good business sense. Sheer demographics will pressure companies to change. Women make up a large part of the available talent pool, and their unique perspective on problem solving and decisionmaking can be an asset. There is also strength in numbers. Women represent a significant consumer base with increasing buying power.

Finally, beyond the economics involved, concerns about social responsibility, shareholder pressure, the threat of litigation, and consumer attitudes increase the likelihood of corporate change.

CONCLUSION

Overall, the gains of the last five years have given women reason to be optimistic about the future. And the strong business reasons for increasing women's representation—the addition of more women to the talent pool, the unique perspective women bring to decisionmaking and problem solving, and women's significant consumer base—are likely to motivate corporations to encourage women's movement into top leadership positions.

Catalyst has projected that by the year 2000 at least one in five senior managers will be women, and women will occupy some 13 percent of Fortune 500 corporate officer positions. By the year 2005, Catalyst projects, women will occupy 17 percent of corporate officer positions.

Of course, women's continued progress into corporate leadership will not happen automatically. In order for women to succeed, companies need to ensure that women receive high-visibility assignments, that succession planning incorporates gender diversity, that formal mentoring programs are instituted, and perhaps—of greatest importance—that managers are held accountable for women's advancement. With a strong commitment from the top, Catalyst's projections are likely to come true.

FOUR

⭐

WOMEN IN UNION LEADERSHIP

Lois Gray

HIGHLIGHTS

THE AMERICAN LABOR MOVEMENT has reached a critical turning point. Faced with shrinking membership and overwhelming economic and technological challenges, unions seek new strategies for survival and growth. Women, who now make up close to a majority of the workforce, are a major—but largely unrealized—force for change.

This chapter examines the evolution of women's struggle for recognition in labor unions and how women today are slowly moving to center stage in the labor movement. It also examines the societal, institutional, and personal factors that still impede women's full representation at the highest levels of labor leadership and the strategies women employ to overcome them. What are the barriers to forging a partnership between organized labor and women members? Why are women underrepresented in labor leadership? Under what circumstances do women become active in labor's cause and achieve leadership recognition? How have unions responded to their potential? And what difference does it make?

- Male leadership and culture dominate the history of American labor unions. Excluded from membership in most unions, women workers nevertheless produced their own heroines, who led struggles for better wages and working conditions and demanded equal treatment and leadership recognition in their unions.
- Today, few of the top elected or appointed officials of American unions are women, but the number of women serving as elected national executive board members, obtaining staff appointments, and assuming leader-

ship roles in local unions and federations is increasing. Women's representation in elected office is greater in unions where they constitute a majority of the membership and in unions that represent occupations traditionally hospitable to women, such as education, nursing, entertainment, and public-sector clerical and administrative work.

- Leadership prospects for women are increasing in the manufacturing and service sectors. Still virtually closed to female leadership are such traditional male preserves as building construction, mining, and transportation.
- Family responsibilities, male bias, and lack of know-how and self-confidence are barriers that women still need to overcome. These challenges, faced by women in other fields, are intensified in the union setting, where leaders are expected to demonstrate extreme dedication and self-sacrifice.
- Career paths of women in union leadership differ from the typical patterns of male leaders who work their way up through the ranks by assuming increasing levels of responsibility at local and regional levels before achieving high office. Some successful union women follow this route; others obtain recognition by excelling as staff specialists hired from the outside for their expertise in a valued professional field. A surprising number move up from clerical positions.
- Factors that contribute to leadership recognition for women in unions are similar to those in other sectors—hard work, performance, visibility, strategic planning, and good luck. Finding a mentor is particularly helpful, but difficult when all the power figures are male. In the political milieu of unions, building a constituency is essential.
- Women have banded together across union lines to form the national Coalition of Labor Union Women (CLUW), an organization that provides opportunities for networking and training in leadership skills. CLUW also articulates and campaigns for issues of concern to women unionists and forges alliances between labor and women's organizations.
- Union responses to the needs and aspirations of women members vary widely. Best practices include: interest surveys of women members; targeted programs on issues of concern to women; opportunities for women to confer with one another through women's committees and women's departments; education and training programs; and affirmative action with goals and timetables for increasing women's representation in staff and leadership positions.
- Women union leaders make a difference through their distinctive leadership styles—which are usually more participatory and inclusive than men's—and by influencing their organizations to become more socially conscious and family-friendly.

INTRODUCTION

If the AFL-CIO does not become a movement of and for working women, we
don't deserve to have a future and we surely will not have one.
　　　　　　　　—Richard Trumka, Secretary-Treasurer, AFL-CIO

Women hold the key to the future of organized labor. Now 39 percent
of the membership, they make up the majority of the newly organized and
still-to-be-organized sectors of the American labor force. Faced with declining membership, unions are giving priority to areas of growth. Women,
according to polls, are more "union-friendly" than men. Heavily concentrated in low-wage jobs, they have much to gain by banding together. On
average, union women earn 38 percent more per hour than nonunion
women. Even when comparing women with similar education and work
experience, union women earn 12 percent more than nonunion women
(Hartmann, Spalter-Roth, and Collins 1994).

　　Thus, women are moving to center stage in the labor movement. In increasing numbers, they affiliate with established unions, most of which are
male dominated. Many are initiating new organizations. The largest group
of unionized women workers are employed in professional and technical
jobs.

　　This chapter focuses on women in union leadership roles, the barriers they
still must overcome, their strategies for achieving recognition, their career
patterns and leadership styles, and their impact on the labor movement. The
primary sources for this chapter include interviews with union officials, including 56 women who hold leadership positions in national unions,[1] sup-
plemented by insights from the literature.

[1]The women labor leaders interviewed for this chapter are elected officials and appointed
staff from the AFL-CIO and from the national headquarters of the AFL-CIO's major affiliated unions (e.g., the Communications Workers of America [CWA], the American Federation of State, County and Municipal Employees [AFSCME], the United Food and
Commercial Workers International Union [UFCW], the United Automobile, Aerospace and
Agricultural Implement Workers of America [UAW], the American Federation of Government Employees [AFGE], the American Federation of Teachers [AFT], and the Service Employees International Union [SEIU]). In addition, interviews were conducted with women
labor leaders at the National Education Association (NEA) and the American Nurses Association (ANA). This chapter also draws on a number of interviews conducted with the women
presidents of several large local unions located in the Northeast.

WOMEN ARE NOT NEW TO UNION LEADERSHIP

Women have always been active in the workplace and in labor organizations. In colonial times, women as well as men were required to work; non-
workers were jailed. Whether working as slaves, indentured servants, or free
women employed for wages, women, like men, rebelled against exploita-
tive working conditions and banded together in protest organizations. When
women found the doors closed to membership in male-dominated unions,
they formed their own organizations. When employers expected women to
work for half the salaries of male workers, women fought back by organizing for equal pay. And when employers tried to enlist women to break
strikes, women joined in solidarity with men.

These struggles produced such legendary heroines as Mother Jones, who
organized coal miners; Sojourner Truth, who fought against slavery; Susan
B. Anthony, the women's suffrage leader who was a delegate to the first convention of the National Labor Unions in 1868; Pauline Newman, who
emerged from the "Great Uprising" of 20,000 New York garment workers in 1909 to become the first full-time woman organizer employed by the
International Ladies' Garment Workers' Union (ILGWU); and Elizabeth
Gurley Flynn, the firebrand from the Industrial Workers of the World
(IWW) who was a leader in the 1912 "Bread and Roses" strike by textile
workers in Lawrence, Massachusetts. In 1907 Agnes Nestor became the first
women to be elected president of a national union, the Glove Workers
(Foner 1979; Wertheimer 1977).

Yet winning leadership recognition in unions has never been easy for
women. When the American Federation of Labor (AFL) was founded in
1898, a woman delegate introduced a resolution calling for the appointment
of women organizers, a proposal that was not implemented until 10 years
later when the AFL appointed its first woman staff member (Wertheimer
1977).

Early in this century, women, rich and poor, came together in the
Women's Trade Union League (WTUL), an organization specifically designed to fight for women's rights in the labor movement and workers' rights
in the women's movement (Kopelov 1984). In 1919, WTUL passed a resolution calling on the U.S. government and the American Federation of
Labor and all its constituent bodies to "guarantee to women workers adequate representation . . . on all policy-making councils, on boards and committees that deal with conditions of employment or standards of life" (Eaton
1990, 205).

The WTUL continued to press for the rights of women workers on the job and in the union through the 1930s and 1940s through legislative initiatives and training and education programs aimed to equip women for activity and leadership. As mass production industries organized during the depression years, women played critical roles in sit-down strikes for union recognition in the automobile and rubber industries. The Congress of Industrial Organizations (CIO), which broke with and challenged the AFL, eliminated the sex and race exclusion clauses that had characterized many of the craft unions and women began to hold office in newly formed labor organizations representing electrical, textile, and tobacco workers (Foner 1980).

With World War II came labor shortages that attracted increasing numbers of women into the labor force where they encountered discriminatory practices such as separate seniority lists. A WTUL survey in 1943 found women to be active in unions, some elected as shop stewards, but few holding "high union posts" (Foner 1980). Exceptions were Eleanor Nelson, who was elected national president of the CIO United Federal Workers; Katherine Lewis (John L. Lewis's daughter), secretary treasurer of District 50 of the United Mine Workers; and Gladys Dickinson, vice president of the Amalgamated Clothing Workers. In 1946 Rose Pesotta resigned her leadership post in the International Ladies' Garment Workers' Union (ILGWU), concluding that "a lone woman vice-president could not adequately represent the women who now make up 85 percent of the International's membership" (Foner 1980, 368).

WHERE ARE THE WOMEN LEADERS IN TODAY'S UNIONS?

The structure and government of American unions resembles those of the United States. The labor movement is decentralized with a division of powers among local, regional, and national units. The basic building block of unionization is the workplace where employees negotiate with their employer. The workplace unit, in many cases combined with other similar units representing employees in the same occupation or the same industry and/or geographic location, constitutes the local union which elects its own officers. Local unions in common occupations (for example, carpenters or teachers) or related industries (such as automobile and steel manufacturing, or health care and retail trade) affiliate to become national unions. (The unions are called "international unions" when they have affiliates in Canada.)

These national unions are the power centers of the American labor move-

THE LEGAL FRAMEWORK FOR WOMEN IN UNIONS

The National Labor Relations Act (NLRA), or Wagner Act, passed in 1935, gave employees in private industry the right to join unions and engage in collective bargaining. This right was protected by penalties on employers who engage in unfair labor practices. In 1947, the NLRA was amended by the Taft Hartley Act to modify legal protections for the right to organize and to outlaw agreements that require union membership as a condition of employment. In 1974, the law was amended again to include hospitals and nursing homes under its protections.

The Labor-Management Reporting Act, or Landrum-Griffin Act, passed in 1959, established a "bill of rights" for union members, internal election procedures, and reporting and disclosure requirements for unions and union officers.

Executive Order 10988, issued in 1962, gave federal employees the right to union representation. Most states currently protect the right of state and municipal employees to organize and bargain.

The Equal Pay Act, passed in 1963, provided equal pay for men and women doing substantially equal work.

The 1964 Civil Rights Act outlawed discrimination based on race, color, sex, national origin, or religion.

ment. Members of local unions determine the structure and policies of the national unions, and elect officers through referendum or delegates assembled in national conventions. As with the U.S. government, unions function under formal constitutions that spell out rules and procedures. In the United States, most national unions are affiliated with the AFL-CIO.

Women are rarely found among the top elected officers in today's national unions, but their numbers are increasing among appointed staff at the national level and elected officers at the regional and local levels. Currently, women hold decisionmaking leadership positions equivalent to chief executive officers in only three national unions: the American Federation of Teachers (AFT), the American Nurses Association (ANA), and the Association of Flight Attendants (AFA). The number of women at this level has not changed over the past 20 years. Two significant changes, however, are the 1995 election of Linda Chávez-Thompson, a Latina, as executive vice president of the national AFL-CIO, and the increase in the number of women serving as international union vice presidents, secretary-treasurers, and executive board members.

As might be expected, women are more likely to achieve top leadership status in labor unions where they constitute a majority—or close to a majority (see Table IV-1). In addition to the AFA, ANA, and AFT, these include the American Federation of Government Employees (AFGE), the American Federation of State, County, and Municipal Employees (AFSCME), the National Education Association (NEA), the Office and Professional Employees International Union (OPEIU), the Service Employees International Union (SEIU), the United Food and Commercial Workers International Union (UFCW), and the Union of Needletrades, Industrial, and Textile Employees (UNITE).[2] Even in these unions, however, the percentage of women in elected decisionmaking posts falls short of their representation in the ranks. In recent AFA elections, men defeated women candidates for two of the three top offices.

Recognition for women is more likely to come through appointment than election. As shown in Table IV-1, in most unions, the percentage of women in charge of headquarters' departments substantially exceeds their representation on executive boards. For example, in the AFL-CIO, elected women members constitute only 13 percent of the Executive Council (the elected officials who make policy for the federation) but appointed women are in charge of 50 percent of union departments—including the important Field Mobilization Department, which supervises a staff of field representatives throughout the United States and coordinates a network of affiliated state and central labor councils.

Even when women constitute 50 percent or more of the membership—as in AFSCME, AFT, SEIU, and UFCW—the female percentage in staff supervisory roles far exceeds the female percentage in elected positions. Exceptions are AFA and ANA, where men hold a disproportionate number of staff positions, despite the predominance of women in the unions' membership and elected policy positions. In the case of ANA, the current national executive director is male. The pattern is also reversed in NEA; its women members are prominent in elected policy positions but continue to

---

[2]On July 1, 1995, the International Ladies' Garment Workers' Union (ILGWU) merged with the Amalgamated Clothing and Textile Workers Union (ACTWU) to form the Union of Needletrades, Industrial and Textile Employees (UNITE).

Table IV-1 • Employed Women by Labor Union Membership and Representation in Leadership Positions, 1999 (in percentages)

Union	Women as a Percentage of		
	Members	Executive Boards	Department Heads
American Federation of Government Employees (AFGE)	46	20	60
American Federation of State, County and Municipal Employees (AFSCME)	52	35	60
Association of Flight Attendants (AFA)	85	79	38
American Federation of Teachers (AFT)	60	40	57
American Nurses Association (ANA)[1]	93	73	70
Bakery, Confectionary and Tobacco Workers (BCT)	33	19	40
Communications Workers of America (CWA)	49	35	20
Hotel Employees and Restaurant Employees International Union (HERE)	48	19	
International Brotherhood of Electrical Employees (IBEW)	30	0	13
International Union of Electronic, Electrical, Salaried, Machine and Furniture Workers (IUE)	40	25	50
Office of Professional Employees International Union (OPEIU)	70	46	15
National Education Association (NEA)[1]	68	33	57
Service Employees International Union (SEIU)	58	30	50
United Automobile, Aerospace and Agricultural Implement Workers of America (UAW)	25	11	10
United Food and Commercial Workers International Union (UFCW)	50	11	25
Union of Needletrades, Industrial and Textile Employees (UNITE)	66	30	40

[1]Not affiliated with the AFL–CIO.

Source: Survey conducted by author, 1999.

depend on a predominantly male staff to administer the organization's business. The national executive director is male, more than half the elected state presidents are women, and four out of five of the state executive directors are men.

Receptivity to women in leadership roles may also reflect the customs and culture of the field a union represents. For example, in theater, movies, music, and dance, women have long occupied "starring" roles in both their professions and their unions. Examples include Patty Duke, former president of the Screen Actors Guild; Ellen Burstyn, former president of Actors' Equity; Shelby Scott, president of the American Federation of Television and Radio Artists; Linda Mays, president of the American Guild of Musical Artists; and Mona Mangan, executive director of Writers Guild East, representing writers for television and motion pictures. In education, another field traditionally open to women, female presidents have emerged in both major unions. Sandra Feldman currently heads AFT, and Mary Hatwood Futrell, an African American woman, is a past president of NEA.

Garment workers' and office workers' unions, which are predominantly female in membership, have only recently elevated women to top office. For example, even though women have played important roles in the history of the needle trades unions, these organizations have always been led by men. In 1999 the UNITE convention increased the proportion of women on its executive board to 30 percent. Historically, OPEIU, which represents female office workers along with fashion models and women in other female-dominated occupations, has been governed by male leaders. At its most recent convention, however, the union dramatically increased the number of female members on the executive board to almost half the total. Women are not found on the executive boards of unions in occupations or industries where the workers are predominantly male, such as building trades, maritime, railroad, and mining (see Table IV-2), although they hold key staff positions in a few of these traditionally male organizations.

Social philosophy may also influence certain unions to adopt a policy of inclusion. For example, in 1944, under the leadership of Walter Reuther, the United Auto Workers (UAW)—which from its inception had a predominantly male constituency—was the first union to establish a women's department and designate a national vice presidency to be filled by a woman (Gabin 1989).

Overall, women's leadership in AFL–CIO-affiliated national unions has been on an upward trend. Many more women are elected to union executive boards today than was the case 20 years ago (see Table IV-3), although—as noted above—the percentage of women in leadership in NEA and ANA decreased during this period. Currently, two AFL–CIO state federations, Florida and South Carolina, have women presidents. In six others,

Table IV-2 • Women Leaders in National Unions by Industrial Sector, 1997 (in percentages)

Industrial Sector	Women as a Percentage of Executive Boards
Arts and entertainment	14
Building trades	0
Education	35
Manufacturing, mining, and agriculture	11
Professional	23
Public employees	21
Service	18
Transportation	7
Total	14

Source: Gifford, *Directory of the United States Labor Organizations*, 1998.

Table IV-3 • Women on Elected Executive Boards of National Unions, 1979 and 1999 (in percentages)

Union	Women as a Percentage of Elected Executive Boards	
	1979	1999
AFGE	0	20
AFSCME	3	35
AFT	25	40
CWA	0	35
HERE	4	19
IUE	4	20
SEIU	15	30
UFCW	3	11
ANA[1]	93	73
NEA[1]	55	33

[1]Not affiliated with the AFL-CIO.

Source: Glassberg, Baden, and Gerstel, *Absent from the Agenda*, 1980; and survey conducted by author, 1999.

women serve as secretary-treasurers (Gifford 1998). In 16 percent of the 50 state federations, a woman has been elected to one of the two top offices, an increase over previous years. The picture is similar for central labor councils (CLCs), which coordinate activities at the local level.

In states and regions, as in national/international unions, women are more likely to hold appointive positions than elective positions. Among AFL-CIO appointees who advise, assist, and coordinate the work of state and local federations, almost half of the state directors are women. The AFL-CIO Field Mobilization Department also has demonstrated a strong commitment to diversity in staff appointments. Amy Dean, a CLC executive from California, was appointed by AFL-CIO President John Sweeney to chair the national AFL-CIO Advisory Committee on Central Labor Councils.

Unions report that women's participation has accelerated at the local level. Unfortunately, this is difficult to document, because unions, with few exceptions, do not monitor or survey their local leadership by gender, race, or ethnicity. Available statistics for women in local union leadership suggest that women's leadership representation in local unions more accurately reflects their union membership than at higher levels.

What kinds of positions do women hold in local unions? Thirty years ago, Alice Cook wrote that women "almost never appear on major negotiating teams. Even when they are a majority, women play the role and are assigned to the status of a minority" (Cook 1968, 324). Historically, women disproportionately carried out the duties of recording secretaries and were rarely elected to positions that served as launching pads for power and recognition (Gray 1998).

Despite increases in the numbers of women attaining high office, gender stereotyping persists. For example, only one of AFGE's 50 collective bargaining councils is headed by a woman. A survey of local officers in the Bakery, Confectionery and Tobacco Workers Union (BCT) found that while three out of four locals have at least one woman officer, women serve mostly as financial and recording secretaries or trustees. A detailed breakdown of leadership positions in the UAW revealed that women hold 13 percent of local presidencies and 50 percent of the recording and financial secretary spots. On the other hand, women occupy 14 percent of the chief steward positions, indicating that they are breaking into the key function of collective bargaining (Gray 1999).

The available evidence indicates that women have a long way to go to achieve leadership in national unions relative to their numbers in the ranks. Still, the movement of women into important staff roles is significant, and their election to local union office, the pool from which top leaders are drawn, bodes well for the future.

WHY SO FEW WOMEN?

Does the fact that women are rarely to be found in the top leadership of American unions mean that there is a glass ceiling that is virtually impenetrable? Are the barriers societal, institutional, or personal—or a combination of the three?

Women are still limited by family responsibilities and society's view of their role in the workplace. Scholars consistently rank this dichotomy as the most important factor standing in the way of female involvement in union activities and leadership (Wertheimer and Nelson 1975; Koziara and Pierson 1980; Needleman and Tanner 1987; Chaison and Andriappan 1982 and 1987; Andriappan and Chaison 1989). An in-depth study of union stewards reported that having a wife at home was an advantage to male stewards, while marriage and family tended to prevent female stewards from attending meetings, volunteering, and traveling—all the activities essential to moving up in leadership (Roby and Uttal 1993). Even for women who make it to the "first rung of leadership," family responsibilities continue to conflict with union responsibilities.

For example, Linda Chávez-Thompson recounts her early years as a staff representative, when she called home to find her little girl crying and begging her to come home. When Ms. Chávez-Thompson was offered a job near home, she took a cut in pay to be with her daughter every night.

The distinctive structure and functions of labor unions also present institutional barriers for women. Growing out of their tradition as "fighting" organizations with limited resources, required to confront well-funded employer opposition, union leaders are expected to devote unlimited hours (including evenings and weekends), to take risks, and to be willing to travel wherever the organization needs their services. This tradition is not only a deterrent to the involvement of women with families but it also reinforces a male culture in which women feel like outsiders, who are not invited to caucus meetings or to "hang out" with male leaders.

Women who want to participate tend to be assigned to stereotyped roles—such as recording secretaries or members of recreation and education committees. Rarely are they included in the core function of collective bargaining, which is seen as requiring the "take-charge" qualities of aggression and assertiveness usually identified with men. Women are perceived as "too emotional" or "too soft" to bargain with tough male managers (Cook 1968). Some report being expected to take notes at meetings. Even in unions made up of predominately female members, such as the AFA, men are sometimes

PROFILE OF LINDA CHÁVEZ-THOMPSON, EXECUTIVE
VICE PRESIDENT, AFL-CIO

Linda Chávez-Thompson was elected executive vice president
of the AFL-CIO in 1995, the first Hispanic woman to serve on the
executive council. Born in Texas, she worked in the cotton fields
with her parents, who were Mexican American sharecroppers. She
began her labor union career by taking a job as bilingual secretary
for a local of the Laborers' International Union (LIUNA). She was
active in community work and volunteered beyond the scope of
her job duties to make speeches and organize for LIUNA.

However, Ms. Chávez-Thompson was disappointed to find herself treated differently from her male counterparts—receiving lower
pay and expense reimbursement—and she left the local to join the
American Federation of State, County, and Municipal Employees
(AFSCME) as an international representative assigned to represent
public employees. There she encountered employers who at first
refused to take her seriously, classifying her as "only a secretary."
Nevertheless, she persisted and achieved gains for the members.
Subsequently, she set her sights on becoming vice president of
AFSCME, with responsibility for leadership of the union in seven
southwestern states.

The road to top office was not easy. Ms. Chávez-Thompson's
boss, who had been her mentor, turned against her, and critics cir-
culated anonymous rumors about her personal life. Her husband,
a union activist, and her children were supportive. What kept her
going was her belief in what she was doing. Her dynamic speaking ability attracted attention. In 1988, she succeeded in her goal
to be elected national vice president of AFSCME.

In this capacity, Ms. Chávez-Thompson acquired a reputation
for organizing the unorganized, and she led a successful policy
campaign to pass a law protecting the rights of public employees to
join unions. When John Sweeney decided to run for president of
the AFL-CIO in 1995, he asked her to join his winning slate. In
her current role, Ms. Chávez-Thompson represents the labor
movement in a wide variety of forums, inspiring crowds with her
enthusiasm for organizing and her campaign for social justice. She
characterizes her leadership style as "inclusive."

picked as spokespersons because it is assumed that they are more outspoken and assertive on grievances.

Overt sexism persists in the labor movement. On the one hand, a woman who is determined or aggressive is considered a "bitch," but, on the other hand, a woman who aspires to leadership is expected to be a superachiever. Many women who make it to the top positions in labor unions report being accused of "sleeping with" the boss to get ahead, a charge never made about men.

Sexism combined with racism is a "double whammy" for women of color. For example, Mary Hatwood Futrell, an African American woman who was elected president of the NEA, says that when she first ran for office at the local level, she was asked to "step aside" and "let a man do it." She also received hate mail, calling her a "nigger" and saying she would ruin the organization. Barbara Easterling, secretary-treasurer of the CWA, found herself ignored and isolated by male staff when she was promoted to a supervisory role.

Women unionists, in this male–dominated environment, encounter difficulties finding mentors and gaining the inside knowledge and networking opportunities that lead to higher positions. Men in power positions tend to seek out other men to be second in command, while women are on their own.

Women report that their leadership skills and capabilities are often underestimated. Women must outperform men in order to receive any recognition. In meetings with male peers, their comments are frequently ignored. On the other hand, when women are selected as spokespersons or appointed to union positions to make up a "balanced slate," they sometimes feel that they are being used to "get out the women's vote" or to demonstrate the organization's interest in women (Needleman 1998).

Even when the leadership of labor unions is unbiased and has good intentions, women, as relative newcomers to leadership, are hampered by the limited number of openings available. Union membership has been shrinking, freezing opportunities for new hires or replacements, and since there are generally no term limits or retirement rules for incumbents, there is little room for upward mobility.

A final roadblock, cited by the women interviewed for this chapter, is personal lack of self-confidence (see also Wertheimer and Nelson 1975; Koziara and Pierson 1980; and Needleman and Tanner 1987). Many fear failure and tend to accept passive roles (Chaison and Andriappan 1982). Gloria Johnson, the current president of the Coalition of Labor Union Women, believes that some women have been "brainwashed" by their past associations with family, friends, and co-workers. Their negative attitudes undermine prospects for networking with other women, which might help them overcome other barriers to leadership.

CAREER PATHS OF WOMEN LEADERS

Union leadership is typically an accidental rather than a planned career choice. Since the vast majority of leaders, male and female, come from the ranks of the membership, they start their careers by working in an occupation that is represented by (or becomes represented by) a union.

Then, through a complex set of circumstances, a worker may emerge as the leadership spokesperson for others in the same occupation. Both male and female union leaders report that they climbed the first rung of the ladder because their associates prevailed upon them to take on leadership responsibilities or because they were particularly dissatisfied with their working conditions or with the incumbent leadership. Many also were motivated by the ideal of advancing the cause of working people (see Quaglieri 1988 for similar findings). Initially at least, they did not think of union leadership as a full-time career commitment.

This "luck-of-the-draw" selection process, combined with the political character of union leadership, presents special problems for women. The career patterns of top leaders include (1) *founders,* who organize a union and become leaders from its earliest days; (2) *inheritors,* who are the beneficiaries of relatives who pass the mantle on to them; (3) *loyalists,* who start at the bottom and work their way to the top; (4) *challengers,* who overthrow incumbents; and (5) *technicians,* who come into the union from outside the ranks with special skills. All the incumbent male leaders have come up through one of these routes, mostly as loyalists, the traditional and accepted path (Gray 1993).

Among women leaders, there are examples of all these career routes. While patterns are similar for men and women, their proportions differ in each of the listed categories. And, for women, there is a sixth route: *secretaries,* who acquire knowledge of the organization and move into professional union roles. Many women leaders have entered the union this way; none of the men have.

There also are women who "founded" their organizations, playing a major role in organizing the members. While few female union founders have careers comparable to such legendary male heroes of labor history as Philip Murray in steel, Harry Bridges in longshore, and Eugene V. Debs in railroads, two examples stand out. Karen Nussbaum organized and became president of 9to5, a unique organization of office workers that functioned as a national working women's organization and later became affiliated with SEIU. She now heads the working women's department of the AFL-CIO. Dolores Huerta, a teacher and social worker, founded, along with César Chávez, the United Farm Workers, and became its vice president.

In labor history, and even today, there are examples of men who "inherited" their leadership positions as the sons of union leaders. This tradition developed in certain skilled trade unions where fathers passed along their occupational skills to their sons, and, in some cases, their union leadership positions as well. This route to the top has been virtually nonexistent for women. Nonetheless, interviews with women leaders indicate that coming from a union family is an important motivating force that helps many persevere to leadership recognition.

Most women who succeed in unions are, like men, *loyalists,* who rise to leadership through the traditional, slow-moving process, starting as rank-and-file members and getting elected to increasingly responsible positions. When this upward mobility is encouraged by incumbents, it is known as "moving through the chairs."

For women, the process is not always easy, as illustrated by the career of Barbara Easterling, international secretary-treasurer of CWA. She was hired as a telephone operator and immediately became active in the local union, motivated by pro-union views acquired from her family. Ms. Easterling volunteered for all kinds of activities and was elected steward and then chief steward. When she became vice president of her local union, some male members, worried that a woman might become president, amended the local bylaws to stipulate that the vice president would not automatically succeed the president in case of illness or death. Nonetheless, Ms. Easterling continued to achieve recognition through her leadership on the job and in the community. When women in her CWA district pressed the director to appoint a woman to the international staff, Barbara was selected. Subsequently, she ran for and was elected executive vice president with the support of the CWA international president. In 1992, she was elected secretary-treasurer, the second highest office in the union.

Kitty Petticord, the elected national women's director of AFGE, also made her mark in her local union of Social Security Administration employees by becoming an expert on safety and health issues, standing up to the employer as a whistleblower for client rights, and helping to fend off a raid by a rival union. These activities brought her to the attention of national officials, who appointed her to staff. Her networking with women local activists resulted in her election to one of the three top offices of her national union.

Sandra Feldman, president of AFT, also came from the ranks, serving as a teacher and local officer before succeeding to the highest office in her union.

A variation of the *loyalist* is the *challenger,* who also comes from the ranks but runs for office in opposition to established officers. Most AFA presidents fit this description. They all started as flight attendants, then progressed to higher levels of responsibility—first as local presidents and then as members of the national committees that negotiate contracts with the airlines—before moving up to the national presidency. Beginning with its breakaway from the Airline Pilots Association, AFA has a history of opposition to incumbent leaders. Three of the five women who have served as president won by defeating their predecessors. Pat Friend, the current president, says that her male colleagues on the AFL-CIO Executive Council frequently question her about why the flight attendants' union, mostly female, is so contentious!

While union leaders usually emerge from the ranks, whether as chosen successors or as challengers, some join the organization because they are hired as technicians or specialists (as attorneys, for example) and subsequently move into executive leadership positions. Given the barriers women face in competing for elective office, they have found acceptance through this route to a greater extent than men.

Many women who hold positions as vice president or department heads entered the labor movement as technicians. For example, Susan Cowell, now vice president of UNITE, prepared for a career in Asian studies at Harvard University and served in the Peace Corps in Korea. Later, while attending Yale University for graduate study, she got "turned on" to union activities when the blue-collar workers went on strike and she volunteered for the picket line. Seeking a union job, Ms. Cowell was first hired as an organizer and was then "discovered" by the union officers, who needed her language skills for an organizing drive of garment workers in Chinatown. From this recognition, she became assistant to the national president, writing speeches and handling public relations. Visibility in this spot, along with the president's support, led to her election to top office.

Susan Philips, recently elected vice president of the United Food and Commercial Workers (UFCW), also came into the union from outside the membership ranks. Inspired to social idealism by her father, a union legislative representative in Washington, D.C., Ms. Philips majored in English and journalism and became a writer for political and labor groups before responding to an advertised opening in the UFCW's publications department. She became known to the executive board in this position and was mentored by a woman vice president, who sponsored Ms. Philips as her replacement when she moved on to another top spot in the union.

In Washington, D.C., headquarters of international unions, and in the AFL-CIO, the number of women in technician or specialist roles is increasing. With the growing recognition of the desirability of female input

PROFILE OF SANDRA FELDMAN, PRESIDENT, AMERICAN FEDERATION OF TEACHERS

Sandra Feldman, one of the few women who serve as president of a national union, is president of the million-member American Federation of Teachers (AFT). Born in a working-class family in Brooklyn—her father was a milkman and her mother worked in a bakery—Ms. Feldman found that school was a "lifeline," opening up a whole new world and a way to make something of herself. Early on, while attending Brooklyn College, she committed herself to the struggle for social justice, becoming heavily involved in democratic socialist politics and the civil rights movement.

As a civil rights activist, Ms. Feldman met Bayard Rustin, the civil rights leader, who became one of her mentors. After acquiring a master's degree in English literature from New York University, she began teaching school and became active in union affairs. She was elected chapter leader, and became recognized for her writing and speaking skills. She came to the attention of Albert Shanker, president of the United Federation of Teachers (UFT), the American Federation of Teachers (AFT) local that represents New York City teachers (it is the largest local in the country). He encouraged Ms. Feldman to take a full-time position with the UFT. As a union field representative, she wrote position papers for Al Shanker and represented the union in a variety of roles, initiating new programs and ideas. When Mr. Shanker was elected to head the national AFT as well as the UFT, he selected Ms. Feldman to be the UFT's executive director, where she supervised the staff and all aspects of the local's work. In 1983 she was elected secretary of the UFT—its second-highest office—and in 1986 she was elected to its highest office.

As president of UFT, the largest local union in the United States, Sandra Feldman became recognized as a children's advocate and an authority on urban education. A veteran of difficult collective bargaining struggles during the fiscal crisis in New York City, she was effective in pursuing the union's cause in the political arena as well and was described as "tough, smart, tenacious, and committed."

In 1997 Al Shanker died and Sandra Feldman was elected to succeed him as head of AFT. (Her successor as president of UFT is

Randi Weingarten, a woman for whom Sandra served as mentor.) As AFT President, Ms. Feldman pursued the goal of uniting all teachers in one powerful organization. The merger agreement she negotiated with the two-million-member National Education Association (NEA) was turned down by the NEA membership. Nonetheless, these two organizations continue to work together as a powerful force not only for representation of teacher interests but also for influencing public policy on education.

Ms. Feldman serves on the executive council of the AFL-CIO and is involved in many community organizations. She is married to a New York businessman.

in decisionmaking, it is likely that more women will be tapped for executive leadership in the future.

Unions in arts and entertainment and sports deviate from the leadership patterns in other unions. Performers in these fields are highly unionized and participate actively in decisionmaking as officers and members of their executive boards but do not want to leave their professions to devote all their time to union work. To represent these organizations in administration and collective bargaining, executive directors are recruited from outside the membership ranks. Mona Mangan, who represents Writers Guild East, is an example of a woman who fills this important and influential role. Coming from a background of political activism, Ms. Mangan completed a law degree and acquired experience handling affirmative action cases for the U.S. Department of Labor before applying for an opening with Writers Guild East. She found this organization, with its democratic structure, a "nice fit" with her social action goals and rose through positions of increasing responsibility to become director, which requires her to match her wits with movie and television moguls in the fast-moving field of entertainment.

Thus, women have followed career paths similar to men—founding unions or working their way up from the bottom, sometimes challenging and defeating incumbent officers, and achieving leadership recognition through contributions as specialists and technicians. However, a surprising number of women union officers, like Linda Chávez-Thompson, began their careers as clericals, surmounted the barriers to women in leadership, and attained decisionmaking roles. This path is unique to women.

Lenore Miller, recently retired as president of the Retail, Wholesale and Department Store Union (which merged with UFCW), and one of the few women to head a national/international union, originally took a speed-writing course because she was unable to find a professional position when she completed her graduate degree. Hired as a clerical worker in the president's office, she made her mark by volunteering for union work outside her own job responsibilities and moved up to become the president's secretary. When an opening developed for the elective office of secretary-treasurer, the president backed her. She eventually succeeded him as president of the international union.

Gloria Johnson, an African American who is the national president of CLUW and a member of the AFL-CIO Executive Council, was hired in 1954 by the International Union of Electronic, Electrical, Salaried, Machine, and Furniture Workers (IUE) as a bookkeeper. Ms. Johnson, who had a bachelor's degree from Howard University, soon began doing research for the union. Her background in civil rights attracted her to the union's political and social action programs, encouraging her to become involved beyond her regular job duties. Ms. Johnson's speaking ability and dynamic leadership of women's activities brought her national fame and reinforced her recognition in the union, where she was appointed social action director and eventually elected to the national executive board.

Another African American woman, Clayola Brown, current vice president of UNITE and member of the AFL-CIO Executive Council, also entered union work as a clerical. After finishing college, Clayola left the rural South where she had grown up in a family of sharecroppers. She had worked in a textile factory and aspired to work for the union, but found that the job of clerk-typist was the only one available to her. Like others, she volunteered for various additional activities and was eventually promoted to a professional position in union education. When the elected office of joint board manager opened, union officials, who were by then aware of her talents, supported her move into this executive role.

PERSONAL STRATEGIES

Analyzing their own career experiences in the labor movement, women in leadership positions offer advice to those who aspire to top office. Getting elected to union office requires patience, perseverance, and hard work by both men and women, but more so for women, who must overcome many barriers. As Sandra Feldman says, "Work your way up" and "be better than anyone." Gloria Johnson was advised by her father, an African American who coped with a white-dominated society, "You can't be just as good; you have to be better."

To become better, women have to learn as much as possible about how their unions function. One way to do this, cited by all those interviewed, is by volunteering for every task, no matter how tedious—from stuffing envelopes and placing phone calls to marching in picket lines and participating in endless meetings. In the process, union activists learn not only the rules and procedures that govern the union but also the ins and outs of union politics.

Several of those interviewed noted that it is important to avoid becoming pigeonholed in "women's" jobs—such as recording secretary—and women's committees, even though filling these roles may be an essential first step on the ladder to recognition. Elaine Bernard, a leading labor educator, says that women need to avoid being thought of as only speaking about women's issues or becoming the "female token." She suggests that the best way to avoid such perceptions is by helping other women break the barriers and joining together in leadership roles (Bernard 1996).

Enrolling in labor education programs where available, whether inside the union or in outside educational institutions, is another way for women to acquire the skills and knowledge they need. Many successful women attribute their start to union women's summer schools and local labor studies courses, which build self-confidence and enhance the public-speaking and communications skills so important to achieving recognition. Experience in community and political activities is also a plus, according to several women leaders, who found that organizing constituencies outside the union developed skills that were transferable to the union setting.

To get ahead, it is important to be visible. This often means taking risks. Many of the women interviewed got their first recognition by speaking out on workers' grievances in meetings with supervisors or on behalf of other women in the union. For example, a Latina member in a predominately female local questioned the white male officer's practice of limiting recruitment for staff positions to white males. As a result, she was given a chance to organize, which led to her appointment as a business agent.

Success calls for strategic planning—setting goals and devising plans for achieving them. For example, Shirley Carr, who was elected to the highest position in the Canadian labor movement (the Canadian counterpart to president of the AFL-CIO), reports that from the time she was first elected union steward,[3] she had a plan that guided her through contests at various levels of union leadership until she made it to the top. In a similar vein, Sandra Feldman suggests that aspiring women leaders should not be so devoted to their current roles at the local level that they ignore the big picture. She

---

[3]Ms. Carr began her career in Local 133 of the Canadian Union of Public Employees.

learned from her mentor, the president of AFT, that she should participate in national union affairs and become known to, as well as learn from, a broader constituency. Anna Marie Taliercio, a local union president in a male-dominated local union of restaurant workers, reports that she made it a point to attend local and state meetings—and to make contacts with officials from other areas—and thus was selected to become vice president of the New York State AFL-CIO.

At one time or another, all the women who achieved leadership in predominately male organizations encountered instances of discrimination and/or sexism. They advise women to rise above such attitudes and to "seek equality not revenge" (Bernard 1996).

Finding a mentor is one of the keys to moving up in any organization, and almost all the women interviewed stressed the role of mentors in their own careers. Many relied on male mentors, who were the power figures in their organizations, while others received help from sympathetic and helpful women. All advise other women to seek help and be prepared to offer help to others.

Several women interviewed acknowledged that, while they worked hard and achieved results, they gained recognition because they were in the "right place at the right time." For example, Dee Maki says she was elected president of the AFA when delegates were deadlocked and looked to her as "a calming influence." Linda Puchala attributes her election to the AFA presidency to the fact that the union had been split into factions by the recall of the previous president and delegates saw her as "a mediator." Several women believe they were elected to the national executive boards of their unions because it was "time to promote a woman."

Whatever the reasons for their success, the experience reported by these and other women union leaders suggests that intensive efforts—learning, doing, planning, communicating, and networking—benefit individual career advancement.

COLLECTIVE ACTION

No matter how effective, individual strategies have limited impact on changing the face of leadership. Unions are political organizations in which decisions are made by voting blocks of members. Therefore, until women achieve power, rather than merely access or individual recognition, there will be no dramatic change in the gender composition of leadership. Bill Fletcher, assistant to AFL-CIO President Sweeney, says that "women need to make things more uncomfortable for union leaders. In the absence of agitation, there is backsliding." He offers the same advice to African Americans and other underrepresented ethnic groups.

Yet there is a dilemma here. Union officials generally view political caucuses as disloyal and discourage their formation. Therefore, members generally approach collective agitation for change with caution. Nonetheless, groups of women and groups organized along racial and ethnic lines do come together from time to time to make demands of leadership. As a result, women (and minorities) are added to leadership slates (see Gabin 1989 for a description of the rebellion of women in the UAW during reconversion after World War II).

The Coalition of Labor Union Women (CLUW) is a national organization that provides a collective forum for union women. Established in 1974, it grew out of regional meetings of union women who wanted to effect changes in their unions. The debates that took place at its founding convention illustrate the tensions associated with separate organizing for women. Among the issues in contention were whether the proposed national organization should function outside and independent of the AFL-CIO, whether membership should be open to women who were not union members, and what stand CLUW should take on longstanding union policies with which delegates might disagree.

One of these policies was seniority, which adversely affects women and minorities in layoffs but protects them against discrimination. Another was reproductive rights, strongly favored by feminists but controversial with male membership. CLUW faced attacks on two fronts: from militant feminists and activists in left-wing organizations—whose agendas threatened to set CLUW on a collision course with the AFL-CIO—and from male leaders, who questioned the need for an organization of women. The convention managed to steer an even course between the twin goals of increasing the rights of women and strengthening their unions (Balser 1987).

Olga Madar, vice president of the UAW, was elected to be CLUW's first president. She was succeeded in 1979 by Joyce Miller, vice president of the Amalgamated Clothing Workers Union. That CLUW had achieved the desired delicate balance was underscored when AFL-CIO President Lane Kirkland invited Joyce Miller to join the executive council. This was a breakthrough for union women, since Joyce Miller, who became the first woman to serve in this decisionmaking body, did not qualify under the traditional rule requiring that only presidents of major national unions be eligible for membership. Later, when there was a question about whether Gloria Johnson, Miller's successor as CLUW president, would be elected to the council, women rallied behind her, and council members eventually supported her bid to serve as a leader and spokesperson for union women.

Currently, CLUW has 81 local chapters that provide leadership training and networking for union women activists at the community level. Among its other major accomplishments, according to officers interviewed, are influencing unions to support issues of concern to women (e.g., pay equity); conducting research and producing publications on a wide variety of subjects, ranging from a report that called attention to the paucity of women in union leadership positions to model collective bargaining clauses; and building alliances between labor unions and women's organizations to achieve common political objectives (Glassberg, Baden, and Gerstel 1980).

CLUW has been especially effective in attracting the participation of African American women and, in several cities, Latinas. Membership in many of the local chapters is predominantly minority. Given the dual barriers that minority women face in their jobs, their unions, and the communities where they live, CLUW is an important source of empowerment. Many local leaders bring to their leadership roles "an impressive degree of political sophistication gained from their activity in the Civil Rights Movement in their communities and in their churches and are not afraid to stand up and let people know where they stand" (Harriford 1993, 404–5). The multiracial, multiethnic composition of CLUW is one of its strengths.

In addition to CLUW, training and self-help networks for union women have grown out of courses offered by university labor education centers. These include annual regional summer schools sponsored by the University and College Labor Education Association, AFL-CIO, and CLUW as well as many local leadership institutes. Follow-up studies from these programs indicate that they have a significant impact in generating increased activism and leadership recognition for participants (Catlett 1986 and Elkiss 1994).

UNION POLICIES

How have unions as institutions responded to the rise of women? What policies and programs have they developed to encourage participation by female members and to facilitate recognition of their leadership? This section takes a look at "best practices" associated with enhanced leadership roles for women.

Recognition of the importance of gender integration is the first step. This may take the form of a policy statement, adopted at the union convention or by the national executive board, which puts the organization on record as promoting equal opportunity within the union as well as in the workplace and the community. For example, SEIU enacted a leadership resolution at its 1992 convention, committing the union to building leadership at all levels so that it would be representative of women and minorities in the membership.

Another useful step is to survey women members to find out how many there are and what is important to them. Gloria Johnson, current president of CLUW, instituted such a survey in the late 1950s, when she was employed in the research department of IUE. The results of her survey laid the groundwork for a women's council and periodic conferences for women members, activities that stimulated activism. Last year, Karen Nussbaum, director of the working women's department of the AFL–CIO, launched a nationwide survey, "Ask a Working Woman," which the AFL–CIO has used to generate interest and support for women's priorities—equal pay, safety and health, child care, and family leave.

It is also important for unions to gather information on the current status of women in the union—where they work, what kinds of jobs they hold, their participation in union activities, and their representation in leadership. Surprisingly, very few unions collect this information. AFSCME and NEA are among those that do. The survey process is valuable as an educational tool contributing to membership awareness. Results provide the basis for assessment and goal setting, as well as a benchmark for evaluating progress. If, as might be expected, the survey indicates that women are not as actively involved as their male counterparts, it may be helpful to identify barriers to women's participation and to create plans for surmounting them. Unions with "best practices" develop affirmative action plans and programs.

Targeting issues of concern to women members in collective bargaining and on the legislative front creates a climate that encourages women to be active and involved in the union. For example, UFCW won a sex discrimination suit against Publix Supermarkets in Florida, overturning a policy that allowed (male) stockers to rise to management positions but denied (female) cashiers the same opportunity (Waldman 1997). The UAW has focused on sexual harassment by filing grievances in the workplace, bringing suits against employers, and offering awareness training to its staff and local officers. AFSCME has pursued the issue of comparable worth (equal pay for jobs of equal value) in a number of successful public-policy initiatives. And the AFL–CIO has played a lead role in promoting equal pay, family leave, child care, and domestic violence prevention, thereby demonstrating support for issues reported as priorities by its women members (Milkman 1995). Campaigns on these issues also afford women members an opportunity to showcase their skills as expert witnesses and speakers, a big step up in leadership recognition.

Ruth Needleman (1998), who has written extensively about women and minorities in unions, concludes that "independent space" and "structured opportunities" are prerequisites for moving union organization and culture in the direction of equal opportunity. "Independent space" means encouraging interaction and self-organization among women and minorities who are outside the dominant culture and leadership cadres of the union so that they can analyze and articulate their own needs and possibilities. Needleman uses the phrase "structured opportunities" to signify leadership pressure for change.

An increasing number of unions offer "independent space"—women's committees and union-sponsored conferences for women. The UAW constitution mandates a women's committee in every local union. Currently, eight national unions support women's departments with full-time staff devoted to organizing and promoting interaction among union women. In AFSCME, for example, the women's department has a staff of six and an annual budget of more than one million dollars (not including staff salaries). The head of AFGE's women's department is one of three national officers elected at conventions.

Nevertheless, holding conferences of female activists is still controversial. Male officers fear the formation of caucuses aimed at challenging the power and policies of incumbents. In many cases, conferences are carefully structured to avoid major policy discussions. Still, interaction and self-organization are increasing, enabling women to hone their leadership skills and acquire knowledge of union practices and politics in a protected environment.

In the past, some of those who were otherwise supportive of female equality voiced a concern that separate structures marginalized women, diverting their energies from succeeding in the mainstream (O'Cleiracain 1986; Baden 1986). For many years, the AFL-CIO considered and rejected the idea of a separate women's department, opting instead to place coordination of women's activities in its civil rights department. But with the election of John Sweeney as AFL-CIO president came the establishment of a working women's department headed by Karen Nussbaum. Under her leadership, the AFL-CIO encourages interaction among women's departments and formulates policy proposals on issues of concern to women. Women also seek independent space on their own, with or without union approval and financial support, by participating in local chapters and national CLUW conferences.

"Structured opportunity," the push from the top, includes efforts to open doors, provide training, share responsibility and power, and include women in visible leadership positions. There are numerous examples of such affirmative action. As noted, while women are still relatively rare in elected positions, union leaders are increasingly appointing women to staff positions. Under John Sweeney's leadership, the AFL-CIO set an example for its affiliates by restructuring headquarters so that women head half of all departments. Even unions with no female representation on their national executive boards are hiring women in key staff positions. The Building and Construction Trades Department of the AFL-CIO has a woman chief of staff; the International Association of Machinists (IAM), a female general counsel; and the Bricklayers Union, a female director of legislation.

Top-level appointments, particularly those that break the stereotype of "women's work"—that is, women's departments, education departments, and recreation departments—and move women into the mainstream collective bargaining and legislative arena, send a message to local unions about women's potential and provide role models for women who aspire to leadership.

Organizing the unorganized has provided a major impetus to appoint women to union staff. Sectors targeted for organizing are predominately female ones in which unionization is low. These include service, public-sector, and professional fields, as well as low-paid manufacturing, agricultural, and home-care jobs.

Furthermore, surveys and public-opinion polls demonstrate that women are more "union-friendly" than men—that is, more likely to favor joining a union (Kochan 1979; Freeman and Medoff 1984; and Bronfenbrenner 1998). Therefore, it is not surprising that young women are being recruited for the AFL-CIO's Organizing Institute (they currently constitute half of the trainees) and for Union Summer, an outreach to college students to encourage their participation in labor activities. For union sponsors, the results are paying off. Women in campaigns involving a female workforce have achieved better "win rates" than their male counterparts (Bronfenbrenner 1998).

Collective bargaining, long a male preserve because of its adversarial character, is also beginning to open to female staff as women assume positions as legal counsels, research directors, and even directors of negotiations. With support from the top, women are making progress in expanding their options with respect to career choices.

Goals and timetables for recruiting women to staff are rare, however. In fact, unions rarely maintain personnel or human resource departments or even affirmative action plans of the type utilized in corporations and government. NEA is one of the few labor organizations with a mandate to track personnel decisions along these lines.

In contrast to affirmative action policies long implemented by unions in Canada and Western Europe, quotas or set-aside positions on executive boards are frowned on in most sectors of the American labor movement (Trebilcock 1991). The first "designated seat" for a woman came when Joyce

Miller, president of CLUW, was invited to join the AFL-CIO Executive Council, breaking a longstanding policy limiting council membership to elected presidents of large national unions.

When John Sweeney was elected president of the AFL-CIO, he added Linda Chávez-Thompson to his slate and successfully persuaded delegates to create a new officer position, executive vice president, that was, in effect, designated to be filled by a Latina. He also enlarged the executive council to include more women and persons of color, ignoring the longstanding rule that council members must be presidents of national unions. In recent years, the New York State AFL-CIO and OPEIU have also enlarged their executive boards to diversify the membership. Nonetheless, no labor organization in the United States has a quota, or proportional representation, for women or minorities in leadership.

The International Confederation of Free Trade Unions, with which the AFL-CIO is affiliated, has recommended that unions "examine their structures and modify them in order to improve the representation of women" (International Labour Office 1999, 18). Its *World Congress Report* noted that when unions reserved seats for women on their national executive councils, the women subsequently were elected to these posts on their own. Among the countries where unions target female representation are Sweden (50 percent) and Norway (40 percent). The Canadian Congress of Labor also reserves seats on its executive board for women. Japan provides reserved seats for representatives of its women's committee (International Labour Office 1999).

Critics note that representation that is reserved on the basis of gender could result in tokenism. Questions have arisen, such as, if women serve on a policymaking board with the president of their own unions, can they express independent views freely and confidently? If a woman holds a designated seat on an all-male executive board, how much influence will she have? Women interviewed for this chapter who hold these positions do not experience these limitations, however. They see themselves as representing a constituency and playing important roles in union decisionmaking.

With all these "best practices," women continue to be underrepresented in union leadership roles. What is needed, according to some veterans of the struggle, is a complete change in union culture with a restructuring of the responsibilities of full-time union officials. They maintain that long hours, constant travel, and the conflict and political intrigue involved in organizing and bargaining—all of which are seen as necessary qualifications for union leadership—are incompatible with family responsibilities and feminine culture. Rather than encouraging women to become more like men, unions should become more women-friendly (Fellner 1993 and Needleman 1993a).

A few unions have already taken steps to become more family-friendly, providing child care at union meetings and conventions, for example. However, these policies are the exception and may only be found in organizations in which women have reached a critical mass in their representation in active membership and leadership positions. The possibility of a dramatic transformation in the responsibilities of leaders in the labor movement (or in business or politics, for that matter) is remote. Therefore, we must rely on incremental steps toward equality of opportunity until women are in a position to influence the culture as well as the policies of their organizations.

WOMEN LEADERS: DO THEY MAKE A DIFFERENCE?

As the number of women in union leadership increases, what is the impact? Do they have a different leadership style? And what are the implications for union policies and priorities? Will a more integrated leadership make the movement more effective in reaching its goals of representing and empowering American workers?

Numerous books and articles have examined, based on corporate experience, whether the leadership style of women executives is different from that of men (Wajcman 1998; Aburdine and Naisbitt 1992; Epstein 1991; Rosener 1990). Some predict that the "feminine" style is the wave of the future, while others argue that to succeed as executives, women must act like the men who hold those leadership posts.

The overwhelming consensus among union leaders interviewed for this chapter is that women bring a distinctively more open, participatory, and "people centered" approach to their leadership roles. In some circumstances, women emulate men. "Pounding the table" and profane language are expected, for example, in the "tough" climate of bargaining with business owners in the garment and trucking industries. Women who are the first to break into male–dominated leadership sometimes "behave like men in women's clothing" because they have to "go it alone." But as more women reach this level, they reportedly develop styles that are "warmer" and more "inclusive."

Describing their own leadership styles, women union leaders use such words as "good listener," "democratic," "willing to share," "open," "inclusive," "consultative," "flexible," and "aiming for consensus." Mary Hatwood Futrell, a former national president of NEA who was trained as a schoolteacher, saw her leadership style in the union as one of sharing knowledge and involving colleagues in the same way she did with her students. Clayola Brown, who adopted a consultative style as a union education director, says that she often won over opponents by actively involving them in decisions. Mary Crayton, an AFL-CIO regional director who started her career as a union secretary, developed what she called a "self-effacing" style—helping others rather than asserting herself, in contrast to the behavior of many male leaders she observed.

Ida Torres, a Latina who is head of her local, officer in her national union, and treasurer of the New York City Central Labor Council, believes that women are "more tender and caring," while men are "afraid to show their emotions." Josephine Le Beau, an African American who is president of AFSCME 1707, a large union of social workers, finds men generally more controlling and women more willing to share information, delegate work, and support the growth and development of staff. According to Dolores Huerta of the Farmworkers, women deal with problems more directly, while men worry about "who's going to get the credit—or the blame."

These observations coincide with findings about women's behavior in nontraditional jobs. Compared with men, women listen more carefully, emphasize cooperation over conflict, and use power differently—not for control but to ensure a fair distribution of resources (Lunneberg 1990).

In considering women's leadership patterns, it is useful to examine organizations of female-concentrated occupations—such as flight attendants, office clericals, and nurses—in which women occupy most leadership positions. Probing into the history of waitress unionism, Sue Cobble (1990) found that women, who were organized in locals that were separate from men, developed a system of "peer management," in which they disciplined and governed themselves in a highly participatory fashion.

The American Nurses Association (ANA) is described by its officers as highly participatory. Staff members are consulted by the executive director about all major decisions, and information is fully shared with staff and officers. There are frequent meetings and focus groups. Men who join the staff have to adjust their style to this way of conducting business.

The organization and representation of women clerical workers at Harvard University also reflected an unusual degree of membership involvement with an emphasis on individual empowerment and cooperative relationships—among the women themselves and with management. Observers noted that this style carried over into contract negotiations (typically an adversarial process in other settings), where many members participated in planning and negotiation (Hurd 1993).

Within the New York City chapter of CLUW, led primarily by African American women, a researcher who monitored meetings for more than a year observed that women have a "different way of doing." Leaders are determined to make CLUW meetings harmonious. If disagreements develop, discussion is postponed until members can work out compromises. The most influential members were those who could get along with everyone, putting the needs of the organization above their own personal ambitions (Harriford 1993).

These examples do not prove that women's leadership styles differ from men in all settings. Nonetheless, experience suggests that in a supportive environment where the number of female leaders has reached a critical mass, women often bring a distinctive approach to their leadership responsibilities.

Policies and priorities in female-led organizations tend to give greater emphasis to social goals in political action and to family and equality issues in collective bargaining. Researchers have observed this pattern not only in the United States but also in Great Britain (Heery and Kelly 1988) and Canada (Briskin and McDermott 1993)—where unions led by women emphasize organizing women workers and promoting their specific interests, while widening the scope of collective bargaining to include such benefits as maternity leave and child care.

The best-case scenario is that with the inclusion of more women in leadership positions, unions will organize more diverse constituencies; strengthen relationships between members and executives through a listening, caring, and participatory approach; broaden the bargaining and political action agenda to give greater attention to the interests of working families; and enhance outreach to community allies.

CONCLUSION

Women's importance and influence in the American labor movement will continue to grow in proportion to their increasing numbers in the workplace. No longer "absent from the agenda," as CLUW charged in 1980, women see their concerns—including family benefits and equal opportunity—becoming priorities for unions that seek to organize the new, predominantly female and minority workforce.

Women unionists have worked for years to gain positions of greater influence in their organizations, using a variety of strategies—both personal and organizational—to overcome a number of barriers. These barriers will continue to exist for some time, both within individual unions and in society at large, but women who believe in the labor movement and in the promise of unions as the best hope for America's working families will continue to challenge them, as they always have.

This chapter has included examples of women who have followed varied and remarkable trajectories to influential positions. These women have exhibited courage and tenacity beyond what it takes to become a male labor leader in male-dominated unions. As we enter the new century, the American labor movement is changing, but the traditional resistance to women's leadership within unions still slows the growth of labor's influence. To the extent that unions realize this, they will benefit from the creative potential and tremendous skills of their female leaders. This will happen even more quickly if these unions develop a keener ability to recognize and recruit leadership from the ranks of their female members and leaders, and develop mechanisms to promote and train women who show commitment and talent.

For their part, women unionists will continue to press for greater access and openness. As more women gain leadership positions, mentor other women, and press for shared priorities—and as unions become more receptive to differences in leadership styles—the labor movement will be better prepared for the challenges of the new century.

FIVE

★

WOMEN IN THE MILITARY: THE STRUGGLE TO LEAD

Judith Youngman

HIGHLIGHTS

WOMEN HAVE SERVED with or in the U.S. military since the American Revolution, yet their struggle for leadership within the armed forces has a long and uneven history.[1] The most dramatic advances came during the 1990s, a decade of "firsts," in which opportunities became available for military women in many nontraditional roles. Yet at the beginning of the twenty-first century, women in the armed services still face policy and cultural constraints on their leadership not faced by most civilian women. As each new career field opens up, a generation must pass before the gender integration process is complete. Meanwhile, women in the military continue to demonstrate their leadership and dedication, challenging prevailing practices and dispelling longstanding assumptions about their abilities.

This chapter reviews the evolution of women's progress in the armed forces—from cooks and laundresses in the late eighteenth century to air and naval combat missions today—and their struggle to break down barriers to women's full participation in the nation's defense.

- Following Operation Desert Storm, Congress repealed all statutory restrictions on women in the armed services. Remaining restrictions are Department of Defense (DOD) combat exclusion, collocation, and privacy policies.
- The Navy has had the greatest success in moving women into nontraditional fields closed to women before the mid-1990s.

[1]The views contained herein are those of the author, and do not necessarily reflect the views of any department or agency of the U.S. government.

- DOD restrictions on women's service limit opportunities for leadership and career advancement and often exclude women from the services' central or elite missions.
- Although enlisted women in most of the services are rising in rank in both staff and operational units, their access to leadership jobs that enhance career development often lags in every service except the Air Force. In all services, the greatest rank-leadership gap for women occurs in senior enlisted leadership of operational units.
  - In all services, African American women experience greater rank-leadership gaps than all other women and African American men.
  - The selection of women for leadership roles often is inhibited by leadership selection processes, career experiences, career development models, and insufficient mentoring.
  - Downsizing and force restructuring in some services adversely affect women's leadership opportunities.
  - Military culture perpetuates gender-discriminatory climates and impedes acceptance of women and their competitiveness for leadership roles.
  - Systemic impediments to women's optimal performance remain, including equipment design, recruiting profiles, training regimens, personnel assignment policies, and even nutritional guidelines.
  - The armed services that provide the greatest career and leadership opportunities for women have the highest retention rates for women.

INTRODUCTION

Since the American Revolution, women have struggled to serve in America's defense. It is significant to note, however, that every advance by women in the military in the nineteenth and twentieth centuries occurred either during or immediately after a war in which women proved their abilities and dedication. Women's struggle to obtain leadership roles in the armed forces reflected a similar pattern. The greater the national defense need, the greater the need for women military leaders.

The 1990s were no exception. Each year brought milestones for military women. In the Persian Gulf War, women commanded platoons and companies of combat-support soldiers, crossed enemy lines, and flew missions over enemy territory. Women died in the line of duty, and women became prisoners of war. Most important, women increasingly thought of themselves as "just soldiers," rather than as auxiliary resources "freeing a man to fight" as in earlier wars. Army Major Marie T. Rossi, a helicopter pilot who was killed in the line of duty during Operation Desert Storm, once said: "I think if you talk to women in the military we see ourselves as soldiers. What I am doing is no greater or less than the man who is flying next to me" (Dane Hansen Productions 1994).

Between 1992 and 1994, following Operation Desert Storm, Congress repealed the remaining statutory restrictions on women serving in combat. During Operation Desert Fox in 1998, women naval aviators became the first American women to fly combat missions. They did so successfully and with little fanfare. In 1999, NATO Yugoslavian operations in Kosovo included Army women combat helicopter pilots.

Today, America's military readiness depends upon the ability of the armed forces to recruit and retain America's daughters, as well her sons, in military service. But women's struggles to serve the nation in the armed forces are far from over. Under Department of Defense (DOD) policies, ground-combat units and submarines remain closed to women. Women are moving only slowly into elite and nontraditional fields and still struggle to obtain leadership roles in the armed forces, even in traditional occupations for women.

Women leaders in the military today, both commissioned and noncommissioned officers, are often more visible and assume greater responsibility for people and assets than their civilian counterparts—and at a younger age. But they still face constraints on their leadership not experienced by women in other professions. Government policies restrict the numbers of women, their access to leadership, and the jobs they hold, while military culture often impedes their advancement.

HISTORICAL BACKGROUND

Although women served in the military as cooks, laundresses, nurses, couriers, and spies throughout the eighteenth and nineteenth centuries, Congress did not authorize a permanent role for military women until the creation of an auxiliary Army Nurse Corps in 1901. In 1908, the Navy followed the Army's example. In World War I, manpower shortages led the Navy and Marine Corps to enroll women in the Reserves. By the end of the war, 34,000 military women had served in the Navy, Marines, Coast Guard, and Army and Navy Nurse Corps.

During World War II, severe manpower shortages forced the armed forces to use women in the war effort as reservists, auxiliarists, and uniformed civilians (including as Women's Air Service Pilots). Overall, nearly 400,000 women served in uniform in the United States, Europe, and the Pacific in a wide range of noncombat capacities. Following World War II, manpower needs, as well as political pressure from women veterans, resulted in permanent status for women in all branches of the armed forces except the Coast Guard.

The Armed Forces Integration Act of 1948 established the parameters for women's military service for more than a generation. The act provided for gender-defined organization and administration and, in the case of the Army, a separate, gender-segregated corps. It also capped women's representation at two percent of each service and limited women's roles to noncombat career fields and naval hospital and transport ships. The greatest constraints on women's service under the 1948 act, however, were in the area of women's leadership (see "Military Women: Milestones").

The 1948 act also limited each service to only one woman colonel or naval captain, although thousands of men held those ranks. Women generals and admirals were not authorized, and women could only command other women. This meant that they were limited to commanding units such as women officer or enlisted training schools or the Women's Army Corps (WAC).

MILITARY WOMEN: MILESTONES

1948   WAC, WAF, WAVES, Women Marines founded
1967   Restrictions on Women's service repealed
1973   All-volunteer force established
1976   Military academies and flight training opened to women
1978   WAC abolished. All women now integral members of services
1981   Promotion lists gender integrated
1988   Risk rule established
1992   Aircraft statutory exclusions repealed
1993   Secretary of Defense opened combat aviation
1993   Combatant vessel statutory exclusions repealed
1994   Secretary of Defense rescinded risk rule and defined combat exclusions
1994   Secretary of Defense opened new Army and Marine Corps positions
1998   Women flew air combat missions and commanded naval combatant ships

No woman could serve more than four years as a colonel or captain without the approval of her service secretary, a requirement not imposed upon men. The 1948 act set a 10 percent limit on women serving as lieutenant colonels and commanders. It also established gender-defined promotion lists for Army, Navy, and Marine Corps women in each grade. Only the new Air Force integrated promotion lists, resulting in men and women competing for promotions.

During Vietnam, the shortage of qualified male volunteers and the increasing unpopularity of the draft provided incentives to revise the 1948 act. Public Law 90-130, signed by President Lyndon B. Johnson on November 8, 1967, created new opportunities for women to assume leadership roles in the armed forces. The law permitted the promotion of women to the ranks of general and admiral, eliminated the restriction of only one woman colonel/captain per service, removed the 10 percent ceiling on the number of female active-duty officers who could serve as lieutenant colonel and commander, and removed the two percent cap on the number of women in the regular armed forces. What the 1967 law did not change were prohibitions on women commanding men. Additional reforms came quickly, though, as a result of increased manpower needs during the Vietnam conflict and new political interest in equal rights for women.

By 1969, the Air Force successfully opened Reserve Officer Training Corps (ROTC) programs to women, with the Army and Navy soon following suit. In 1973, the all-volunteer force replaced the draft-based military. The Army and Navy opened flight training to women. By the mid-1970s, the success of the all-volunteer force depended upon the increased representation and utilization of women—and their leadership. The senior military staff colleges (which train service leaders) admitted women students, staff, and faculty.

In 1976, under congressional mandate, the federal service academies also opened their doors to women. New jobs in all but combat and direct combat-support fields were available to women in all services, including flight training, Air Force missile systems, and naval sea duty. The Coast Guard opened all jobs to women, thus eliminating combat restrictions on women in the Coast Guard. By 1978, with the disbanding of the WAC, gender-defined administration of women was ended. Women were integrated into the regular armed forces at last.

During the 1980s, the numbers of women in the military continued to increase, reaching nearly 12 percent of all personnel by the end of the decade. In 1981, Congress abolished separate promotion tracks for women and men officers with passage of the Defense Officer Personnel Management Act. In 1987 and 1988, a DOD task force on women recommended a clearer standard for evaluating women's access to noncombatant positions. The resulting new "risk rule" specified that those noncombatant positions posing a substantial risk of injury, death, or capture should remain closed to women, even to women who were not in combat units.

The Persian Gulf War focused attention on women in the military as no previous war had. More than 40,000 women (including women on active duty and those in the Reserves and National Guard) served in the Gulf, representing more than seven percent of U.S. forces. Women commanded combat-support units, engaged in ground fire fights with Iraqi forces, accepted the surrender of Iraqi soldiers, provided air cover, and refueled aircraft and armor units in close proximity to enemy forces. They died in the line of duty and were taken prisoners of war. What surprised some military planners was the broad public acceptance not only of women serving in Desert Storm but also of women casualties and prisoners of war.

Following the Gulf War, the 1992 Defense Authorization Act repealed combat aircraft exclusion laws. In 1993, Secretary of Defense Les Aspin opened combat aviation to women and expanded assignments on noncombatant ships. In 1994, the Defense Authorization Act repealed laws prohibiting women from permanent assignment aboard combatant vessels. Also in 1994, Secretary Aspin, by internal DOD memorandum, rescinded the risk rule, defined direct ground combat as the basis for closing positions to women, established a new assignment rule for women, and required the services to review all positions closed to women. As a result of these policy changes, more than 260,000 new positions have been opened to military women since 1993.

WOMEN IN THE MILITARY AFTER DESERT STORM

At century's end, no statutes or laws restricted women's numbers, roles, and leadership in America's armed forces. Current restrictions result from policies of the Department of Defense (DOD) and the individual armed forces.

Under the 1994 DOD women's assignment rule, women cannot be assigned to units below the brigade level whose primary mission is direct ground combat, or to units required to physically collocate and remain with direct ground-combat units. It is important to note that women are excluded from serving in combat and collocated units even during peacetime, since the armed services organize and "train as we fight." Special Operations Forces and other special operations units also remain closed to women, as do Navy and Coast Guard vessels that lack berthing for women, including all submarines. Finally, any woman can be excluded from a position in which job-related physical requirements would exclude the vast majority of women service members.

How have these DOD assignment policies been implemented by each of the services? The central missions of today's Army remain ground-combat missions. Consequently, 91 percent of Army occupations, but only 67 percent of actual positions, are open to women. Combat occupations that remain closed include the central missions of infantry and armor, and such elite units as Special Forces and Rangers (see Figure 7-3 in the "Statistical Portrait").

Navy women today can serve in 96 percent of Navy occupations, including those on combatant ships. Submarines remain closed, as do elite Special Warfare (SEAL) units. Women can serve in 94 percent of all Navy positions because submarine fleet and SEAL positions represent a small percentage of all positions in that service. In reality, however, women have access to only 91 percent of Navy positions. On Navy ships, women and men are housed in separate berthing areas. This necessitates the redesign of most existing ships. About 13 percent of all shipboard bunks are designated for women. This means that women cannot be given approximately 87 percent of sea-duty assignments that are technically open to them. Sea-bunk unavailability limits the assignment of women—especially enlisted women—to certain ships and missions, although the Navy is continuing to request funds from Congress to convert more ships for gender-integrated crews. No service is more ground-combat-oriented, and thus affected by the combat exclusion policy, than the Marine Corps. While women can serve in 93 percent of Marine Corps occupations, they can serve in only 62 percent of positions. Since the Marine Corps is organized as expeditionary forces deployable on naval ships, access to shipboard assignments for Marines is critical for career advancement. Berthing for women Marines remains limited on naval ships, however, further restricting their competitiveness for career advancement.

The Air Force is currently the most gender-integrated of all the armed forces. More than 99 percent of all Air Force occupations and positions are open to women. Remaining closed are specialized positions normally collocated with Special Operations Forces units.

All Coast Guard occupations and positions officially are open to women under present assignment policies. However, leadership progress for officer and enlisted personnel begins on small cutters, where berthing for enlisted women is frequently limited. Thus, the exclusion of women from positions on smaller cutters early in their careers can limit their leadership opportunities later on.

COMBAT, COLLOCATION, AND WOMEN AT RISK

Current combat and collocation policies restrict women's access to experience in combat competencies essential for future career opportunities. Current DOD combat exclusion policies often are justified by questioning women's ability to perform combat-related jobs—especially their physical strength and aggressiveness. But women's performance suggests that they can compete.

Occupationally defined physical requirements have not been developed for military occupations. Existing physical fitness tests measure general fitness. While studies of aggression note differences between men and women, 30 percent of women fall above the mean in measures of aggression, while 30 percent of men fall below the mean (Reinisch and Sanders 1986). Army field exercises assessing women's performance under combat conditions validate that many women can do the job (Johnson 1978; Coyle 1989).

Combat exclusion and collocation policies remain based upon unproven assumptions about women in combat. Yet combat-support units resolved concerns years ago about women's aggressiveness and ability to engage in violence, as well as concerns relating to privacy and women's physical ability to perform many jobs. For example, the Marine Corps requires Marine Combat Training (MCT) for women. Stated reasons for providing such training, when combat is closed to women, are that modern battlefield lines are fluid and all Marines must be trained to defend themselves when attacked. Since MCT was introduced in 1997, women have earned recognition as "honor graduates" at rates equal to, or greater than, the rates of men.

Marine policy regarding women appears based on an assumption similar to the one underlying the assignment of women in the Army's field artillery branch. In the early 1980s, women in field artillery were allowed to become specialists in target acquisition (a noncombat job), but not in directing cannon fire (a combat job), even though soldiers in these two positions might stand side by side. Today, in Army field artillery, women are excluded from the Multiple Launch Rocket System (MLRS), a mobile missile system attached to ground-combat units above the brigade level. But women in the Signal Corps are allowed to move ahead of the MLRS unit (closer to combat) to "set markers."

Until Congress repealed the ban on women in combat aircraft, women could serve on Air Force KC-10 refueling crews, but not on fighter planes. During combat operations, KC-10s can come under fire while refueling fighters, yet they possess few defensive weapons. Fighter aircraft, on the other hand, are equipped to defend against enemy attack. Ironically, women have served on KC-10 crews in combat operations since U.S. strikes against Libya in the 1980s, but could not serve on fighter aircraft until Congress repealed the restrictions after Operation Desert Storm.

Thus, it appears that while women can be targets of enemy air, missile, and ground-combat actions and can engage in defensive combat actions, DOD policies prohibit them from offensive combat. Even though Secretary Aspin in 1994 repealed the rule prohibiting women from being at risk for injury, death, or capture, a *de facto* risk rule exists still in the armed forces. Policies protect women from the risks of using force offensively but not from the risks of using force defensively, even outside the ground-combat arms and their collocated units.

The effects of the *de facto* risk rule, combat, collocation, and privacy policies are clear: women are excluded from the central missions of the Army and Marine Corps and from most elite units in all services.

SERVICE MISSIONS, ELITE UNITS, AND WOMEN'S LEADERSHIP

Despite DOD limitations on women's service, since 1995 women have assumed new leadership positions in all services as they have gained experience and longevity in career fields opened since the 1970s. For example, Air Force women officers have commanded the space shuttle, commanded a Flying Wing, and served as fighter and fighter test pilots. By 1997, Coast Guard women officers commanded medium-endurance cutters and Coast Guard air stations.

In 1998, several significant advancements occurred for women in the Navy. Five women naval officers were selected to command combatant ships. Women naval aviators flew combat missions in Operation Desert Fox. And Vice Admiral Patricia Tracey, who, in 1996, became the first woman to achieve three-star rank in any of the armed forces, was appointed Assistant Secretary of Defense for Military Personnel Policy.

Women's leadership roles expanded in the Army and Marine Corps as well. A woman officer assumed command of an Army air defense artillery battalion. Lieutenant General Claudia Kennedy served as Army Deputy Chief of Staff for Intelligence, the only woman to command a combat-support branch previously closed to women in any service. And two women served as command sergeants major at three-star commands. From 1996 to 1998, Marine Corps Lieutenant General Carol Mutter (now retired) served as Deputy Commandant for Manpower and Personnel, the highest-ranking woman in Marine Corps history.

What are the prospects for opening more military occupations to women in the years ahead? In the short term, women's status in the armed forces is unlikely to change, despite women's successes during the Gulf War and in subsequent deployments to Somalia, Haiti, Bosnia, the Persian Gulf, and Kosovo. Secretary of Defense William S. Cohen, citing lack of public and congressional pressure, repeatedly has stated that he will not reconsider DOD policies regarding women. Historically, however, expanding opportunities for women did not result from congressional and public pressure, but from manpower shortages or recruiting shortfalls. At the beginning of the twenty-first century, both of these difficulties threaten the readiness of the armed services.

With the percentage of women in the military rising annually, women increasingly will compete against other women for leadership positions in the career fields currently open to them. Denying women experience in the central missions and elite units of their services will undermine their ability to compete with men for senior leadership positions well into the twenty-first century.

WOMEN'S REPRESENTATION IN THE ARMED FORCES

Since the advent of the all-volunteer force in 1973, the percentages of women among active duty and reserve personnel have increased dramatically, from 1.6 percent in 1973 to 14 percent in 1999 (see Table 7-1 and Figure 7-1 in the "Statistical Portrait").[2]

This trend is likely to continue as the number of women recruited into the armed forces increases. In fiscal year 1998, women accounted for 27 percent of Air Force enlisted recruits and 20 percent of Army enlisted recruits. Military career opportunities opened in the mid-1990s are attracting a new generation of American women. At the same time, the services are recruiting women more aggressively, finding that women recruits—especially enlisted recruits—have higher educational levels and mental aptitude scores than males, and help keep the quality of recruits high. This is true even in the Marine Corps, which, until recently, never actively recruited women.

The opening of career opportunities in the 1990s, coupled with the increased recruitment of women, has skewed women's representation dramatically throughout the services by rank and career fields. First, women are underrepresented in operational career fields, many of which opened to women only in the past decade. Second, women are overrepresented in lower-officer and enlisted ranks in all services. Third, women leaders are nearly nonexistent in newly opened, nontraditional career fields.

[2]Unless otherwise noted, the statistics in this chapter come from either the U.S. Department of Defense or the individual services.

WOMEN IN TRADITIONAL AND NONTRADITIONAL FIELDS

Women officers and enlisted personnel remain concentrated in such traditional military career fields for women as health care, support, administration, supply, and training. Nearly three-quarters of women officers and two-thirds of enlisted women still serve in these administrative and staff fields.

Women officers and enlisted personnel are overrepresented in the lower ranks overall (see Table 7-3 in the "Statistical Portrait"). Even though the number of women in senior enlisted and officer ranks has increased dramatically since the 1970s, their representation is far lower than the total representation of women in every service.

The underrepresentation of women among senior noncommissioned and commissioned officers will change only as women rise through the ranks during a military career of 20 years or more. This generational-change phenomenon is especially important in understanding the career progression of women in newly opened nontraditional fields. In the military, leaders within different military career fields "grow" within those fields over a career. Leaders are not recruited from outside their service and rarely from outside their career field. Consequently, once a career field is opened to women, it takes a generation before women can assume leadership roles in that field. The gender-integration process in the armed services thus repeats itself every time a new occupation or career field opens to women.

The Navy appears to be the most successful of the services in integrating women into positions that have opened since 1994 and developing them to assume leadership roles. Although surface combat ships were only opened to women in the mid-1990s, by 1999, six women had been selected for command of combat ships. In addition, by 1999, more than 6,900 women were serving on combatant ships, more than double the number in 1996. In contrast, by 1998, fewer than 2,800 Army enlisted women served in positions opened since 1994 (although more than 13,000 positions were opened during that period). In 1998, the first Army woman achieved command of an air defense artillery battalion, but only after the branch had been open to women for 20 years, allowing women to move up through the ranks.

WOMEN LEADERS: THE RANK-LEADERSHIP GAP

Unlike the practice in many civilian occupations, promotion to higher rank in the armed services does not necessarily translate into a leadership role, especially within the enlisted ranks. At the senior enlisted ranks (E7–E10), certain jobs are defined within each senior rank as "key" leadership jobs. These jobs share similar characteristics in all services: They are "troop" leadership positions, not staff positions. They are related to "critical" missions or capabilities of the services. They influence the policies and performance of the service, branch, or unit, and enhance the promotability and career advancement of service members. Examples of key leadership jobs in which women are underrepresented include command and senior enlisted advisors of larger units—such as Army brigades, Navy fleets, or Air Force wings—and senior enlisted instructors at training bases.

Service data show that enlisted women in most of the services are rising in rank in both staff and operational units. But their access to leadership jobs that enhance career development often lags in every service except the Air Force. In all services, the greatest rank-leadership gap for women occurs in senior enlisted leadership of operational units.

In all services, African American women also experience greater rank-leadership gaps than all other women or African American men.

Leadership Selection and Development of Women

The reasons for women's rank-leadership gaps differ within each service, just as service force structures and missions differ. But rank-leadership gaps for military women across the services reflect similar patterns. The cumulative career experiences of women may ill prepare them for leadership. In addition, leadership selection processes and criteria can disadvantage women because they may be unrelated to job requirements or operational readiness. The lack of clear career development models and mentoring for women, especially in nontraditional career fields, may impede women's selection for leadership positions, while professional military education may inadequately prepare them for senior military leadership. Downsizing, outsourcing, and privatization also may reduce future leadership opportunities.

Career Experiences

Critical experiences early in a military career affect later leadership opportunities for women in all services. For Air Force pilots, for example, selection as a general's aide at the junior ranks of lieutenant or captain substantially enhances future competitiveness for command of operational units. Early experience as a general's aide provides women with both a command leadership laboratory and invaluable mentoring and career guidance by a senior officer.

Navy women frequently lack experience and skills that can be obtained only through assignments at sea early in their careers because, until the 1990s, women were denied access to combatant ships and sufficient opportunities for sea duty. Senior enlisted women, therefore, seldom obtained early qualifications to lead operational units later in their careers.

How important is the timing of the "right" career experiences for commissioned and noncommissioned officers? General Henry H. Shelton, chairman of the Joint Chiefs of Staff, concluded, "It takes about 20 years to grow a colonel in the Army, Air Force, and Marine Corps or a captain in the Navy and an equal amount of time to get a great sergeant major or senior chief. Waiting until the sixteenth year of someone's career to begin providing those challenges that help a leader mature is far too late. If we want women to succeed at higher levels of command then we've got to let them 'earn their spurs' early in their careers and challenge them at every opportunity. Getting women the early operational experience they need to develop their skills is an imperative of today's challenging environment" (U.S. Department of Defense 1998, 2–3).

LEADERSHIP SELECTION

Selection criteria and processes for filling leadership positions disadvantage women in some services. Historically, Army selection criteria for senior enlisted leadership positions often excluded women outright. Today, selection processes often make women less promotable. For instance, first sergeant positions in Army training commands are key leadership jobs that enhance promotability and competitiveness for future leadership positions. Until 1998, however, only first sergeants from combat career fields could serve in gender-integrated basic training units. Today, some first sergeant positions remain limited to combat soldiers. This policy, which "codes" jobs as requiring combat experience, automatically excludes women, since ground-combat fields are closed to them.

Army command sergeants major are the senior noncommissioned officers responsible for all enlisted personnel in a unit. The command sergeant major selection process for major commands usually requires nomination by a senior officer. This nomination-based system contributes to a network-driven selection process for these competitive command positions. Since most senior officers in the Army are men, the nomination system functions as a predominantly male network. The Army is the only armed service in which senior enlisted personnel are nominated for a senior leadership role.

Army enlisted women may be the most disadvantaged by leadership selection processes of all military women. But women in all the armed services describe disadvantages. If a woman wants a key leadership job, she pursues opportunities for leadership in "hardship" tours and undesirable locations that men try to avoid.

The Marine Corps offers few key leadership opportunities for senior enlisted women, even in leadership of gender-integrated units and leadership in hardship tours. Women commissioned and noncommissioned officers frequently lack critical combat skills required for selection to a leadership role. In the Marine Corps, even noncombat leadership positions may be coded to require combat qualifications or operational experience in combat units that women do not possess.

Like the Marine Corps, the Coast Guard has few women in senior officer and enlisted ranks overall. Only one woman has risen to flag rank in the active duty Coast Guard, Rear Admiral Vivian Crea. The most senior women officers in the Coast Guard, captains and commanders, increasingly are selected for operational commands, both at sea and ashore. But few women noncommissioned officers assume operational commands.

CAREER DEVELOPMENT

Women's assumption of leadership roles also can be hampered by the lack of career development models and mentoring, especially in nontraditional military occupations.

As women reach higher ranks as commissioned and noncommissioned officers, operational assignments often are replaced by high-visibility staff positions. Serving in staff positions—especially multiple staff positions in Washington, D.C., or regional commands—can impede women's selection for operational leadership assignments. Commanders in operational career fields simply do not get to know women assigned to staff positions in headquarters units. Thus, women are left out of informal mentoring networks in operational occupations.

Women of all ranks, officer and enlisted, disproportionately serve in human resources staff positions as equal opportunity officers, diversity trainers, and the like. Staff equal opportunity assignments, although important to the service and to the progression of women as a class of military personnel, nonetheless remove women from operational units and career experiences. Equal opportunity assignments also necessitate special training, adding to the time away from operational units.

In most nontraditional career fields, military women frequently lack career development models. Women military nurses know what it takes to become head of the Army, Navy, or Air Force nurse corps. But a woman F-16 pilot has a much dimmer picture of the career steps necessary to compete successfully for command of the Pacific Air Forces in 25 years.

Effective mentoring of military women is essential for their success, especially in nontraditional fields. But such mentoring is in its infancy. In nontraditional fields in the Army, Navy, Air Force, and Marine Corps, only men have long-term career experience. But men are often hesitant to mentor women officers or enlisted personnel, citing concerns that they will be perceived as fraternizing or being overly supportive of women. Yet mentoring, and informal networks accessed through mentoring, are more important for individual career success and advancement in the armed services than in any other profession, since experiences outside the military do not prepare individuals for careers inside the military.

America's armed services are among the largest organizations in the world. They encompass multiple occupations and diverse subcultures. Military personnel never obtain a permanent job or place of work, nor do they ever have a stable supervisor. Personnel are transferred to new jobs and new locations every one to four years, depending upon their occupations and assignments. Military careers are "up or out" career paths. If you are not promoted in rank on schedule, with promotion based upon your performance as well as your career experiences and skills, then you are forced out of the service.

Mentors and networks provide continuity within this career environment in which peers, supervisors, jobs, and locations change regularly. Mentors provide informal career guidance, support, and opportunities at each stage of service members' careers. Too often, women in the military are not mentored sufficiently, which leaves them out of the informal networks essential for career development. General Shelton has expressed his concerns about the lack of effective mentoring of military women, noting that ". . . mentoring isn't just about giving career advice over a few drinks at the NCO or Officers' Club. Nor is mentoring sponsorship or favoritism. Mentoring is a process of thoughtful and deliberate advice, education, and counsel designed to assist in professional growth and an important step in helping provide the leaders of tomorrow. It is hard for me to imagine an officer, NCO, or DOD civilian succeeding without the benefit of sound advice from experienced superiors. Yet, by sometimes putting artificial gender barriers around the mentoring process, we've prevented women from gaining the full benefits of the process" (U.S. Department of Defense 1998, 2).

PROFESSIONAL MILITARY EDUCATION AND LEADERSHIP DEVELOPMENT

In civilian professions, academic degrees, professional certifications, and an occasional specialized training program are prerequisites for career advancement. However, there are no civilian educational institutions comparable to those designed to develop leaders in America's armed services. Military colleges and schools offer professional education considered essential for future leaders in the commissioned and noncommissioned officer corps. Attendance is sometimes by competitive selection, and often determines which officers and noncommissioned officers will be selected for key leadership positions within a service.

For example, the Army maintains a multilevel educational continuum for professional officers. The first two professional military schools a commissioned officer attends focus on training in the officer's primary career field. Army officers receive vocational training in basic and advanced courses that they need to serve as junior officers in leadership roles at the platoon and company levels. Following company command, a "leadership cut" for Army officers occurs in selections for the year-long program at the Command and General Staff College (C&GS) that prepares majors to assume command of a battalion or to serve as a brigade executive officer, key leadership jobs necessary for career advancement. Normally, approximately 50 percent of Army majors are selected for C&GS. Officers not selected for C&GS may be selected to take the course by correspondence, a less valued option. While the Army plans to offer an intermediate-level educational program equivalent to C&GS to all majors by the year 2004, it does not plan a fundamental review of the curriculum to identify gender disparities.

After serving in battalion command or in a brigade staff position, an Army officer must complete a year-long course at the Army War College (or a comparable program at the Air War College, Naval War College, or Industrial College of the Armed Forces) to compete effectively for brigade command. Selection for the war college as senior lieutenant colonels or junior colonels ideally prepares officers for future brigade command. The war college curriculum focuses on national security, strategy, and military doctrine most critical to the central war-fighting missions of each service, e.g., ground, air, or naval strategy. Finally, following brigade command, those colonels the Army deems competitive for general officer often are selected for the National War College, the joint service school that educates many future general and flag officers of all services.

Sequential professional military education requirements exist in all the armed forces. In all services, the selection of officers for military school at the earliest opportunity in their careers enhances their competitiveness for selection to rank-appropriate key leadership positions. All services have similar professional military education requirements for noncommissioned officers, especially at the senior ranks.

Women officers and noncommissioned officers have graduated from senior service schools since restrictions on women's rank were eliminated in the 1970s. But the professional military education offered at service schools still may benefit women, as a group, less than their male counterparts. In most years, women are underrepresented as students and faculty at service schools, and especially as students at the war college of their own service. For example, a yearly cohort at a war college may have a class made up of 15 percent women, but half of those women will be Department of State or Department of Defense civilians and women officers from other services. Male students, however, overwhelmingly are drawn from the war college's own service.

While military women take the same curricula as their male counterparts, they may gain less benefit for their career development from the military education experience. Underrepresentation of women on faculties results in few female role models and mentors for both women and men. The "quota of one"—meaning that women students are widely distributed throughout the program—still dominates most service colleges and schools.

Virtually all military colleges and schools divide year-group classes into small seminars, whose members rotate through the curriculum together. A typical seminar has one woman, rarely more than two. While the small-group model reflects service demographics, women can be marginalized within their small groups. In addition to being in the minority of one or two in a group of fifteen, a woman lacks the combat experiences of most of her male peers and instructors. She is perceived as less of an expert in the war-fighting focus of the war college. Women still learn the curricula, and some excel. However, they do not receive equal mentoring and networking opportunities within their (frequently noncombat) career fields. Nor do the curricula of military colleges and schools address the unique challenges women may face as military leaders.

THE EFFECTS OF MILITARY DOWNSIZING

The future of women leaders in the armed forces can only be brighter than the past. The opening of new positions to women in the past decade has provided them with new career opportunities, and they are performing well in these new roles. As the current generation of military women matures within the services early in the twenty-first century, more women will reach higher ranks, and more will be selected for leadership positions in the commissioned and noncommissioned officer corps. But unless additional positions are opened up in the decade ahead, military downsizing, outsourcing, and privatization—coupled with increasing numbers of women in the services—could limit women's future opportunities.

Downsizing, outsourcing, and privatization have reduced the number of leadership jobs overall in the services. For instance, new classes of Coast Guard cutters open to women are replacing older cutters, some of which were closed to women. But new high-technology cutters have much smaller crews than older cutters, limiting berthing for women. Downsizing has also led to the decommissioning of naval vessels and to base closings, thereby limiting the places where women can serve. Outsourcing and privatization replace military jobs with civilian contractors, especially in support functions where women disproportionately serve.

Downsizing also is changing the size of units deployed in combat areas, i.e., from brigade to battalion level in the Army. Since women can serve in combat units, and with collocated units, at the brigade but not the battalion level, deployment of smaller units closes positions to them that were once open. Examples include the occupational specialties in the Army Corps of Engineers and Signal Corps, career fields open to women for a generation.

Restructuring of the armed forces following downsizing may result in consolidation of noncombat and combat fields, restricting women's competitiveness for key leadership positions within the combined career field. Air Force security forces, for example, are open to women. But security forces now undertake antiterrorism activities considered ground combat, from which women are excluded. Will women officers and noncommissioned officers be competitive for senior leadership roles in Air Force security forces in the future if women are denied antiterrorism experience within the career field today?

Overall, military women still struggle daily for access to experiences, competencies, mentoring, and networking that are essential to compete for leadership in the nation's armed forces. Despite downsizing, outsourcing, and privatization, women's representation in the armed services is increasing. But force restructuring could result in the channeling of women into certain career paths in nontraditional fields for women because of current combat, collocation, and privacy policies. Women still lack combat competencies necessary to compete for senior leadership positions in many recently opened nontraditional fields. As women continue to be concentrated in certain occupations, especially in the Army and Marine Corps, they increasingly may compete against one another for midlevel leadership positions.

MILITARY CULTURE AND WOMEN LEADERS

Military readiness in the twenty-first century will depend upon the continued accession and retention of women, even in nontraditional careers. Since the advent of the all-volunteer force in the 1970s, every service has reported the same experience: women recruits help keep recruit quality high, and women encounter fewer disciplinary and substance abuse problems than their male counterparts. The gender-integrated force appears better suited to post–cold war military missions, such as peacekeeping, than male-only combat units (Segal and Segal 1993; Miller and Moskos 1995).

But the future place of women in the armed forces, and especially their assumption of leadership positions in the central and elite missions of the services, is still uncertain. Most uncertain is the influence that increased numbers of women in leadership roles will have in shaping the policies, missions, and operations of the armed forces. Limitations on women's leadership result not only from DOD policies, but also from a military culture that has yet to fully accept women as equal partners in the nation's defense.

At the turn of the century, several aspects of military culture impede the integration of women and their competitiveness for leadership roles. The emergence in the 1980s of the so-called warrior culture defining an innately masculine ideal provides a rationale for continuing to exclude women from combat and collocated positions. The resistance within the armed forces to adopting occupationally defined physical performance standards perpetuates the perception that women cannot meet the physical requirements of the combat arms. The slowness of the armed forces in removing systemic impediments to women's performance, such as ill-designed gear and inadequate nutrition standards, further impedes women's optimal on-the-job performance. And inconsistency within DOD in challenging gender-discriminatory climates not only undermines women's performance, but also may contribute to higher attrition rates for women than men.

THE WARRIOR CULTURE

For 200 years, America's defense depended upon a small cadre of professional soldiers and masses of citizen soldiers who served during times of war and peace. Professional soldiers provided the military expertise for planning and training—and eventually for leading the nation's armed forces into battle. But in every war, America's combat soldiers were citizen soldiers who served in the military for a "tour of duty" or two. The citizen soldier embodied the obligations and rights of citizenship, including the willingness to risk life and limb in the nation's defense. Popular acceptance of war throughout American history primarily rested on the public's support for America's sons and daughters in harm's way.

Professional and citizen soldiers fought for cause, country, and comrades, and to return home. They fought to uphold freedom and end tyranny. They fought to preserve American values and interests and to liberate, but not to conquer. The citizen soldier matured in the military and in combat, proving himself ready to accept the obligations of citizenship. He was respected for this commitment. The citizen soldier's effectiveness in combat was based on his dedication to duty, his teamwork, and the leadership of military professionals in the art of war and strategy (Ambrose 1998; Moskos 1975; Bacevich 1998; Lehman 1994).

The warrior ideal that emerged in the late twentieth century bears little resemblance to the citizen or professional soldier. The warrior is motivated to fight by bonds with other warriors and his superior moral and physical strength. He is driven by his aggressive nature to prove his masculinity in combat. The warrior is revered in the warrior culture for his embodiment of virtue and masculinity (Snider 1999; Gibson 1994; Collins 1998).

In general, most contemporary discussions of the warrior culture are based on its masculine nature. Advocates of the warrior culture nearly always criticize the presence of women in the military and oppose women in combat. The warrior culture asserts that:

- women impede male bonding;
- women are less aggressive;
- men will seek to protect women;
- women lack the physical strength for combat;
- privacy between men and women is difficult to maintain;
- sex, both forced and consensual, will interfere with unit cohesion;
- women do not want to serve in combat; and
- Americans will not tolerate women killing, being held as prisoners of war, or coming home in body bags.

What the warrior culture usually ignores, however, is behavioral and scientific research that challenges its conclusions about male bonding and aggression. It also ignores the fact that many concerns about women in combat have been addressed for decades in combat-support units. These concerns include privacy; unit cohesion; sex; women's aggressiveness, ability to engage in violence, and "will to kill" in the line of duty; women's physical ability to perform jobs previously considered too physically challenging for them; and even what the American people will tolerate regarding women at war. The criticisms of military women appear to be based on unproven assumptions that are unrelated to women's abilities and performance in the military to date.

The future effects of the warrior culture on women in the military are potentially great, however. The inherently masculine warrior ideal excludes women outright. In fact, warrior arguments are the dominant reasons given today for keeping ground-combat and collocated positions closed to women. For instance, it is hard to interpret the current DOD collocation restriction on women—namely, that women cannot serve in units that accompany ground-combat units—without concluding that women cannot be put "at risk" or that they are incapable of the offensive use of force.

The most significant impact of the warrior culture, however, may be on unit cohesion and military readiness itself. The warrior culture posits two classes of soldiers: one with unlimited access to all fields and leadership roles in the services and one with access limited by gender. Neither class is based upon ability or performance. The warrior culture's greatest consequence, therefore, may be the tensions generated by the *de facto* gendered caste system it creates within military units and the armed forces themselves.

SYSTEMIC IMPEDIMENTS TO WOMEN'S PERFORMANCE

Military women in the all-volunteer force have met the challenges of expanded roles in the armed forces. What is little known, however, is that military women succeed despite handicaps not experienced by their male counterparts. These handicaps result from systemic impediments to the optimal performance of women—impediments that the armed services have only started to identify and address. Women's performance continues to be impeded by systems and equipment designed for men, including recruiting profiles, personnel assignment policies, physical training regimens and standards, combat gear design, and even nutritional guidelines for military meals.

Critics of military women often claim that women lack the physical strength and aggressiveness essential for forward-deployed occupational specialties. But such differences may not be exclusively defined by gender. They also may be related to differences in the types of men and women recruited. Recruiting strategies and profiles target men who participate in high school competitive sports, an indicator of fitness and competitiveness. Service recruiting strategies for women are just beginning to similarly target women high school athletes, especially those involved in competitive sports.

Equipment and gear are typically designed for male physiology and tested only upon men. In summer 1998, the Army for the first time included women soldiers in tests of a new pack design. The pack being replaced, the ALICE (All Purpose, Lightweight Individual Carrying Equipment), concentrated weight load on the upper back, which fit male physiology well. The new MOLLE (Modular Lightweight Load Carriage Equipment) pack more evenly distributes weight across the back. Following weight-load testing of the MOLLE pack on women, the prototype was modified to better accommodate both male and female physiology before it was distributed in the field. Other gear not designed for women (and described by women as impeding their job performance) includes combat boots, flak jackets, and battle dress and dungaree uniforms—all used in operational units. Women's uniforms generally are designed to meet appearance standards rather than performance standards. It was only in 1998, for example, that the Navy lifted the requirement that women assigned to ships—including combatant ships—take their skirts and heels to sea.

Female physical fitness frequently is a source of criticism of military women. In fact, the Federal Advisory Committee on Gender-Integrated Training and Related Issues recommended in 1997 a toughening of physical fitness standards in basic training. But in a report released in 1998, the Institute of Medicine (IOM) of the National Academy of Sciences reached a different conclusion. Noting the incidences of stress fractures in basic training, the IOM recommended more gradual physical conditioning for both men and women. Noting that women suffered more stress fractures in basic training, the IOM concluded: "When men and women of equal fitness level are compared, however, the gender differences in injury rate disappear" (Institute of Medicine 1998, 77). The U.S. Military Academy similarly found that when women shortened their strides in training exercises, rather than adapting to male cadet strides, women's injury rate was reduced to that of men.

The IOM study, *Assessing Readiness in Military Women,* further concluded that little correlation exists between the physical training regimens and standards of the services and job-specific physical requirements of positions classified as "heavy" or "very heavy." Similarly, women who exceed current military height-weight standards during basic training performed better on tests of strength than women who meet the standards. The IOM study concluded that height-weight standards for women related more to appearance than to performance, fitness, nutrition, or health.

The U.S. Army Research Institute of Environmental Medicine also studied women's physical capabilities as they relate to load carriage and lifting performance potential. The institute tested whether a physical conditioning program specifically designed to increase women's load carriage and lifting performance would improve their success in performing military tasks rated "heavy" and "very heavy." After the women had undergone 14 weeks of conditioning, the institute concluded that ". . . a specially designed and implemented physical training program can be very effective in improving the ability of women to perform physically demanding military jobs. A great majority of women undergoing such training could qualify for military jobs categorized as 'very heavy' under the present classification system" (U.S. Army Research Institute of Environmental Medicine 1996, 8).

Military nutrition standards similarly do not optimize women's health and physical readiness. The 1998 IOM project investigated nutrition standards and availability as they related to the performance of military women. The IOM suggested that the "nutrient density of operational (field) rations and military dining hall menus may make it difficult for women to obtain recommended levels of calcium, iron, and folic acid while balancing energy intake with expenditure" (Institute of Medicine 1998, 13). Such nutritional deficiencies in military women affect not only strength and endurance performance, but stress fracture levels as well.

Personnel assignment policies continue to disadvantage women, especially those seeking a military career, because they reflect the assumptions that service members are unmarried or reside in a traditional family structure. Neither assumption is accurate in the twenty-first-century military. The military is a more married force than at any time since the 1930s. By definition, military women with families are in nontraditional families. Additionally, military women disproportionately are married to military men, creating dual-career military families, including spouses serving in different services. Military personnel assignment policies rarely reflect these realities. With a small range of choices at best, military personnel are assigned by their service to new jobs, locations, and types of assignments every one to four years, consistent with the traditional career path within their career field. If a service member wishes to remain competitive for career advancement, there is limited flexibility in career paths and in the personnel assignment system.

Most disadvantaged by this system are dual-career couples with dependent children who struggle to balance assignments and families, especially operational and overseas assignments that equally benefit both careers. This system has a particularly negative impact on military women who are more likely than military men to marry other service members.

What do these systemic impediments to the performance of military women suggest? They suggest that if the armed forces were to recruit women the way they recruit men (targeting women who engage in competitive sports), to issue women gear and equipment that complement their physiology (as they do men), to develop physical fitness and nutrition standards that meet female physiological needs, to develop occupationally defined physical performance standards (rather than male physiology–defined physical fitness standards), and to design physical conditioning programs for female as well as male physiology, then women's already competitive performance in the armed forces could improve even more.

Improved physical performance could expand occupational opportunities for women, since current DOD policy denies women jobs requiring physical capabilities that only a few women possess. Improved physical performance also could increase individual competitiveness for promotion and career advancement. More family-friendly personnel assignment policies could improve retention of women and men alike. Only in the past five years have the armed forces begun to question the prevailing assumption underlying military culture—that the military is designed for men, and women must fit into the male model.

THE IMPORTANCE OF CLIMATE

Every few years, sexual harassment within military culture becomes a topic of national debate. Usually, an egregious incident of sexual assault or harassment in a single service, such as the Navy Tailhook Convention or the Army's Aberdeen training base scandal, precipitates media attention and congressional review.

But the nature and implications of gender–discriminatory climates in the military are far more diverse than the latest national debate suggests. Gender climates differ dramatically between different services, as they do within each of the services on a unit-by-unit, and career-field-by-career-field, basis. Gender-discriminatory climates negatively affect unit cohesion and military readiness. They also may be a primary factor in higher attrition rates for women than men, in slowing the entrance of women into newly opened nontraditional fields, in the perpetuation of systemic impediments to women's performance, and in women's selection for leadership roles.

In most of the services, men and women alike increasingly note "realistic gender environments." Realistic environments are those in which gender–discriminatory incidents may occur, but in which both men and women express trust in the processes and leadership to resolve the discrimination fairly. The question is, Why does military culture still tolerate gender-discriminatory environments where they exist?

The most recent cross-service cultural assessments measuring gender climates were conducted in 1988 and 1995 by the DOD's Defense Manpower Data Center (1988, 1996). These two studies provide insight into patterns of gender discrimination within the cultures of the armed forces.

On virtually all measures of gender discrimination, ranging from sexual assault to hostile environments, climate *patterns* were similar for all services in 1988 and 1995, except for the Navy. The service with the lowest rates of gender discrimination across all measures was the Air Force, followed by the Navy, Army, and Coast Guard. The service with the highest rates, from rape to harassment, was the Marine Corps. Between 1988 and 1995, gender discrimination dropped in all services, but the drops in the Marine Corps and Coast Guard were not significant.

In the Navy, however, rates of gender discrimination dropped by a dramatic 13 percent. Following the Tailhook Convention in the early 1990s, the Navy resolved to improve gender climates. The positive effects of its early efforts were measured in the 1995 survey.

In 1988 and 1995, patterns of gender discrimination in the services inversely correlated with women's roles. The Air Force—which has opened more than 99 percent of all positions and occupations to women and which has conducted gender-integrated basic training for more than 20 years—consistently has had the lowest levels of every form of gender discrimination of any service. The Navy—with gender-integrated training, the second largest number of positions and occupations open to women, and the largest number of women moving into nontraditional occupations—has had the second-lowest levels of all forms of gender discrimination. The Army, with only 67 percent of positions open to women, has had the third lowest levels of discrimination of all forms. It is in the Marine Corps that gender discrimination is most pervasive. This is not surprising given that, in the Marine Corps, less than six percent of the personnel are women, only 62 percent of the positions are open to women, and the highest level of gender segregation of any service exists.

Women's Attrition and Military Culture

Gender-discrimination patterns within the services also inversely correlate with attrition rates for military women, which—especially during their first enlistment—are higher than attrition rates for military men in all services but the Navy. Currently, attrition rates for both men and women may be too high to maintain optimal military readiness in the long term.

During the first 12 months of service, Marine Corps women have the highest attrition, Army women the second highest, Navy women the third highest, and Air Force women the lowest. Only in the Navy are attrition rates higher for men than women during the first 12 months in the service.

For the first three years in the service, the patterns are the same. Marine Corps and Army women have the highest attrition rates: nearly 44 percent leave their service, compared with slightly more than 30 percent of Marine and Army men. Slightly more Navy men continue to leave than Navy women. Air Force women have the lowest attrition rates of all service women. Indeed, Army and Marine Corps men leave at rates comparable to Air Force women.

What do these data suggest? The parallels between the levels of gender integration in a service, gender climates, and women's attrition are compelling. Women stay longer in the services that offer more opportunities, greater gender integration, and more favorable climates. These parallels merit study within DOD, which they are not yet receiving.

REDRESSING CULTURAL CONSTRAINTS

The armed forces are just beginning to address the many cultural constraints impeding the performance and progress of women in the military. Yet redressing cultural constraints improves women's performance and their competitiveness for leadership selection. It also enhances unit performance, thereby improving military readiness.

Since the mid-1990s, the armed services increasingly have appeared willing to challenge prevailing practices in the gender-integrated military. The Navy developed a methodical plan for gender-integrating all-male naval combatant vessels. The Navy's integration strategy included assigning a "critical mass" of women to a ship and phasing in integration. The assignment of "first-rate" junior women officers, especially graduates of the U.S. Naval Academy, preceded the full integration of crews. Women noncommissioned officers, and finally junior enlisted women, followed. Climate assessments and training also accompanied the phased-in integration process. Although combatant vessels were not opened to women until 1994, today more than 6,900 women serve on combatant ships, or three out of every four women serving at sea.

Although all ground-combat positions remain closed to Army women, the Army recently took the lead in questioning longstanding assumptions about women's physical capabilities, physiology, and the need to redesign equipment for female physiology. The Marine Corps tested women's endurance under combat and field conditions in 1997 when it introduced the Crucible endurance test at the end of basic training and Marine Combat Training for all women. During the Crucible, women succeed but they succeed differently from men. While men physically "power through" endurance tests as individuals, women work strategically and succeed as teams. Women honor graduates of Marine Combat Training demonstrate that women, too, can excel in combat skills.

Overall, remediation of cultural constraints affecting the participation, performance, and acceptance of women in the armed services can only enhance military readiness and the selection and performance of women leaders.

WOMEN IN THE MILITARY: THE STRUGGLE TO LEAD

Throughout American history, women have struggled for leadership in America's armed forces. The 1990s was a decade of many firsts for military women—in air and naval combat, leadership of operational units, service in nontraditional occupations, and space. But achieving firsts does not mean that women's struggle for leadership is over.

At the beginning of the twenty-first century, military women still confront the effects of federal laws and policies that limit their roles and leadership. They are impeded by their small numbers in all services. Career uncertainties still result from leadership selection criteria and processes that disadvantage women. Women are limited by continued exclusion from the central and elite missions of their services and by cultural constraints imposed by organizations designed for men.

The assumption of key leadership positions by women commissioned and noncommissioned officers is constrained by the military's unique organization and by the historical underrepresentation of women in the senior ranks. Since the military "grows" its own leaders, senior officers in newly opened military occupations cannot be recruited from outside the military, from the individual service, or even, sometimes, from the career field itself. For this reason, senior women leaders in a career field lag behind junior women personnel by nearly a generation, impeding role-modeling, mentoring, and networking for women. As every new career field opens to women, the generation-long gender integration process begins again. With most career fields that reflect the central and elite missions of some services remaining closed to women today, the gender-integration process could continue throughout the twenty-first century.

In civilian professions today, the ideal leader may be perceived as male. But organizations increasingly value the consensus-building, organizational, communications, and other skills that women bring. In the military, the ideal leader is defined as masculine, not just male. Masculine strengths are valued; feminine strengths are denigrated. Military women individually struggle to obtain the skills and experiences necessary to perform at optimal levels. They strive for leadership in the armed services as individuals who have proven their abilities and dedication.

Women's struggle for leadership is also about more than individual career advancement. In the mid-1990s, the U.S. Supreme Court commented on the current status of women in America in its decision in *United States v. Virginia Military Institute,* which required the admission of women at Virginia Military Institute (VMI). The Court ruled: "[This] Court has repeatedly recognized that neither federal nor state government acts compatibly with the equal protection principle when a law or official policy denies to women, simply because they are women, full citizenship stature—equal opportunity to aspire, achieve, participate in and contribute to society based upon their individual talents and capacities" (518 U.S. 532).

Women's struggle for leadership in the armed forces may be carried out by individual women. But their collective struggle to share equally in the defense of the nation represents the final stage in the American woman's long journey to full citizenship.

AMERICAN WOMEN TODAY: A STATISTICAL PORTRAIT

Section I:
Demographics[1]

This section contains the basic statistics about the U.S. population, with particular attention to the female population. Here are data on median age, life expectancy, and the racial and Hispanic/non-Hispanic mix, as they are now and as they are projected to be 30 years from now. Also in this section is information about marital status, family characteristics, living arrangements, and divorce and fertility rates. In many cases, data from earlier years provide a context for the current data.

The numbers in this section confirm what many have observed about the United States today—that we are an increasingly diverse society racially and ethnically; that our older population is growing; that young people are marrying later than they used to; that an increasing number are not marrying at all; and that most wives are in the paid workforce.

- Females outnumber males in the U.S. population as a whole and among non-Hispanics of every race, but males have the edge among people of Hispanic origin (see Table 1-1).
- The majority of people in the age groups under 30 are male; the majority in the age groups over 30 are female. The older the age group, the greater the female majority (see Figure 1-2).
- The baby boomers, now middle-aged or close to it, swell the midsections of the U.S. population age profile. Thirty years from now, they will produce a bulge at the top (see Figure 1-3).

[1]The editors are deeply indebted to Vanessa Wight for her creative, patient, and meticulous work, not only in tracking down and gathering the source materials for every section of the "Statistical Portrait" in this edition, but also in preparing all the tables and figures for publication.

- Life expectancy is projected to increase for American women and men of every race in the next half century. Although women will retain the edge in life expectancy, gender differences are projected to narrow somewhat (see Table 1-3).
- U.S. fertility rates have generally declined over the last 40 years (see Figure 1-5).
- Although the median ages of every racial and ethnic group are projected to increase between now and 2030, it is the non-Hispanic white population—already the "oldest"—that is expected to age the most (see Table 1-4).
- Although people who have never married still account for a minority of Americans, that minority has grown (see Figure 1-6).
- Age at first marriage has been rising for people of both sexes, and the age difference between the typical bride and the typical groom has been steadily narrowing (see Figure 1-7).
- Married-couple families with working wives account for close to half of all American families, whatever their type, and for more than 60 percent of married-couple families (see Table 1-6).
- The proportion of American children in two-parent families, which has been shrinking for years, was below 70 percent in 1998 (see Table 1-7).
- The ratio of women to men widens as people age, and the widening accelerates in the upper ages. In the age group over 95, there are nearly four times as many women as men (see Figure 1-9).
- By age 75, whether they are black, white, or Hispanic, most women are no longer living with a spouse (see Table 1-9). Indeed, a woman over 65 is more than twice as likely as a man to find herself alone in old age (see Figure 1-10).

Table 1-1 • Population of the United States by Race, Hispanic Origin, and Sex, July 1, 2001 (projected)[1]

In the U. S. population overall, females outnumber males by over six million (roughly five percent), and although the imbalance is greatest among non-Hispanic blacks and whites, females predominate in all the groups shown here except Hispanics (who may be of any race). The comparative youth of the Hispanic population accounts for this, since as a general rule males outnumber females in the age groups under 30 (*see* Table 1-4 and Figure 1-2).

	Number
White, non-Hispanic	
Females	100,890,000
Males	96,761,000
Black, non-Hispanic	
Females	17,902,000
Males	16,052,000
American Indian, Eskimo, and Aleut, non-Hispanic	
Females	1,059,000
Males	1,020,000
Asian/Pacific Islander, non-Hispanic	
Females	5,718,000
Males	5,234,000
Hispanic[2]	
Females	16,036,000
Males	16,245,000
All races	
Females	141,606,000
Males	135,312,000

[1]Resident population of the 50 states and the District of Columbia.
[2]Persons of Hispanic origin may be of any race—in other words, Hispanic origin is not a *racial* category. Until fairly recently, most of the government sources that presented data by race and Hispanic origin included persons of Hispanic origin both in the racial category to which they belonged *and* in the category "persons of Hispanic origin." Today, some of these sources present data by Hispanic and non-Hispanic origin; that is, persons of Hispanic origin, whatever their race, are shown by origin but not by race, and persons not of Hispanic origin are shown by race.

Source: Bureau of the Census, *Population Projections of the United States by Age, Sex, Race, and Hispanic Origin: 1995 to 2050,* 1996, Table 2.

Figure 1-1 • Population of the United States by Sex, Race, and Hispanic Origin, July 1, 2001 (projected)(percent distributions)[1]

The proportion of non-Hispanic blacks is slightly larger among females than among males; the proportion of Hispanics is slightly larger among males than among females. In other respects, the distributions of the two sexes are nearly identical.

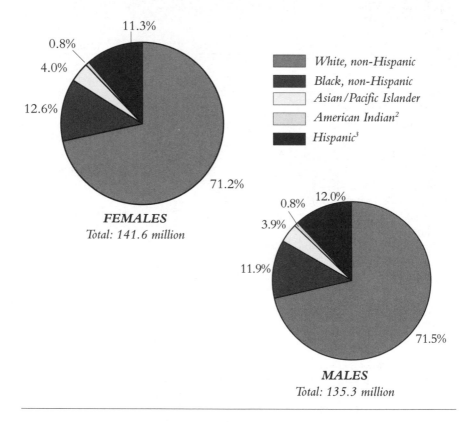

FEMALES
Total: 141.6 million

MALES
Total: 135.3 million

White, non-Hispanic
Black, non-Hispanic
Asian/Pacific Islander
American Indian[2]
Hispanic[3]

[1] Resident population of the 50 states and the District of Columbia.
[2] Includes Eskimo and Aleut.
[3] Persons of Hispanic origin may be of any race. In this figure, Hispanics are not included in the racial categories. *See* footnote to Table 1-1.

Source: Bureau of the Census, *Population Projections of the United States by Age, Sex, Race, and Hispanic Origin: 1995 to 2050,* 1996, Table 2.

Figure 1-2 • Population of the United States by Age and Sex, July 1, 2001 (projected)[1]

There are more males than females among people under 30. In the age groups over 30, however, women are in the majority, and the older the population, the greater the female edge. In the population over 80, there are nearly two women for every man (*see also* Figure 1-9).

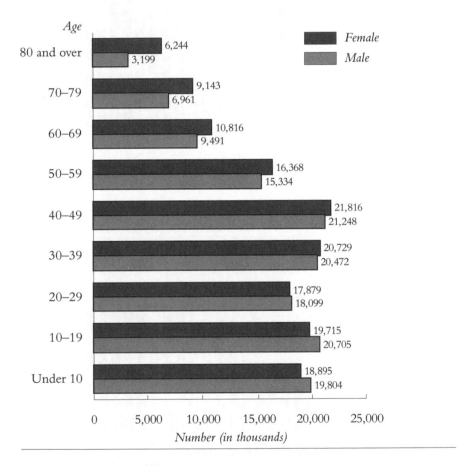

[1]Resident population of the 50 states and the District of Columbia.

Source: Bureau of the Census, *Population Projections of the United States by Age, Sex, Race and Hispanic Origin: 1995 to 2050,* 1996, Table 2.

Figure 1-3 • Population of the United States in 2001 and 2030 by Age and Sex (projected) (percent distributions)

This figure shows how the U.S. population is distributed by age and sex today and how it is projected to be distributed in 2030. The baby boomers, now middle-aged or nearly so, account for the bulge in the middle of the 2001 distribution; as they move into old age, the bulge will appear in the upper part of the 2030 distribution.

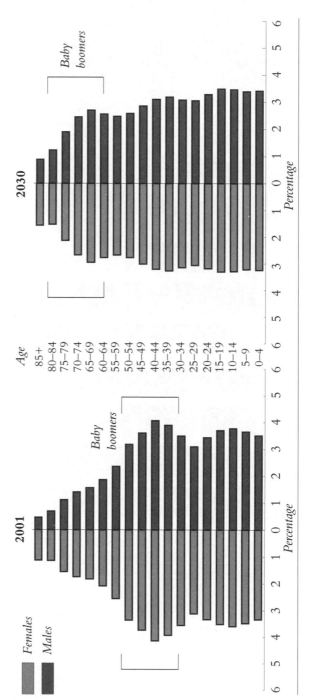

Source: Bureau of the Census, *Population Projections of the United States by Age, Sex, Race, and Hispanic Origin: 1995-2050,* 1996, Table 2.

Figure 1-4 • Population of the United States by Race and Hispanic Origin, 2001 and 2030 (projected)(percent distributions)[1]

Between now and 2030, according to Census Bureau projections, the U.S. population will increase by 70 million. The proportion that is of Hispanic origin will grow from less than one in eight (11.7 percent) to nearly one in five (18.9 percent). The proportion that is of Asian/Pacific Islander origin, currently at four percent, will increase to nearly seven percent. Non-Hispanic whites will account for six in 10 Americans in 2030, compared with more than seven in 10 today.

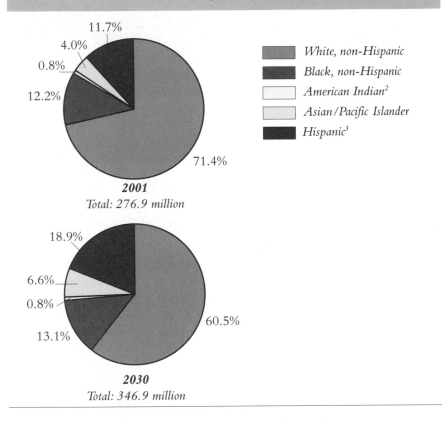

■ *White, non-Hispanic*
■ *Black, non-Hispanic*
□ *American Indian[2]*
▨ *Asian/Pacific Islander*
■ *Hispanic[3]*

2001
Total: 276.9 million

2030
Total: 346.9 million

[1] Resident population of the 50 states and the District of Columbia.
[2] Includes Eskimo and Aleut.
[3] Persons of Hispanic origin may be of any race. In this figure, Hispanics are not included in the racial categories. *See* footnote to Table 1-1.

Source: Bureau of the Census, *Population Projections of the United States by Age, Sex, Race, and Hispanic Origin: 1995 to 2050*, 1996, Table 2.

Table 1-2 • Life Expectancy at Birth and at Age 65 by Sex, Race, and Hispanic Origin, 2001 (in years)

Regardless of race or Hispanic origin, a female is likely to live longer than her male counterpart. The differences by gender in life expectancy are wider at birth than at age 65, most conspicuously so in the case of blacks (10.3 years versus 4.0 years).

| | Life Expectancy (years of life remaining) | | | |
| | At Birth | | At Age 65 | |
	Females	Males	Females	Males
All races	79.8	73.1	19.5	16.0
Non-Hispanic				
White	80.6	74.4	19.6	16.2
Black	74.5	64.2	17.7	13.7
American Indian, Eskimo, and				
Aleut	80.7	72.2	22.8	18.2
Asian/Pacific Islander	85.2	79.8	23.2	19.0
Hispanic[1]	82.9	75.2	22.5	19.3

[1]Persons of Hispanic origin may be of any race. In this table, Hispanics are not included in the racial categories. *See* footnote to Table 1-1.

Source: Bureau of the Census, *Population Projections of the United States by Age, Sex, Race, and Hispanic Origin: 1995–2050,* 1996, Tables B–1 and B–2, middle assumptions.

Table 1-3 • Life Expectancy at Birth and at Age 65 by Sex and Race, 1950 and Projected 2001, 2030, and 2050[1]

The Census Bureau has projected that life expectancy will increase for American women and men of every race in the next half century, and that the gender differences will narrow somewhat. However, if the projections prove accurate, life expectancy will still be shorter for black Americans than for their counterparts of other races.

| | Life Expectancy (years of life remaining) | | | |
| | At Birth | | At Age 65 | |
	Females	Males	Females	Males
All races				
1950	71.1	65.6	15.0	12.8
2001	79.8	73.1	19.5	16.0
2030	82.4	76.9	21.2	18.5
2050	84.3	79.7	22.4	20.3
White				
1950	72.2	66.5	15.1	12.8
2001	80.6	74.3	19.8	16.3
2030	83.7	78.7	21.9	19.3
2050	85.9	82.0	23.6	21.6
Black				
1950	62.7	58.9	14.9	12.9
2001	74.8	64.6	17.9	13.8
2030	77.6	67.9	19.3	15.4
2050	79.7	70.8	20.3	16.5
Native American[2]				
2001	81.0	72.7	22.7	18.3
2030	83.8	76.5	24.3	20.5
2050	85.7	79.3	25.5	22.1
Asian/Pacific Islander				
2001	85.1	79.6	23.1	19.0
2030	86.8	82.0	24.3	20.7
2050	88.1	83.9	25.3	21.9

[1]Data for Native American and Asian/Pacific Islander are not available for 1950.
[2]American Indian, Eskimo, and Aleut.

Source: National Center for Health Statistics, *Health, United States, 1998,* 1998, Table 29; and Bureau of the Census, *Population Projections of the United States by Age, Sex, Race, and Hispanic Origin: 1995–2050,* 1996, Tables B–1 and B–2, middle assumptions.

Figure 1-5 • U.S. Fertility Rates by Race and Hispanic Origin of Mother, 1950–1997[1,2]

In the U.S. population overall, fertility rates (the number of live births in a given year per 1,000 women age 15–44) have generally declined over the last 40 years. In recent years, Hispanics have had the highest fertility rates.

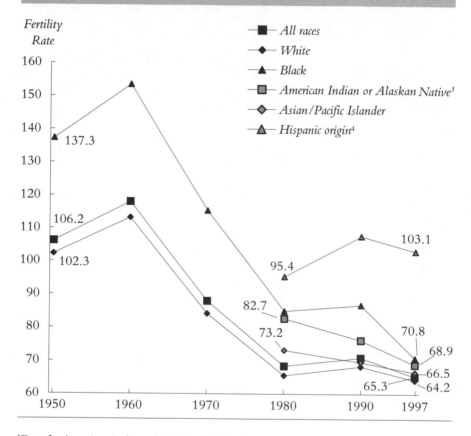

[1]Data for American Indians, Asian/Pacific Islanders, and persons of Hispanic origin are not available for the years 1950, 1960, and 1970.
[2]Except for 1950, 1960, and 1970, rates are based on race of mother.
[3]Includes Eskimo and Aleut.
[4]Persons of Hispanic origin may be of any race. *See* footnote to Table 1-1.

Source: Bureau of the Census, *Statistical Abstract of the United States: 1980*, 1980, Table 88; National Center for Health Statistics, *Health, United States, 1998*, 1998, Table 3; and *National Vital Statistics Report 47*, no. 4, 1998, Table 3.

Table 1-4 • Median Ages of the U.S. Population by Sex, Race, and Hispanic Origin, July 1, 2001, and July 1, 2030 (projected)

Differences by sex, race, and Hispanic origin in fertility rates and life expectancy are reflected in median ages. Comparatively long life expectancy, together with a low fertility rate in recent years, has already made non-Hispanic whites the "oldest" population in the United States, and will age it faster than other groups over the next three decades. Comparing Hispanic females (who may be of any race) with non-Hispanic white females provides the most dramatic contrast: as of mid-2001, there will be a difference of more than 12 years in their median ages; by mid-2030, that difference will have widened to nearly 14 years.

| | Median Age in Years | | | |
| | 2001 | | 2030 | |
	Female	Male	Female	Male
All races	37.1	34.7	39.7	37.2
Non-Hispanic				
White	39.9	37.6	44.5	42.2
Black	32.0	28.2	34.9	30.2
American Indian, Eskimo, and				
Aleut	29.0	27.2	31.2	29.7
Asian/Pacific Islander	32.8	30.7	35.6	32.4
Hispanic[1]	27.6	26.5	30.8	28.7

[1]Persons of Hispanic origin may be of any race. In this table, Hispanics are not included in the racial categories. *See* footnote to Table 1-1.

Source: Bureau of the Census, *Population Projections of the United States by Age, Sex, Race, and Hispanic Origin: 1995 to 2050*, 1996, Table 2.

Table 1-5 • Marital Status by Sex, Race, and Hispanic Origin, 1998 (percent distributions)[1]

The never married account for a smaller proportion of women than of men (20.5 percent versus 26.9 percent) in part because the female population is "older" than the male population (see Figure 1-2 and Table 1-4). But other factors must be at work to account for the large percentages of both black women and black men who have never married.

Marital Status	All Races[2]		White		Black		Hispanic[3]	
	Women	Men	Women	Men	Women	Men	Women	Men
Married, spouse present	54.0	58.2	57.2	60.7	31.0	39.7	52.8	50.1
Married, spouse absent	3.9	3.5	3.2	3.1	8.0	5.6	7.5	7.4
Widowed	10.8	2.7	11.0	2.6	10.7	3.7	6.3	1.3
Divorced	10.8	8.8	10.7	8.7	13.1	10.1	9.1	6.4
Never married	20.5	26.9	17.8	24.8	37.3	40.9	24.3	34.8
Total number (in thousands)	102,403	95,009	84,953	80,385	12,794	10,297	9,753	10,082
Total percentage[4]	100.0	100.0	100.0	100.0	100.0	100.0	100.0	100.0

[1]Persons age 18 and over.
[2]Includes Asian/Pacific Islanders and Native Americans, not shown separately (data not available).
[3]Persons of Hispanic origin may be of any race. In this table, Hispanics are included in the racial categories as well as in the Hispanic category. See footnote to Table 1-1.
[4]Percentages may not total 100.0 due to rounding.

Source: Bureau of the Census, Marital Status and Living Arrangements: March 1998, 1999, Table 1.

Figure 1-6 • Never-Married Adults by Sex, Race, and Hispanic Origin, 1980 and 1998[1]

In 1998, the never married accounted for larger proportions of the black, white, and Hispanic populations of both sexes than was the case in 1980.

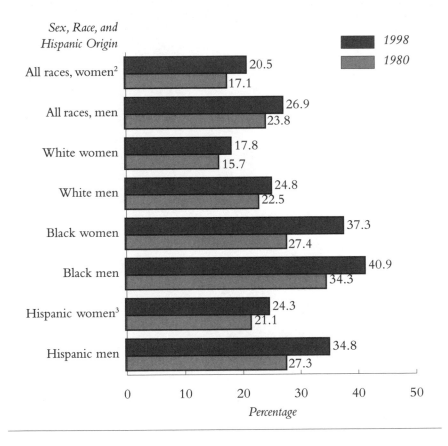

[1]Persons 18 years and over.
[2]Includes Asian/Pacific Islanders and Native Americans, not shown separately (data not available).
[3]Persons of Hispanic origin may be of any race. In this figure, Hispanics are included in the racial categories as well as in the Hispanic category. *See* footnote to Table 1-1.

Source: Bureau of the Census, *Marital Status and Living Arrangements: March 1998,* 1999, Table 1.

Figure 1-7 • Median Age at First Marriage by Sex, 1890–1998

In the 1950s and 1960s, American women and men married at earlier ages than their counterparts in the decades before and since. The trend over the last 30 years is notable not only because the age at first marriage has been increasing for both sexes but also because the difference between the sexes in age at first marriage has been narrowing.

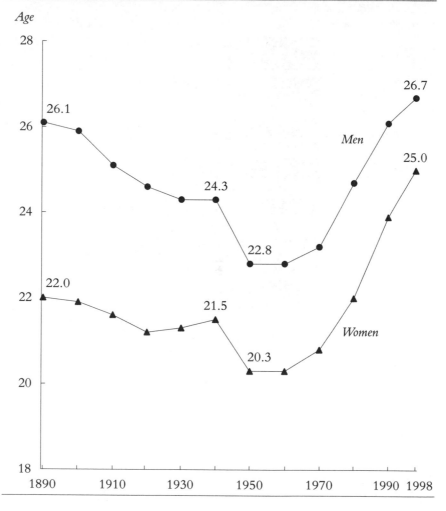

Source: Bureau of the Census, *Marital Status and Living Arrangements: March 1998,* 1999, Table MS-2.

Figure 1-8 • The Divorce Rate, 1950–1998

The divorce rate—the number of divorces in a given year per 1,000 persons in the population—declined by more than one-fourth (27 percent) between 1980 and 1998.

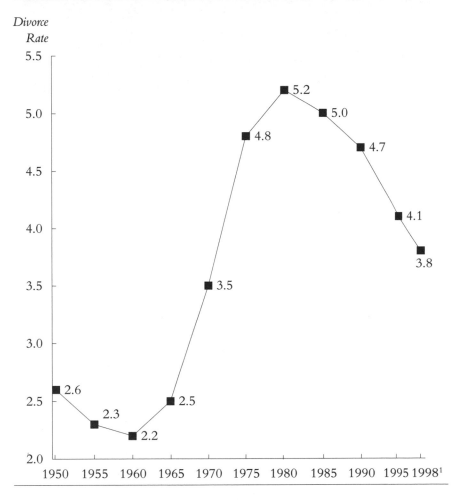

Divorce Rate

¹For the 12 months ending with August 1998.

Source: Bureau of the Census, *Statistical Abstract of the United States: 1998*, 1998, Table 92, and National Center for Health Statistics, *National Vital Statistics Report* 47, no. 14, 1998, Table 1.

Table 1-6 • Families by Family Type, Race, and Hispanic Origin, 1970, 1980, 1990, and 1997 (percent distributions)[1]

This table shows how the "mix" of American family types changed over the waning decades of the twentieth century. Between 1970 and 1997, the proportion of families headed by women grew from 11.5 percent to 17.8 percent, while the proportion headed by men more than doubled, from 2.4 percent to 5.5 percent. Married-couple families with working wives, who in 1970 represented only about one-third of all families and were in the minority even among married couples, accounted for close to half (47.3 percent) of all families in 1997 (and for more than 60 percent of all married-couple families).

Family Type	1970	1980	1990	1997
All races[2]				
Married couple	86.1	81.7	78.6	76.6
Wife in paid labor force	33.8	41.0	45.7	47.3
Wife not in paid labor force	52.3	40.7	32.9	29.3
Male head, no spouse present	2.4	3.2	4.4	5.5
Female head, no spouse present	11.5	15.1	17.0	17.8
Total percentage	100.0	100.0	100.0	100.0
Total number (in thousands)	51,948	60,309	66,322	70,884
White				
Married couple	88.3	85.1	82.8	80.8
Wife in paid labor force	33.6	42.0	47.5	49.3
Wife not in paid labor force	54.7	43.1	35.2	31.5
Male head, no spouse present	2.3	3.0	4.0	5.3
Female head, no spouse present	9.4	11.9	13.2	14.0
Total percentage	100.0	100.0	100.0	100.0
Total number (in thousands)	46,535	52,710	56,803	59,515

(continued)

[1]Percentages may not total 100.0 due to rounding.
[2]Includes Asian/Pacific Islanders and Native Americans, not shown separately (data not available).

Table 1-6 (continued)

Family Type	1970	1980	1990	1997
Black				
Married couple	65.6	53.7	47.8	46.6
Wife in paid labor force	35.5	32.0	31.4	32.3
Wife not in paid labor force	30.2	21.7	16.3	14.3
Male head, no spouse present	3.8	4.6	6.3	6.7
Female head, no spouse present	30.6	41.7	45.9	46.7
Total percentage	100.0	100.0	100.0	100.0
Total number (in thousands)	4,928	6,317	7,471	8,408
Hispanic[3, 4]				
Married couple	—	73.1	69.3	69.0
Wife in paid labor force	—	33.8	35.2	38.1
Wife not in paid labor force	—	39.4	34.2	30.9
Male head, no spouse present	—	5.1	6.9	7.8
Female head, no spouse present	—	21.8	23.8	23.2
Total percentage	—	100.0	100.0	100.0
Total number (in thousands)	—	3,235	4,981	6,961

[3]Persons of Hispanic origin may be of any race. In this table, Hispanics are included in the racial categories as well as in the Hispanic category. *See* footnote to Table 1-1.
[4]Data by Hispanic origin are not available for 1970.

Source: Bureau of the Census, *Historical Income Tables,* <http://www.census.gov/hhes/income/histinc/>; and *Money Income in the United States: 1997,* 1998, Table 4.

Table 1-7 • Children's Living Arrangements by Race and Hispanic Origin, 1975, 1985, 1995, and 1998 (percent distributions)[1]

Overall, as of 1998, fewer than seven in 10 American children lived with two parents, although the proportions who did were much larger among white and Hispanic children and much smaller among black children. However, in 1998, a black child was slightly more likely to be living with two parents than had been the case just three years earlier. The reverse was true of a white child.

Living Arrangements	1975	1985	1995	1998
All races[2]				
Living with two parents	80.3	73.9	68.7	68.1
Living with mother only	15.5	20.9	23.5	23.3
Living with father only	1.5	2.5	3.5	4.4
Other	2.7	2.7	4.3	4.1
Total percentage	100.0	100.0	100.0	100.0
Total number (in thousands)	66,087	62,475	70,254	71,377
White				
Living with two parents	85.4	80.0	75.8	74.0
Living with mother only	11.3	15.6	17.8	18.2
Living with father only	1.5	2.4	3.4	4.6
Other	1.8	2.0	3.0	3.2
Total percentage	100.0	100.0	100.0	100.0
Total number (in thousands)	55,500	50,836	55,327	56,124
Black				
Living with two parents	49.4	39.5	33.1	36.2
Living with mother only	40.9	51.0	52.0	51.1
Living with father only	1.8	2.9	4.1	3.7
Other	7.9	6.6	10.8	8.9
Total percentage	100.0	100.0	100.0	100.0
Total number (in thousands)	9,472	9,479	11,301	11,414

(continued)

[1]Percentages may not total 100.0 due to rounding.
[2]Includes Asian/Pacific Islanders and Native Americans, not shown separately (data not available).

Table 1-7 (continued)

Living Arrangements	1975	1985	1995	1998
Hispanic[3, 4]				
Living with two parents	—	67.9	62.9	63.6
Living with mother only	—	26.6	28.4	26.8
Living with father only	—	2.2	4.2	4.4
Other	—	3.3	4.4	5.1
Total percentage	—	100.0	100.0	100.0
Total number (in thousands)	—	6,057	9,843	10,863

[3]Persons of Hispanic origin may be of any race. In this table, Hispanics are included in the racial categories as well as in the Hispanic category. *See* footnote to Table 1-1.
[4]Data for persons of Hispanic origin are not available for 1975.

Source: Bureau of the Census, *Marital Status and Living Arrangements: March 1998,* 1999, Tables 4, CH-1, CH-2, CH-3, and CH-4.

Table 1-8 • Households with Unrelated Partners by Sex of Partners and Presence of Children, 1998 (numbers in thousands)[1]

In 1998, some 5.9 million households consisted of unrelated people living together as partners; of these, about 1.7 million (not quite 30 percent) were same-sex partnerships. Although there are far more likely to be children in the household when the partners are heterosexual than when they are of the same sex, children are present in only a minority of unrelated-partner households.

Household Type	Number of Households	With Children	
		Number	Percentage
Partners of opposite sex	4,236	1,520	35.9
Female householder, male partner	1,885	724	38.4
Male householder, female partner	2,352	796	33.8
Partners of same sex	1,674	167	10.0
Both partners female	810	135	16.7
Both partners male	865	32	3.7
Total	5,911	1,687	28.5

[1]Partners over age 18; children under age 15.

Source: Bureau of the Census, *Marital Status and Living Arrangements: March 1998*, 1999, Table 8.

Figure 1-9 • Ratio of Women to Men in the Population Age 65 and Over by Age, 1997 (number of women per 100 men in a given age group)

This figure illustrates how the ratio of women to men widens in the elderly population. In the youngest elderly group (people from 65 to 69), there are about six women for every five men. Among the oldest old (95 and up), there are nearly four women for every man.

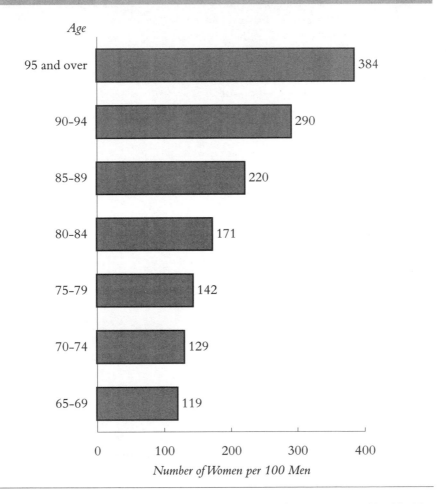

Source: Bureau of the Census, *Statistical Abstract of the United States: 1998*, 1998, Table 16.

Table 1-9 • Living Arrangements of Women Age 65 and Over by Age, Race, and Hispanic Origin, 1998 (percent distributions)[1]

Given the gender difference in life expectancy, it is not surprising that, whether they are white, black, or of Hispanic origin, women between 65 and 75 are more likely than their older counterparts to be living with a spouse. However, as this table makes clear, there are substantial differences by race and Hispanic origin in older women's living arrangements. For example, in all three age groups shown here, Hispanic women (who may be of any race) are considerably less likely than either white or black women to be living alone.

	Living Alone	Living with Spouse	Living with Others[2]	Total Percentage	Total Number
Age 65–74					
All races[3]	30.2	52.4	17.3	100.0	9,882
White	29.8	55.1	15.1	100.0	8,651
Black	37.6	29.8	32.6	100.0	956
Hispanic[4]	21.7	44.0	34.3	100.0	586
Age 75–84					
All races	50.4	32.1	17.5	100.0	6,754
White	51.3	33.2	15.5	100.0	6,108
Black	44.9	19.8	35.2	100.0	494
Hispanic	37.7	29.2	33.1	100.0	281
Age 85 and over					
All races	61.7	10.9	27.4	100.0	1,923
White	63.4	11.1	25.5	100.0	1,731
Black	47.4	7.5	45.1	100.0	174
Hispanic	33.8	8.4	57.7	100.0	70

[1]Noninstitutional population.
[2]Most of these women live with family members, either in their own households or in the family members' households.
[3]Includes Asian/Pacific Islanders and Native Americans, not shown separately (data not available).
[4]Persons of Hispanic origin may be of any race. In this table, Hispanics are included in the racial categories as well as in the Hispanic category. *See* footnote to Table 1-1.

Source: Bureau of the Census, *Marital Status and Living Arrangements: March 1998,* 1999, Table 7.

Figure 1-10 • Living Arrangements of Women and Men Age 65 and Older, 1998[1]

A woman is more than twice as likely as a man to find herself alone in old age, a phenomenon largely explained by her longer life expectancy and the strong likelihood that she married an older man.

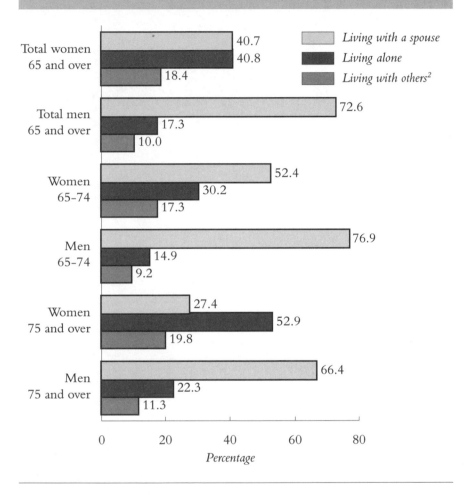

[1]Noninstitutional population.
[2]Most of these women and men live with family members, either in their own households or in the family members' households.

Source: Bureau of the Census, *Marital Status and Living Arrangements: March 1998*, 1999, Table 7.

SECTION 2:

EDUCATION

IN THIS SECTION is evidence that the longstanding female educational deficit is melting away—indeed, it has disappeared among younger women. At a time when employers place a high premium on an educated workforce, more women than men are earning undergraduate and master's degrees. In the age groups under 35, a larger proportion of women than of men are college graduates. More and more women are earning doctoral or professional degrees. The result presumably will be better employment and advancement opportunities for the growing percentage of American women who are well educated, and rosier economic prospects for them over time.

But prospects look increasingly bleak for people who lack schooling, a disproportionate number of whom are of Hispanic origin. The educational deficit among Hispanics is reflected in low current earnings and lack of benefits (see Section 5), with troubling implications for their long-term economic well-being.

- Compared with white and black Americans, those of Hispanic origin are educationally disadvantaged: less than 56 percent are high school graduates (see Table 2-1).
- Although white women are still more likely than black women to have a high school diploma, the proportion of high school graduates among black women more than doubled between 1970 and 1998 (see Figure 2-1).
- Whether white, black, or Hispanic, women between the ages of 25 and 35 are more likely to be college graduates than their male counterparts in the same age group (see Table 2-2).
- Racial and ethnic diversity has increased among college undergraduates of both sexes (see Table 2-3).

- Women are and will continue to be overrepresented among college and university graduate and undergraduate students. The ratio of women to men is particularly lopsided among part-time students (see Figure 2-3).
- Over the last quarter of the twentieth century, women overtook men in earning associate, bachelor's, and master's degrees, and significantly narrowed men's lead in earning doctoral and first professional degrees (see Table 2-4).
- Women have been and remain heavily overrepresented among undergraduates awarded degrees in certain fields, such as the health professions, education, and English. Still, the proportions of women have been growing in such traditionally male-dominated fields as engineering and the physical sciences (see Table 2-5).
- In 20 years, women's share of law degrees awarded annually almost doubled, their share of M.D. degrees more than doubled, and their share of degrees in dentistry more than tripled. Blacks and Hispanics were underrepresented among the female recipients of these first professional degrees; Asian/Pacific Islanders were overrepresented in dentistry and medicine (see Table 2-6).
- Despite women's dramatic gains in law, medicine, and dentistry, they are still in the minority among the recipients of first professional degrees awarded annually in those fields. But women outnumber men by nearly two to one among the recipients of degrees awarded annually in veterinary medicine and pharmacy (see Figure 2-4).
- Over a 20-year period when the number of Ph.D.'s awarded annually to women more than doubled, the proportions of women's doctorates earned in education, humanities, and the social sciences decreased; the proportions earned in life sciences, physical sciences, and engineering increased (see Figure 2-5).
- Most of the males on the faculties of America's four-year colleges and universities have tenure; most of their female colleagues do not. This state of affairs has remained essentially unchanged over the years (see Figure 2-6).

Table 2-1 • Educational Attainment of Women and Men Age 25 and Over by Race and Hispanic Origin, 1998 (in percentages)

The serious educational deficit among people of Hispanic origin is obvious in this table. Less than 56 percent of Hispanic women and men are high school graduates; close to 30 percent did not attend high school at all.[1]

	No High School	Some High School, No Diploma	High School Diploma or More	Some College, No Degree	Associate Degree, No More	Bachelor's Degree or More	Postgraduate Degree[2]	Number (in thousands)
				Percentage With				
All races[3]								
Women	7.4	9.7	82.9	17.3	8.0	22.4	6.6	89,835
Men	7.5	9.7	82.8	17.1	6.9	26.5	9.4	82,376
White								
Women	7.2	9.0	83.8	17.2	8.2	22.8	6.7	75,016
Men	7.4	9.1	83.6	17.1	7.1	27.3	9.7	70,062
Black								
Women	7.4	15.8	76.7	19.2	7.0	15.4	5.0	10,798
Men	8.9	16.0	75.2	19.0	5.3	13.9	3.7	8,578
Hispanic[4]								
Women	29.1	15.7	55.3	12.5	5.4	10.9	2.5	7,989
Men	28.2	16.2	55.7	12.7	4.7	11.1	3.8	8,055

[1]Many of the foreign-born Hispanics in the United States have little schooling. *See The American Woman 1999–2000*, Table 2-4.

[2]Postgraduate degrees include master's, professional, and doctorate degrees.

[3]Includes Asian/Pacific Islanders and Native Americans, not shown separately (data not available).

[4]Persons of Hispanic origin may be of any race. In this table, Hispanics are included in the racial categories. *See* footnote to Table 1-1.

Source: Bureau of the Census, *Educational Attainment in the United States: March 1998 (Update)*, 1998, Table 1.

Table 2-2 • Educational Attainment of Women and Men Age 25 and Over by Age, Race, and Hispanic Origin, 1998 (in percentages)

Young women have closed one longstanding gender gap: in every group shown here, women between the ages of 25 and 35 are more likely than their male contemporaries to be college graduates.

	High School Graduate or More		Bachelor's Degree or More	
	Women	*Men*	*Women*	*Men*
All races[1]				
Total 25 and over	82.9	82.8	22.4	26.5
25–34	89.0	86.8	28.7	26.2
35–44	89.0	87.0	25.8	26.9
45–54	87.9	86.6	25.9	31.8
55–64	78.9	80.2	17.9	26.4
65 and over	66.6	67.6	11.2	19.8
White				
Total 25 and over	83.8	83.6	22.8	27.3
25–34	89.5	86.5	30.1	26.7
35–44	89.6	87.6	26.7	27.8
45–54	89.1	87.6	26.2	32.9
55–64	81.1	81.9	17.6	27.1
65 and over	69.0	69.8	11.5	20.8
Black				
Total 25 and over	76.7	75.2	15.4	13.9
25–34	86.9	87.1	15.6	15.0
35–44	85.9	81.5	16.5	14.1
45–54	82.0	77.0	19.5	18.2
55–64	64.7	63.0	15.5	12.4
65 and over	44.0	41.9	7.7	6.0

(continued)

[1]Includes Asian/Pacific Islanders and Native Americans, not shown separately (data not available).

Table 2-2 (continued)

	High School Graduate or More		Bachelor's Degree or More	
	Women	*Men*	*Women*	*Men*
Hispanic origin[2]				
Total 25 and over	55.3	55.7	10.9	11.1
25–34	63.7	59.9	12.3	9.9
35–44	60.4	60.1	12.5	13.0
45–54	55.5	54.3	11.7	12.5
55–64	46.3	49.2	8.3	11.6
65 and over	27.7	32.0	4.5	6.8

[2]Persons of Hispanic origin may be of any race. In this table, Hispanics are included in the racial categories as well as in the Hispanic category. *See* footnote to Table 1-1.

Source: Bureau of the Census, *Educational Attainment in the United States: March 1998 (Update)*, 1998, Table 3.

Figure 2-1 • Women Age 25 and Over Who Completed Four Years of High School or More by Race and Hispanic Origin, 1960–1998 (in percentages)

Over the nearly three decades shown here, black women made the most dramatic gains in educational attainment as measured by the percentage of high school graduates. As of 1998, more than three-fourths of black women over age 25 had at least a high school diploma, compared with less than one-third in 1970.

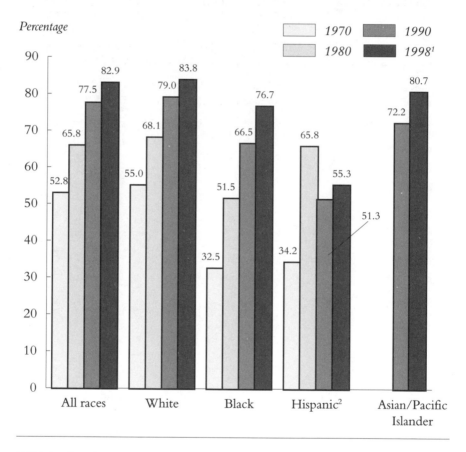

[1]1996 data have been substituted for 1998 data for Asian/Pacific Islanders (1998 data were not available).
[2]Persons of Hispanic origin may be of any race. In this figure, Hispanics are included in the racial categories as well as in the Hispanic category. *See* footnote to Table 1-1.

Source: Bureau of the Census, *Statistical Abstract of the United States: 1998*, 1998, Table 261.

Table 2-3 • College Enrollment of Women and Men by Race and Hispanic Origin, 1980, 1990, and 1996 (percent distributions)[1]

Diversity has increased among college undergraduates of both sexes, although somewhat more among women than men. The distribution by race and Hispanic origin of female undergraduates is similar in some respects to that of the population as a whole (*see* Table 1-1); the dissimilarities involve Asian/Pacific Islanders, who are somewhat overrepresented among undergraduates, and Hispanics, who are slightly underrepresented.

	Women			Men		
	1980	*1990*	*1996*[2]	*1980*	*1990*	*1996*[2]
Non-Hispanic						
White	81.9	78.4	72.0	83.5	79.6	73.9
Black	10.9	10.8	12.5	8.8	8.5	9.7
Asian/Pacific Islander	2.2	3.8	5.5	2.6	4.8	6.6
American Indian or Alaskan Native	0.8	0.9	1.1	0.7	0.8	1.0
Hispanic[3]	4.1	6.1	9.0	4.3	6.2	8.8
Total percentage[4]	100.0	100.0	100.0	100.0	100.0	100.0
Total number (in thousands)	5,402	6,487	6,720	4,858	5,254	5,266

[1]Fall enrollment of undergraduates, excluding non–U.S. citizens on temporary visas.
[2]Data for 1996 are preliminary.
[3]Persons of Hispanic origin may be of any race. In this table, Hispanics are not included in the racial categories. *See* footnote to Table 1-1.
[4]Percentages may not total 100.0 due to rounding.

Source: National Center for Education Statistics, *Digest of Education Statistics, 1998,* 1999, Table 207.

Figure 2-2 • Women Enrolled in College or University Undergraduate or Graduate Programs by Age, 1975, 1985, 1996, and Projected 2000 and 2008 (percent distributions)[1]

Women over 30 account for almost one-third of the women currently enrolled at all levels in U.S. colleges and universities.

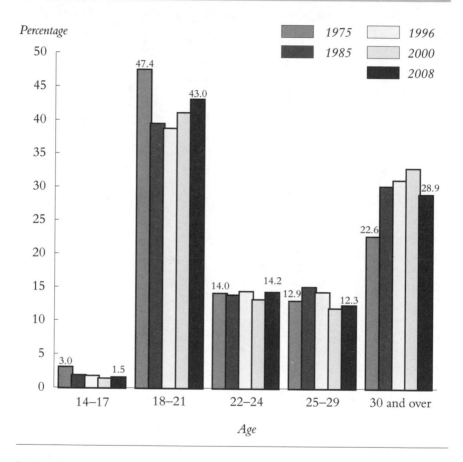

[1]Fall enrollments. Includes undergraduates, students in graduate programs, and students seeking first professional degrees (i.e., in law, medicine, etc.).

Source: National Center for Education Statistics, *Digest of Education Statistics, 1998,* 1999, Table 174.

Figure 2-3 • Ratio of Women to Men Enrolled at All Levels in Colleges and
Universities by Full- or Part-Time Status, 1975, 1985, 1996, and Projected 2000
and 2008[1]

The current and projected overrepresentation of women in college and university student bodies—undergraduate and graduate—is illustrated here. The ratio
of women to men is particularly lopsided among part-time students.

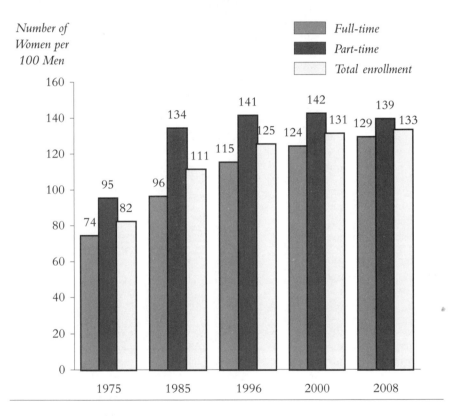

[1]Fall enrollments. Includes undergraduates, students in graduate programs, and students
seeking professional degrees (i.e., in law, medicine, etc.).

Source: National Center for Education Statistics, *Digest of Education Statistics, 1998*, 1999,
Table 174.

Table 2-4 • Recipients of Postsecondary Degrees by Sex, 1975/76, 1995/96, and Projected 2001/02

This table shows the remarkable gains that women have made in postsecondary education. In the minority among degree recipients at every level just two decades earlier, by 1995/96 women were in the majority among associate, bachelor's, and master's degree recipients. And, although women are still underrepresented at the first professional and doctoral degree levels, they seem to be on the way to closing those gaps.

Degree	1975/76	1995/96	Percent Change 75/76– 95/96	Projected 2001/02
Associate, total number	391,454	555,216	41.8	550,000
Number of women	181,458	335,702	85.0	339,000
Women as a percentage of degree recipients	46.4	60.5	—	61.6
Bachelor's, total number	925,746	1,164,792	25.8	1,195,000
Number of women	420,821	642,338	52.6	685,000
Women as a percentage of degree recipients	45.5	55.1	—	57.3
Master's, total number	311,771	406,301	30.3	422,000
Number of women	144,523	227,220	57.2	231,000
Women as a percentage of degree recipients	46.4	55.9	—	54.7
Professional, total number[1]	62,649	76,734	22.5	72,400
Number of women	9,757	31,986	227.8	31,800
Women as a percentage of degree recipients	15.6	41.7	—	43.9
Doctoral, total number	34,064	44,652	31.1	47,200
Number of women	7,797	17,811	128.4	20,000
Women as a percentage of degree recipients	22.9	39.9	—	42.4

[1]First professional degrees (i.e., in law, medicine, etc.).

Source: National Center for Education Statistics, Digest of Education Statistics, 1998, 1999, Table 244.

Table 2-5 • Women Awarded Undergraduate Degrees in Selected Fields, 1975/76, 1985/86, and 1995/96 (in percentages)

Certain fields have always attracted more women than men. For example, in the three years shown here, women were consistently and heavily overrepresented among undergraduates awarded degrees in the health professions, education, and English. Nevertheless, female representation has been increasing in some fields of study where few women were found a generation ago, such as engineering and the physical sciences.

Field	Degrees Awarded to Women as a Percentage of All Degrees Awarded		
	1975/76	*1985/86*	*1995/96*
Biological/life sciences	34.6	48.1	52.7
Business	19.8	45.7	48.6
Computer and information sciences	19.8	35.7	27.5
Education	72.8	75.9	75.1
Engineering	3.2	13.1	16.1
English language and literature	61.7	65.8	66.0
Health professions	78.8	85.0	81.6
Mathematics	40.1	46.3	45.7
Physical sciences	19.2	27.5	36.0
Psychology	54.5	69.0	73.0
Social sciences	37.7	43.8	47.9
Visual and performing arts	60.9	61.8	59.2
All fields	45.5	50.8	55.1

Source: National Center for Education Statistics, *Digest of Education Statistics, 1998,* 1999, Tables 244, 278, 280, 282, 283, 284, 286, 289, 290, 291, 293, 295, and 297.

Table 2-6 • Women Awarded First Professional Degrees in Dentistry, Medicine, and Law by Race and Hispanic Origin, 1976/77, 1986/87, and 1995/96 (percent distributions)[1]

More than twice as many women were awarded degrees in medicine and law in 1995/96 as in 1976/77. The number of women awarded dentistry degrees more than tripled; women's share of dentistry degrees quintupled. Asian/Pacific Islanders were clearly a factor in this development: they accounted for one in five dentistry degrees awarded to women in 1995/96.

	Dentistry			Medicine			Law		
	1976/77	1986/87	1995/96	1976/77	1986/87	1995/96	1976/77	1986/87	1995/96
Non-Hispanic									
White	82.8	77.6	64.8	86.7	83.5	69.2	90.5	88.0	77.3
Black	12.0	8.5	7.9	9.5	7.1	9.7	5.8	6.3	9.8
Asian/Pacific Islander	3.0	9.2	21.2	1.9	5.5	15.6	1.7	2.1	6.7
American Indian or Alaskan Native	0.5	0.2	0.2	0.2	0.6	0.6	0.4	0.5	0.7
Hispanic[2]	1.6	4.5	5.9	1.7	3.3	4.9	1.6	3.1	5.5
Total percentage[3]	100.0	100.0	100.0	100.0	100.0	100.0	100.0	100.0	100.0
Degrees awarded to women									
Number	367	1,095	1,252	2,543	4,949	6,211	7,630	14,440	17,186
As a percentage of all degrees	7.3	23.7	36.0	19.1	32.4	41.0	22.5	40.2	43.6

[1]Data exclude non-U.S. citizens on temporary visas.
[2]Persons of Hispanic origin may be of any race. In this table, Hispanics are not included in the racial categories. See footnote to Table 1-1.
[3]Percentages may not total 100.0 due to rounding.

Source: National Center for Education Statistics, *Digest of Education Statistics, 1980,* 1980, Table 112; *Digest of Education Statistics 1990,* 1991, Table 240; and *Digest of Education Statistics 1998,* 1999, Table 274.

Figure 2-4 • First Professional Degrees Awarded in Selected Fields by Sex of Recipients, 1995/96[1]

Despite their dramatic gains in dentistry, medicine, and law, women were still in the minority among the recipients of first professional degrees in these fields in 1995/96. Among those awarded degrees in veterinary medicine and pharmacy, however, women outnumbered men by nearly two to one.

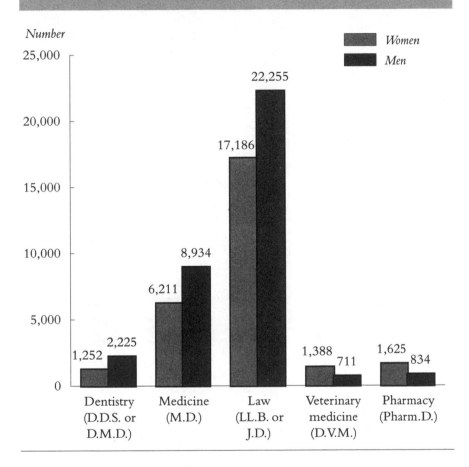

[1]Data exclude non-U.S. citizens on temporary visas.

Source: National Center for Education Statistics, *Digest of Education Statistics, 1998,* 1999, Table 274.

Figure 2-5 • Doctoral Degrees Awarded to Women in 1975/76 and 1995/96 by Field of Study (percent distributions)[1]

Among the women who were awarded doctorates in 1995/96, those who took degrees in engineering, life sciences, and physical sciences were considerably better represented than had been the case 20 years earlier.

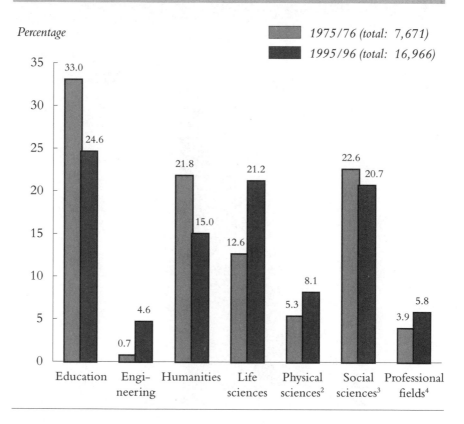

[1]Percentages may not total 100.0 due to rounding.
[2]Includes mathematics, computer science, physics, astronomy, chemistry, and earth, atmospheric, and marine sciences.
[3]Includes psychology.
[4]Includes business and management and other professional fields but excludes first professional degrees and some nonresearch doctorates such as those in theology.

Source: National Center for Education Statistics, *Digest of Education Statistics, 1977–1978*, 1978, Table 121; and *Digest of Education Statistics, 1998*, 1999, Table 298.

Figure 2-6 • Full-Time Faculty with Tenure in Public and Private Colleges and Universities by Sex, 1980/81, 1990/91, and 1996/97 (in percentages)[1]

Most of the males on the faculties of America's four-year colleges and universities have tenure; most of their female colleagues do not. This state of affairs has remained essentially unchanged over the years.

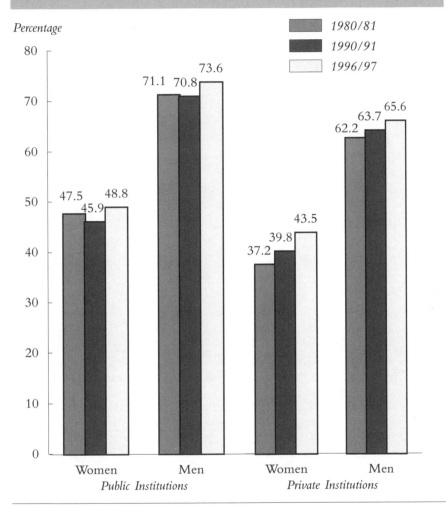

[1]Four-year institutions.

Source: National Center for Education Statistics, *Digest of Education Statistics, 1998,* 1999, Table 240.

SECTION 3:

HEALTH

MANY OF THE tables and figures in this section document continuing racial disparities in the health of American women and their infants. Black women's death rates from nearly every major cause still exceed white women's. Black, Native American, and Hispanic women are still less likely to have timely prenatal care than white women. A black mother is more than twice as likely as a white mother to have a low-birthweight baby—that is, a baby whose survival may be in doubt. Indeed, one in seven black babies dies in infancy, a proportion more than twice that of white babies. AIDS remains far more prevalent among black women and teenage girls than among their counterparts of other races.

Not all the statistics in this section are grim, however. Black and white women's death rates from heart disease and stroke are much lower than they were 30 years ago. Deaths from breast cancer have been declining. Smoking is far less prevalent among women age 18–64 than it was 30 years ago, improving the prospect that in the future lung cancer will lose its present primacy as the leading cause of cancer death in women.

- Although most expectant mothers in the United States have early prenatal care, those who are Native American, black, or Hispanic are considerably more likely than Asian and non-Hispanic white women to have either late prenatal care or none at all (see Table 3-3).
- Black women are twice as likely as white women to have low-birthweight babies—more than one in eight compared with one in 16. Black women's babies are also more than twice as likely as white women's babies to die before their first birthday (see Figure 3-1 and Table 3-4).

- A generation ago, both white and black women were far more likely to die from heart disease than from cancer. This is no longer the case for white women, but it is still true for black women (see Table 3-5).
- Cancer death rates in relation to incidence rates are higher for black women than for white women except in the case of lung cancer, which is the leading cause of cancer death for American women overall. However, white and black women's death rates from lung cancer are notably higher than for women of other races, or for Hispanic women (see Table 3-6, Figure 3-2, and Table 3-7).
- With the notable exception of women who are over 65, adult women today are far less likely to smoke than were their counterparts 30 years ago (see Figure 3-3).
- The number of new AIDS cases in females age 13 and over dropped in the late 1990s among blacks as well as whites, but in 1998—as in every year since at least 1989—black women and teenage girls accounted for a disproportionate number of female AIDS victims over age 13 (see Figure 3-4 and Table 3-8).
- Reported cases of chlamydia—the most prevalent of all sexually transmitted diseases—have increased sharply since 1985. Over 80 percent of the more than half million chlamydia cases are female (see Figure 3-5 and Table 3-9).

Table 3-1 • Contraception Use by Females Age 15–44 by Race and Hispanic Origin, 1995 (percent distributions)[1]

Both white and black women who are not of Hispanic origin are more likely than their Hispanic counterparts to use contraception.

	All Races[2]	Non-Hispanic White	Non-Hispanic Black	Hispanic[3]
Contraception users as a percentage of females age 15–44	**64.2**	**66.0**	**62.2**	**58.9**
Users of a particular method as a percentage of females age 15–44				
Female sterilization	17.8	16.3	24.9	21.6
Male sterilization	7.0	9.0	1.1	2.4
Birth control pill	17.3	18.8	14.8	13.6
Implant	0.9	0.7	1.4	1.2
Injectable	1.9	1.6	3.3	2.8
Intrauterine device	0.5	0.5	0.5	0.9
Diaphragm	1.2	1.5	0.5	0.4
Condom	13.1	13.0	12.5	12.1
Other[4]	4.5	4.7	3.1	3.9
Contraception nonusers as a percentage of all females age 15–44[5]	**35.8**	**34.0**	**37.8**	**41.1**
Total percentage	100.0	100.0	100.0	100.0
Total number (in thousands)	60,201	42,522	8,201	6,702

[1]Percentages may not total 100.0 due to rounding.
[2]Includes Asian/Pacific Islanders and Native Americans, not shown separately (data not available).
[3]Persons of Hispanic origin may be of any race. *See* footnote to Table 1-1.
[4]Includes abstinence and natural family planning, withdrawal, morning-after pill, and other methods not shown separately.
[5]Nonusers include women who are sterile, pregnant or postpartum, or seeking pregnancy, as well as women who have never had sexual intercourse.

Source: National Center for Health Statistics, *Fertility, Family Planning, and Women's Health: New Data from the 1995 National Survey of Family Growth,* 1997, Tables 41 and 42.

Table 3-2 • Legal Abortions by Week of Gestation, 1976, 1985, and 1996

In all three of the years shown here, close to nine in every 10 legal abortions were performed in the first trimester—i.e., before the thirteenth week of gestation; most of the rest occurred in the second trimester.

Week of Gestation[1]	Percent Distributions		
	1976	*1985*	*1996*
8 weeks or less	47.0	50.3	54.6
9–10 weeks	28.1	26.6	22.6
11–12 weeks	14.4	12.5	11.0
13–15 weeks	4.5	5.9	6.0
16–20 weeks	5.1	3.9	4.3
21 weeks or more	0.9	0.8	1.5
Total percentage	100.0	100.0	100.0
Total number	988,267	1,328,570	1,221,585

[1]Week of gestation is calculated from last menstrual period.

Source: Centers for Disease Control and Prevention, *Abortion Surveillance: Preliminary Analysis—United States, 1996*, 47, no. 47, December 4, 1998, Table 1.

Table 3-3 • Prenatal Care for Mothers with Live Births in 1996 by Race and Hispanic Origin (in percentages)

Native American, black, and Hispanic mothers (those of Cuban origin excepted) are considerably less likely than Asian and non-Hispanic white women to have prenatal care early in their pregnancies, and more likely to have either late care or no care at all.

	Percentage of Live Births for Which Mothers Received	
	Early Prenatal Care[1]	Late or No Prenatal Care[2]
All mothers with live births	81.9	4.0
White	84.0	3.3
Black	71.4	7.3
American Indian or Alaskan Native	67.7	8.6
Asian/Pacific Islander	81.2	3.9
Chinese	86.8	2.5
Japanese	89.3	2.2
Filipino	82.5	3.3
Hawaiian and part-Hawaiian	78.5	5.0
Other Asian/Pacific Islander	78.4	4.6
Hispanic[3]	72.2	6.7
Mexican American	70.7	7.2
Puerto Rican	75.0	5.7
Cuban	89.2	1.6
Central and South American	75.0	5.5
Other Hispanic	74.6	5.9
White, non-Hispanic	87.4	2.4
Black, non-Hispanic[4]	71.5	7.3

[1]Care began in the first trimester.
[2]No prenatal care or prenatal care began during the third trimester.
[3]Persons of Hispanic origin may be of any race. In this table, Hispanics are included in the racial categories. See footnote to Table 1-1.
[4]Selected states.

Source: National Center for Health Statistics, Health, United States, 1998, 1998, Table 6.

Figure 3-1 • Low-Birthweight Births in 1996 by Mothers' Race and Hispanic Origin (low-birthweight births as a percentage of all live births)

More than one in eight (13 percent) of black women who gave birth in 1996 had low-birthweight babies—a proportion twice that of white mothers. Puerto Rican mothers also had a higher-than-average percentage of low-birthweight babies. Low birthweight (less than 2,500 grams, or about five and one-half pounds) is associated with infant mortality (*see* Table 3-4).

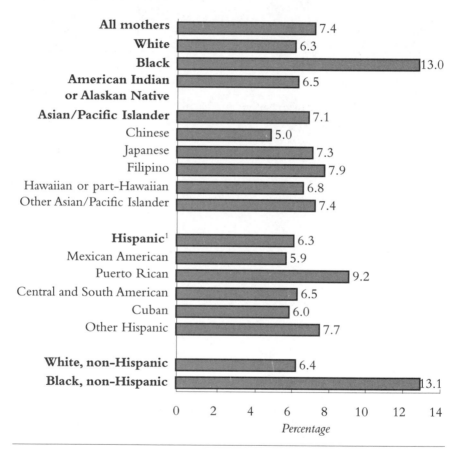

[1]Persons of Hispanic origin may be of any race. In this figure, Hispanics are included in the racial categories. *See* footnote to Table 1-1.

Source: National Center for Health Statistics, *Health, United States, 1998*, 1998, Table 11.

Table 3-4 • Infant Mortality Rates for Babies Born in the United States in 1995 by Mothers' Race and Hispanic Origin (number of infant deaths in the first year of life per 1,000 live births)

Babies born to Native American or Puerto Rican mothers are at higher-than-average risk of early death, but the risk for babies born to black mothers is far greater—more than 14 percent (one in seven) die before their first birthday.

	Mortality Rate
All races	7.6
White	6.3
Black	14.6
American Indian or Alaskan Native	9.0
Asian/Pacific Islander	5.3
Chinese	3.8
Japanese	5.3[1]
Filipino	5.6
Hawaiian and part–Hawaiian	—[2]
Other Asian/Pacific Islander	5.5
Hispanic[3]	6.3
Mexican American	6.0
Puerto Rican	8.9
Cuban	5.3
Central and South American	5.5
Other Hispanic	7.4
White, non-Hispanic	6.3
Black, non-Hispanic	14.7

[1]Infant mortality rates for groups with fewer than 10,000 births are considered unreliable.
[2]Rate not published.
[3]Persons of Hispanic origin may be of any race. In this table, Hispanics are included in the racial categories as well as in the Hispanic category. *See* footnote to Table 1-1.

Source: National Center for Health Statistics, *Health, United States, 1998*, 1998, Table 20.

Table 3-5 • White and Black Women's Death Rates from Selected Causes, 1970 and 1996[1]

A generation ago, both white and black women were far more likely to die from heart disease than from cancer. While this is no longer the case for white women, it is still true for black women, even though their death rate from heart disease has dropped by nearly 40 percent. Deaths from stroke, pneumonia, accidents, and liver disease have been greatly reduced for women of both races. Nevertheless, black women's death rates from most of the causes shown here still exceed white women's rates.

	White Women's Death Rates		Black Women's Death Rates	
	1970	1996	1970	1996
Heart disease	167.8	92.9	251.7	153.4
Malignant neoplasms (cancers)	107.6	107.6	123.5	130.7
Cerebrovascular diseases (e.g., stroke)	56.2	22.9	107.9	39.2
Unintentional injuries (accidents)	27.2	17.6	35.3	20.5
Pneumonia and influenza	15.0	10.1	29.2	12.9
Diabetes mellitus	12.8	10.7	30.9	29.4
Chronic liver disease and cirrhosis	8.7	4.4	17.8	5.7
Suicide	7.2	4.4	2.9	2.0
Chronic obstructive pulmonary disease	5.3	18.3	—	13.1
Homicide and legal intervention	2.2	2.5	15.0	10.2
Nephritis, nephrotic syndrome, and nephrosis (diseases of the kidneys)	—	3.1	—	8.5
HIV/AIDS	—	1.8	—	20.2

[1]Deaths per 100,000 resident population; rates are age-adjusted.

Source: National Center for Health Statistics, *National Vital Statistics Report* 47, no. 9, 1998, Table 14.

Table 3-6 • Incidence and Death Rates among Women from Selected Cancers by Cancer Site and Race, 1996 (per 100,000 women)[1]

Of the cancers shown here, three—cancers of the breast, uterus, and ovary—are more common among white women than black women. Lung and cervical cancers are more common among black women than white women. However, except in the case of lung cancer, death rates in relation to incidence rates are higher for black women than for white women.

	Incidence[2]			Death Rate		
	All Races	White	Black	All Races	White	Black
Breast	110.7	113.3	100.3	24.3	24.0	30.8
Lung and bronchus	42.3	43.7	47.2	34.3	35.0	33.5
Uterus (except cervix)	21.1	21.8	15.7	3.3	3.1	5.9
Ovary	14.1	15.3	8.5	7.4	7.6	6.1
Cervix	7.7	7.0	10.6	2.7	2.4	5.2

[1]These rates are age-adjusted to the distribution of the 1970 U.S. standard population, which explains why they differ from the National Center for Health Statistics rates shown in Figure 3-2 and Table 3-7.
[2]Cancer diagnosed in 1996.

Source: National Cancer Institute, *SEER Cancer Statistics Review, 1973–1996 Initial Content: Tables and Graphs*, 1999, Tables IV-4, V-3, VII-3, XV-3, XV-6, and XX-3.

Figure 3-2 • Women's Death Rates from Breast and Lung Cancer, 1950–1996

Although fewer American women are dying of breast cancer, more are dying of lung cancer.

Death Rate

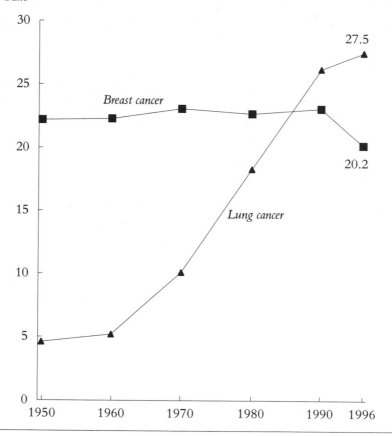

Source: National Center for Health Statistics, *Health, United States, 1998*, 1998, Tables 41 and 42.

Table 3-7 • Women's Death Rates from Breast and Lung Cancer by Race and Hispanic Origin, 1980–1996[1]

White and black women's death rates from lung cancer are notably higher than those for women in the other groups shown here.

	Breast Cancer			Lung Cancer		
	1980	*1990*	*1996*	*1980*	*1990*	*1996*
White	22.8	22.9	19.8	18.2	26.5	28.0
Black	23.3	27.5	26.5	19.5	27.5	27.6
American Indian or Alas- kan Native	8.1	10.0	12.7	8.1	13.5	16.0
Asian/Pacific Islander	9.2	10.0	8.9	9.5	11.3	10.9
Hispanic[2,3]	—	14.1	12.8	—	8.7	8.6

[1]Rates are age-adjusted to the 1940 U.S. standard population, which explains why they differ from the National Cancer Institute rates shown in Table 3-6.
[2]Persons of Hispanic origin may be of any race. In this table, Hispanics are included in the racial categories as well as in the Hispanic category. *See* footnote to Table 1-1.
[3]Data for women of Hispanic origin are not available for 1980.

Source: National Center for Health Statistics, *Health, United States, 1998,* 1998, Tables 41 and 42.

Figure 3-3 • Women Smokers by Age, 1965 and 1995 (current smokers as a percentage of all women in their age group)

With the notable exception of women who are over 65, adult women today are far less likely to smoke than were their counterparts in 1965.

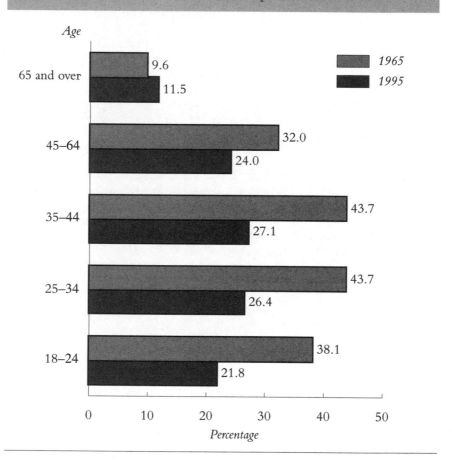

Source: National Center for Health Statistics, *Health, United States, 1998*, 1998, Table 62.

Figure 3-4 • AIDS Cases in Females Age 13 and Over by Race and Hispanic Origin, 1989–1997[1]

The Centers for Disease Control reported a slight decline between 1996 and 1998 in the number of newly reported AIDS cases among women and teenaged girls. Nevertheless, in 1998—as in every year since at least 1989—black women and girls accounted for a disproportionate number of female AIDS cases.

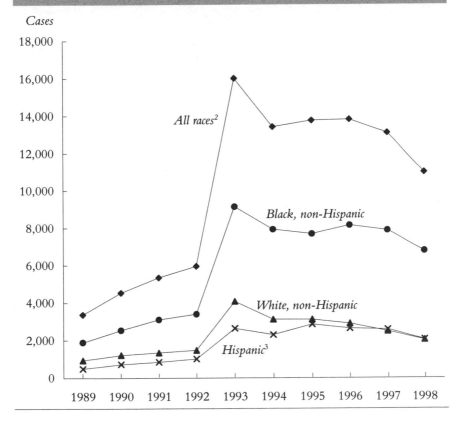

[1]The AIDS case reporting definitions were expanded in 1993.
[2]Includes Asian/Pacific Islanders and Native Americans, not shown separately (data not available).
[3]Persons of Hispanic origin may be of any race. *See* footnote to Table 1-1.

Source: National Center for Health Statistics, *Health, United States, 1993,* 1994, Table 61, and *Health, United States, 1995,* 1996, Table 56; and Centers for Disease Control and Prevention, *HIV/AIDS Surveillance Report* 7, no. 2, 1995, Table 10; 8, no. 2, 1996, Table 10; 9, no. 2, 1997, Table 10; and 10, no. 2, 1998, Table 19.

Table 3-8 • Distribution of Newly Reported AIDS Cases among Females Age 13 and Over by Race and Hispanic Origin, 1998

The overrepresentation of blacks among the women and teenage girls who have AIDS can be seen all too clearly here. In 1998, when black women and girls accounted for about 12 percent of the U.S. female population over age 13, they accounted for nearly 62 percent of the newly reported cases of AIDS in females over age 13.

	Percent Distribution of Female AIDS Cases	Percent Distribution of All Females Age 13 and Over
Non-Hispanic		
White	18.5	74.2
Black	61.9	11.9
Asian/Pacific Islander	0.5	3.6
American Indian or		
Alaskan Native	0.3	0.7
Hispanic[1]	18.8	9.6
Total percentage	100.0	100.0
Total number	10,998	113,320,000

[1]Persons of Hispanic origin may be of any race. In this table, Hispanics are not included in the racial categories. *See* footnote to Table 1-1.

Source: Centers for Disease Control and Prevention, *HIV/AIDS Surveillance Report* 10, no. 2, 1998, Table 19; Bureau of the Census, *Population Projections of the United States by Age, Sex, Race, and Hispanic Origin: 1995 to 2050,* 1996, Table 2.

Figure 3-5 • Reported Cases of Selected Sexually Transmitted Diseases in the United States, 1955–1997 (both sexes)[1]

This figure tracks reported cases—among both sexes—of the three sexually transmitted diseases that are currently most prevalent. While the incidences of syphilis and gonorrhea have been declining since 1975, reported cases of chlamydia—the most prevalent of all sexually transmitted diseases—have increased sharply.

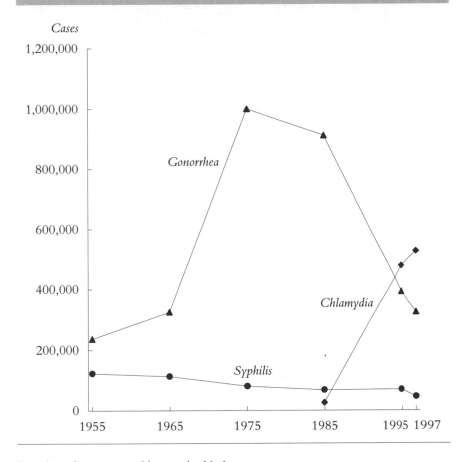

[1]Number of cases reported by state health departments.

Source: Centers for Disease Control and Prevention, *Sexually Transmitted Disease Surveillance, 1997*, 1998, Table 1.

Table 3-9 • Reported Cases of Sexually Transmitted Diseases in the United States, 1997

Men slightly predominate among people with syphilis and gonorrhea. Women overwhelmingly predominate among people with chlamydia, accounting for over 82 percent of the more than half million chlamydia cases reported in 1997. According to the Centers for Disease Control, untreated chlamydia infections can have serious long-term consequences for women's reproductive health, including sterility and ectopic pregnancy.

	Total Number of Cases	Percentage Female
Chlamydia trachomatis	526,653	82.9
Gonorrhea	324,901	49.8
Syphilis	46,537	48.0
Chancroid	243	28.4
Genital herpes	8,204	59.8
Other and nonspecified pelvic inflammatory disease (PID)	4,215	99.9

Source: Centers for Disease Control and Prevention, *Sexually Transmitted Disease Surveillance, 1997*, 1998, Table 2.

SECTION 4:

EMPLOYMENT

AS THE NEW century begins, American women's commitment to the paid workforce is stronger than ever. As of 1998, 70 percent of women between the ages of 16 and 65 were in the labor force. Seventy-seven percent of women in their mid-to-late twenties were in the workforce, a record high for women in that age group. Seventy-nine percent of women in their mid-to-late forties—the peak years of labor force participation for women, at least up to now—were in the workforce, also a record high. In fact, labor force participation was higher than ever before among women in every age group, among married women, and among women with children, even young children.

What is most telling about these statistics is not so much that record proportions of women are entering the paid labor force but that record proportions of women are staying in it. Some of the reasons for this can be inferred from the statistics on earnings (see Section 5) and on family income (see Section 6). These show that, as of 1998, the typical working woman was earning more than ever before and her earnings were making an important difference to family income.

Furthermore, compared with women workers of earlier generations, today's women have more to gain by continuing to work and more to lose by dropping out. The growing proportion of college-educated women in the population and the growing proportion of managers and professionals in the female workforce suggest that many women are in jobs that not only pay reasonably well but also offer economic rewards for those who stay the course. And women in more routine jobs that require computer skills, which must be continually upgraded, may hesitate to take time out of the workforce lest their skills become obsolete.

- Labor force participation has continued to increase among black, white, and Hispanic women and to decrease among black, white, and Hispanic men (see Table 4-3).
- Even when unemployment was lower than usual among blacks and Hispanics, it was higher than among whites. Black women's unemployment rate has generally been at least twice white women's (see Table 4-5 and Figure 4-2).
- The majority of working women work year round, full time. Most of the women who work part time apparently do so by choice (see Figure 4-3 and Table 4-7).
- There has been a modest increase in the number of women in labor unions and a steep drop in the number of union men. As a result, the female presence in the ranks of union members is larger than it used to be (see Table 4-10 and Figure 4-8).
- As the female workforce grew in the 1990s, the proportion of women workers holding managerial and professional jobs rose and the proportion in administrative support jobs dropped. However, black and Hispanic women are less well represented than white women in managerial and professional occupations (see Tables 4-11 and 4-12).
- The percentages of women have increased in many once largely male professional and technical white-collar occupations, although they remain minuscule in traditionally male blue-collar occupations (see Table 4-13).
- Even among children under six, children with a stay-at-home parent are in the minority. Close to two-thirds of mothers who have children under six are in the workforce (see Table 4-20 and Figures 4-11 and 4-12).

Figure 4-1 • Women in the Labor Force, 1948–1998[1]

The increase in American women's labor force participation over the second half of the twentieth century was generally steady and incremental, although it accelerated in the 1970s and slowed down somewhat after that. By 1998, nearly three in every five women were in the labor force—compared with fewer than one in every three women 50 years earlier—and more than 45 percent of American workers were women.

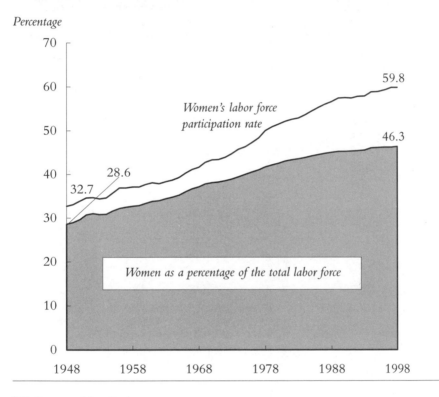

[1]Civilians age 16 and over.

Source: Bureau of Labor Statistics, *Handbook of Labor Statistics*, 1989, Table 2; and *Employment and Earnings*, January 1999, Tables 1 and 2.

Table 4-1 • Women in the Labor Force, 1948–1998[1]

Comparing the labor force participation rate at the beginning and end of each decade shows that participation increased fastest in the 1970s—i.e., by eight percentage points.

Year	Women's Labor Force Participation Rate	Women as a Percentage of Total Labor Force	Year	Women's Labor Force Participation Rate	Women as a Percentage of Total Labor Force
1948	32.7	28.6	1974	45.7	39.4
1949	33.1	29.0	1975	46.3	40.0
1950	33.9	29.6	1976	47.3	40.5
1951	34.6	30.7	1977	48.4	41.0
1952	34.7	31.0	1978	50.0	41.7
1953	34.4	30.8	1979	50.9	42.1
1954	34.6	30.9	1980	51.5	42.5
1955	35.7	31.6	1981	52.1	43.0
1956	36.9	32.2	1982	52.6	43.3
1957	36.9	32.5	1983	52.9	43.5
1958	37.1	32.7	1984	53.6	43.8
1959	37.1	32.9	1985	54.5	44.2
1960	37.7	33.4	1986	55.3	44.5
1961	38.1	33.8	1987	56.0	44.8
1962	37.9	34.0	1988	56.6	45.0
1963	38.3	34.4	1989	57.4	45.2
1964	38.7	34.8	1990	57.5	45.2
1965	39.3	35.2	1991	57.4	45.3
1966	40.3	36.0	1992	57.8	45.4
1967	41.1	36.7	1993	57.9	45.5
1968	41.6	37.1	1994	58.8	46.0
1969	42.7	37.8	1995	58.9	46.1
1970	43.3	38.1	1996	59.3	46.2
1971	43.4	38.2	1997	59.8	46.2
1972	43.9	38.5	1998	59.8	46.3
1973	44.7	38.9			

[1]Civilians age 16 and over.

Source: Bureau of Labor Statistics, Handbook of Labor Statistics, 1989, Table 2; and Employment and Earnings, January 1999, Tables 1 and 2.

Table 4-2 • Women's Labor Force Participation Rates by Age and Five-Year Birth Cohort, Selected Years 1953–1998[1]

Reading across this table, one can trace labor force participation over time by women in each of the 10 five-year cohorts; reading down, one can compare labor force participation at a particular age by women of different cohorts. The 1949–53 and 1954–58 cohorts are the heart of the baby boom generation (usually considered people born between 1946 and 1960).

Labor Force Participation at Age

Year(s) Born	20–24	25–29	30–34	35–39	40–44	45–49	50–54	55–59	60–64	65–69	Age in 1998
1929–33	44.3	35.7	37.0	46.4	54.1	59.8	58.5	53.3	37.1	17.8	65–69
1934–38	46.4	37.4	41.9	52.5	62.5	65.3	64.8	57.1	39.1		60–64
1939–43	47.6	43.2	48.2	60.9	69.3	72.9	69.9	61.3			55–59
1944–48	54.6	51.8	59.8	68.2	75.9	76.5	73.0				50–54
1949–53	61.2	64.3	68.0	74.6	78.1	78.8					45–49
1954–58	68.5	69.8	71.9	75.5	78.6						40–44
1959–63	69.9	73.6	73.4	75.6							35–39
1964–68	72.7	73.9	75.4								30–34
1969–73	71.3	77.3									25–29
1974–78	73.0										20–24

[1]Data for 1958, 1963, 1968, 1973, and 1978 are for the total labor force. Data for subsequent years are for the civilian labor force.

Source: Bureau of Labor Statistics, *Employment and Earnings*, January 1964, Table A-16; January 1969, Table A-1; January 1974, Table 1; January 1979, Table 3; January 1984, Table 3; January 1989, Table 3; January 1994, Table 3; and January 1999, Table 2; *Labor Force Statistics Derived from the Current Population Survey, 1948–87*, 1988, Table B-4; and *Handbook of Labor Statistics*, 1989, Table 5.

Table 4-3 • Labor Force Participation Rates by Sex, Race, and Hispanic Origin, 1948, 1958, 1968, 1978, 1988, 1998, and Projected 2006[1]

Black women consistently have been more likely than white women to be in the paid workforce, but that is projected to change by 2006. In all the groups shown here, labor force participation has continued to increase for women and decrease for men.

	Labor Force Participation Rates						
	1948	*1958*	*1968*	*1978*	*1988*	*1998*	*2006*
Women							
All races[2]	32.7	37.1	41.6	50.0	56.6	59.8	61.4
White	—	35.8	40.7	49.4	56.4	59.4	62.0
Black	—	—	—	53.1	58.0	62.8	61.3
Hispanic[3]	—	—	—	—	53.2	55.6	57.2
Men							
All races	86.6	84.2	80.1	77.9	76.2	74.9	73.6
White	—	84.3	80.4	78.6	76.9	75.6	74.3
Black	—	—	—	71.5	71.0	69.0	69.6
Hispanic	—	—	—	—	81.9	79.8	77.1

[1]Civilian labor force age 16 and over.
[2]Includes Asian/Pacific Islanders and Native Americans, not shown separately (data not available).
[3]Persons of Hispanic origin may be of any race. In this table, Hispanics are included in the racial categories as well as in the Hispanic category. *See* footnote to Table 1-1. (Data by Hispanic origin are not available for years before 1980.)

Source: Bureau of Labor Statistics, *Handbook of Labor Statistics*, 1989, Table 5; "Labor Force 2006: Slowing Down and Changing Composition," *Monthly Labor Review*, November 1997, Table 4; *Employment and Earnings*, January 1999, Table 5.

Table 4-4 • Labor Force Participation and Unemployment Rates of People of Hispanic Origin by Sex and Origin, 1998 (numbers are in thousands)[1]

As can be seen in Table 4–3, Hispanic women are less likely to be in the labor force than American women overall. However, this table shows that labor force participation by Hispanics of both sexes varies considerably by place of origin.

	Mexican	Puerto Rican	Cuban	Other[2]	Total
Women					
Total number	6,280	1,105	535	2,415	10,335
Labor force number	3,435	576	264	1,471	5,746
Labor force participation rate	54.7	52.2	49.2	60.9	55.6
Unemployment rate	8.6	8.2	8.6	7.3	8.2
Men					
Total number	6,937	975	527	2,295	10,734
Labor force number	5,660	672	387	1,852	8,571
Labor force participation rate	81.6	68.9	73.5	80.7	79.8
Unemployment rate	6.5	8.5	4.1	5.9	6.4

[1]Civilian labor force age 16 and over.
[2]"Other," which was derived by subtracting persons of Mexican, Puerto Rican, and Cuban origin from the total Hispanic population, includes persons of Central and South American origin.

Source: Bureau of Labor Statistics, *Employment and Earnings,* January 1999, Table 6.

Table 4-5 • Unemployment Rates by Sex, Race, and Hispanic Origin, 1948–1998[1]

Unemployment was very low overall in 1998, and lower than usual among black and Hispanic people of both sexes. Still, unemployment remained a much greater problem among blacks and Hispanics than among whites.

Year	All Races[2]		White		Black		Hispanic[3]	
	Women	Men	Women	Men	Women	Men	Women	Men
1948	4.1	3.6	—	—	—	—	—	—
1958	6.8	6.8	6.2	6.1	—	—	—	—
1968	4.8	2.9	4.3	2.6	—	—	—	—
1978	7.2	5.3	6.2	4.6	13.8	11.8	—	—
1988	5.6	5.5	4.7	4.7	11.7	11.7	8.3	8.1
1998	4.6	4.4	3.9	3.9	9.0	8.9	8.2	6.4

[1]Civilian workers age 16 and over.
[2]Includes Asian/Pacific Islanders and Native Americans, not shown separately (data not available).
[3]Persons of Hispanic origin may be of any race. In this table, Hispanics are included in the racial categories as well as in the Hispanic category. *See* footnote to Table 1-1.

Source: Bureau of Labor Statistics, *Handbook of Labor Statistics*, 1989, Table 28; and *Employment and Earnings,* January 1999, Table 5.

Table 4-6 • Labor Force Participation and Unemployment Rates by Sex, Veteran Status, Race, and Hispanic Origin, 1998 (numbers are in thousands, persons are age 20 and over)

Black and Hispanic veterans of both sexes are considerably more likely to be in the labor force and less likely to be unemployed than their counterparts who are not veterans. This is not, however, the situation among white female veterans, who, compared with white female nonveterans, are marginally less likely to be in the workforce and somewhat more likely to be unemployed. The comparatively low labor force participation rate among male veterans, especially white male veterans, is no doubt related to age distribution—a substantial percentage are over 65 (*see* Figure 7-6).

	Women		*Men*	
	Veterans	*Not Veterans*	*Veterans*	*Not Veterans*
All races[1]				
Total number	1,448	97,339	23,634	67,155
Percent in the labor force	63.3	60.4	59.4	82.9
Unemployment rate	5.1	4.0	3.1	3.9
White				
Total number	1,164	80,910	20,976	55,989
Percent in the labor force	59.2	59.7	58.6	84.2
Unemployment rate	5.0	3.4	2.8	3.3
Black				
Total number	249	11,962	2,191	7,531
Percent in the labor force	81.4	64.5	65.7	74.5
Unemployment rate	5.1	7.9	4.7	8.1
Hispanic[2]				
Total number	66	9,215	512	8,703
Percent in the labor force	71.3	57.0	59.2	84.8
Unemployment rate	5.0	7.1	2.5	5.6

[1]Includes Asian/Pacific Islanders and Native Americans, not shown separately (data not available).
[2]Persons of Hispanic origin may be of any race. In this table, Hispanics are included in the racial categories as well as in the Hispanic category. *See* footnote to Table 1-1.

Source: Bureau of Labor Statistics, unpublished data from 1998 annual averages of the Current Population Survey.

Figure 4-2 • Unemployment Rates of White, Black, and Hispanic Women, 1978–1998[1]

This figure shows women's unemployment rates by race and Hispanic origin over two decades. While the peaks and valleys are roughly parallel, especially for the years before 1992, the unemployment rate among black women has remained at least twice the rate among white women.

Unemployment Rate

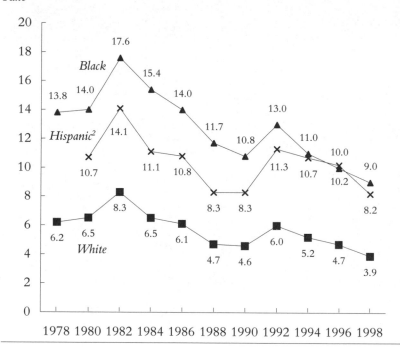

[1]Unemployed women as a percentage of the female civilian labor force age 16 and over.
[2]Persons of Hispanic origin may be of any race. In this figure, Hispanics are included in the racial categories as well as in the Hispanic category. *See* footnote to Table 1-1.

Source: Bureau of Labor Statistics, *Handbook of Labor Statistics*, 1989, Table 28; and *Employment and Earnings*, January 1991, Tables 3 and 40; January 1993, Tables 3 and 40; January 1996, Table 5; January 1997, Table 5; and January 1999, Table 5.

Figure 4-3 • Employed Women by Year-Round, Full-Time Status, 1970–1997

Only a minority (about 40 percent) of the approximately 38 million women who worked in 1970 worked year round full time. By 1997, of the nearly 68 million women who worked, a solid majority (about 56 percent) worked year round full time.

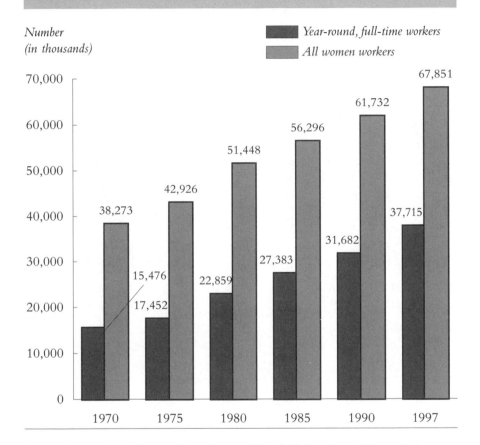

*Number
(in thousands)*

■ *Year-round, full-time workers*

■ *All women workers*

Source: Bureau of the Census, *Money Income of Households, Families, and Persons in the United States: 1991,* 1992, Table B-16; *Money Income in the United States: 1995,* 1996, Table 10; and *Money Income in the United States: 1997,* 1998, Table 10.

Figure 4-4 • Work Schedules of Women with Work Experience, 1997 (percent distributions)

Most women who work full time work year round. Of the 47.8 million women who had full-time jobs in 1997, close to four in five (78.9 percent) worked year round, compared with less than half of the women who had part-time jobs.

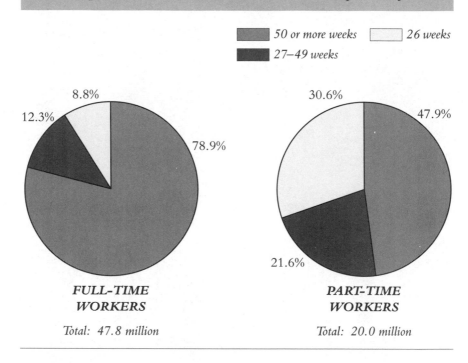

50 or more weeks   26 weeks

27–49 weeks

FULL-TIME WORKERS

Total: 47.8 million

PART-TIME WORKERS

Total: 20.0 million

Bureau of the Census, *Money Income in the United States: 1997*, 1998, Table 10.

Table 4-7 • Employed Women and Men by Full- or Part-Time Status and Race, 1998 (percent distributions)[1]

Whether they are black or white, women are less likely than their male counterparts to work full time, although black women are somewhat more likely than white women to have full-time jobs. Black women are also more likely than white women to be on involuntary part time, that is, to be working part time when they want to be working full time.

Work Status	All Races[2]		White		Black	
	Women	Men	Women	Men	Women	Men
Full time[3]	74.6	89.6	73.2	89.7	81.9	89.6
Part time	25.4	10.4	26.8	10.3	18.1	10.4
Voluntary	23.0	8.8	24.6	8.9	14.3	7.8
Involuntary	2.5	1.6	2.3	1.4	3.8	2.5
Total percentage[4]	100.0	100.0	100.0	100.0	100.0	100.0
Total number (in thousands)	57,573	68,304	47,615	58,535	7,316	6,648

[1]Civilians age 16 and over. Excludes employed workers reporting "not at work."
[2]Includes Asian/Pacific Islanders and Native Americans, not shown separately (data not available).
[3]Includes a small number of workers who usually work full time but who were on an involuntary part-time schedule.
[4]Percentages may not total 100.0 due to rounding.

Source: Bureau of Labor Statistics, *Employment and Earnings*, January 1999, Table 8.

Figure 4-5 • Workers Holding Multiple Jobs by Sex, 1978 and 1998 (percent distributions)

Between 1978 and 1998, the number of "moonlighters"—people holding down more than one job—increased by some 3.4 million; women accounted for most (72 percent) of that increase. By 1998, close to half (47.3 percent) of all multiple jobholders were women, compared with less than 30 percent two decades earlier.

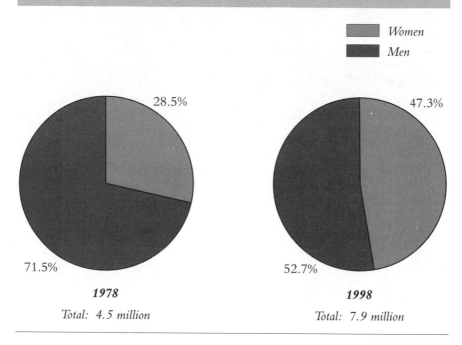

Women

Men

28.5%

71.5%

1978

Total: 4.5 million

47.3%

52.7%

1998

Total: 7.9 million

Bureau of Labor Statistics, "Multiple Jobholding Up Sharply in the 1980's," *Monthly Labor Review*, July 1990, Table 1; and *Employment and Earnings*, January 1999, Table 36.

Table 4-8 • Characteristics of Multiple Jobholders by Sex, 1998[1] (percent distributions)

About two-thirds of the men with multiple jobs, compared with just over half of the women, have at least one full-time job. Thirty percent of the women have two part-time jobs, compared with just over 12 percent of the men.

	Women	*Men*
Age		
Under 25	16.6	12.0
25–54	74.3	77.3
55 or over	9.1	10.7
Total percentage	100.0	100.0
Race		
White	85.6	86.7
Black	10.6	9.7
Other[2]	3.8	3.6
Total percentage	100.0	100.0
Hispanic (percentage of total)[3]	5.4	7.2
Marital status		
Married, spouse present	46.7	63.8
Never married	29.6	24.3
Widowed, divorced, or separated	23.7	11.9
Total percentage	100.0	100.0
Full- or part-time status		
Primary job full time, secondary job part time	49.9	62.4
Both jobs full time	2.1	4.5
Both jobs part time	30.0	12.3
Hours vary on primary or secondary job	17.5	20.3
Primary job part time, secondary job full time	0.5	0.5
Total percentage	100.0	100.0
Total number (in thousands)	3,748	4,178

[1]Workers age 16 or over.

[2]Includes Asian/Pacific Islanders and Native Americans, not shown separately (data not available).

[3]Persons of Hispanic origin may be of any race. In this table, Hispanics are included in the racial categories as well as in the Hispanic category. *See* footnote to Table 1-1.

Source: Bureau of Labor Statistics, *Employment and Earnings,* January 1997, Table A–36; and January 1999, Table 36.

Figure 4-6 • Workers on Goods-Producing and Service-Producing Nonfarm Payrolls by Sex, 1970–1998

In 1970, there were two service-producing workers for every goods-producing worker; by 1998, there were four service-producers for every goods-producer. Among women workers, the ratio is far more lopsided—in 1998, about eight service-producers for every goods-producer.

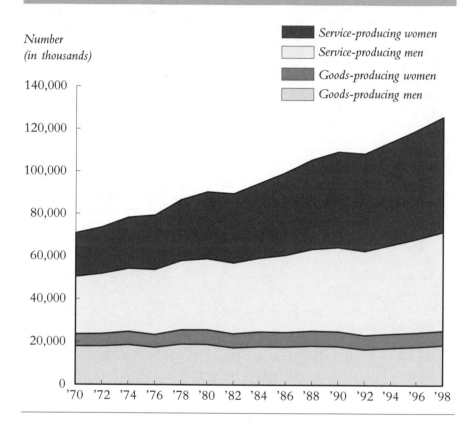

Source: Bureau of Labor Statistics, *Handbook of Labor Statistics*, 1989, Tables 68 and 73 (as corrected in *BLS Bulletin 2340*, March 1990); and unpublished data, 1999, <http://146.142.4.24/cgi-bin/dsrv?ee>.

Table 4-9 • Employed Persons by Industry and Sex, 1988 and 1998 (percent distributions)

The services industry, a part of the service-producing sector, is by far the dominant employer of American women, and its dominance has been increasing: in 1998, it employed 48.2 percent of all women workers, up from 44 percent in 1988. The services industry is also the single largest employer of men (25.3 percent in 1998).[1] Men, however, are still distributed more evenly across American sectors and industries than women.

Industry	Women 1988	Women 1998	Men 1988	Men 1998
Agriculture	1.3	1.4	3.9	3.6
Goods-producing				
Mining	0.2	0.1	1.0	0.8
Construction	1.4	1.3	10.9	10.9
Manufacturing durable goods	6.6	5.6	14.6	12.9
Manufacturing nondurable goods	7.0	5.2	8.0	7.1
Service-producing				
Transportation and public utilities	4.3	4.5	9.3	9.3
Wholesale trade	2.5	2.5	5.2	5.0
Retail trade	19.2	18.6	14.4	15.3
Finance, insurance, and real estate	9.1	8.3	5.1	5.0
Services[2]	44.0	48.2	22.6	25.3
Public administration	4.5	4.2	4.9	4.7
Total percentage[3]	100.0	100.0	100.0	100.0
Total number (in thousands)	51,696	60,771	63,271	70,693

[1] For more detail about the industries classified as "services industries," *see The American Woman 1999-2000,* Table 4-11.
[2] Includes private households.
[3] Percentages may not total 100.0 due to rounding.

Source: Bureau of Labor Statistics, *Employment and Earnings,* January 1989, Table 25; and January 1999, Table 17.

Figure 4-7 • Employed Women and Men by Nonagricultural Industry, 1998 (percent distributions)[1,2]

This figure (which, unlike the preceding table, excludes agricultural workers) illustrates the extent to which women workers are concentrated in just two industries—services and wholesale and retail trade. In 1998, these industries, both in the service-producing sector of the economy, together employed more than 70 percent of all female nonagricultural workers.

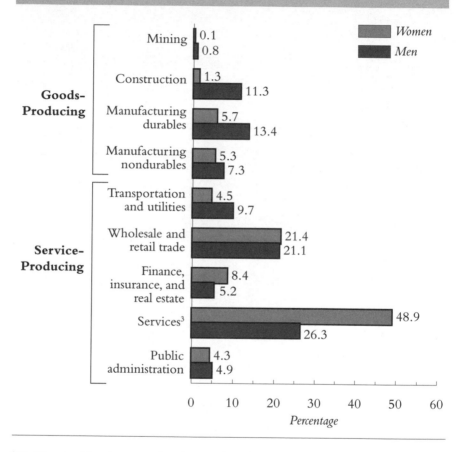

[1]Civilians age 16 and over employed in nonfarm industries.
[2]Percentages may not total 100.0 due to rounding.
[3]Includes private households.

Source: Bureau of Labor Statistics, *Employment and Earnings*, January 1999, Table 14.

Table 4-10 • Labor Union Membership by Sex, Race, and Hispanic Origin, 1988 and 1998 (numbers in thousands)

The number of women labor union members rose by 380,000, or more than six percent, between 1988 and 1998. However, because the total number of employed women grew at nearly three times that rate, union members as a proportion of all working women slipped from 12.6 to 11.4 percent. Both the number and the proportion of men in labor unions dropped precipitously, by 1.2 million and 4.2 percentage points, respectively, over the decade.

	Total Employed[1]		Union Members[2]		Union Members as a Percentage of Total Employed	
	1988	1998	1988	1998	1988	1998
Women						
All races[3]	47,495	55,757	5,982	6,362	12.6	11.4
White	40,393	45,831	4,638	4,952	11.5	10.8
Black	5,674	7,443	1,121	1,123	19.8	15.1
Hispanic[4]	3,088	5,015	384	534	12.4	10.6
Men						
All races	53,912	60,973	11,019	9,850	20.4	16.2
White	46,783	51,700	9,294	8,166	19.9	15.8
Black	5,502	6,452	1,438	1,337	26.1	20.7
Hispanic	4,535	7,360	837	937	18.5	12.7

[1]Wage-and-salary workers age 16 and over.
[2]Employed members of labor unions or employee associations similar to unions.
[3]Includes Asian/Pacific Islanders and Native Americans, not shown separately (data not available).
[4]Persons of Hispanic origin may be of any race. In this table, Hispanics are included in the racial categories as well as in the Hispanic category. *See* footnote to Table 1-1.

Source: Bureau of Labor Statistics, *Employment and Earnings,* January 1989, Table 59; and January 1999, Table 40.

Figure 4-8 • Labor Union Members by Sex, 1988 and 1998 (percent distributions)[1]

The modest increase in the number of women in labor unions (*see* Table 4-10), together with the significant decrease in the number of union men, accounts for the growing female presence in the ranks of union members, up from just over 35 percent in 1988 to just over 39 percent in 1998.

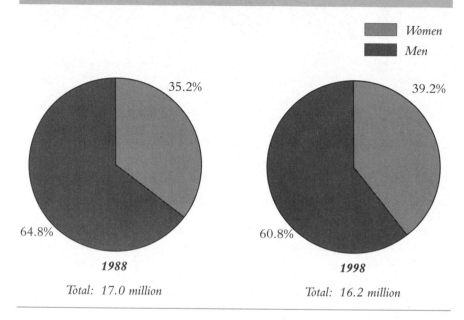

Women
Men

35.2%

39.2%

64.8%

60.8%

1988

1998

Total: 17.0 million

Total: 16.2 million

[1]Members of a labor union or an employee association that is similiar to a labor union.

Source: Bureau of Labor Statistics, *Employment and Earnings*, January 1989, Table 59; and January 1999, Table 40.

Table 4-11 • Employed Women and Men by Occupation, 1988 and 1998 (percent distributions)

Two shifts that occurred between 1988 and 1998 in the occupational distribution of women workers are especially noteworthy: the rise in the proportion in managerial and professional occupations, and the drop in the proportion in administrative support occupations.

Occupation	Women		Men	
	1988	*1998*	*1988*	*1998*
Managerial and professional	**25.2**	**31.4**	**25.5**	**28.1**
Executive, administrative, and managerial	10.8	13.9	13.6	15.0
Professional specialty	14.4	17.4	11.9	13.1
Technical, sales, and administrative support	**44.6**	**40.7**	**19.7**	**19.5**
Technicians and related support	3.3	3.8	2.9	2.8
Sales occupations	13.0	13.1	11.1	11.1
Administrative support, including clerical	28.3	23.8	5.7	5.6
Service occupations	**17.9**	**17.5**	**9.6**	**10.2**
Private household	1.7	1.3	0.1	0.1
Protective service	0.5	0.7	2.6	2.8
Other service	15.7	15.4	6.9	7.3
Precision production, craft, and repair	**2.3**	**2.0**	**19.7**	**18.7**
Operators, fabricators, and laborers	**8.9**	**7.4**	**20.9**	**19.5**
Machine operators, assemblers, and inspectors	6.4	4.8	7.6	6.9
Transportation and material moving occupations	0.8	0.9	6.9	6.8
Handlers, equipment cleaners, helpers, and laborers	1.6	1.7	6.4	5.8
Farming, forestry, and fishing	**1.1**	**1.1**	**4.5**	**4.0**
Total percentage[1]	**100.0**	**100.0**	**100.0**	**100.0**
Total employed (in thousands)	51,696	60,771	63,273	70,693

[1]Percentages may not total 100.0 due to rounding.

Source: Bureau of Labor Statistics, *Employment and Earnings,* January 1989, Table 21; and January 1999, Table 10.

Table 4-12 • Employed Women by Occupation, Race, and Hispanic Origin, 1998 (percent distributions)[1]

The occupational distribution of America's working women overall (*see* Table 4-11) conceals some large differences by race and Hispanic origin. For example, the proportion of Hispanic women employed as operators, fabricators, or laborers is nearly twice that of white women, and black and Hispanic women are much more heavily concentrated than white women in service occupations.

Occupation	*White*	*Black*	*Hispanic*[2]
Managerial and professional	**32.6**	**23.2**	**17.3**
Executive, administrative, and managerial	14.6	10.1	8.1
Professional specialty	18.1	13.0	9.2
Technical, sales, and administrative support	**41.1**	**39.1**	**37.4**
Technicians and related support	3.8	3.5	2.7
Sales occupations	13.4	11.4	12.6
Administrative support, including clerical	24.0	24.2	22.1
Service occupations	**16.3**	**25.0**	**26.7**
Private household	1.3	1.5	4.7
Protective service	0.6	1.7	0.6
Other service	14.4	21.9	21.4
Precision production, craft, and repair	**1.9**	**2.0**	**3.0**
Operators, fabricators, and laborers	**6.8**	**10.4**	**13.7**
Machine operators, assemblers, and inspectors	4.3	7.0	10.1
Transportation and material moving occupations	0.8	1.4	0.8
Handlers, equipment cleaners, helpers, and laborers	1.6	2.0	2.8
Farming, forestry, and fishing	**1.2**	**0.3**	**1.9**
Total percentage[3]	**100.0**	**100.0**	**100.0**
Total number (in thousands)	50,327	7,685	5,273

[1] Data were not available for Native Americans and Asian/Pacific Islanders.
[2] Persons of Hispanic origin may be of any race. In this table, Hispanics are included in the racial categories as well as in the Hispanic category. *See* footnote to Table 1-1.
[3] Percentages may not total 100.0 due to rounding.

Source: Bureau of Labor Statistics, *Employment and Earnings*, January 1999, Table 10; and unpublished data from 1998 annual averages of the Current Population Survey.

Table 4-13 • Women Employed in Selected Occupations, 1983 and 1998[1]

The proportions as well as the numbers of women have increased in many once largely male professional and technical white-collar occupations, but while more women were in many traditionally male blue-collar occupations in 1998 than in 1983, their percentages remained minuscule (*see also* Table 4-15).

Occupation	Number of Women (in thousands)		Women as a Percentage of Total Employed	
	1983[2]	*1998*	*1983*[2]	*1998*
Airplane pilots and navigators	1	4	2.1	3.4
Architects	13	28	12.7	17.5
Automobile mechanics	4	7	0.5	0.8
Carpenters	16	16	1.4	1.2
Clergy	16	39	5.6	12.0
Computer programmers	144	174	32.5	28.5
Data processing equipment repairers	9	46	9.3	16.9
Dental assistants	151	225	98.1	98.1
Dentists	8	31	6.7	19.8
Economists	37	64	37.9	46.3
Editors and reporters	98	140	48.4	51.0
Financial managers	138	376	36.6	53.3
Lawyers and judges	103	272	15.8	28.6
Librarians	168	173	87.3	83.4
Managers, medicine and health	52	574	57.0	79.2
Mechanical engineers	7	23	2.8	7.0
Physicians	82	197	15.8	26.6
Registered nurses	1,315	1,879	95.8	92.5
Social workers	262	512	64.3	68.4
Teachers, elementary school	1,125	1,639	83.3	84.0
Teachers, postsecondary	220	389	36.3	42.3
Telephone installers/repairers	24	28	9.9	12.0
Welders and cutters	27	30	5.0	5.1

[1]Civilians age 16 and over.
[2]1983 is the earliest year for which the occupational data are comparable to 1998 data.

Source: Bureau of Labor Statistics, *Employment and Earnings,* January 1984, Table 22; and January 1999, Table 11.

Table 4-14 • Women Employed in Selected Occupations by Race and Hispanic Origin, 1998

Shown here is the representation of whites, blacks, and Hispanics among the women employed in all but two of the occupations shown in Table 4-13.[1] The reader should be aware, however, that the racial/ethnic breakdowns for occupations employing fewer than 75,000 women may not be reliable.

Occupation	Number of Women (all races, in thousands)[2]	Percentage of Employed Women Who Are		
		White	Black	Hispanic[3]
Architects	28	92.9	—	3.6
Automobile mechanics	7	71.4	28.6	—
Carpenters	16	93.7	6.2	18.7
Clergy	39	84.6	12.8	7.7
Computer programmers	174	81.0	8.0	3.4
Data processing equipment repairers	46	82.6	6.5	8.7
Dental assistants	225	91.1	6.2	11.6
Dentists	31	83.9	—	3.2
Economists	64	90.6	4.7	10.9
Editors and reporters	140	90.7	8.6	2.9
Financial managers	376	87.0	9.0	4.0
Lawyers and judges	272	89.7	5.9	3.3
Librarians	173	93.1	5.2	4.6
Managers, medicine and health	574	90.1	6.6	5.4
Mechanical engineers	23	91.3	—	4.3
Physicians	197	77.2	6.6	5.6
Registered nurses	1,879	84.9	9.1	3.2
Social workers	512	75.2	22.3	5.1
Teachers, college and university	389	84.6	6.9	3.6
Teachers, elementary school	1,639	86.6	10.8	5.2
Telephone installers/repairers	28	78.6	21.4	7.1
Welders and cutters	30	90.0	10.0	16.7

[1]Airplane pilots/navigators and firefighters are not shown here because the Current Population Survey found no black or Hispanic women in these occupations in 1998.
[2]Includes Asian/Pacific Islanders and Native Americans, not shown separately (data not available).
[3]Persons of Hispanic origin may be of any race. *See* footnote to Table 1-1.

Source: Bureau of Labor Statistics, unpublished data from 1998 annual averages of the Current Population Survey.

Table 4-15 • Women Employed in Selected Nontraditional Technical and Trade Occupations, 1983 and 1998[1,2]

Unlike Table 4-13, which shows an eclectic sampling of occupations that are both traditional and nontraditional for women, this table shows nontraditional, mostly fairly well-paid, blue-collar occupations. All these occupations employed more workers in 1998 than in 1983 and most are likely to continue to grow. Women have made the least progress proportionately in the construction trades, although in 1998 there were several thousand more female painters and electricians than in 1983.

Occupation	Number of Women (in thousands)		Women as a Percentage of Total Employed	
	1983[3]	1998	1983[3]	1998
Aircraft engine mechanics	2	6	2.5	3.7
Electrical and electronic equipment mechanics	50	96	7.4	11.1
Electricians	9	16	1.5	1.9
Firefighters	2	5	1.0	2.3
Heating, air conditioning, and refrigeration mechanics	1	5	0.5	1.5
Industrial machinery repairers	12	12	2.2	2.1
Industrial truck and tractor equipment operators	21	48	5.6	8.9
Machinists	19	31	4.1	5.7
Painters, construction and maintenance	23	28	4.9	4.7
Plumbers, pipefitters, and steamfitters	5	5	1.1	0.9
Police and detectives, public service	23	69	5.7	11.5
Truck drivers[4]	69	158	3.1	5.3

[1]Civilians age 16 and over.
[2]"Nontraditional" occupations are defined by the U.S. Department of Labor as those in which less than 25 percent of the workers are women.
[3]1983 is the earliest year for which the occupational data are comparable to 1998 data.
[4]For 1983, we aggregated "truckdrivers, heavy" and "truckdrivers, light."

Source: Bureau of Labor Statistics, *Employment and Earnings,* January 1984, Table 22; January 1999, Table 11; and unpublished data from 1998 annual averages of the Current Population Survey.

Table 4-16 • Women Employed in Selected Nontraditional Technical and Trade Occupations by Race and Hispanic Origin, 1998[1,2]

Black and Hispanic women (respectively, 12.6 and 8.7 percent of employed women overall) appear to be overrepresented among electrical/electronic equipment mechanics and in policing. Both are nontraditional occupations that now employ a fair number of women and pay reasonably well (*see* Table 5-4).

Occupation	Number of Women (all races, in thousands)[3]	Percentage of Employed Women Who Are		
		White	*Black*	*Hispanic*[4]
Aircraft engine mechanics	6	66.7	16.7	16.7
Electrical and electronic equipment mechanics	96	80.0	14.6	10.4
Electricians	16	87.5	6.2	—
Firefighters	5	—[5]	—	—
Heating, air conditioning, and refrigeration mechanics	5	60.0	20.0	—
Industrial machinery repairers	12	58.3	33.3	—
Industrial truck and tractor equipment operators	48	66.7	31.2	6.2
Machinists	31	83.9	12.9	6.5
Painters, construction and maintenance	28	92.9	3.6	7.1
Plumbers, pipefitters, and steamfitters	5	—[5]	—	—
Police and detectives, public service	69	63.8	36.2	10.1
Truck drivers	158	84.8	12.7	6.3

[1]Civilians age 16 and over.
[2]"Nontraditional" occupations are defined by the U.S. Department of Labor as those in which less than 25 percent of the workers are women.
[3]Includes Asian/Pacific Islanders and Native Americans, not shown separately (data not available).
[4]Persons of Hispanic origin may be of any race. *See* footnote to Table 1-1.
[5]The CPS data, which are rounded to the nearest thousand, showed no black or Hispanic women in this occupation in 1998, but *see* comments on Table 4-14.

Source: Bureau of Labor Statistics, unpublished data from 1998 annual averages of the Current Population Survey.

Table 4-17 • Contingency Rates by Occupation and Sex, February 1995 and February 1997

The contingent workforce shrank a bit between 1995 and 1997, and contingent workers accounted for smaller proportions of the workers employed in the majority of the occupational categories shown here. However, the contingent proportion increased slightly among women workers in administrative support, technician, and farming, forestry, and fishing occupations—and among men in the latter two occupational categories.

| | *Contingent Workers as a Percentage of All Workers in Occupation[1]* | | | |
| | *1995* | | *1997* | |
Occupation	*Women*	*Men*	*Women*	*Men*
Total, all occupations	5.3	4.5	4.8	4.0
Executive, administrative, and managerial	3.2	2.3	2.8	1.9
Professional specialty	7.0	6.6	5.8	6.2
Technicians and related support	3.6	4.8	3.7	5.6
Sales occupations	3.4	2.0	2.5	1.7
Administrative support, including clerical	5.7	6.0	6.1	5.5
Service occupations	6.5	4.7	5.7	4.1
Precision production, craft, and repair	4.9	4.5	4.7	4.1
Operators, fabricators, and laborers	5.7	5.4	4.6	4.4
Farming, forestry, and fishing	4.3	5.9	5.2	6.0
Total number (in thousands)	3,039	2,995	2,828	2,746

[1]Contingent workers as measured by the Bureau of Labor Statistics using the broadest of three alternative definitions (Estimate No. 3). This definition "effectively included all wage and salary workers who did not expect their jobs to last" plus self-employed persons and independent contractors who had been employed in these arrangements for a year or less and who expected to remain in these arrangements for a year or less.

Source: Bureau of Labor Statistics, "A Profile of Contingent Workers," *Monthly Labor Review*, October 1996, Table 2; and unpublished data from the February 1995 and February 1997 Current Population Surveys.

Table 4-18 • Contingent and Noncontingent Workers by Selected Demographic Characteristics, February 1997 (percent distributions)

Compared with a typical member of the noncontingent workforce, the typical contingent worker is younger, more likely to be Hispanic, and more likely to be female.

	Contingent Workers[1]		Noncontingent Workers	
	Female	Male	Female	Male
Age				
16–19	12.2	12.6	4.7	4.2
20–24	18.6	17.3	9.2	8.9
25–34	24.6	25.0	24.6	25.3
35–44	21.0	20.7	28.1	28.2
45–54	14.6	12.6	21.4	20.6
55–64	6.9	7.8	9.4	9.7
65 and over	2.2	4.1	2.6	3.1
Total percentage[2]	100.0	100.0	100.0	100.0
Race				
White	82.3	81.6	83.8	86.5
Black	11.3	10.9	12.2	9.3
Other[3]	6.5	7.5	4.0	4.2
Total percentage[2]	100.0	100.0	100.0	100.0
Hispanic[4]	10.5	14.3	8.0	10.5
Total number (in thousands)	2,828	2,746	55,983	65,185
Percentage of workers	50.7	49.3	46.2	53.8

[1]Contingent workers as measured by the Bureau of Labor Statistics using the broadest of three alternative definitions (Estimate No. 3). This definition "effectively included all wage and salary workers who did not expect their jobs to last" plus self-employed persons and independent contractors who had been employed in these arrangements for a year or less and who expected to remain in these arrangements for a year or less.
[2]Percentages may not total 100.0 due to rounding.
[3]"Other" was derived by subtracting whites and blacks from the "all races" total. Specific data for Asian/Pacific Islanders and Native Americans were not available.
[4]Persons of Hispanic origin may be of any race. In this table, Hispanics are included in the racial categories as well as in the Hispanic category. *See* footnote to Table 1-1.

Source: Bureau of Labor Statistics, "Contingent Work: Results From the Second Survey," *Monthly Labor Review*, November 1998, Table 1.

Figure 4-9 • Employed Women and Men in Alternative Work Arrangements, February 1997 (percent distributions)

The term "alternative work arrangements" encompasses several quite different arrangements: independent contracting, on-call work, work for a contract firm, and "temping" through an agency. Although independent contractors account for the majority of the workers of both sexes who are in alternative arrangements, the majority is much larger among the men (72.6 percent versus 58.8 percent for women). On-call workers rank second for both sexes, but account for a considerably larger share of the women than of the men. The proportion of temps is twice as big among the women as among the men.

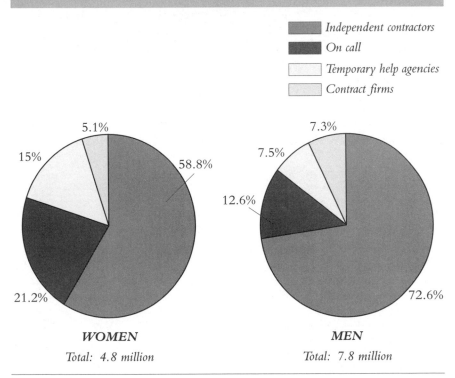

WOMEN
Total: 4.8 million

MEN
Total: 7.8 million

Source: Bureau of Labor Statistics, "Workers in Alternative Work Arrangements: A Second Look," *Monthly Labor Review,* November 1998, Table 6.

Table 4-19 • Self-Employed Women and Men by Occupation, 1998 (percent distributions)[1]

The occupational profiles of self-employed women and men differ considerably, both from each other and from the profiles of wage-and-salary workers. For example, 23 percent of self-employed women are in personal service occupations, compared with less than two percent of self-employed men and less than three percent of wage-and-salary women.

Occupation	Percent Distribution of Self-Employed Workers		Percent Distribution of Wage-and-Salary Workers	
	Women	*Men*	*Women*	*Men*
Managerial and professional	**35.7**	**38.1**	**31.5**	**28.2**
Executive, administrative, and managerial	16.2	21.9	13.9	14.9
Professional specialty	19.5	16.2	17.6	13.3
Technical, sales, and administrative support	**29.3**	**19.2**	**41.6**	**20.3**
Technicians and related support	0.6	0.9	3.9	3.0
Sales occupations	20.0	17.5	12.9	11.0
Administrative support, including clerical	8.7	0.7	24.8	6.2
Service occupations	**28.3**	**3.8**	**17.0**	**11.2**
Personal service occupations	23.2	1.8	2.8	0.7
All other service occupations	5.2	2.0	14.2	10.5
Precision production, craft, and repair	**3.0**	**29.0**	**1.9**	**18.5**
Construction trades	0.8	19.6	0.1	7.0
All other precision production, craft, and repair	2.3	9.4	1.8	11.5
Operators, fabricators, and laborers	**3.3**	**8.4**	**7.7**	**21.1**
Farming, forestry, and fishing	**0.3**	**1.4**	**0.2**	**0.8**
Total percentage[2]	**100.0**	**100.0**	**100.0**	**100.0**
Total number (in thousands)	**3,482**	**5,480**	**56,389**	**62,630**

[1]Excludes persons self-employed in the agricultural industry.
[2]Percentages may not total 100.0 due to rounding.

Source: Bureau of Labor Statistics, unpublished data from 1998 annual averages of the Current Population Survey.

Figure 4-10 • Labor Force Participation Rates of Married Women by Race and Hispanic Origin, 1978–1998[1]

> Working has long been the norm for married women who are black, and although it is now the norm for white and Hispanic married women as well, black wives continue to have the highest labor force participation rate.

Labor Force Participation Rate

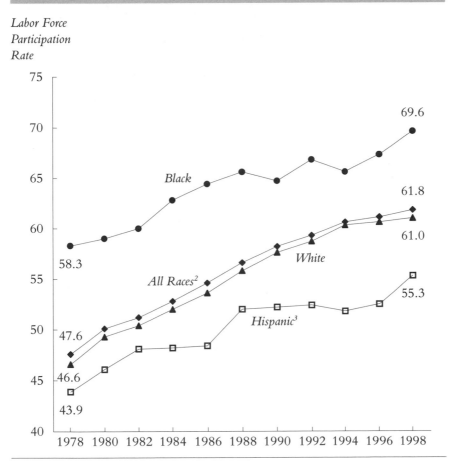

[1]Married women with spouse present.
[2]Includes Asian/Pacific Islanders and Native Americans, not shown separately (data not available).
[3]Persons of Hispanic origin may be of any race. *See* footnote to Table 1-1.

Source: Bureau of Labor Statistics, unpublished data from the March 1976, 1978, 1980, 1982, 1984, 1986, 1988, 1990, 1992, 1994, 1996, and 1998 Current Population Surveys.

Table 4-20 • Children with Working Parents by Children's Age and Living Arrangements, 1997[1]

Children with a stay-at-home parent are in the minority. In 1997, this was the case even for children under six, whether they lived with one parent or two.

Children's Living Arrangements	Age of Children			
	Total Under 18	Under 6	6–11	12–17
Live with both parents	48,386	16,463	16,471	15,452
Both parents employed				
Number	28,936	8,675	9,923	10,337
Percentage	59.8	52.7	60.2	66.9
Live with mother only	16,740	5,622	5,654	5,464
Mother employed				
Number	10,505	3,032	3,699	3,774
Percentage	62.8	53.9	65.4	69.1
Live with father only	3,059	1,077	958	1,023
Father employed				
Number	2,456	827	778	852
Percentage	80.3	76.8	81.2	83.3

[1]Does not include children who live with neither parent.

Source: Bureau of the Census, *Marital Status and Living Arrangements: March 1997 (Update)*, 1998, Table 6.

Figure 4-11 • Children with Mothers in the Labor Force by Children's Age, 1978, 1988, and 1998 (in percentages)

As of 1998, the mothers of a solid majority (59 percent) of children under six were in the workforce, although, not surprisingly, children of school age are more likely than younger children to have working mothers (nearly 70 percent of school-age children do).

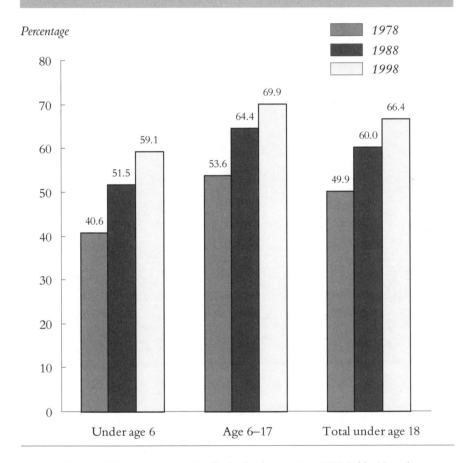

Source: Bureau of Labor Statistics, *Handbook of Labor Statistics*, 1989, Table 59; and unpublished data from the March 1998 Current Population Survey.

Figure 4-12 • Labor Force Participation Rates of Mothers with Children under 18 by Children's Age, 1978–1998[1]

In 1978, it was not the norm for a mother with a child under six to work, and even less common if her child was a toddler (under three). But by 1998, nearly two in every three mothers with children under six, and more than three in five with toddlers, were in the workforce.

*Labor Force
Participation
Rate*

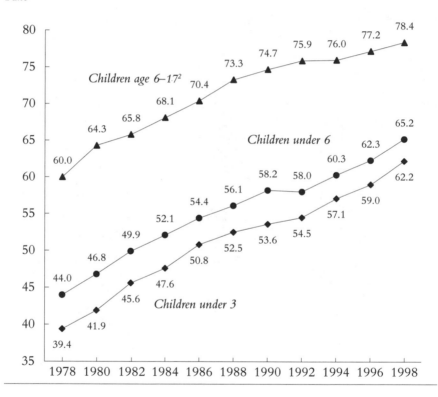

[1]Includes single women, married women with spouse present, and widowed, divorced, and separated women.
[2]None younger than six.

Bureau of Labor Statistics, *Handbook of Labor Statistics*, 1989, Table 56; and unpublished data from the March 1990, 1992, 1994, 1996, and 1998 Current Population Surveys.

Figure 4-13 • Employment Status of Mothers with Children under Age 18 by Children's Age, 1998 (percent distributions)[1]

Of all mothers with children under 18, more than 70 percent are in the paid labor force—that is, they are either working or looking for work—and half are employed full time. Only about 28 percent are not in the labor force at all. Women with young children are considerably more likely than women with school-age children to be out of the labor force entirely, but they are only slightly more likely to work part time.

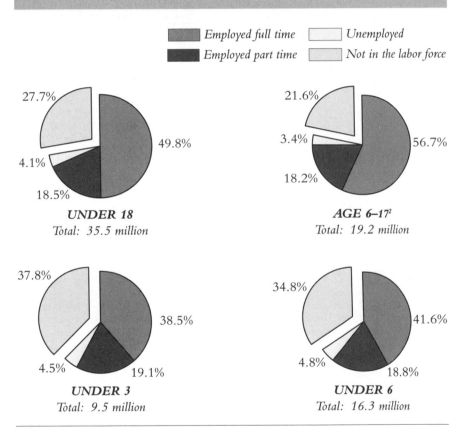

Employed full time　　*Unemployed*
Employed part time　　*Not in the labor force*

UNDER 18
Total: 35.5 million

AGE 6–17[2]
Total: 19.2 million

UNDER 3
Total: 9.5 million

UNDER 6
Total: 16.3 million

[1]Percentages may not total 100.0 due to rounding.
[2]None younger than six.

Source: Bureau of Labor Statistics, unpublished data from the March 1998 Current Population Survey.

Table 4-21 • Employed Mothers by Full-Time Work Status and Age of Children, 1978, 1988, and 1998[1]

The number of working mothers—especially mothers with small children—increased considerably between 1978 and 1998. However, only among the working mothers of school-age children was the percentage of full-time workers higher in 1998 than it had been in 1978.

Age of Children	Employed Mothers (numbers in thousands)		
	1978	1988	1998
Under 18			
Total employed	15,142	20,132	24,209
Percentage full time	70.6	72.9	72.9
Age 6–17[2]			
Total employed	9,845	12,028	14,370
Percentage full time	71.5	75.3	75.7
Under 6			
Total employed	5,297	8,104	9,839
Percentage full time	69.0	69.4	68.8
Under 3			
Total employed	2,768	4,492	5,454
Percentage full time	68.2	68.3	66.9

[1]Women age 16 and over.
[2]None younger than six.

Source: Bureau of Labor Statistics, *Handbook of Labor Statistics,* 1989, Table 56; and unpublished data from the March 1998 Current Population Survey.

Table 4-22 • Child–Care Arrangements for Young Children of Working Mothers by Race and Hispanic Origin, 1994 (percent distributions)[1]

> Having their children cared for by a relative while they work is the most common arrangement used by working mothers in every group shown here. For Hispanic mothers, it is more common than all the other arrangements combined.

Care Provided by	All Races[2]	White	Black	Hispanic Origin[3]
Relatives	**49.1**	**47.2**	**49.8**	**58.0**
Father	18.4	19.6	11.0	16.9
Grandparent	16.3	14.2	22.1	22.4
In child's home	5.9	4.9	7.6	8.0
In another home	10.4	9.2	14.6	14.4
Other relative	8.9	6.8	13.9	16.5
In child's home	3.4	2.4	5.2	7.3
In another home	5.5	4.5	8.6	9.2
Mother while she works[4]	5.5	6.5	2.8	2.2
Nonrelatives	**20.5**	**21.3**	**14.8**	**20.7**
Babysitter in child's home	5.1	5.5	1.5	5.7
Family day-care provider	15.4	15.8	13.3	15.0
Organized facilities	**29.3**	**30.7**	**33.8**	**19.3**
Day-care center	21.6	23.3	22.9	12.8
Nursery/preschool	7.8	7.4	10.9	6.5
Other[5]	**1.0**	**0.8**	**1.6**	**2.0**
Total percentage[6]	**100.0**	**100.0**	**100.0**	**100.0**
Total number of children (in thousands)	10,288	7,523	1,162	1,205

[1]Primary care arrangements for children under age five.
[2]Includes Asian/Pacific Islanders and Native Americans, not shown separately (data not available).
[3]Persons of Hispanic origin may be of any race. *See* footnote to Table 1-1.
[4]Includes mothers working at home or away from home.
[5]Includes preschoolers in kindergarten and school-based activities.
[6]Percentages may not total 100.0 due to rounding.

Source: Bureau of the Census, *Who's Minding Our Preschoolers? Fall 1994 (Update)*, 1997, Table C.

SECTION 5:
EARNINGS AND BENEFITS

TWO MEASURES OF earnings are used in this section: the median weekly earnings of full-time workers and the median annual earnings of full-time workers who worked year round. By either measure, America's working women are making more money than ever before.

After dipping slightly in the mid-1990s, women's real (inflation-adjusted) weekly earnings resumed what was a gently upward trend during most of the 1980s and 1990s. The median for women was about 14 percent higher in 1998 than in 1978. The median for men, however, was nine percent lower in 1998 than in 1978.

Women's gains and men's losses were spread quite unequally across the population. Both white and black women gained, but white women gained considerably more than black women. Both white and black men lost, but black men lost considerably more than white men. As a result, the earnings gap between white and black women widened, as did the gap between white and black men.

The annual earnings of year-round, full-time workers (plotted for 1980–1997 and adjusted for inflation) show largely similar trends—white women's earnings up more than black women's; white men's earnings down; Hispanic men's earnings down steeply. However, the annual earnings of Hispanic women and black men were essentially the same in 1997 as they had been in 1980.

Race and ethnic discrimination and other factors that cannot be easily quantified are no doubt implicated in earnings differences. Nevertheless, the data on earnings by educational attainment, together with the data on earnings by occupation, powerfully suggest that to be educationally disadvantaged is to be "earnings disadvantaged," and vice versa.

- Increases in women's median earnings were responsible for most of the narrowing of the wage gap (the ratio of women's earnings to men's earnings) between 1978 and 1998 (see Table 5-1 and Figure 5-1).

- The wage gap is narrowest among young workers (see Figure 5-2 and Table 5-2).

- The earnings of black and Hispanic workers of both sexes have consistently been lower than those of white workers, and the wage gap has consistently been narrower for black and Hispanic workers than for whites (see Table 5-3).

- The most lucrative wage-and-salary jobs require a postgraduate degree and/or highly specialized training. When it comes to unskilled and semiskilled occupations, those in which men predominate pay much better than those in which women predominate (see Table 5-4).

- Between 1987 and 1997, working women and men who lacked a college degree saw their real earnings erode; women and men who had a bachelor's degree or better saw their real earnings increase. However, although higher education pays off for women as well as for men, it rewards men better than it rewards women (see Table 5-7).

- Women who work year round, full time are slightly more likely than their male counterparts to be in an employer-sponsored pension plan. Black women are nearly as likely as white women to be in a plan, Hispanic women much less likely (see Table 5-8).

- Roughly two-thirds of white and black workers of both sexes who work year round, full time have health insurance coverage through their own jobs. Their Hispanic counterparts are less likely to have coverage (see Table 5-9).

- One in seven women age 55–64 has no health insurance at all (see Figure 5-9).

- The number of people without health insurance has continued to grow. Children under 18 constitute the largest single component of America's uninsured (see Figure 5-8 and Table 5-10).

Table 5-1 • Median Weekly Earnings by Sex and Female-to-Male Earnings Ratios, 1978–1998[1]

After inflation, women workers' earnings were nearly 14 percent higher in 1998 than in 1978; men's earnings were nine percent lower. As a consequence, the wage gap—the ratio of women's to men's earnings—was significantly narrower in 1998 than in 1978, although not quite as narrow as in 1993 (*see* Figure 5-1).

	Median Earnings		Ratio of Women's
	Women	*Men*	*to Men's Earnings*
Current dollars			
1978[2]	166	272	61.0
1979	182	291	62.6
1980	201	312	64.4
1990	346	481	71.9
1991	366	493	74.2
1992	380	501	75.8
1993	393	510	77.1
1994	399	522	76.4
1995	406	538	75.5
1996	418	557	75.0
1997	431	579	74.4
1998	456	598	76.3
1998 dollars[3]			
1978	401	657	61.0
1998	456	598	76.3
Percent change	+13.7	-9.0	—

[1]Median usual weekly earnings of full-time wage-and-salary workers.
[2]May 1978.
[3]The CPI-U-X1 was used to inflate the earnings series.

Source: Bureau of Labor Statistics, *Handbook of Labor Statistics*, 1989, Table 41; *Employment and Earnings*, January 1991, Table 54; January 1993, Table 54; January 1995, Table 37; January 1996, Table 37; January 1997, Table 37; and January 1999, Table 37; and unpublished data from the May 1978 Current Population Survey.

Figure 5-1 • Median Weekly Earnings by Sex, 1978–1998 (in constant 1998 dollars)[1,2]

The wage gap narrowed during most of the period shown here because men's earnings declined and women's earnings increased. As men's earnings began to recover in the mid-1990s, the narrowing trend stalled, even though women's earnings continued to rise.

1998 Dollars

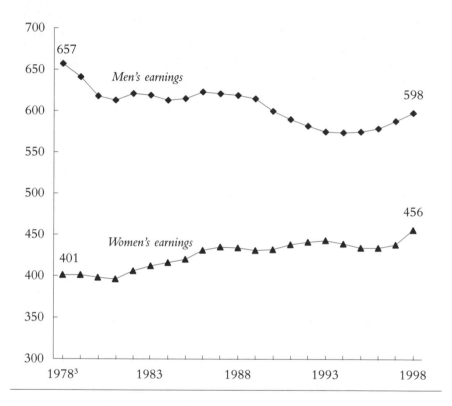

[1]Median usual weekly earnings of full-time wage-and-salary workers.
[2]The CPI-U-X1 was used to inflate the earnings series.
[3]May 1978.

Source: Bureau of Labor Statistics, *Handbook of Labor Statistics*, 1989, Table 41; *Employment and Earnings*, January 1991, Table 54; January 1993, Table 54; January 1995, Table 37; January 1996, Table 37; January 1997, Table 37; and January 1999, Table 37; and unpublished data from the May 1978 Current Population Survey.

Figure 5-2 • Female-to-Male Earnings Ratios among Workers Age 25–64 by Age, 1978–1998[1]

The female-to-male earnings ratio—commonly known as the wage gap—is narrowest among young workers.[2] Between 1978 and 1998, although the wage gap narrowed in all of the four 10-year age groups shown here, it remained narrowest (82.9 percent) in the 25–34 group. The most dramatic change occurred in the 35–44 age group, where the gap narrowed by nearly 21 percentage points, from just under 53 percent in 1978 to nearly 74 percent in 1998.

Earnings Ratio

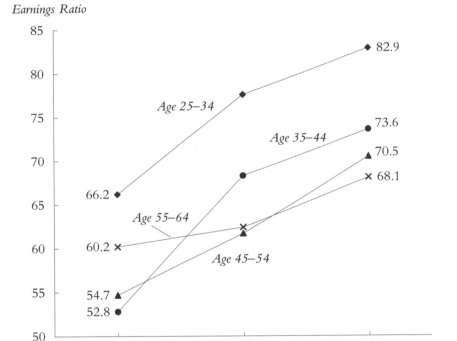

[1]Based on usual median weekly earnings of full-time wage-and-salary workers.
[2]The editors elected to focus on the earnings of workers between 25 and 65. We omitted the 16–24 group (where the earnings ratio was around 91 percent in 1998) because many of these workers have yet to finish their education. We omitted the group age 65 and over because large standard errors accompany the BLS earnings data for these workers (relatively few people in this age group are employed full time).

Source: Bureau of Labor Statistics, unpublished data from the May 1978 Current Population Survey and the 1998 Current Population Survey (annual averages).

Table 5-2 • Female-to-Male Earnings Ratios among Workers Age 25–64 by Age, 1998[1,2]

As a general rule, the older the workers, the wider the wage gap between men and women. The minor exception in 1998 was in the 55–59 age group, where the wage ratio was marginally narrower than in the 50–54 age group.

| | Median Weekly Earnings (in 1998 dollars) | | |
Age	Women	Men	Earnings Ratio
16 years and over	456	598	76.3
25 years and over	485	639	75.9
25–29	433	507	85.4
30–34	471	587	80.2
35–39	489	657	74.4
40–44	507	699	72.5
45–49	521	724	72.0
50–54	509	741	68.7
55–59	495	719	68.8
60–64	433	657	65.9

[1]Based on usual median weekly earnings of full-time wage-and-salary workers.
[2]The editors elected to focus on the earnings of workers between 25 and 65. We omitted the group between 16 and 25 (where the earnings ratio was around 91 percent in 1998) because many of these workers have yet to finish their education. We omitted the group age 65 and over because large standard errors accompany the BLS earnings data for these workers (relatively few people in this age group are employed full time).

Source: Bureau of Labor Statistics, unpublished data from the 1998 Current Population Survey (annual averages).

Table 5-3 • Women's and Men's Median Weekly Earnings and Female-to-Male Earnings Ratios by Race and Hispanic Origin, 1978–1998[1]

The earnings of black and Hispanic workers of both sexes have consistently been lower than those of white workers, and the female-to-male wage ratios have consistently been narrower for black and Hispanic workers than for whites.

	Median Weekly Earnings (in constant 1998 dollars)				
	1978[2]	1983	1988	1993	1998
All races[3]					
Women	401	412	434	443	465
Men	657	619	619	575	598
Earnings ratio	61.0	66.7	70.2	77.1	76.3
White					
Women	403	416	438	452	468
Men	671	633	641	591	615
Earnings ratio	60.1	65.6	68.4	76.5	76.1
Black[4]					
Women	379	378	397	393	400
Men	526	480	478	442	468
Earnings ratio	72.0	78.8	83.0	88.8	85.5
Hispanic[5]					
Women	—[6]	—	358	353	337
Men	—	—	423	390	390
Earnings ratio	—	—	84.7	90.5	86.4

[1]Median usual weekly earnings of full-time wage-and-salary workers.
[2]May 1978.
[3]Includes Asian/Pacific Islanders and Native Americans, not shown separately (data not available).
[4]"Black and other" in 1978.
[5]Persons of Hispanic origin may be of any race. In this table, Hispanics are included in the racial categories as well as in the Hispanic category. *See* footnote to Table 1-1.
[6]Data on median usual weekly earnings of Hispanic workers by sex were not available for 1978 and 1983.

Source: Bureau of Labor Statistics, *Handbook of Labor Statistics*, 1989, Table 41; *Employment and Earnings*, January 1999, Table 37; and unpublished data from the May 1978 Current Population Survey.

Table 5-4 • Median Weekly Earnings of Workers in Selected Occupations, 1998

If overall median weekly earnings are the benchmark, it is obvious that while not all jobs requiring higher education pay very high salaries, the most lucrative wage-and-salary jobs require a postgraduate degree and/or highly specialized training. When it comes to unskilled and semi-skilled occupations, those in which men predominate, such as truck drivers, pay a good deal better than those in which women predominate, such as cashiers.

Occupations	Earnings of Wage-and-Salary Workers (both sexes, in dollars)	Women as a Percentage of All Workers[1]
All occupations	523	46.2
Aircraft engine mechanics	780	3.7
Airplane pilots and navigators	1,383	3.4
Architects	872	17.5
Automobile mechanics	493	0.8
Carpenters	490	1.2
Cashiers	267	78.2
Clergy	593	12.0
Computer programmers	843	28.5
Data processing equipment repairers	641	16.9
Dental assistants	369	98.1
Dentists	—[2]	19.8
Electrical and electronic equipment repairers	665	11.1
Electrical and electronic technicians	642	16.9
Economists	900	46.3
Editors and reporters	723	51.0
Financial managers	852	53.3
Firefighters	734	2.3

(continued)

[1]Women's representation among all workers in occupation, i.e., including those who are not full-time wage-and-salary workers.
[2]Dentists who are full-time wage-and-salary workers are too few in number for a reliable estimate of median earnings.

Table 5-4 (continued)

Occupations	Earnings of Wage-and-Salary Workers (both sexes, in dollars)	Women as a Percentage of All Workers
Heating, air conditioning, and refrigeration mechanics	594	1.5
Industrial machinery repairers	608	2.1
Industrial truck and tractor equipment operators	452	8.9
Lawyers and judges	1,218	28.6
Librarians	665	83.4
Machinists	594	5.7
Managers, medicine and health	716	79.2
Mechanical engineers	998	7.0
Painters, construction, and maintenance	402	4.7
Physicians	1,156	26.6
Plumbers, pipefitters, and steamfitters	593	0.9
Police and detectives, public service	723	11.5
Registered nurses	739	92.5
Sales workers, apparel	296	80.2
Sales workers, motor vehicle and boats	587	11.1
Social workers	579	68.4
Teachers, college and university	907	42.3
Teachers, elementary school	691	84.0
Telephone installers and repairers	750	12.0
Truck drivers	516	5.3
Welders and cutters	518	5.1

Source: Bureau of Labor Statistics, Employment and Earnings, January 1999, Tables 11 and 39.

Table 5-5 • Female-to-Male Earnings Ratios by Occupation, 1998[1]

The wage gap is far from uniform across occupational categories. In some cases, the differences reflect the concentration of women and/or minorities in the less well-paid jobs in the overall category. (For example, women heavily predominate among the workers in the lower-paying sales occupations, such as apparel sales and cashiers; men predominate in the relatively high-paying sales occupations, such as automobile and boat sales [see Table 5-4].)

Occupation	Earnings Ratio 1998
All occupations	76.3
Managerial and professional specialty	72.4
Executive, administrative, and managerial	68.4
Professional specialty	76.2
Technical, sales, and administrative support	69.1
Technicians and related support	72.9
Sales occupations	59.8
Administrative support, including clerical	80.7
Service occupations	76.1
Protective service	78.5
All other service occupations[2]	90.8
Precision production, craft, and repair	69.5
Mechanics and repairers	86.6
Construction trades	74.9
Precision production occupations	64.2
Operators, fabricators, and laborers	71.7
Machine operators, assemblers, and inspectors	69.5
Transportation and material moving occupations	71.9
Handlers, equipment cleaners, helpers, and laborers	85.9
Farming, forestry, and fishing	88.6

[1]Usual median weekly earnings of full-time wage-and-salary workers.
[2]Excluding workers in private households.

Source: Bureau of Labor Statistics, Employment and Earnings, January 1999, Table 39.

Table 5-6 • Median Annual Earnings by Sex, Race, and Hispanic Origin, 1980–1997 (in constant 1998 dollars)[1,2]

> During the 1980s and most of the 1990s, real (inflation-adjusted) annual earnings continued to increase for women who worked year round, full time, although only white women could claim substantial gains, and Hispanic women barely held their own. The real median earnings of white and—especially—Hispanic men were lower in 1997 than in 1980.

			Median Annual Earnings			Net Change 1980–
	1980	*1985*	*1990*	*1995*	*1997*	*1997*
Women						
All races[3]	22,176	23,668	24,721	24,062	25,362	+14.4
White	22,335	23,929	25,002	24,505	25,726	+15.2
Black	21,137	21,675	22,498	22,102	22,378	+5.9
A/PI[4]	—	—	26,594	26,607	28,214	—
Hispanic[5]	19,170	19,793	19,545	18,373	19,269	+0.5
Men						
All races	36,862	36,652	34,518	33,687	34,199	-7.2
White	37,942	37,966	36,018	34,410	35,741	-5.8
Black	26,831	26,478	26,332	26,127	26,844	—[6]
A/PI	—	—	33,379	33,770	35,222	—
Hispanic	26,852	25,830	23,865	21,796	21,952	-18.2

[1]Earnings of people who worked year round, full-time. Unlike the weekly earnings figures, which are based on the earnings of wage-and-salary workers, the annual earnings figures include the self-employed. For the years before 1990, data are for civilian workers only.
[2]The CPI-U-X1 was used to inflate the earnings series.
[3]Includes Native Americans, not shown separately (data not available).
[4]Data for Asian/Pacific Islanders are not available for years before 1988.
[5]Persons of Hispanic origin may be of any race. In this table, Hispanics are included in the racial categories as well as in the Hispanic category. *See* footnote to Table 1-1.
[6]Less than one tenth of one percent.

Source: Bureau of the Census, *Historical Income Tables*, P-31, P31-A, P31-B, P31-C, P31-D, <http://www.census.gov/hhes/income/histinc/>.

Figure 5-3 • Median Annual Earnings by Sex and Race, 1975–1997 (in constant 1998 dollars)[1,2,3]

White men may have lost ground since 1985, but they are still America's highest earners, with Asian/Pacific Islander men a close second. Asian/Pacific Islander women are doing well, too—better than black men. In the late 1990s, there were gains for the year-round, full-time workers in all the groups shown here.

Dollars

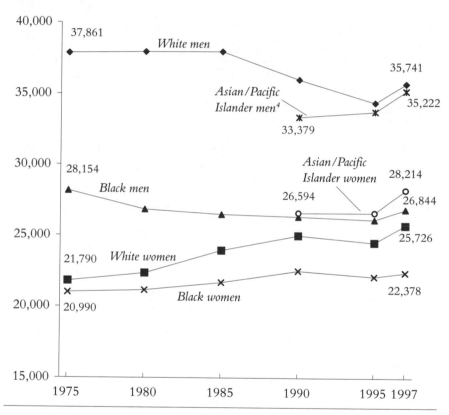

[1]Earnings of people who worked year round, full time. For years before 1990, data are for civilian workers only.
[2]The CPI-U-X1 was used to inflate the earnings series.
[3]Includes Native Americans, not shown separately (data not available).
[4]Data for Asian/Pacific Islanders are not available for years before 1988.

Source: Bureau of the Census, *Historical Income Tables*, P31-A, P31-B, P31-C, P31-D, <http://www.census.gov/hhes/income/histinc/>.

Figure 5-4 • Median Annual Earnings by Sex and Hispanic Origin, 1975–1997 (in constant 1998 dollars)[1,2]

Of all year-round, full-time workers, only Hispanic women had lower annual earnings in 1998 than Hispanic men. By the time the prosperity of the late 1990s brought a halt to the long decline in Hispanic men's earnings, they had dropped considerably below the earnings of women overall.

Dollars

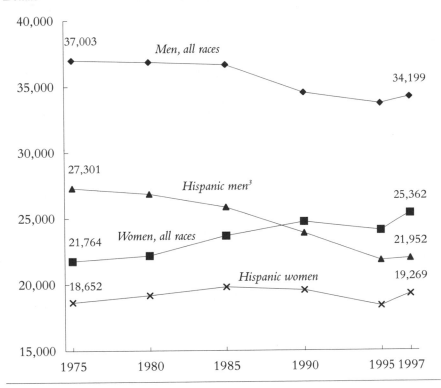

[1]Earnings of people who worked year round, full time. For years before 1990, data are for civilian workers only.
[2]The CPI-U-X1 was used to inflate the earnings series.
[3]Persons of Hispanic origin may be of any race. In this figure, Hispanics are included in the racial categories as well as in the Hispanic category. *See* footnote to Table 1-1.

Source: Bureau of the Census, *Historical Income Tables*, P-31 and P31-D, <http://www.census.gov/hhes/income/histinc/>.

Table 5-7 • Mean Annual Earnings by Educational Attainment and Sex, 1987 and 1997 (in constant 1998 dollars)[1,2]

> The difference higher education makes to earnings is dramatically illustrated here. On average, people of both sexes who lacked a college degree saw the purchasing power of their earnings erode between 1987 and 1997; people of both sexes who had a bachelor's degree or better saw their real earnings increase. But while there is no question that higher education pays off for both sexes, it rewards men more handsomely than it rewards women.

	Women's Mean Earnings		Men's Mean Earnings	
	1987	1997	1987	1997
Total, all levels	27,041	29,717	42,881	44,390
Less than 9th grade	16,202	15,190	25,434	23,100
9–12 (no diploma)	18,848	18,884	30,601	28,068
High school graduate	23,278	23,009	35,506	33,119
Some college (no degree)	27,744	26,976	41,974	33,980
Associate degree[3]	—	30,240	—	41,095
Bachelor's degree or more	37,332	42,274	60,885	67,427
Professional degree[3]	—	75,231	—	121,922

[1]Earnings of year-round, full-time workers age 18 and over.
[2]The CPI-U-X1 was used to inflate the earnings series.
[3]Data not available for 1987.

Source: Bureau of the Census, *Money Income of Households, Families, and Persons in the United States: 1987*, 1988, Table 36; and *Money Income in the United States: 1997*, 1998, Table 9.

Table 5-8 • Pension Plan Availability and Coverage by Workers' Sex and Work Experience, and by Race and Hispanic Origin of Women, 1997[1]

Of all the women who work year round, full time, about two-thirds work for employers who offer a pension plan and over half are included in a plan. These proportions slightly exceed those for men who work year round, full time. However, Hispanic women, whatever their work schedules, are less likely than black or white women to be in a plan.

		Percentage	
		With Pension	*Worker*
	Number	*Plan Offered*	*Included*
	(in thousands)	*at Work*	*in Plan*
Total with work experience[2]			
Women, all races[3]	67,851	54.8	39.8
White	56,028	54.9	39.9
Black	8,702	55.2	40.1
Hispanic[4]	5,856	39.6	26.9
Men, all races[3]	76,731	54.3	43.9
Year round, full time			
Women, all races	37,715	66.3	55.9
White	30,606	66.6	56.2
Black	5,313	66.3	55.2
Hispanic	3,143	48.6	38.4
Men, all races	54,933	62.0	54.6
Year round, part time			
Women, all races	9,592	39.4	19.9
White	8,366	39.4	20.0
Black	853	42.8	20.8
Hispanic	746	30.2	14.1
Men, all races	4,288	32.8	13.5

[1] "Pension plan" refers to an employer- or union-provided pension or retirement plan.
[2] Total includes workers who did not work year round.
[3] Includes Asian/Pacific Islanders and Native Americans, not shown separately (data not available).
[4] Persons of Hispanic origin may be of any race. In this table, Hispanics are included in the racial categories as well as in the Hispanic category. *See* footnote to Table 1-1.

Source: Bureau of the Census, Current Population Survey, March 1998, Table NC8, <http://ferret.bls.census.gov/macro/031998/noncash/8_000.htm>.

Figure 5-5 • Employed Women in Employer-Provided Pension Plans and Employed Women with Employer-Provided Health Insurance by Employer Size, 1997 (percent distributions)

The larger her employer's workforce, the more likely it is that a woman will have pension coverage or health insurance (or both) through her job. The majority of women who have these benefits work for employers with at least 1,000 employees, although the majority of employed women overall work for smaller employers.

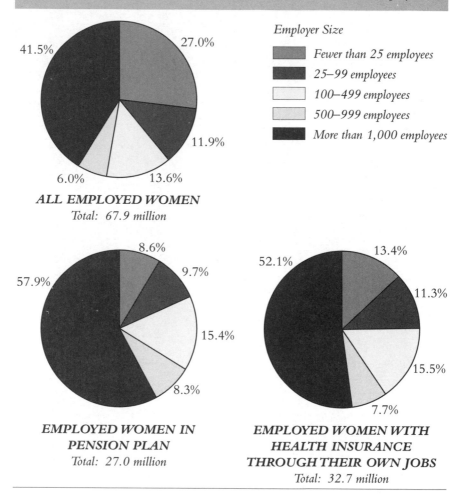

Employer Size
- Fewer than 25 employees
- 25–99 employees
- 100–499 employees
- 500–999 employees
- More than 1,000 employees

ALL EMPLOYED WOMEN
Total: 67.9 million

EMPLOYED WOMEN IN PENSION PLAN
Total: 27.0 million

EMPLOYED WOMEN WITH HEALTH INSURANCE THROUGH THEIR OWN JOBS
Total: 32.7 million

Source: Bureau of the Census, Current Population Survey, March 1998, Tables NC7 and NC8, <http://ferret.bls.census.gov/macro/031998/noncash/7_000.htm> and <.../8_000.htm>.

Table 5-9 • Year-Round, Full-Time Workers Covered by Health Insurance
through Their Own Jobs by Sex, Race, and Hispanic Origin, 1997 (numbers are
in thousands)[1]

The majority of people who work year round, full time have health insurance
through their jobs. White men are slightly more likely than white women to
have such coverage; the reverse is true for black workers. Least likely to have
coverage are Hispanic men.

| | | With Health Insurance through Own Jobs[2] | |
	Number of Workers	*Number*	*Percent*
All races[3]			
Women	37,715	25,078	66.5
Men	54,933	37,448	68.2
White			
Women	30,606	20,212	66.0
Men	47,241	32,460	68.7
Black			
Women	5,313	3,680	69.3
Men	5,172	3,439	66.5
Hispanic[4]			
Women	3,143	1,713	54.5
Men	5,976	2,969	49.7

[1]Workers age 15 and over.
[2]With employer-provided group health insurance in their own names.
[3]Includes Asian/Pacific Islanders and Native Americans, not shown separately (data not
available).
[4]Persons of Hispanic origin may be of any race. In this table, Hispanics are included in the
racial categories as well as in the Hispanic category. *See* footnote to Table 1-1.

Source: Bureau of the Census, Current Population Survey, March 1998, Table NC7,
<http://ferret.bls.census.gov/macro/031998/noncash/7_000.htm>.

Figure 5-6 • Women and Men Age 18–64 with Private Health Insurance by Source of Coverage, 1997 (percent distributions)[1]

Of all adults under age 65 who had private health insurance coverage for all or part of 1997, more than half of the women and about three-quarters of the men had coverage through their own jobs. However, women were much more likely than men to have coverage through a family member's job, and slightly more likely to have coverage that was not related to employment.

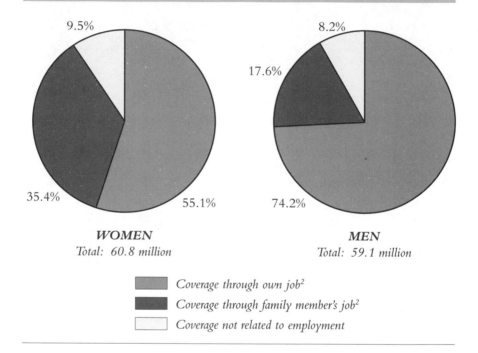

WOMEN
Total: 60.8 million

MEN
Total: 59.1 million

  Coverage through own job[2]
  Coverage through family member's job[2]
  Coverage not related to employment

[1]People with coverage for all or part of the year.
[2]Coverage related to current or past employment.

Source: Bureau of the Census, Current Population Survey, March 1998, Table 24, <http://ferret.bls.census.gov/macro/031998/pov/new24_000.htm>.

Figure 5-7 • Women Age 18–64 with Private Health Insurance by Age and Source of Coverage, 1997 (percent distributions)[1]

Of those women between the ages of 60 and 65 who have private health insurance, one in five has coverage that is unrelated to employment. These women, a few years short of eligibility for Medicare, almost certainly have had to buy individual policies, which are generally far more expensive than employer-provided group policies and often provide fewer benefits. (One in seven women between the ages of 55 and 65 has no health insurance at all [*see* Figure 5-9].)

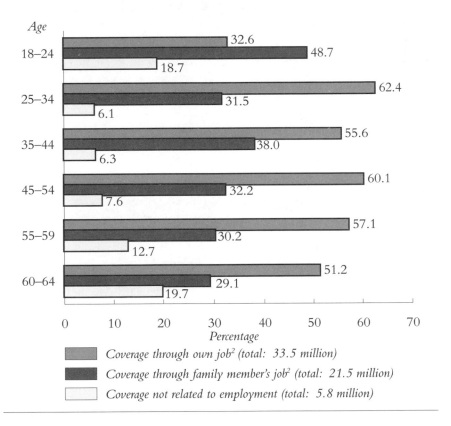

Age

Age	Coverage through own job	Coverage through family member's job	Coverage not related to employment
18–24	32.6	48.7	18.7
25–34	62.4	31.5	6.1
35–44	55.6	38.0	6.3
45–54	60.1	32.2	7.6
55–59	57.1	30.2	12.7
60–64	51.2	29.1	19.7

Percentage

Coverage through own job[2] (total: 33.5 million)
Coverage through family member's job[2] (total: 21.5 million)
Coverage not related to employment (total: 5.8 million)

[1]Women with coverage for all or part of the year.
[2]Coverage related to current or past employment.

Source: Bureau of the Census, Current Population Survey, March 1998, Table 24, <http://ferret.bls.census.gov/macro/031998/pov/new24_000.htm>.

Figure 5-8 • Health Insurance Coverage for People of All Ages by Sex and Type of Insurance, 1987 and 1997 (in percentages)[1,2]

The percentage of the U.S. population without health insurance has continued to grow. In 1987, about 12 percent of females and 14 percent of males lacked coverage of any kind throughout the year; by 1997, these proportions approached 15 percent and 18 percent, respectively.

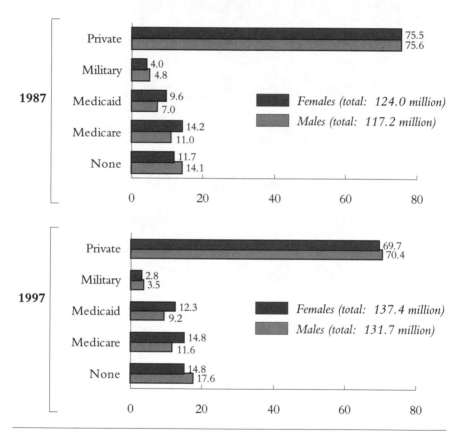

[1]The "insured" had coverage for all or part of the year; the uninsured had no coverage at any time during the year.

[2]Percentages for each sex total more than 100.0 percent because some insured had coverage from more than one source.

Source: Bureau of the Census, Current Population Survey, March 1998, Table HI-1, <http://www.census.gov/income/hlthins/hi01.txt>.

Figure 5-9 • People with and without Health Insurance Coverage by Age and Sex, 1997

Among people under age 55, women are more likely than men to have some form of health insurance coverage. Nevertheless, given the importance of regular checkups for women in their reproductive years, it is disturbing that one in four women between 18 and 25, and nearly one in five between 25 and 35, have no coverage.

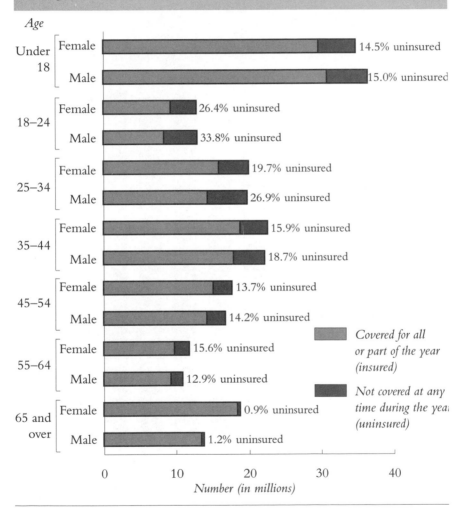

Source: Bureau of the Census, Current Population Survey, March 1998, Table 24, <http://ferret.bls.census.gov/macro/031998/pov/new24_000.htm>.

Figure 5-10 • Number of People without Health Insurance Coverage by Sex, 1987–1997[1]

Between 1987 and 1997, the number of Americans without health insurance increased by 12 million. More than 43 million people—20.3 million females and 23.1 million males—had no health insurance coverage of any kind at any time during 1997.

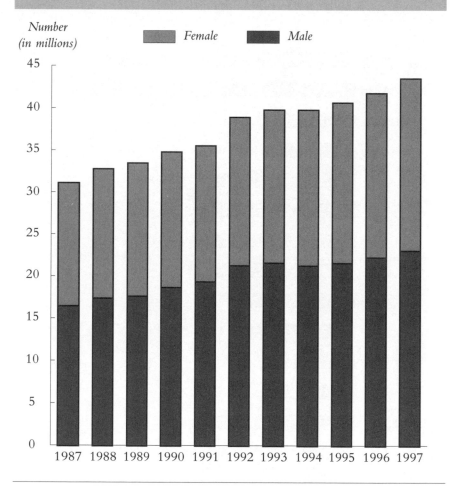

Number (in millions)

Female   Male

[1]Persons of all ages who had no health insurance coverage of any kind during the year.

Source: Bureau of the Census, Current Population Survey, March 1998, Table HI-1, <http://www.census.gov/income/hlthins/hi01.txt>.

Figure 5-11 • Women and Men Age 16–64 without Health Insurance Coverage by Work Experience, 1997 (percent distributions)[1]

Most of the adults of working age who were uninsured in 1997 had some work experience in that year; in fact, nearly 30 percent of the women and more than 46 percent of the men worked full time throughout the year. But people who did not work at all accounted for a much larger proportion—more than one-third—of the uninsured women than of the uninsured men.

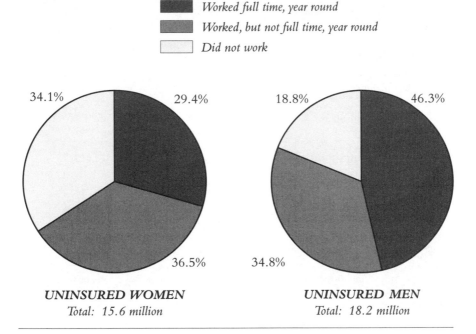

■ *Worked full time, year round*

■ *Worked, but not full time, year round*

☐ *Did not work*

UNINSURED WOMEN
Total: 15.6 million

UNINSURED MEN
Total: 18.2 million

[1]Not covered at any time during the year.

Source: Bureau of the Census, Current Population Survey, March 1998, Table 24, <http://ferret.bls.census.gov/macro/031998/pov/new24_000.htm>.

Table 5-10 • People without Health Insurance Coverage by Family Relationship, 1997 (percent distribution)[1,2]

Minor children constitute the largest single component of America's uninsured (23.4 percent). Virtually tied for second place are adult children who live with their parents (14.5 percent) and wives (14.4 percent).

	Number of Uninsured (in thousands)	Percentage of Uninsured
People living in families	**34,854**	**80.7**
Wives	6,238	14.4
Husbands	5,468	12.7
Female householders	2,364	5.5
Children under age 18	10,110	23.4
Children over age 18	6,257	14.5
Other[3]	4,417	10.2
Members of unrelated subfamilies[4]	389	0.9
People not living in families	**8,345**	**19.3**
Unrelated females	3,010	7.0
Unrelated males	4,946	11.4
Total	**43,198**	**100.0**

[1]Persons who had no health insurance coverage at any time during the year.
[2]Unrelated individuals under age 15 are excluded.
[3]Could include male householders with no spouse present, as well as other relatives.
[4]"Unrelated subfamilies" who live in the household of someone to whom they are not related by birth, marriage, or adoption, include 180,000 children under 18.

Source: Bureau of the Census, Current Population Survey, March 1998, Table 24, <http://ferret.bls.census.gov/macro/031998/pov/new24_000.htm>.

SECTION 6:
ECONOMIC SECURITY

AMERICAN FAMILIES OF all types were doing better financially in 1997 than they had been five years earlier, at least in terms of real (inflation-adjusted) income. However, only married couples with working wives and families headed by women had higher real incomes than their counterparts 20 years earlier. Married couples without working wives and families headed by men actually lost ground between 1977 and 1997. In light of the increase in women's median earnings over the same period (see Section 5), and the decrease in men's, it is hard to avoid the conclusion that, in general, it has been women's earnings that have fueled the growth in their families' income.

Nevertheless, many American women and their families are poor. The fact that the typical woman who heads a family with children is a little better off than her counterpart of 20 years ago doesn't alter the fact that her income remains the lowest, by far, of any family type. Not surprisingly, the poverty rate among female-headed families with children is very high—in 1997, it was 41 percent overall—and even higher among black and Hispanic families.

Poverty rates are comparatively high among women over 65, who are much more likely than their male contemporaries to be poor. The risk of poverty is even higher for older women who live alone or are over 75, and highest for those who are Hispanic or black.

- The median incomes for families of every type were higher in 1997 than they had been five years earlier, but the median for married-couple families with working wives still outpaced by far the medians for other family types (see Figure 6-1).
- For black families of every type, median real income was higher in 1997 than it had been 10 years earlier, but, except for female-headed families,

Hispanic families lost ground. Among whites, the median increased only for families with wives in the workforce, although white families of every type still had much higher incomes than their black and Hispanic counterparts (see Table 6-1).

- Close to 80 percent of all women between the ages of 15 and 65 had wage-and-salary income in 1997 (see Table 6-2).
- Compared with men over 65, women over 65 have much less personal income, receive income from fewer sources, and, as a rule, average less income from any given source. Being black or Hispanic deepens older women's economic disadvantage (see Tables 6-3 and 6-4).
- Females are more likely than their male contemporaries to be poor. This is the case at every age and in every racial group for which poverty data are available.
- A female-headed family with children is far more likely to be poor than a family of another type. A white family of any type, with or without children, is less likely to be poor than its black or Hispanic counterparts. A Hispanic family of any type, with or without children, is more likely to be poor than its white or black counterparts (see Figures 6-3 and 6-4 and Table 6-6).
- One in eight women over age 65 is poor, compared with about one in 14 men over 65. Of older women who live alone, one in five is poor (see Figure 6-5 and Table 6-8).

Figure 6-1 • Median Family Income by Family Type, 1977–1997 (in constant 1998 dollars)[1]

After taking inflation into account, median income was higher in 1997 than in 1992 for families of all types, but the income of married couples in which the wife worked still far outpaced that of other family types. In 1997, the typical married couple with a wife in the labor force had an income that was more than half again as high as the couple without a working wife and nearly three times as high as the family with a female householder.[2]

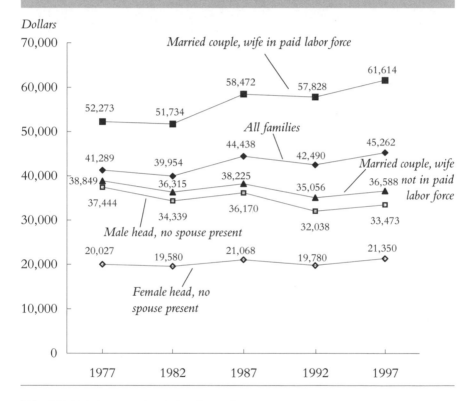

[1]The CPI-U-X1 was used to inflate the median incomes.
[2]In 1997, both spouses were in the labor force in 91 percent of the 33.4 million couples with wives in the labor force. In about 43 percent of the 2.9 million couples where the wives were the only working spouses, the husbands were over age 60.

Source: Bureau of the Census, *Historical Income Tables*, Table F-7, <http://www.census.gov /hhes/income/histinc/>.

Table 6-1 • Median Income of White, Black, and Hispanic Families by Family
Type, 1987, 1992, and 1997 (in constant 1998 dollars)[1]

For black families of every type, real (inflation-adjusted) income was higher in
1997 than in 1987; for black families overall, the median was up by a net of 10
percent. But income dropped for Hispanic families of every type except those
headed by women. The news was mixed for whites: only families with wives in
the workforce had more purchasing power in 1997 than in 1987. However, white
families of every type still had much higher incomes than their black and Hispanic counterparts.

	Median Income		
	1987	*1992*	*1997*
White			
All family types	46,468	44,927	47,482
Married couple	50,843	49,381	52,909
Wife in paid labor force	59,333	58,631	62,398
Wife not in paid labor force	39,281	35,839	36,909
Female-headed, no spouse present	24,411	23,145	23,357
Male-headed, no spouse present	38,042	34,136	35,344
Black			
All family types	26,410	24,517	29,048
Married couple	39,187	39,879	46,079
Wife in paid labor force	48,259	48,555	52,507
Wife not in paid labor force	24,632	24,469	29,205
Female-headed, no spouse present	14,125	13,760	17,142
Male-headed, no spouse present	25,899	24,017	26,054
Hispanic[2]			
All family types	29,128	27,366	28,580
Married couple	34,989	32,746	34,442
Wife in paid labor force	45,007	42,954	42,939
Wife not in paid labor force	26,147	23,729	24,119
Female-headed, no spouse present	13,918	14,759	15,228
Male-headed, no spouse present	28,215	22,533	25,941

[1]The CPI-U-X1 was used to inflate the median incomes.
[2]Persons of Hispanic origin may be of any race. In this table, Hispanics are included in the
racial categories as well as in the Hispanic category. *See* footnote to Table 1-1.

Source: Bureau of the Census, *Historical Income Tables*, Tables F7A, F7B, and F7D, <http://
www.census.gov/hhes/income/histinc/>.

Figure 6-2 • Median Income of Families with Children by Family Type, 1977–1997 (in constant 1998 dollars)[1]

> Overall, the median income for families with children is only slightly lower than for families in general ($44,223 versus $45,262 in 1997; *see* Figure 6-1); however, the contrast between the median for married couples with children and the median for female-headed families with children is stark—in 1997, the former was more than three times the latter.

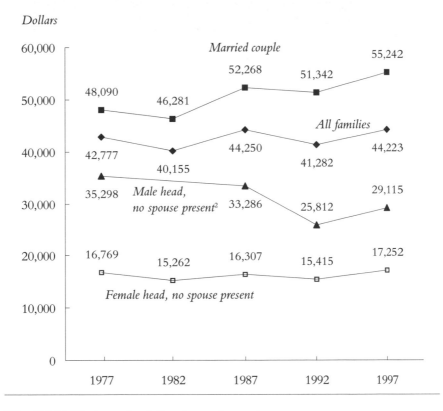

[1]The CPI-U-X1 was used to inflate the earnings series.
[2]Data not available for 1982.

Source: Bureau of the Census, *Historical Income Tables*, Table F-10, <http://www.census.gov/hhes/income/histinc/>.

Table 6-2 • Sources of Personal Income for Women Age 15–64 by Race and Hispanic Origin, 1997[1]

Work is by far the most common source of income for women of working age and yields by far the most income. In 1997, close to 80 percent of all women between the ages of 15 and 65 had wage-and-salary income averaging $21,313. Black women were slightly more likely than white and Hispanic women to have wage-and-salary income, but earned less than white women. Comparatively few black and Hispanic women have income from assets, such as interest and dividends, and those who do usually average less income than white women from these sources—Hispanic women's dividends being the exception.

| | Women with Income from Source | | Mean Income from Source (in dollars) |
	Number (in thousands)	Percentage	
Total with income[2]			
All races	79,354	100.0	20,581
White	65,197	100.0	20,939
Black	10,406	100.0	18,172
Hispanic origin[3]	7,193	100.0	15,140
Wage and salary			
All races	62,491	78.7	21,313
White	51,263	78.6	21,604
Black	8,341	80.2	19,012
Hispanic origin	5,597	77.8	16,530
Self-employment[4]			
All races	4,419	5.6	12,998
White	3,953	6.1	12,815
Black	257	2.5	11,585
Hispanic origin	238	3.3	9,189

(continued)

[1]The income shown in this table is personal income. In the case of a woman who lives alone, or who is the sole support of a family, her personal income constitutes the household's entire income.
[2]Totals comprise women who had personal income from any source in 1997. However, not every source of income is detailed in this table.
[3]Persons of Hispanic origin may be of any race. In this table, Hispanics are included in the racial categories as well as in the Hispanic category. *See* footnote to Table 1-1.
[4]Excludes farm self-employment, from which 558,000 women had income in 1997.

Table 6-2 (continued)

| | Women with Income from Source | | Mean Income from Source (in dollars) |
	Number (in thousands)	Percentage	
Unemployment compensation			
All races	2,433	3.1	2,319
White	1,822	2.8	2,239
Black	497	4.8	2,640
Hispanic origin	282	3.9	2,321
Social Security			
All races	4,829	6.1	6,536
White	3,916	6.0	6,574
Black	770	7.4	6,422
Hispanic origin	372	5.2	5,635
AFDC[5]			
All races	2,508	3.2	3,528
White	1,461	2.2	3,458
Black	917	8.8	3,410
Hispanic origin	574	8.0	4,037
Interest			
All races	42,511	53.6	1,345
White	37,661	57.8	1,402
Black	2,984	28.7	805
Hispanic origin	2,208	30.7	645
Child support			
All races	4,757	6.0	3,699
White	3,913	6.0	3,904
Black	751	7.2	2,659
Hispanic origin	435	6.0	3,216
Dividends			
All races	12,738	16.1	2,374
White	11,669	17.9	2,386
Black	580	5.6	2,199
Hispanic origin	362	5.0	3,437

[5]Excludes 102,000 women who also receive another kind of public assistance.

Source: Bureau of the Census, Current Population Survey, March 1998, Table PinC-12, <http://ferret.bls.census.gov/macro/031998/perinc/12_000.htm>.

Table 6-3 • Sources of Personal Income for People Age 65 and Over by Sex, 1997[1]

On average, men over 65 have nearly 80 percent more personal income than women over 65, and receive income from a larger variety of sources. Moreover, with an occasional exception, men average more income from any given source than women do—in important instances, much more income. For example, older men are not only more than twice as likely as older women to receive pension income but the amount the men average is more than 75 percent larger. Older men are more likely than older women to have income from assets (i.e., interest, dividends, rents and royalties) and, except for dividends, average more from these sources.

| | People with Income from Source | | Mean Income from Source (in dollars) |
	Number (in thousands)	Percentage	
Total with income[2]			
Women	18,093	100.0	14,820
Men	13,308	100.0	26,543
Earnings			
Women	2,188	12.1	12,695
Men	2,735	20.6	28,705
Social Security			
Women	16,804	92.9	7,596
Men	12,037	90.4	10,217
Supplemental Security Income (SSI)			
Women	1,008	5.6	3,118
Men	355	2.7	3,832
Survivors' benefits			
Women	1,335	7.4	7,766
Men	199	1.5	11,642
Pensions			
Women	4,009	22.2	7,354
Men	6,204	46.6	13,078

(continued)

[1]The income shown in this table is personal income. In the case of an individual who lives alone, or who is the sole support of a family, personal income would constitute the household's entire income.

[2]Totals comprise people who had income from any source in 1997. However, not every source of income is detailed in this table.

Table 6-3 (continued)

| | People with Income from Source | | Mean Income from Source (in dollars) |
	Number (in thousands)	Percentage	
Interest			
Women	10,812	59.8	3,798
Men	8,517	64.0	4,192
Dividends			
Women	3,266	18.1	4,948
Men	3,084	23.2	4,614
Rents and royalties			
Women	1,579	8.7	5,381
Men	1,453	10.9	5,450

Source: Bureau of the Census, Current Population Survey, March 1998, Table PinC-12, <http://ferret.bls.census.gov/macro/031998/perinc/12_000.htm>.

Table 6-4 • Sources of Personal Income for White, Black, and Hispanic Women
Age 65 and Over, 1997[1]

As Table 6-3 shows, older women have much lower incomes, on average, than older men. Being black or Hispanic deepens women's disadvantage. Compared with white women, black and Hispanic women have fewer sources of income and, as a rule, less income from any given source. One notable exception is the average pension income received by black women which, in 1997, was nearly $1,500 more than that received by white women.

| | Women with Income from Source | | Mean Income from Source (in dollars) |
	Number (in thousands)	Percentage	
Total with income[2]			
White	16,155	100.0	15,165
Black	1,555	100.0	11,540
Hispanic[3]	863	100.0	9,249
Earnings			
White	1,938	12.0	12,883
Black	191	12.3	9,991
Hispanic	80	9.3	—[4]
Social Security			
White	15,104	93.5	7,635
Black	1,421	91.4	7,343
Hispanic	734	85.1	5,923

(continued)

[1]The income shown in this table is personal income. In the case of a woman who lives alone or who is the sole support of a family, her personal income constitutes the household's entire income.

[2]Totals comprise women who had income from any source in 1997. However, not every source of income is detailed in this table.

[3]Persons of Hispanic origin may be of any race. In this table, Hispanics are included in the racial categories as well as in the Hispanic category. See footnote to Table 1-1.

[4]The unpublished Census Bureau data on which this table was based show more than $17,112 in average earnings for older Hispanic women with earnings in 1997. The editors decided to omit this figure, which is based on a relatively small sample, because it is twice as high as the comparable figure for 1995 and seems inconsistent with the overall income average for Hispanic older women.

Table 6-4 (continued)

	Women with Income from Source		Mean Income from Source (in dollars)
	Number (in thousands)	Percentage	
Supplemental Security Income (SSI)			
White	675	4.2	2,960
Black	264	17.0	3,106
Hispanic	211	24.4	3,278
Survivors' benefits			
White	1,237	7.7	7,830
Black	79	5.1	7,462
Hispanic	31	3.6	—[5]
Pensions			
White	3,635	22.5	7,218
Black	297	19.1	8,700
Hispanic	102	11.8	5,683
Interest			
White	10,216	63.2	3,873
Black	441	28.4	1,633
Hispanic	242	28.0	1,831
Dividends			
White	3,161	19.6	4,961
Black	41	2.6	—[5]
Hispanic	24	2.8	—[5]
Rents and royalties			
White	1,504	9.3	5,246
Black	42	2.7	—[5]
Hispanic	36	4.2	—[5]

[5]The number of women reporting income from this source was too small for a reliable estimate of mean income.

Source: Bureau of the Census, Current Population Survey, March 1998, Table PinC-12, <http://ferret.bls.census.gov/macro/031998/perinc/12_000.htm>.

Table 6-5 • Poverty Rates of Individuals by Sex, Age, Race, and Hispanic Origin, 1997 (numbers are in thousands)

Females are more likely than their male contemporaries to be poor. This is the case at every age and in every group shown here.

	Females			Males		
	Total	In Poverty		Total	In Poverty	
	Number	Number	Percent	Number	Number	Percent
Total	137,105	20,387	14.9	131,376	15,187	11.6
Age						
Under 18	34,702	6,934	20.0	36,367	7,179	19.7
18 and over	102,403	13,453	13.1	95,009	8,008	8.4
18–24	12,568	2,657	21.1	12,633	1,760	13.9
25–44	42,235	5,629	13.3	41,580	3,382	8.1
45–64	29,041	2,744	9.4	27,271	1,915	7.0
65 and over	18,558	2,423	13.1	13,524	953	7.0
Race						
White	112,154	13,944	12.4	109,047	10,452	9.6
Black	18,382	5,317	28.9	16,076	3,799	23.6
Asian/Pacific Islander	5,426	826	15.2	5,056	642	12.7
Hispanic[1]	14,968	4,463	29.8	15,670	3,845	24.5

[1]Persons of Hispanic origin may be of any race. In this table, Hispanics are included in the racial categories as well as in the Hispanic category. *See* footnote to Table 1-1.

Source: Bureau of the Census, *Poverty in the United States: 1997*, 1998, Table 2; and unpublished data from the March 1998 Current Population Survey.

Figure 6-3 • Poverty Rates of Families with Children by Family Type, 1977–1997[1]

Single-parent families, whatever the sex of the custodial parent, are far more likely to be poor than two-parent families are. However, the poverty rate for female-headed families with children is more than double the rate for male-headed families with children.

Poverty Rate

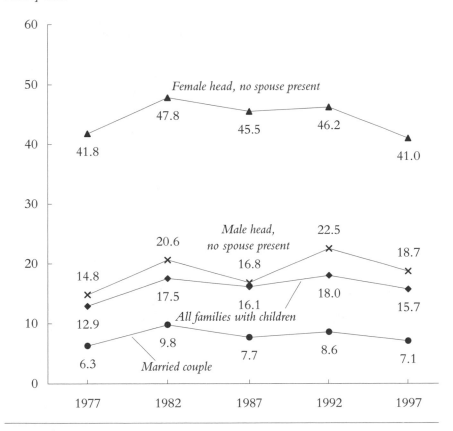

[1]Families that include related children under 18.

Source: Bureau of the Census, *Poverty in the United States: 1997*, 1998, Table C-3.

Figure 6-4 • Poverty Rates of Families by Family Type and Presence of Children, 1997

As a whole, families that do not include minor children are rarely poor. Their poverty rates are much lower than the rates for their counterparts of the same family type that do include children. But, having a female head increases a family's risk of poverty even when there are no children present.

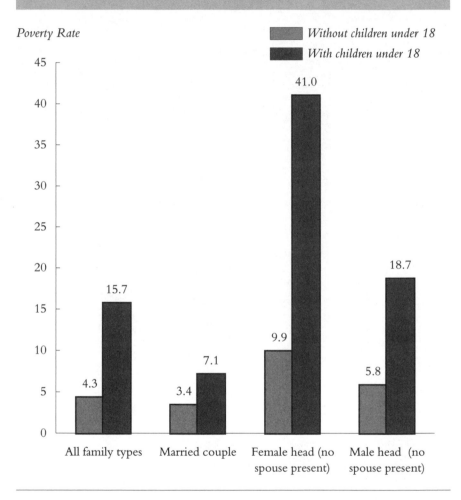

Source: Bureau of the Census, *Poverty in the United States: 1997*, 1998, Table C-3.

Table 6-6 • Poverty Rates of White, Black, and Hispanic Families by Family Type and Presence of Children, 1997[1]

The type of family and the presence or absence of minor children are not the only factors that affect a family's risk of poverty—race and ethnicity are involved, as well. A white family of any type, with or without children, is less likely to be poor than its black or Hispanic counterparts. A Hispanic family of any type, with or without children, is more likely to be poor than its white or black counterparts.

| | *Percentage in Poverty* | | | |
| | *All Family Types* | *Married-Couple Families* | *Families with* | |
			Female Head[2]	*Male Head[2]*
White families, total	8.4	4.8	27.7	11.9
Families with children	13.0	6.7	37.6	17.5
Families without children	3.7	3.1	8.4	4.6
Black families, total	23.6	8.0	39.8	19.6
Families with children	30.5	9.0	46.9	25.6
Families without children	9.6	6.5	14.7	12.0
Hispanic[3] families, total	24.7	17.4	47.6	21.7
Families with children	30.4	21.0	54.2	30.5
Families without children	11.2	9.5	20.6	8.6

[1]Related children under age 18.
[2]With no spouse present.
[3]Persons of Hispanic origin may be of any race. In this table, Hispanics are included in the racial categories as well as in the Hispanic category. *See* footnote to Table 1-1.

Source: Bureau of the Census, *Poverty in the United States: 1997*, 1998, Table C–3.

Table 6-7 • Poverty Rates of Unrelated Individuals by Sex and Age, 1997 [1]

Poverty rates are high among unrelated individuals of both sexes. (These are people who live alone or in the households of nonrelatives.) Still, at every age, female unrelated individuals are more likely than their male counterparts to be poor.

	Females		Males	
	Total Number (in thousands)	Percentage in Poverty	Total Number (in thousands)	Percentage in Poverty
Under 18	135	94.0	107	86.7
18–24	2,548	41.4	2,645	30.5
25–34	3,334	17.3	5,216	11.9
35–44	2,579	17.9	4,378	14.7
45–54	2,844	20.0	3,022	16.0
55–59	1,259	25.1	981	18.7
60–64	1,285	27.0	704	24.8
65–74	3,163	22.4	1,377	15.6
75 and over	4,720	22.8	1,375	16.9
Total	21,868	24.0	19,804	17.4

[1]Unrelated individuals are people who live alone or with nonrelatives.

Source: Bureau of the Census, Current Population Survey, March 1998, Table 1, <http://ferret.bls.census.gov/macro/031998/pov/new1_000.htm>.

Figure 6-5 • Poverty Rates of People Age 65 and Over and Age 75 and Over by Sex, 1987–1997

People who think that poverty is no longer a significant problem for America's older people are overlooking older women. One in eight women over age 65 is poor, compared with about one in 14 men over 65. The poverty rate among women over 75 is more than twice that among men over 75.

Poverty Rate

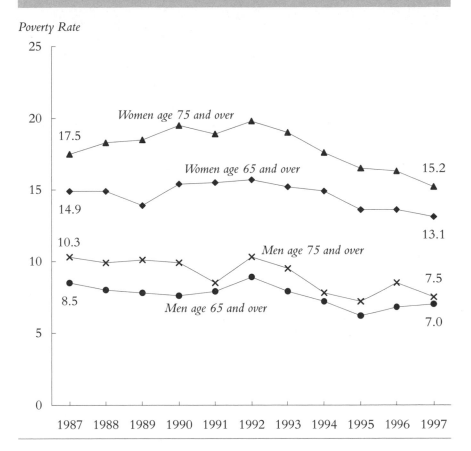

Source: Bureau of the Census, *65+ in the United States,* 1996, Table 4-4; *Income, Poverty, and Valuation of Noncash Benefits: 1993,* 1995, Table 8; *Income, Poverty, and Valuation of Noncash Benefits: 1994,* 1996, Table 9; *Poverty in the United States: 1987,* 1989, Table 11; *Poverty in the United States: 1988 and 1989,* 1991, Tables 5 and 24; *Poverty in the United States: 1990,* 1991, Table 6; *Poverty in the United States: 1991,* 1992, Table 6; *Poverty in the United States: 1995,* 1996, Table 2; *Poverty in the United States: 1996,* 1997, Table 2; and *Poverty in the United States: 1997,* 1998, Table 2.

Table 6-8 • Women Age 65 and Over Living Alone by Ratio of Income to Poverty Level, Race, and Hispanic Origin, 1997 (in percentages)

Being poor or perilously close to it is the reality for most older women who live alone. Of the 7.6 million women over 65 who lived alone in 1997, more than 22 percent had incomes at or below $7,698 (the 1997 poverty threshold for single people over 65). Only one-third had more than twice the threshold ($15,396). Because the great majority of older women who live alone are white, the overall statistics largely reflect the situation of white women. Hispanic and black women are in far worse straits.

	Race and Hispanic Origin			
Women Age 65 and Over Living Alone	*All Races[1]*	*White*	*Black*	*Hispanic[2]*
Percentage with income below				
100 percent of poverty	22.4	20.4	40.0	54.0
125 percent of poverty	35.8	33.4	57.2	71.0
150 percent of poverty	47.8	45.4	70.7	79.7
200 percent of poverty	66.0	64.5	81.0	89.8
Total number (in thousands)	7,577	6,807	663	256

[1]Includes Asian/Pacific Islanders and Native Americans, not shown separately (data not available).

[2]Persons of Hispanic origin may be of any race. In this table, Hispanics are included in the racial categories as well as in the Hispanic category. *See* footnote to Table 1-1.

Source: Bureau of the Census, *Poverty in the United States: 1997,* 1998, Tables 1 and 2.

Table 6-9 • The Housing Cost Burden by Household Type and Tenure, Selected Age Groups, 1997[1]

Whatever their household type, renters typically spend a much larger proportion of income for housing than owners do. Older householders of both sexes who rent have a heavy housing cost burden, but the heaviest is borne by older women who live alone—55 percent of their income went to housing in 1997 (and this was exclusive of any public subsidy they might have received).

	Housing Costs as a Percentage of Income[2]	
	Owners	Renters
Two-or-more-person households		
Married couples, all ages	13.9	22.8
Age 25–29	17.5	21.7
Age 30–34	18.0	21.5
Age 35–44	16.5	22.4
Age 45–64	11.8	21.8
Age 65 and over	14.1	38.6
Female householders, all ages	21.2	44.6
Age 65 and over	15.7	42.1
Male householders, all ages	17.7	32.9
Age 65 and over	14.9	49.0
One-person households		
Female householders, all ages	23.0	44.1
Age 65 and over	24.7	55.0
Male householders, all ages	15.6	27.3
Age 65 and over	18.7	43.0

[1]The age group refers to the age of the person identified as the householder. In the case of married couples, this is usually—but not necessarily—the husband.
[2]Median housing costs; median income.

Source: Bureau of the Census and Department of Housing and Urban Development, *American Housing Survey for the United States in 1997,* 1999, Tables 3-20, 3-21, 4-20, and 4-21.

SECTION 7:
WOMEN IN THE MILITARY

THE LAST STATUTORY barriers to women's full participation in the defense of this country fell in the mid-1990s when Congress repealed the laws that prohibited women from serving on combat ships and aircraft. The repeal opened the pathway to the top enlisted and officer positions for women in the Navy and the Air Force.

However, certain Defense Department policies keep women from participating in the full range of military duties. By policy, women cannot serve on Navy submarines or in the SEALS. By policy, women cannot serve in units whose primary mission is ground combat—infantry, armor, special forces, and most artillery units—or in units that routinely collocate with ground-combat units. This policy effectively denies women access to most top positions in the Army and Marine Corps.

There are also systemic blocks to women's progress and full participation in the military, long a male institution whose equipment, procedures, standards, and ideals were designed by and for men. Men served in the military because it was a responsibility of citizenship; women were permitted to serve only when there were insufficient men or when certain skills deemed womanly, such as nursing, were required. Women's roles in the military were ancillary, artificially determined, and limited by law, policy, and idealizations of femininity and masculinity. Judith Youngman discusses these matters more fully in Chapter Five.

This situation began to change in the early 1970s when the military draft ended and the all-volunteer force began. Since then, the numbers of women in the armed services have gradually increased and women's roles have gradually expanded. By the early 1990s, women had served with distinction in military operations in Grenada, Panama, and the Gulf War. Their superb service in the Gulf War convinced Congress to repeal the statute that forbade women to serve on aircraft or ships with combat missions. Women now command warships, and, in 1998, women flew in air combat missions for the first time in U.S. history.

- Women currently constitute 14 percent of U.S. service personnel, but they are not spread evenly through the services or the ranks. The Marine Corps has the smallest percentage of women; the Air Force has the largest (see Table 7-1).
- Since 1972, the percentage of enlisted women has grown almost ninefold and the percentage of women officers has more than tripled. Nevertheless, compared with their overall representation in the services, women are underrepresented in the senior officer and enlisted ranks. However, it takes 15 to 20 years to reach these ranks, so the situation should gradually improve (see Figures 7-1 and 7-2 and Tables 7-2 and 7-3).
- All occupations and positions in the Coast Guard are open to women, as are 99 percent of those in the Air Force. Ninety-six percent of Navy occupations and 91 percent of Navy positions are open to women. However, although most Army and Marine Corps occupations are open to women, a third of Army positions and nearly two-fifths of Marine Corps positions are closed to them (see Figure 7-3).
- A disproportionate number of military women are in health care and support and administration occupations. To some extent, this is because most women currently on active duty entered military service before the major changes to the combat restriction laws in 1991 and 1994 expanded occupational opportunities for women (see Figures 7-4 and 7-5).

Table 7-1 • Active Duty Servicewomen by Branch of Service, Rank, Race, and Hispanic Origin, May 31, 1999

As of May 31, 1999, women in the military (including the Coast Guard) numbered 194,219—14 percent of the total active force. The Air Force has the highest percentage of women; the Marine Corps has the lowest. The Army has the highest percentage of African American women; the Marine Corps has the highest percentage of women of Hispanic origin. The Navy is the only service with a higher percentage of women serving in its officer ranks than in its enlisted ranks.

Service and Rank[1]	Number of Women	Women as a Percentage of Total Personnel	Percent Distribution of Women[2]			
			White	Black	Hispanic	Other
Total DOD forces[3]						
Enlisted	160,383	14.1	50.8	34.9	7.9	6.4
Officers	30,425	13.9	75.1	14.7	3.5	6.7
Army						
Enlisted	58,119	15.0	38.7	47.0	7.2	7.1
Officers	10,219	13.2	67.3	21.8	4.1	6.8
Navy						
Enlisted	39,572	12.8	52.0	30.9	10.2	6.9
Officers	7,711	14.3	78.9	10.3	4.7	6.1
Marine Corps						
Enlisted	9,060	5.9	55.8	23.5	14.4	6.2
Officers	866	4.8	77.1	12.5	5.0	5.4
Air Force						
Enlisted	53,632	18.7	62.3	26.6	5.7	5.3
Officers	11,629	16.7	79.3	11.6	2.0	7.1
Coast Guard						
Enlisted	2,726	10.0	73.4	12.8	7.5	6.3
Officers	685	9.8	81.3	7.3	4.5	6.9

[1]Officers include warrant officers.
[2]Percentages may not total 100.0 due to rounding.
[3]Defense Department (DOD) forces do not include the Coast Guard, which, in peacetime, is part of the Department of Transportation.

Source: U.S. Department of Defense, Defense Manpower Data Center, unpublished data, May 31, 1999.

Figure 7-1 • Active Duty Servicewomen in the Department of Defense Services by Officer/Enlisted Status, 1972–1999 (in percentages)[1]

Since 1972, the year before the beginning of the all-volunteer force, the percentage of enlisted women has grown almost ninefold and the percentage of women officers has more than tripled.

Percentage

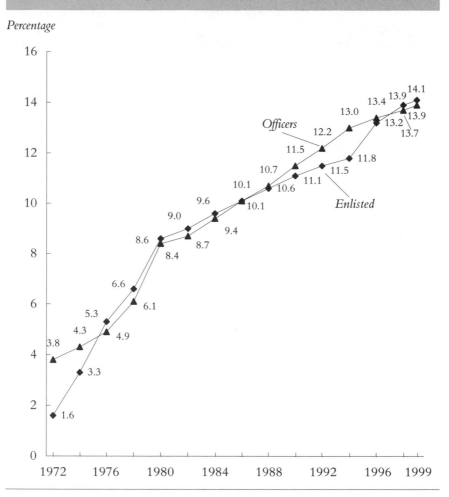

[1]Does not include the Coast Guard, which, in peacetime, is part of the Department of Transportation.

Source: U.S. Department of Defense, Defense Manpower Data Center, unpublished data, August 1997 and May 31, 1999.

Figure 7-2 • Women in Senior Enlisted and Officer Pay Grades by Branch of
Service, Selected Years, 1972–1999 (in percentages)

A key, yet usually overlooked, measure of women's status in the military is their
growing seniority. These charts depict women as a percentage of the three senior
enlisted pay grades and as a percentage of pay grade O6 (colonel or Navy captain). More women are now reaching the flag/general officer ranks, and each of
the DOD services has, has had, or soon will have a woman serving at the three-
star level (vice admiral/lieutenant general).

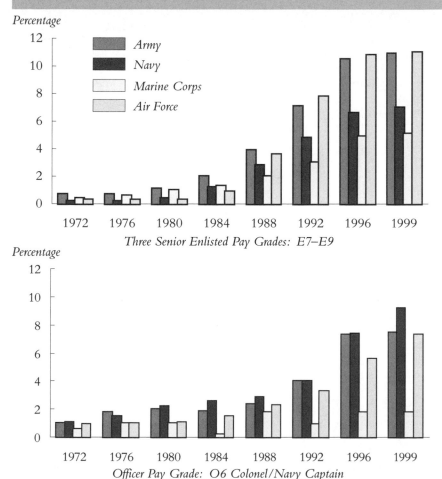

Source: U.S. Department of Defense, Defense Manpower Data Center, unpublished data,
August 1997 and May 31, 1999.

Table 7-2 • Active Duty Servicewomen by Pay Grade Grouping and Branch of Service, May 31, 1999[1]

Women are still underrepresented in the senior enlisted and officer ranks. However, it takes 15-20 years to reach these ranks, so the situation should gradually improve. (It should be noted that, as this is written, the Air Force has nominated a woman for lieutenant general and the Coast Guard has selected an active-duty woman for promotion to rear admiral [lower half[2]]. A woman rear admiral [upper half] of the U.S. Public Health Service currently serves as Chief of the Coast Guard's Health and Safety.)

Service and Pay Grade Grouping	Number of Women	Women as a Percentage of Total Personnel in Pay Grade
Army		
Officers, total	10,219	13.2
General (O7–O10)	7	2.8
Senior (O6)	274	7.6
Midgrade (O4–O5)	2,914	12.5
Junior (O1–O3, W1–W5)	7,024	14.2
Enlisted, total	58,119	15.0
Senior (E7–E9)	5,706	10.9
Midgrade (E5–E6)	17,100	13.6
Junior (E1–E4)	35,313	16.8
Navy		
Officers, total	7,711	14.3
Flag (O7–O10)	9	4.1
Senior (O6)	311	9.3
Midgrade (O4–O5)	2,517	14.3
Junior (O1–O3, W1–W5)	4,874	14.8
Enlisted, total	39,572	13.1
Senior (E7–E9)	2,284	7.0
Midgrade (E5–E6)	11,245	9.2
Junior (E1–E4)	26,043	16.8

(continued)

[1]Excludes women selected for, but not yet actually serving in, each pay grade grouping as of May 31, 1999.
[2]Rear admiral (lower half) is the equivalent of brigadier general. The rank insignia is one silver star. Rear admiral (upper half) is the equivalent of major general. The rank insignia is two silver stars.

Table 7-2 (continued)

Service and Pay Grade Grouping	Number of Women	Women as a Percentage of Total Personnel in Pay Grade
Marine Corps		
Officers, total	866	4.8
General (O7–O10)	1	1.3
Senior (O6)	11	1.8
Midgrade (O4–O5)	149	2.9
Junior (O1–O3, W1–W5)	705	5.7
Enlisted, total	9,060	5.9
Senior (E7–E9)	687	5.1
Midgrade (E5–E6)	2,023	5.2
Junior (E1–E4)	6,350	6.2
Air Force		
Officers, total	11,629	16.7
General (O7–O10)	8	2.9
Senior (O6)	293	7.3
Midgrade (O4–O5)	3,674	14.0
Junior (O1–O3, W1–W5)	7,654	19.6
Enlisted, total	53,632	18.7
Senior (E7–E9)	4,190	11.0
Midgrade (E5–E6)	15,293	13.8
Junior (E1–E4)	34,149	24.6
Coast Guard		
Officers, total	685	9.8
Flag (O7–O10)	0	0
Senior (O6)	5	1.5
Midgrade (O4–O5)	117	6.4
Junior (O1–O3, W1–W5)	563	11.6
Enlisted, total	2,726	10
Senior (E7–E9)	152	4.3
Midgrade (E5–E6)	964	8.7
Junior (E1–E4)	1610	12.5

Source: U.S. Department of Defense, Defense Manpower Data Center, unpublished data, May 31, 1999.

Table 7-3 • Women as a Percentage of Personnel in Military Pay Grades, Department of Defense Services, 1999

Women now constitute 14.1 percent of the total armed forces (Army–14.7; Navy–13.1; Marine Corps–5.8; Air Force–18.3). Since it takes 15-20 years to reach the senior enlisted and officer pay grades, and since the percentage of military personnel who were female was considerably smaller 15-20 years ago (*see* Figure 7-1) than is the case today, women constitute a smaller share of the population of the senior pay grades.

Pay Grade	Total DOD[1]	Army	Navy	Marine Corps	Air Force
Officers					
O7–O10	2.8	2.1	4.1	1.3	2.9
O6	7.6	7.6	9.3	1.8	7.3
O5	11.8	11.6	13.0	3.2	12.5
O4	13.5	13.1	15.3	2.7	15.0
O3	15.7	15.4	15.3	3.5	18.6
O2	16.9	17.7	15.8	7.1	21.1
O1	17.1	18.2	15.1	8.2	22.0
W5	1.1	0.3	—[2]	4.2	—[3]
W4	2.8	2.3	3.8	3.8	—[3]
W3	4.2	4.0	3.9	6.4	—[3]
W2	8.4	8.8	6.7	7.2	—[3]
W1	8.4	9.0	—[2]	6.0	—[3]
Enlisted					
E9	6.0	5.9	3.1	2.6	9.8
E8	8.9	10.0	6.3	4.8	12.2
E7	10.0	11.7	7.8	5.6	11.0
E6	9.8	12.2	8.6	5.1	11.5
E5	12.5	14.8	9.8	5.4	15.2
E4	17.1	17.5	15.4	6.1	23.2
E3	17.5	17.1	18.8	6.5	26.1
E2	15.7	15.5	17.1	6.4	25.6
E1	15.7	14.2	16.5	5.9	25.5

[1]Does not include the Coast Guard, which, in peacetime, is part of the Department of Transportation.
[2]Navy personnel who are warrant officers serve in pay grades W2, W3, and W4 only.
[3]The Air Force does not have any personnel serving in the warrant officer ranks.

Source: U.S. Department of Defense, Defense Manpower Data Center, unpublished data, May 31, 1999.

Figure 7-3 • Positions and Occupations Currently Open to Active Duty Women by Branch of Service, 1999 (in percentages)[1]

The term "occupation" refers to an occupational specialty. The term "position" refers to a particular job in a given unit. For example, the occupation of hospital corpsman is open to Navy women, but the position of hospital corpsman aboard a submarine is closed to them. The major fields closed to women include infantry, armor, special forces/SEAL, and submarine warfare. All are associated with ground combat except submarine warfare, which remains closed due to "habitability" (i.e., close living quarters) aboard submarines.

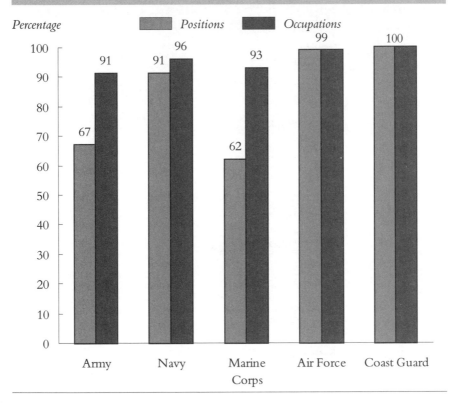

[1]The most recent major changes with respect to the occupations and positions open to military women were made in 1994. In 1999, the Navy opened Coastal Mine Hunters and Mine Counter Measure (MCM) ships to women. Enlisted women do not serve on MCM's.

Source: U.S. Department of Defense, Office of the Assistant Secretary of Defense, Public Affairs News Release no. 449–94, July 29, 1994; and Staff of the Office of the Chief of Naval Operations, unpublished data, 1999.

Figure 7-4 • Occupational Profile of Active Duty Enlisted Personnel in the Department of Defense Services by Sex, 1999 (percent distributions)[1,2]

Most women currently on active duty entered military service before the major changes to the combat restriction laws, which opened new occupations and positions to them, were made in 1991 and 1994. That explains, to some extent, the disproportionate number of women in health care and support and administration. It will be interesting to see if these proportions change now that women entering the services have more options.

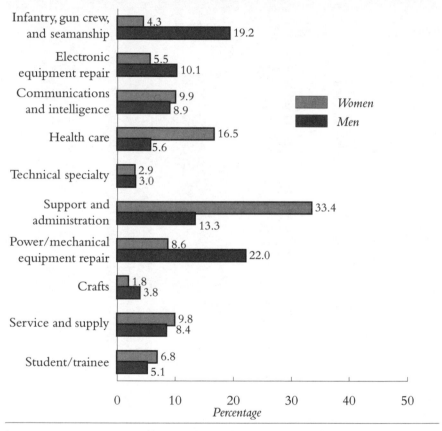

[1]Does not include the Coast Guard, which, in peacetime, is part of the Department of Transportation.
[2]Percentages may not total 100.0 due to rounding.

Source: U.S. Department of Defense, Defense Manpower Data Center, unpublished data, May 31, 1999.

Figure 7-5 • Occupational Profile of Active Duty Officers in the Department of Defense Services by Sex, 1999 (percent distributions)[1,2]

The changes in the combat restriction laws in 1991 and 1994 opened air and sea combat positions to women officers. However, infantry, armor, and most field artillery and special forces positions remain closed to them. Thus, women in the Navy and Air Force can now enter most of their services' key warfighting occupations, whereas women in the Army and Marine Corps can enter only aviation combat positions.

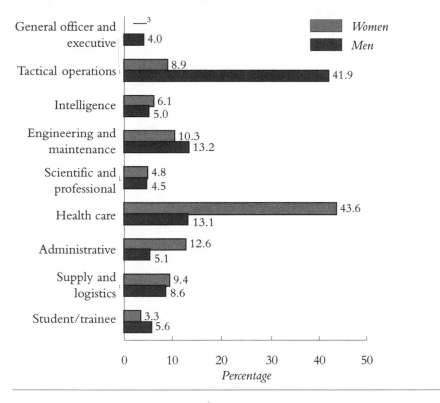

[1]Does not include the Coast Guard, which, in peacetime, is part of the Department of Transportation.
[2]Percentages may not total 100.0 due to rounding.
[3]Less than one-tenth of one percent.

Source: U.S. Department of Defense, Defense Manpower Data Center, unpublished data, May 31, 1999.

Table 7-4 • Women Graduates of U.S. Service Academies, 1980, 1990, and 1999

The first women to attend the service academies graduated in 1980. Since that time, the percentage of women in each graduating class has gradually increased. The most dramatic increase has been in the proportion of women in the graduating classes of the Coast Guard Academy, where, in the class of 1999, women constituted almost a third of the graduates.

Service Academy	Women as a Percentage of Graduates			Number of Women in Class of 1999
	Class of 1980	Class of 1990	Class of 1999	
Air Force	10.9	10.4	14.7	140
Coast Guard	9.2	12.6	31.5	42
Military (West Point)	6.8	9.8	13.4	125
Naval Academy	5.8	9.7	15.2	132

Source: Department of Defense, unpublished data provided by each service academy, June 1993 and June 1999; and Department of Transportation, unpublished data provided by the Coast Guard Academy, June 1993 and June 1999.

Figure 7-6 • Female and Male Veterans by Age, 1998 (numbers are in thousands)

Most women veterans served either during World War II or after 1972, when the all-volunteer force was implemented. As more military occupations and positions have opened to women over the last 25 years, more women have been able to serve. So even though the percentage of adult citizens who are veterans has been shrinking, the percentage of veterans who are women has been growing and will continue to grow.

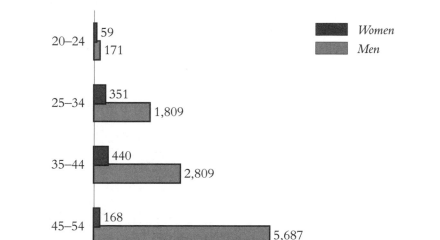

Age

Source: Bureau of Labor Statistics, unpublished data from the 1998 Current Population Survey (annual averages).

Figure 7-7 • Female and Male Veterans by Race, 1998 (percent distributions)[1]

This chart depicts veterans by race. It is interesting to note that white males represent 88 percent of all male veterans, while white women represent a smaller percentage of all female veterans—80 percent. Whereas African American men represent 9.3 percent of male veterans, African American women represent over 17 percent of female veterans. Based on current active-duty populations, the percentage of women veterans who are African American is projected to grow over the coming years.

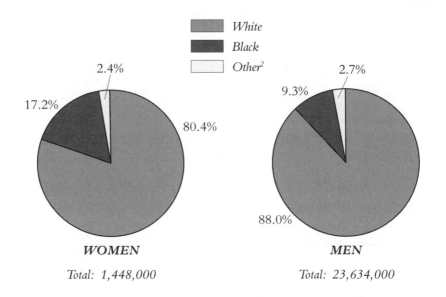

☐ White
☐ Black
☐ Other[2]

WOMEN

2.4%
17.2%
80.4%

Total: 1,448,000

MEN

2.7%
9.3%
88.0%

Total: 23,634,000

[1]People age 20 years and over.
[2]Includes Asian/Pacific Islanders and Native Americans, not shown separately (data not available).

Source: Bureau of Labor Statistics, unpublished data from the 1998 Current Population Survey (annual averages).

SECTION 8:
ELECTIONS AND OFFICIALS

THIS SECTION INCLUDES several figures and tables about the gender gap at the polls. The statistics about voters' preferences on which the figures and tables are based were taken from exit polls and other postelection surveys that were conducted for the New York Times Company by Voter News Service, an independent polling firm. This is a first for *The American Woman*'s "Statistical Profile," which, as a rule, eschews statistics from nongovernment sources. However, our government does not collect statistics about how people vote.[1]

The national election of the year 2000 will precede publication of this book by a few months. If the patterns of the last five presidential elections and the last 10 elections for the House of Representatives are again evident, there will be a gender gap in voters' preferences. Whether it will affect the outcome depends on several variables, such as the size of the gap and the percentage of women who vote compared with the percentage of men who vote. From this vantage point, it seems safe only to assume that women will turn out to vote in larger proportions than men, as they have in every presidential election from 1980 through 1996.

- Women voters have outnumbered male voters in presidential-year national elections since at least 1964; beginning with 1980, women have been more likely than men to vote (see Table 8-1).
- In each of the five presidential elections from 1980 through 1996, there was a gender gap in voters' preferences: women were more likely than

[1]The Census Bureau collects statistics on the number and demographic characteristics of people who report having voted, but, unfortunately, not even its 1998 statistics will be released in time for them to appear in this edition of *The American Woman*.

men to vote for the Democratic candidate. However, women were not necessarily more likely to vote for the Democratic candidate than for the Republican candidate (see Figure 8-1).

- The gender gap in voting preferences waxed and waned in the presidential elections from 1980 through 1996; it was at its widest in 1996, when female voters were 11 percentage points more likely than male voters to vote for the Democratic candidate. More important to the outcome was that the Democratic candidate received an absolute majority (54 percent) of women's votes (see Figure 8-2).

- As measured by the percentage of female and male voters who voted for Democratic presidential candidates, the gender gap has been consistently narrowest among voters who are high school graduates but have gone no further with their education, and widest among college graduates (see Table 8-2).

- At least since 1980, men have been more likely than women to vote for Republican candidates for the House of Representatives. This gender gap widened sharply in 1994, when 58 percent of male voters voted Republican and 53 percent of female voters voted Democratic. The 1994 elections gave the Republicans a majority in the House for the first time in decades (see Figure 8-3).

- Women's progress in winning seats in state legislatures has been a "leading indicator" of their progress in winning seats in Congress. Women have also made great strides in gaining statewide executive office. However, at no level are women approaching parity with men (see Table 8-3).

- Over the seven-year period shown here, the number of female federal judges increased by 73 percent. As of 1998, about one in five federal judgeships was held by a woman, up from roughly one in eight in 1991 (see Table 8-4).

Table 8-1 • Voter Participation in National Elections in Presidential Election Years by Sex, 1964–1996

Female voters have outnumbered male voters in presidential-year national elections since at least 1964; beginning with 1980, women have been more likely than men to vote—that is, women's representation among voters has been larger than their representation in the population of voting age. The reverse is true for men.

	People Who Reported Voting as a Percentage of the Voting Age Population		Number Who Reported Voting (numbers are in thousands)	
	Women	*Men*	*Women*	*Men*
1964	67.0	71.9	39,183	37,476
1968	66.0	69.8	40,967	38,016
1972	62.0	64.1	44,869	40,917
1976	58.8	59.6	45,624	41,098
1980	59.4	59.1	49,304	43,782
1984	60.8	59.0	54,499	47,393
1988	58.3	56.4	54,550	47,675
1992	62.3	60.2	60,509	53,311
1996	55.5	52.8	56,066	48,910

Source: Bureau of the Census, *Historical Time Series Tables*, Table 5, <http://www.census.gov/population/www/socdemo/voting.html>.

Figure 8-1 • How Women and Men Reported Voting in Presidential Elections, 1980–1996 (percent distributions)[1]

This figure shows how people said they voted in each of the presidential elections from 1980 through 1996, by the party of the candidate for whom they voted.[2] In all five elections, women were more likely than men to vote for the Democratic candidate, but not necessarily more likely to vote for the Democratic candidate than for the Republican candidate. Third-party candidate Ross Perot, a major factor in the outcome in 1992, had more success with men than with women.

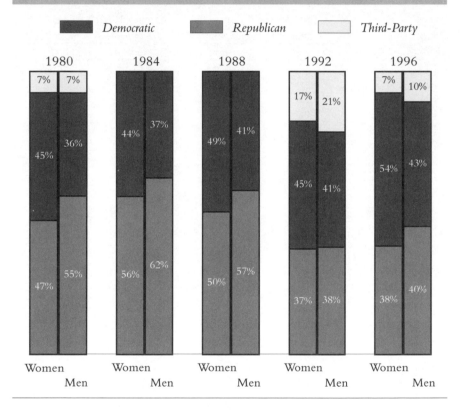

[1]1980: Reagan (R), Carter (D), Anderson; 1984: Reagan (R), Mondale (D); 1988: Bush (R), Dukakis (D); 1992: Clinton (D), Bush (R), Perot; 1996: Clinton (D), Dole (R), Perot.
[2]In 1980, 1992, and 1996, there were third-party candidates of some consequence; votes for these candidates are designated "other." Votes for minor-party candidates are omitted.

Source: The New York Times Company, "The Vote Under a Microscope," *The New York Times*, 1997, <http://www.nytimes.com/library/politics/elect-port.html>.

Figure 8-2 • People Who Reported Voting for the Democratic Party Candidate in Presidential Elections by Sex, 1980–1996 (in percentages)

A "gender gap" in voting preferences is visible in Figure 8-1, but it can be seen more clearly in this figure, which shows the percentages of female and male voters, respectively, that voted for the Democratic candidate.[1] The gap waxes and wanes; it was at its widest in 1996, when female voters were 11 percentage points more likely than male voters to vote for the Democratic candidate. The 1996 election was the only one of the five shown here in which the Democratic candidate received an absolute majority (54 percent) of women's votes.

Percentage

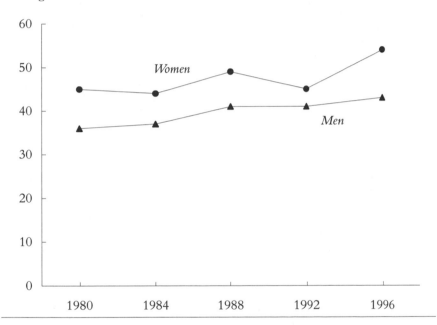

[1]The difference in the likelihood to vote for the Democratic candidate gives the clearest picture over time of the gender gap in these presidential elections. This is because, in 1992 and 1996, the picture was complicated by a third-party candidate who apparently drew more votes from people who would otherwise have voted Republican than from people who would otherwise have voted Democratic.

Source: The New York Times Company, "The Vote Under a Microscope," *The New York Times*, 1997, <http://www.nytimes.com/library/politics/elect-port.html>.

Table 8-2 • People Who Reported Voting Democratic (D) or Republican (R) in Presidential Elections by Educational Attainment and Sex, 1980–1996 (in percentages)

As measured by the percentage of female and male voters who voted for the Democratic candidate, the gender gap has been consistently narrowest among voters who are high school graduates but have gone no further with their education, and widest among college graduates.[1]

	1980[2]		1984		1988		1992[2]		1996[2]	
	R	D	R	D	R	D	R	D	R	D
High school graduates										
Women	50	44	58	41	50	50	38	43	34	56
Men	53	42	62	37	50	49	33	43	36	46
Some college										
Women	52	39	58	41	54	45	39	42	38	53
Men	59	31	65	33	60	38	37	40	44	42
College graduates[3]										
Women	42	44	52	47	49	51	36	48	39	53
Men	59	28	63	36	63	36	42	40	49	41

[1]The difference in the likelihood to vote for the Democratic candidate gives the clearest picture over time of the gender gap in these presidential elections. This is because, in 1992 and 1996, the picture was complicated by a third-party candidate who apparently drew more votes from people who would otherwise have voted Republican than from people who would otherwise have voted Democratic.

[2]Percentages do not total 100.0 because votes for the third-party candidates are not included.

[3]Includes those with postgraduate education.

Source: The New York Times Company, "The Vote Under a Microscope," *The New York Times*, 1997, <http://www.nytimes.com/library/politics/elect-port.html>.

Figure 8-3 • People Who Reported Voting for the Republican Candidate in Elections for the U.S. House of Representatives by Sex, 1980–1998 (in percentages)

Since 1980, at least, men have been more likely than women to vote for Republican candidates for the U.S. House of Representatives. This gender gap widened sharply in 1994, as the male vote went heavily Republican (58 percent, up from 48 percent in 1992) while the percentage of women voting Republican rose slightly (to 47 percent from 45 percent in 1992). The result: Republicans gained a majority in the House for the first time in decades.

Percentage

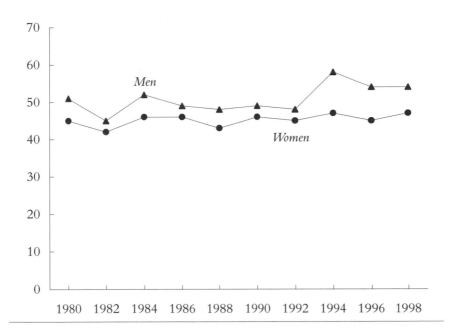

Source: The New York Times Company, "A Look at Voting Patterns of 115 Demographic Groups in House Races," *The New York Times*, 1998, <http://www.nytimes.com/library/politics/camp/110998voter3.html>.

Table 8-3 • Women in Elective Office, Selected Years, 1979–1999

State legislatures are the traditional breeding grounds for politicians with congressional ambitions and women's progress in winning state legislative seats has been a "leading indicator" of their progress in winning seats in Congress. Women have also made great strides in gaining statewide executive office. But women's representation in the highest federal and statewide elective offices (e.g., governorships) remains very small. Ruth Mandel discusses this subject more fully in Chapter One.

Elected Officeholders	Women as a Percentage of All Officeholders											Number of Women
	1979	1981	1983	1985	1987	1989	1991	1993	1995	1997	1999	1999
Members of Congress	3.2	4.3	4.5	4.7	4.7	5.8	6.0	10.1	10.7	11.8[1]	12.1	65
House[2]	3.7	4.8	5.1	5.3	5.3	6.7	6.4	10.8	11.0	12.4[1]	12.9	56
Senate	1.0	2.0	2.0	2.0	2.0	2.0	4.0	7.0	9.0	9.0	9.0	9
Statewide executive officials[3]	10.7	10.5	10.5	13.3	13.9	14.3	18.2	22.2	25.9	25.4	27.6	89
Governors[4]	4.0	—	—	4.0	6.0	6.0	6.0	6.0	2.0	4.0	6.0	3
State legislators	10.3	12.1	13.3	14.8	15.7	17.0	18.3	20.5	20.6	21.6	22.3	1,656
Mayors of 100 largest cities	—	—	—	7.0	11.0	17.0	19.0	19.0	17.0	12.0	16.0	16

[1] 105th Congress. Excludes Susan Molinari who resigned in mid-1997. Includes four women elected to the House in special elections in 1998.
[2] Excludes nonvoting delegates. As of December 1999, there were two women delegates.
[3] Includes some women filling elective positions by appointment or constitutional succession. Excludes officials elected to executive posts by state legislatures, judges, and elected members of university boards of trustees and boards of education.
[4] As of June of each year.

Source: Center for the American Woman and Politics (CAWP), *Women in the U.S. Congress 1917–2001*, January 1999; *Statewide Elective Executive Women: 1969–1999*, February 1999; *Women in State Legislatures 1999*, May 1999; *Women in Elective Office 1999*, August 1999; and *Statewide Elective Executive Women 1999*, September 1999.

Table 8-4 • Women on the Federal Bench, 1991 and 1998[1]

> Over the seven-year period shown here, the number of female federal judges increased by 73 percent. As of 1998, about one in five federal judgeships was held by a woman, up from roughly one in eight in 1991.

	Women			
	1991		*1998*	
	Number	*As a Percentage of All Active Judges*	*Number*	*As a Percentage of All Active Judges*
Supreme Court	1	11.1	2	22.2
Circuit courts[2]	19	12.2	36	19.0
District courts[3]	54	9.7	115	18.2
Bankruptcy courts	39	13.3	62	18.1
U.S. magistrates (full-time)	59	18.2	83	20.2

[1]As of September 1991 and 1998, respectively.
[2]Includes the Temporary Emergency Court of Appeals.
[3]Includes territorial courts; Claims Court; Court of International Trade; Special Court, Regional Rail Reorganization Act of 1973; and Judicial Panel on Multidistrict Litigation.

Source: Administrative Office of the United States Courts, *Annual Report on the Judiciary Equal Employment Opportunity Program for the Twelve-Month Period Ended September 30, 1991*, 1991; and unpublished data, September 1998.

WOMEN IN CONGRESS

The Congressional Caucus for Women's Issues: Achievements in the 105th Congress

Lesley Primmer Persily

INTRODUCTION

THE 1996 ELECTIONS ushered in two more years of divided national government. President Clinton was reelected to a second term in the White House, and a slimmed-down Republican majority returned to Congress. Although the 105th Congress (1997–1998) is destined to be remembered as the one that impeached William Jefferson Clinton, it also served as the backdrop for several notable milestones for women in politics: the number of women in the House of Representatives and the Senate reached a new high of 66 (including delegates); Madeleine Albright became the first woman to serve as Secretary of State; and the Congressional Caucus for Women's Issues turned 20.

"It's nice to know that women's issues, which too often were relegated to the back benches of politics, are now front and center because of what you have done over the past 20 years," First Lady Hillary Rodham Clinton told caucus members at a twentieth-anniversary gala celebration attended by the President, First Lady, and Secretary of State. "You've not only made women's issues ones to be reckoned with, but you've made it clear that women's issues are . . . America's issues."

When the 105th Congress came to a close, the caucus had won several important policy battles, the most hard-fought of which was the requirement that federal health plans provide contraceptive coverage for their enrollees. With a display of bipartisan cooperation that often eludes party leaders in Congress, the caucus thus began its third decade of advocacy on behalf of women in this country and the world over.

A MUST-PASS LEGISLATIVE AGENDA

As one of the caucus's first orders of business, members elected new leaders for the 105th Congress: Representative Nancy Johnson (R-CT) and Delegate Eleanor Holmes Norton (D-DC) as cochairs, and Representatives Sue Kelly (R-NY) and Carolyn Maloney (D-NY) as vice chairs. Electing new leaders every two years is one of the caucus's major recent changes. After more than a decade with Representatives Patricia Schroeder (D-CO) and Olympia Snowe (R-ME) at the helm, the caucus voted in 1994 to impose a two-year limit on the terms of its officers.

In 1995, the new Republican-led House had voted to abolish legislative service organizations like the caucus, forcing it to give up its six-member staff and $250,000 budget. But rather than fold the organization, the congresswomen restructured it into an informal caucus with staff support provided primarily by the personal staff of its officers. A new nonprofit organization called Women's Policy, Inc. (WPI) took over the information services the caucus had provided through its weekly and monthly newsletters.

Caucus membership expanded and changed in the 105th Congress, becoming more bipartisan and including women of widely divergent political views. Following an active recruitment effort by Republican cochair Nancy Johnson, the caucus membership roster listed 39 Democrats and 15 Republicans, including many conservatives who had previously eschewed membership in the organization. (The caucus had included just seven Republican members in the 104th Congress.) Among the new members were Representatives Jennifer Dunn (R-WA), Linda Smith (R-WA), Barbara Cubin (R-WY), and Helen Chenoweth (R-ID). Only two newly elected women—Representatives Jo Ann Emerson (R-MO) and Anne Northup (R-KY)—chose not to join the caucus during the 105th Congress.

Congresswomen Johnson and Norton also instituted changes in the way the caucus pursued its legislative agenda. In an effort to involve as many congresswomen as possible in the caucus's advocacy work, the new leaders created 14 issue-oriented legislative teams and named a Republican and a Democrat to head each one. While some of the teams were very active—holding hearings and drafting legislation—others never got off the ground. In some cases, the teams brought together congresswomen from opposite ends of the political spectrum who had little interest in working with each other.

Together, the legislative teams covered a wide range of policy priorities. Some were organized around legislation due to be reauthorized in the 105th

Congress, including the Violence Against Women Act, the Higher Education Act, and federal job training and vocational education programs. Others were formed to address policy initiatives that the congresswomen wanted to push in the new Congress, including preventive health services for women, child care, health care insurance reform, juvenile justice, and pensions and retirement benefits. Still others were aimed at long-standing caucus interests such as women in the military, teen pregnancy, women-owned businesses, HIV/AIDS, and international women's rights.

The new cochairs also decided to abandon a caucus tradition of introducing omnibus legislative packages composed of individual members' bills and organized around a central theme, like women's health or economic equity. (The caucus had introduced the Economic Equity Act in every Congress since 1980, and the Women's Health Equity Act in every Congress since 1990.)

Instead, Congresswomen Johnson and Norton worked with their colleagues to develop a list of "must-pass" legislative measures. To win a place on the list, a bill must have garnered bipartisan support and been the subject of a congressional hearing. Caucus members imposed these criteria to bolster prospects for final passage of the bills before the 105th Congress ended. The caucus did not draw up the priority list until midway through the second session, leaving members only a few months to push the bills through both houses of Congress and onto the President's desk for a signature.

Caucus members met separately with House Speaker Newt Gingrich (R-GA) and Democratic Minority Leader Richard Gephardt (D-MO) to seek support for their policy agenda. While noncommittal, both congressional leaders expressed support for the bipartisan caucus's efforts.

By the time the 105th Congress adjourned, three of the caucus's seven legislative priorities had become law:

- **Contraceptive coverage:** Health plans participating in the federal government's health benefits program are now required to cover contraceptives for federal workers and their dependents if they also cover other prescription drugs. The provision had been part of a more expansive bill that would have required all health plans to cover the five forms of contraception approved by the Food and Drug Administration (FDA): oral contraceptives, intrauterine devices, Norplant, Depo Provera, and diaphragms.

  The contraceptive coverage provision proved to be one of the year's most contentious and difficult-to-resolve issues, with Congress reaching a final agreement on the bill only after it granted an exemption for individual health care providers.

- **Mammography quality standards:** Congress will continue to ensure the safety and accuracy of mammography facilities by requiring annual inspections and accreditation. The original Mammography Quality Standards Act was passed in 1992. The updated version, enacted by the 105th Congress, requires mammography facilities to notify women directly of mammogram results, so that women no longer have to wait for their doctors to provide the information. The measure received near-unanimous support in both the House and the Senate.

- **Women and Science Commission:** Congress approved the creation of a commission to examine ways to encourage more women and minorities to pursue careers in science, engineering, and technology. The commission also is charged with exploring ways to increase female and minority participation in undergraduate and graduate programs in engineering, physics, and computer science. This legislation received unanimous support in both houses of Congress.

The four caucus priorities that did not become law were:

- **Violence against women prevention:** Congress failed to reauthorize the Violence Against Women Act (VAWA), legislation enacted in 1994 to provide $1.67 billion over six years for a variety of programs dealing with domestic and sexual violence—including battered women's shelters, rape education and prevention initiatives, training for federal judges, and a national domestic violence hot line. During consideration of a bill to protect children from sexual solicitation on the Internet, the House voted in favor of an amendment to reauthorize key portions of the landmark law, including state grants for law enforcement and prosecution efforts and grants to encourage pro-arrest policies. The House-passed amendment also included a number of provisions from a new policy initiative known as VAWA II, which included funding for research and prevention efforts. Although these provisions won easy approval by the House, they were stripped out of the Internet bill by the Senate Judiciary Committee. Congress has, however, continued to fund programs authorized under the act. The caucus endorsed the reauthorization of the 1994 legislation, but not the VAWA II initiative.

- **Child care:** Congress failed to act on legislation to increase the general availability and affordability of child care. (It did approve a new grant program to fund child-care centers on college campuses.) The tobacco settlement bill, which died in the Senate, had offered the best chance for major new federal support for child care. Before killing the bill, the Senate voted to require states to spend 25 percent of revenues from the tobacco settlement on child-care activities.

- **Federal contracting for women-owned businesses:** Congress also failed to act on a nonbinding resolution to encourage federal agencies to review recommendations for improving women-owned businesses' access to federal contracts.

- **Prohibition on genetic discrimination by health insurers:** Although President Clinton gave the effort his personal attention, the 105th Congress failed to act on legislation to prevent group health plans and insurance providers from discriminating against individuals and their family members on the basis of genetic information. The prohibition was narrowly applied to managed-care plans participating in Medicare and Medicaid.

OTHER GAINS FOR WOMEN

In addition to their must-pass agenda, caucus members championed a number of other measures important to women. Some of these were enacted by the 105th Congress, among them new grant programs to expand child care and prevent sexual assault on college campuses and expanded Medicare coverage for bone mass measurement and mammography screening. Several politically popular federal programs were also reauthorized in the 105th Congress, including the Women, Infants, and Children's Supplemental Food Program (WIC) and Head Start.

Additional policy gains for women during the 105th Congress include:

HEALTH CARE

- **Breast and ovarian cancer research:** As it has since the early 1990s, Congress allocated funds from the defense budget for women's health research, including $135 million for breast cancer and $10 million for ovarian cancer. Congress reauthorized the breast and ovarian cancer research program at the National Institutes of Health (NIH) and the Centers for Disease Control and Prevention's (CDC) National Breast and Cervical Cancer Early Detection program. Congress also approved the creation of a special stamp to raise money for breast cancer research.
- **Osteoporosis and other women's health research:** A small sum ($2.5 million) in the defense budget was earmarked for osteoporosis research. Congress also reauthorized NIH's osteoporosis research program and research on diethylstilbestrol (DES) and aging. The same legislation authorized a new research program on cardiovascular disease in women. In addition, Congress expanded an earlier requirement that NIH include women and minorities in clinical trials to cover trials sponsored by the FDA.
- **Breast cancer surgery:** Congress voted to require health plans to cover reconstructive breast surgery following a mastectomy. However, it failed to act on a companion proposal to allow physicians and patients to deter-

mine the appropriate length of a hospital stay following breast cancer surgery.

- **Preventive health benefits under Medicare:** Congress expanded Medicare coverage to include annual mammograms for disabled beneficiaries over 39, waiving the deductible. (Under the previous law, Medicare covered annual mammograms for beneficiaries aged 50-64, and mammograms every two years for beneficiaries under 50 and over 65.) In addition, coverage for bone mass measurement is now available to Medicare beneficiaries at high risk of developing osteoporosis, including estrogen-deficient women.
- **Health care coverage:** Congress approved $24 million to help states expand health coverage and services for uninsured, low-income children. It also prohibited discrimination based on genetic information or domestic violence in managed-care plans participating in Medicare and Medicaid, and accelerated the deduction for health care coverage purchased by the self-employed.
- **Date-rape drug restrictions:** Congress placed new importation restrictions on certain controlled substances, such as the insomnia drug Rohypnol, that have been used to incapacitate women, making them more vulnerable to sexual assault.

HIGHER EDUCATION

- **Campus-based child care:** Congress approved $45 million for campus-based child-care programs that serve primarily low-income students. The funds can be used to establish new child-care centers or to expand existing ones. Individual colleges will be allowed to set the amount of the dependent-care allowance for purposes of determining eligibility for Pell grants, a federal grant program for low-income students.
- **Campus crime prevention:** The Higher Education Act included a $10 million grant program to help colleges reduce violent crime against women. Funds will be used to strengthen campus sexual assault policies and services and to encourage cooperation between college campuses and local law enforcement. Congress also approved expanded campus crime reporting, requiring schools to include in their crime reports crimes that occur on public grounds or off-campus property. The legislation also funded a national baseline study to examine how colleges and universities handle reports of sexual assault.
- **Campus athletic disclosure requirement:** Colleges and universities will be required to submit annual reports to the secretary of education de-

tailing the total revenue and expenses for men's and women's athletic programs. The secretary will report the information to Congress and notify high schools of its availability.

FAMILY POLICY

- **Child support:** Congress approved bills to improve state child-support-enforcement efforts and to strengthen federal penalties for the most egregious cases of nonpayment of child support. The measure to improve state enforcement efforts also requires the federal government to ensure that medical-support provisions in child-support orders requiring parents to pay children's health care costs are properly carried out.
- **Tax reform:** Beginning in 1999, families with children under age 17 will receive a $500-per-child tax credit. Congress revised the tax code to allow certain higher-income filers to claim personal tax credits against dependent care and adoption expenses, as well as the $500 per child credit, without triggering the minimum tax that is imposed on those in the upper-income bracket.
- **IRA reform:** Congress approved legislation to allow nonworking spouses to save the full $2,000 annually in an Individual Retirement Account, regardless of the working spouse's pension plan.

WOMEN-OWNED BUSINESSES

Congress provided $8 million in Fiscal Year 1999 for the Women's Business Center program at the Small Business Administration (SBA), double the amount of the previous year. Operating in most states, these centers provide a broad range of training and counseling services to women business owners in the areas of finance, management, and marketing. It also approved funding for a national survey of women-owned businesses.

OTHER ACTION IMPORTANT TO WOMEN

Aided by a more moderate Senate, supporters of a woman's right to choose held the line for the most part against new efforts to restrict reproductive choice. The Senate rejected House-backed provisions that would have required parental notification for adolescents seeking contraceptive services, barred FDA testing or approval of drugs that chemically induce abortions, and reinstated abortion restrictions on international family planning providers.

The Senate derailed House-passed legislation to make it illegal to circumvent a state's parental consent law by taking a minor across state lines to obtain an abortion. It also sustained President Clinton's veto of legislation to outlaw a controversial abortion procedure widely known as partial-birth abortion.

Another top priority of House Republicans—legislation to permit private-sector employers to offer compensatory time in place of overtime pay to their workers—fell victim to a Senate filibuster. In addition, bipartisan majorities in both houses rejected high-profile, Republican-led efforts to end affirmative action for disadvantaged minority and women-owned businesses that compete for federal transportation construction contracts. By an even larger margin, the House rejected an amendment to the Higher Education Act that would have prohibited any public college or university that receives federal funds from using racial or gender preferences in the admission of students.

Still, there were losses for women in the 105th Congress. Military personnel, federal employees, and poor women will continue to have less access to abortion services because of federal funding restrictions. For the first time, the Hyde Amendment, prohibiting the use of federal funds to pay for abortions, was applied to Medicare and the new child health block grant.

On the economic front, Congress eliminated a 10.5 percent set-aside for vocational education services targeted at displaced homemakers, single parents, and pregnant women—the only federal funding source targeted directly toward these special-needs populations. The vocational education reauthorization approved by Congress eliminated the requirement that states maintain a full-time sex equity coordinator responsible for administering sex equity programs.

The 105th Congress compiled an even longer list of missed opportunities—legislative measures that could have significantly improved the health and economic status of scores of American women, had they been enacted. The failure to pass legislation to increase the availability and affordability of quality child care, protect the rights of managed-care patients, or remedy tax inequities incurred by two-earner couples also translated into losses for women in the 105th Congress.

One of the most controversial and high-profile legislative initiatives in the 105th Congress was the Patients' Bill of Rights. Eager to quiet Democratic demands for action on managed-care legislation, the House Republican leadership hurriedly pushed through a patients' protection bill to ensure coverage for emergency room care, remove gag rules on the information physicians can give patients, and permit patients direct access to obstetrician-gynecologists.

Meanwhile, women's health advocates backed a bipartisan alternative that would have ensured that health care decisions be made by doctors rather than health plans, guaranteed ongoing access to specialists and clinical trials, and given doctors the right to prescribe drugs that are not on lists approved by managed-care plans. It also would have prevented health plans from forcing women who undergo breast cancer surgery to leave the hospital early.

Both measures died after the Senate failed repeatedly to reach an agreement on the amount of time and the number of amendments that could be considered during debate on managed-care legislation.

Patients' rights legislation is certain to occupy a prominent place on the congressional agenda in the 106th Congress as will the effort to reduce the marriage penalty paid by many two-earner couples. The Senate failed to take up a House-approved measure to increase the standard deduction for married couples filing jointly to twice what is currently allowed for individual taxpayers.

CAUCUS HEARINGS

The caucus held seven hearings or public forums on issues of concern to the congresswoman. The topics covered included the following:

- **Early child development:** Witnesses described how new research methods have changed the understanding of how the brain develops and how it is molded by environmental experiences. This new understanding of early child development has fueled renewed debate about the need for better family leave policies and higher quality child care.
- **Women-owned businesses:** Caucus members explored the obstacles women-owned businesses face in obtaining government contracts. Witnesses said that federal agencies have been unwilling to meet the five-percent federal goal for awarding government contracts to women-owned businesses.
- **Contraceptive technology:** This hearing focused on the limited contraceptive options available to women in the United States. Following the forum, the caucus sent letters to medical schools, health insurers participating in the Federal Employee Health Benefits Plan, and the White House to encourage more training and education of health care providers, and more access to contraceptives.
- **Title IX:** Witnesses discussed the history and accomplishments of Title IX, which prohibits sex discrimination in educational programs at institutions receiving federal funds. A number of witnesses criticized the government for a decrease in Title IX enforcement efforts.
- **Equal pay:** The caucus held a town hall meeting to hear from pay equity advocates and working women, and to discuss why women's wages

continue to lag behind those of men. A report prepared for the caucus by the Congressional Research Service (CRS) said that the wage gap has narrowed over the last several decades. According to the report, in the 1960s and 1970s, women earned 60 cents for every dollar earned by men, whereas in 1996, they earned 74 cents for every dollar earned by men.

- **Tamoxifen use:** Shortly after the release of new research findings that the drug tamoxifen decreased the incidence of breast cancer by nearly half in women at high risk for the disease, the caucus held an informational hearing to discuss the risks and benefits of the drug.
- **Breast-feeding in the workplace:** A caucus hearing focused on the need to amend the 1978 Pregnancy Discrimination Act to ensure that women cannot be fired or discriminated against for breast-feeding in the workplace.

LOOKING AHEAD

The 105th Congress adjourned in the throes of a historic presidential impeachment process that seriously strained bipartisan relations within both the caucus and the House at large. Republican efforts to exploit the Clinton scandal were credited with bolstering Democrats' political fortunes among a scandal-weary electorate.

The 1998 elections once more pushed the number of women in Congress to a record high of 67—again, including delegates—in the 106th Congress. Of the women incumbents who sought reelection, all but one—Senator Carol Moseley-Braun (D-IL)—won reelection. Seven new women were sworn in on the opening day of the 106th Congress, six Democrats and one Republican—all supportive of a woman's right to reproductive choice. This group of congresswomen was very different from the one that had come to the Hill at the start of the 105th Congress.

With a razor-thin Republican majority in the House of Representatives, a presidential election campaign already in high gear, and a long list of pressing policy issues, ranging from child care to Social Security reform, the influence of the bipartisan women's caucus in the 106th Congress is likely to be substantial.

WOMEN IN THE 106TH CONGRESS[1]

ON NOVEMBER 3, 1964, when Patsy Mink, the senior woman in the 106th Congress, was elected to her first term, she was one of 10 women (and the only minority woman) among the 434 individuals elected that year to the House of Representatives. Two women were in the Senate. Exactly 34 years later, on November 3, 1998, Representative Mink was one of 56 women—a record number—elected to the House.[2] Nine women were in the Senate.[3]

To be one of the 535 individuals who make the laws for a country of more than 270 million surely can be considered having arrived at the top, and women have unquestionably made progress in getting there. Since Congresswoman Mink's first term, the female presence in Congress has increased from two percent to 12 percent. Nevertheless, if representation even roughly commensurate with the female share of the American population is the goal, we are far from reaching it.

Only 27 states, plus the District of Columbia and the Virgin Islands, currently have women in their congressional (House and/or Senate) dele-

---

[1]The information in the paragraphs preceding the congressional biographies was compiled from three sources: *Congressional Quarterly* of January 9, 1999; *Congress at Your Fingertips: 106th Congress, 1st Session 1999,* 1999; and *Women in the United States Congress 1917–1998,* 1998. Please see References for the full citations.

[2]The total is 58 if the two women elected as delegates from the District of Columbia and the U.S. Virgin Islands are included in the count. Delegates from U.S. territories and the District of Columbia cannot vote on matters before the full House, although they may vote in committee.

[3]The 1998 election did not increase the number of women in the Senate because, although Blanche Lambert Lincoln was newly elected, Carol Moseley-Braun, the only incumbent woman up in 1998, was not reelected.

gations. California and Maine share the distinction of having women in both Senate seats. California can claim the added distinction of having the most women—13, or 25 percent—in its House delegation. New York is next with six (19 percent) in the House, followed by Florida with five (22 percent). Of the 23 states that have no women in their delegations to the 106th Congress, six—Alaska, Delaware, Iowa, Mississippi, New Hampshire, and Vermont—have *never* sent a woman to Congress.

The demographic profile of the women elected to the 106th Congress differs from that of their male colleagues in several interesting respects. In the House, on average, the women are older than the men—the average age of the women representatives is about three years older than the average for the House overall. The freshman women are four years older, on average, than their male peers. Senate women, on the other hand, are typically younger than Senate men—there is a 12-year difference in average age.

Minorities are much better represented among the women in the House than among the men. (No minority women currently serve in the Senate.) Of the women House members (not counting the women delegates, both of whom are African Americans), 18 (one-third) are minority women—12 African Americans, five Hispanics, and one Asian American. In contrast, minorities account for only 11 percent of the male members of the House.

The women in Congress are considerably more likely than their male counterparts to be Democrats—six of the nine women senators (66 percent) are Democrats, as are 39 of the 56 women members of the House (70 percent). The comparable percentages for the men are 43 percent in the Senate, 46 percent in the House. A few women hold positions in the leadership of their respective political parties in Congress, but no women are in the very top positions in the leadership of either party.

Although older than the typical congressman, the typical congresswoman has less seniority. Only nine of the women in the House (16 percent) have served more than five terms, and none has served more than 12.[4] Over one-third of the men have served more than five terms, and 22 have served more than 12. No full committee in either the House or the Senate is chaired by a woman, and only one (in the House) has a woman as its ranking minority member (that is, the senior Democratic member). However, each of the three Republican women in the Senate chairs at least one subcommittee (two chair two), and five of their Democratic counterparts are the ranking minority members on at least one subcommittee. Eight of the Republican women in the House are subcommittee chairs; 14 of the Democratic women

[4]If Representative Mink's service had been continuous, she would now be in her seventeenth term.

are ranking members on House subcommittees. (In theory, at least, a ranking member is in line to become chair if her party gains the majority in the next election.)

The typical congresswoman is about as likely as the typical congressman to have had experience in elective public office before coming to Congress. Close to 70 percent of the women in the House held city, county, or state elective office before their election to Congress, compared with 72 percent of the men in the House. Eight (89 percent) of the nine women senators held prior elective office, compared with about 85 percent of the male senators.

Of course, the "typical congresswoman" is a fiction. In reality, as Ruth Mandel points out in Chapter One, elected women can differ as greatly from one another in political philosophies and priorities as elected men can. Some of these differences can be inferred from the very brief biographies that follow.

All the women in the 106th Congress, including delegates, are profiled here. The biographies are followed by a list of the members of the bipartisan Congressional Caucus for Women's Issues, which is chaired in the 106th Congress by Representatives Sue Kelly (R-NY) and Carolyn Maloney (D-NY).[5]

Representative Tammy Baldwin *(Democrat, Second District, Wisconsin)* was elected to the House in 1998. She is the first woman to be elected to Congress from Wisconsin. A committed advocate for health care, seniors, and programs to assist the disabled, she serves on the Budget Committee and the Judiciary Committee.

Congresswoman Baldwin began her career in elective office in 1986 as a member of the Dane County (Wisconsin) Board of Supervisors; after four terms as a supervisor, she was elected to the Wisconsin Assembly, where—in her first term—she was named chair of the Committee on Elections, Constitutional Law, and Corrections.

Congresswoman Baldwin was born and raised in the congressional district she now represents. She graduated from Smith College with a major in mathematics and government and earned her law degree from the University of Wisconsin Law School.

---

[5]The caucus is a House organization; it has no senators among its members. However, the four women senators who previously served in the House were active in the caucus while in the House.

Representative Shelley Berkley *(Democrat, First District, Nevada),* who was elected to the House in 1998, serves on the Transportation and Infrastructure Committee and the Veterans' Affairs Committee. She previously held elective office in the Nevada Assembly and, more recently, on the Nevada University and Community College System Board of Regents.

Congresswoman Berkley is a lawyer whose private-sector positions have included vice president of government and legal affairs for the Sands Hotel and in-house counsel for Southwest Gas Corporation. Her community activities have ranged from serving as president of the Las Vegas Public Broadcasting System affiliate to founding the Southern Nevada Association of Women Attorneys.

A graduate of the University of Nevada, Las Vegas, Congresswoman Berkley received her law degree from the University of San Diego School of Law. She is the mother of two sons.

Representative Judy Biggert *(Republican, Thirteenth District, Illinois)* was elected to the House in 1998. She serves on the Banking and Financial Services Committee, the Government Reform Committee, and the Science Committee. Before coming to Congress, she was elected three times to the Illinois legislature, where she was assistant Republican House leader.

Her legislative record reflects a commitment to improving education, reducing taxes, and reducing crime and violence, including domestic violence.

Before coming to Congress, Representative Biggert practiced law, specializing in real estate, estate planning, and probate. She has a B.A. from Stanford University and a J.D. from Northwestern University School of Law. Married to Rody Biggert, she has four children and one grandchild.

Representative Mary Bono *(Republican, Forty-fourth District, California)* was first elected to Congress in April 1998, in a special election to fill the House seat left vacant by the death of her husband, Sonny Bono. She was reelected to a full term in November 1998. She serves on the Judiciary Committee, the Armed Services Committee, and the Small Business Committee.

Congresswoman Bono strongly advocates returning authority to local government, particularly in education. She opposes the existing federal tax structure, and favors tax relief and reducing the federal bureaucracy. She believes it is the responsibility of the federal government to maintain a strong national defense.

Congresswoman Bono, although born in Cleveland, has been a Californian for most of her life. She has a B.A. in art history from the University of Southern California. She is the mother of two children.

Senator Barbara Boxer *(Democrat, California)* was elected to the Senate in 1992, following 10 years in the House of Representatives. She sits on the Budget Committee, the Environment and Public Works Committee, and the Foreign Relations Committee, where she is the ranking Democrat on the International Operations Subcommittee.

During her tenure in the House, Senator Boxer led the fight for federal funding of abortions for women who were victims of rape or incest. In both the House and the Senate, she championed the Family and Medical Leave Act and the Violence Against Women Act. She also has worked to draw attention and resources to women's health issues, such as breast cancer.

Born in Brooklyn, New York, in 1940, Senator Boxer has a B.A. in economics from Brooklyn College. She is married and the mother of two adult children. Before coming to Congress, she was for six years a member of the Marin County (California) Board of Supervisors.

Representative Corrine Brown *(Democrat, Third District, Florida)*, first elected to Congress in 1992, serves on the Transportation and Infrastructure Committee and the Veterans' Affairs Committee. She is the ranking Democrat on the latter's Oversight and Investigations subcommittee. Her legislative priorities include education, aging, economic development, and women's issues.

Congresswoman Brown holds B.S. and M.A. degrees from Florida A&M University and an education specialist degree from the University of Florida. She has been a member of the faculties at Florida Community College of Jacksonville, the University of Florida, and Edward Waters College. She was born in 1946 in Jacksonville, where she still resides.

Representative Lois Capps *(Democrat, Twenty-second District, California)* was first elected to Congress in March 1998, in a special election to fill the House seat left vacant by the death of her husband, Walter Capps. She was reelected to a full term in November 1998. She currently serves on the Commerce Committee, where her major focus is on enacting a strong patients' bill of rights. Her other priorities include Medicare reform, mental health, the environment, and high-technology and communications issues.

Congresswoman Capps, who was born in Wisconsin, earned a B.S. degree with honors in nursing from Pacific Lutheran University. She also has a master's degree in religion from Yale University and a master's degree in education from the University of California, Santa Barbara. Congresswoman Capps was married to the late Walter Capps for 37 years. She has three grown children.

Representative Julia Carson *(Democrat, Tenth District, Indiana)* was first elected to the House in 1996. She is a member of the Banking and Financial Services Committee and the Veterans' Affairs Committee.

In 1972, Congresswoman Carson successfully ran for the Indiana House of Representatives; after two terms, she was elected to the Indiana Senate, where her concerns included health care, child support, and the plight of the poor.

Congresswoman Carson, who was born in 1938, has two children. She resides in Indianapolis.

Representative Helen Chenoweth-Hage *(Republican, First District, Idaho)* was first elected to the House in 1994. She serves on the Agriculture Committee, the Veterans' Affairs Committee, the Government Reform Committee, and the Resources Committee, where she chairs the Subcommittee on Forests and Forest Health. Her priorities include balancing the budget, lowering taxes, and shrinking the size of government.

Born in eastern Kansas in 1938, Representative Chenoweth-Hage moved to Idaho in 1964. She served as state executive director of the Idaho Republican Party from 1975 to 1977. She went on to serve as chief of staff to then-Congressman Steve Symms (R-ID). She and Wayne Hage were married in 1999.

Delegate Donna Christian-Christensen *(Democrat, At Large, U.S. Virgin Islands)*, formerly Donna Christian-Green, was first elected to Congress in 1996. She is the fourth person and the first woman to be elected delegate to the House of Representatives from the U.S. Virgin Islands. She serves on the Small Business Committee and is the ranking Democrat on its Subcommittee on Rural Enterprises, Business Opportunities and Special Small Business Programs. She also serves on the Resources Committee.

Delegate Christian-Christensen has an M.D. from the George Washington University School of Medicine. Her medical career ranged from private family practice to serving as Acting Commissioner of the U.S. Virgin Islands Department of Health. She has been a trustee of the National Medical Association since 1995.

Delegate Christian-Christensen, who has two daughters, is married to Christian Christensen.

Representative Eva Clayton *(Democrat, First District, North Carolina)* was first elected to the House in November 1992, in a combination general and special election, to fill the seat left vacant by the death of her predecessor. She is not only the first woman elected to Congress from North Carolina but also the first woman to be elected president of a Democratic congressional "freshman class." An advocate for rural health care, housing assistance, and job training, Congresswoman Clayton serves on the Budget Committee and the Agriculture Committee, and is the ranking Democrat on the latter's Subcommittee on Department Operations, Oversight, Nutrition and Forestry.

Representative Clayton was born in 1934 in Savannah, Georgia. Before coming to Congress, she served as a member of the Warren County Board of Commissioners. She is married to Theaoseus T. Clayton, Sr. They have four children and five grandchildren.

Senator Susan M. Collins *(Republican, Maine)* was elected to the Senate in 1996. She serves on the Labor and Human Resources Committee, the Special Committee on Aging, and the Governmental Affairs Committee, where she is the first freshman and the first woman to chair the Subcommittee on Investigations.

Her priorities include helping small businesses create jobs, improving access to education for youngsters, and campaign finance reform.

Her career before her election to the Senate included serving as staff director for the Senate Subcommittee on the Oversight of Government Management and as Maine's commissioner of professional and financial regulation under Governor John R. McKernan.

Born in 1952 in Caribou, Maine, Senator Collins is a magna cum laude graduate of St. Lawrence University, with a degree in government. She resides in Bangor.

Representative Barbara Cubin *(Republican, At Large, Wyoming)* was first elected to the House in 1994. She is a member of the Commerce Committee and the Resources Committee, where she chairs the Subcommittee on Energy and Mineral Resources. She also serves as a deputy whip in the Republican leadership.

Before coming to Congress, Representative Cubin served in both houses of Wyoming's legislature. A fifth-generation Wyomingite, Representative Cubin is married to Frederick Cubin, M.D. They have two children in college. She is a graduate of Creighton University.

Representative Patricia Danner *(Democrat, Sixth District, Missouri)* was first elected to Congress in 1992. She is a member of the Transportation and Infrastructure Committee and the International Relations Committee.

Before her election to the U.S. House, Congresswoman Danner served for 10 years in the Missouri Senate, where she worked on legislation to provide tuition waivers for displaced homemakers. She also authored Missouri's Extended Day Child Care Act, which provided funds for after-school child-care services.

Congresswoman Danner, who was born in 1934 in Louisville, Kentucky, earned her B.A. from Northeast Missouri State University. She is married and has four children.

Representative Diana DeGette *(Democrat, First District, Colorado),* first elected to Congress in 1996, is a member of the Commerce Committee, serving on three of its subcommittees: Health and the Environment; Finance and Hazardous Materials; and Oversight and Investigations.

In her first term, Representative DeGette was the author of legislation streamlining public-health programs for children and increasing funding for environmental programs. Early in the 106th Congress, she introduced legislation to protect and preserve 1.4 million acres of Colorado wilderness.

Congresswoman DeGette, who was born in 1957, is a graduate of Colorado College and New York University Law School. Before her election to Congress, she served in the Colorado legislature. A resident of Denver, she is married to Lino Lipinsky. They have two children.

Representative Rosa L. DeLauro *(Democrat, Third District, Connecticut)* was first elected to Congress in 1990. In 1999, after two terms as chief deputy whip, she was elected by her colleagues to the position of assistant to the Democratic leader, making her the highest-ranking woman Democrat in the House of Representatives.

A member of the Appropriations Committee, Congresswoman DeLauro serves on its Labor, Health, Human Services, and Education Subcommittee and its Agriculture Subcommittee. She has made improving health care a top priority during her tenure, authoring legislation to guarantee 48-hour minimum hospital stays for mastectomies and to increase funding for research on women's health.

Congresswoman DeLauro, who was born in New Haven, Connecticut, in 1943, has been in public service for much of her life. She was the first woman to serve as executive assistant to the mayor of New Haven and was chief of staff to U.S. Senator Christopher Dodd (D-CT). Before her election to the House, she was the executive director of EMILY's List, a nationwide network of political donors helping to elect pro-choice Democratic women. She and her husband, Stanley Greenberg, have three grown children.

Representative Jennifer Dunn *(Republican, Eighth District, Washington),* first elected to Congress in 1992, serves on the House Ways and Means Committee. Her policy priorities include retirement security, tax relief, IRS oversight, hitech issues, and international trade policy. Since 1997, Congresswoman Dunn has spearheaded the effort to close the "gender gap" in American politics. She translates issues from a woman's perspective, thus communicating how policies affect women.

From 1981 to 1992—before her election to Congress—Representative Dunn was chair of the Washington State Republican Party.

Congresswoman Dunn was born in Seattle in 1941. She holds a B.A. from Stanford University. She is the mother of two children.

Representative Jo Ann Emerson *(Republican, Eighth District, Missouri),* was first elected to Congress in 1996, in a combined special and general election. The special election was to fill the vacancy left by the death of her husband, Bill Emerson, in the 104th Congress. The general election was to a full term in the 105th Congress. Representative Emerson is the first Republican woman from her state to serve in the U.S. House of Representatives. A member of the Appropriations Committee, she serves on three of its subcommittees: Agriculture; Treasury, Postal Service and General Government; and the District of Columbia.

Before coming to Congress, Representative Emerson was senior vice president of public affairs for the American Insurance Association. She also served as deputy director of communications for the Republican National Committee.

Representative Emerson, who was born in Bethesda, Maryland, in 1950, graduated from Ohio Wesleyan University. She has two daughters and two stepchildren.

Representative Anna Eshoo *(Democrat, Fourteenth District, California)* was elected to her first term in Congress in 1992. She sits on the Commerce Committee.

Before coming to Congress, she served for 10 years on the San Mateo County Board of Supervisors, where she was responsible for securing funds for California's first freestanding nursing facility for AIDS patients. In Congress, she has played an active role in women's health issues, introducing legislation to guarantee insurance coverage of breast reconstructive surgery following a mastectomy.

Representative Eshoo, who was born in New Britain, Connecticut, in 1942, has an A.A. from Cañada College in Redwood City, California. She is the mother of two children.

Senator Dianne Feinstein *(Democrat, California)* was first elected to the Senate in November 1992 to complete the unexpired term of Pete Wilson (R–CA), who had been elected governor of California. She was reelected in 1994 to a full six-year term. Senator Feinstein sits on the Appropriations Committee, where she is the ranking Democrat on the Legislative Branch Subcommittee; the Rules and Administration Committee; and the Judiciary Committee, where she is the ranking Democrat on the Technology, Terrorism, and Government Information Subcommittee.

Senator Feinstein, who was born in San Francisco in 1933, was mayor of that city from 1978 to 1988. Before that, she was a member of the San Francisco Board of Supervisors. She received her B.A. from Stanford University. Married to Richard C. Blum, Senator Feinstein has one daughter, three stepdaughters, and one granddaughter.

Representative Tillie Fowler *(Republican, Fourth District, Florida)* was first elected to the House of Representatives in 1992. She is a member of the Armed Services Committee and the Transportation and Infrastructure Committee, where she chairs the Subcommittee on Oversight, Investigations and Emergency Management. As the vice chair of the House Republican Conference, Congresswoman Fowler is the highest-ranking woman in the House leadership in the 106th Congress. (She has announced, however, that she will not run for reelection in 2000.)

She began her career of public service as a legislative assistant to Representative Robert Stephens, Jr. (D-GA), and then served as general counsel in the White House Office of Consumer Affairs during the Nixon Administration. Before her election to Congress, she was a member of the Jacksonville (Florida) City Council for seven years and council president for two years.

Congresswoman Fowler was born in 1942 in Milledgeville, Georgia. She holds both a B.A. and a law degree from Emory University. She is married to L. Buck Fowler and has two daughters.

Representative Kay Granger *(Republican, Twelfth District, Texas)* was first elected to Congress in 1996. She is the first Republican woman from Texas to serve in the U.S. House of Representatives, where she is a member of the Appropriations Committee.

Her legislative priorities include balancing the federal budget, strengthening defense, and lifting government regulation on small business.

Before coming to Congress, Representative Granger served three terms as mayor of Fort Worth; before that, she served two years on the Fort Worth City Council and seven years on the Zoning Commission. She received her B.S. and an honorary Doctorate of Humane Letters from Texas Wesleyan University. She is the mother of three grown children and lives in Fort Worth.

Representative Darlene Hooley *(Democrat, Fifth District, Oregon)* was first elected to the House in 1996. She is a member of the Banking and Financial Services Committee and the Budget Committee.

A former teacher, Congresswoman Hooley became a neighborhood activist in the mid-1970s, advocating for safe playgrounds. She was elected in 1976 to the West Linn (Oregon) City Council, where she served for four years. She was then elected to the Oregon legislature, where she authored landmark welfare reform legislation and pay equity legislation. In 1987, she was appointed to fill a vacancy on the Clackamas County Board of Commissioners. She was subsequently elected, and several times reelected, to the board.

Representative Hooley, who was born in 1939, received her B.S. from Oregon State University. She lives in West Linn.

Senator Kay Bailey Hutchison *(Republican, Texas),* the first woman to represent Texas in the Senate, was first elected to that body in June 1993 to fill the unexpired term of Lloyd Bentsen (D-TX), who had been appointed U.S. Secretary of the Treasury. In November 1994 she was reelected to a full, six-year term.

Senator Hutchison sits on four committees: the Appropriations Committee, where she chairs the District of Columbia Subcommittee; the Commerce, Science and Transportation Committee, where she chairs the Surface Transportation and Merchant Marine Subcommittee; the Environment and Public Works Committee; and the Rules and Administration Committee. She also serves as Deputy Majority Whip. She is chair of the Board of Visitors of the U.S. Military Academy, and serves as an American delegate to the Helsinki Commission.

Before coming to the Senate, Senator Hutchison was Texas state treasurer—the first Republican woman to be elected to statewide office in Texas. She also served in the Texas legislature and as vice chair of the National Transportation Safety Board in the Ford Administration.

Raised in La Marque, Texas, Senator Hutchison is a graduate of the University of Texas at Austin and the University of Texas School of Law. She is married to Ray Hutchison. They live in Dallas.

Representative Sheila Jackson Lee *(Democrat, Eighteenth District, Texas),* first elected to the House in 1994, sits on the Science and Judiciary Committees. She is the ranking Democrat on the latter's Immigration and Claims Subcommittee.

Before coming to Congress, Representative Jackson Lee was a member of the Houston City Council. Earlier she served as an associate municipal court judge. She is a graduate of Yale University and holds a J.D. from the University of Virginia Law School. She is married to Dr. Elwyn C. Lee and has two children.

Representative Eddie Bernice Johnson *(Democrat, Thirtieth District, Texas)* was first elected to the House in 1992. She sits on the Transportation and Infrastructure Committee and the Science Committee, and is the ranking Democrat on the latter's Basic Research Subcommittee.

Before her election to Congress, Representative Johnson was a business entrepreneur, professional nurse, and health care administrator. When she was elected to the Texas House of Representatives, she became the first African American woman since 1935 to be elected to public office in Texas. She left the legislature in 1977 to become the regional director of the Department of Health, Education, and Welfare during the Carter Administration. In 1986 she was elected to a seat in the Texas Senate, which she held until her election to Congress.

Representative Johnson, who received her nursing preparation at St. Mary's College of Notre Dame, is a graduate of Texas Christian University. She earned a master's degree in public administration from Southern Methodist University. Born in 1935 in Waco, Texas, she is the mother of one child.

Representative Nancy Johnson *(Republican, Sixth District, Connecticut)* was first elected to Congress in 1982. The 106th Congress marks her ninth term in the House. She has been a member of the Ways and Means Committee since 1988, when she became the first Republican woman ever appointed to that committee. She currently chairs its Subcommittee on Human Resources— the first woman ever to chair a Ways and Means subcommittee. She also sits on its Subcommittee on Health, where she has been a leader in health care reform efforts. She is particularly proud of her success in getting bipartisan support for the Children's Health Care bill, now law, which guarantees health insurance to millions of children.

Representative Johnson, who was born in Chicago, received her bachelor's degree from Radcliffe College. Before coming to Congress, she served three terms in the Connecticut State Senate. She and her husband, Theodore Johnson, have three daughters.

Representative Stephanie Tubbs Jones *(Democrat, Eleventh District, Ohio)* was elected to Congress in 1998. She serves on the Banking and Financial Services Committee and the Small Business Committee. Her special concerns include health care (particularly patients' rights and long-term care), Social Security, education, and housing and community development. She is the original sponsor of the Child Abuse Protection and Enforcement Act of 1999.

Before coming to Congress, Representative Jones served as Cuyahoga County (Ohio) prosecutor and as a judge in both the Common Pleas and Municipal Courts. She earned her undergraduate and law degrees at Case Western Reserve University. Congresswoman Jones was born in 1949 in Cleveland, where she has lived all her life. She is married to Mervyn Jones; they have one son.

Representative Marcy Kaptur *(Democrat, Ninth District, Ohio)*, first elected to Congress in 1982, is the senior Democratic woman in the House of Representatives. She sits on the Appropriations Committee and is the ranking Democratic member of its Agriculture Subcommittee.

Congresswoman Kaptur has long advocated for U.S. workers and small businesses, particularly those with female entrepreneurs, as well as for tighter restrictions on trade and tougher lobbying restrictions on top-level federal officials. Mental health issues are also a priority, and she has pushed for the creation of a congressional advisory committee on mental illness. Her other interests include making sure that the U.S. Capitol contains art that reflects women's roles in society.

Born in 1946 in Toledo, Ohio, Representative Kaptur earned her B.A. from the University of Wisconsin and her M.A. in urban planning from the University of Michigan. She practiced as an urban planner for 15 years before seeking public office and was a doctoral candidate in urban studies at the Massachusetts Institute of Technology. She also served as an urban adviser during the Carter Administration and as the first deputy director of the National Cooperative Consumer Bank.

Representative Sue W. Kelly *(Republican, Nineteenth District, New York)* was first elected to the House in 1994. She is a member of the Banking and Financial Services Committee, the Transportation and Infrastructure Committee, and the Small Business Committee, where she chairs the Subcommittee on Regulatory Reform and Paperwork Reduction. In 1999, Representative Kelly was named cochair of the Congressional Caucus for Women's Issues.

Before coming to Congress, Representative Kelly worked as an educator, small-business owner, patient advocate, rape crisis counselor, and community leader. She is a graduate of Denison University and has a master's degree in health advocacy from Sarah Lawrence College.

Congresswoman Kelly was born in 1936 in Lima, Ohio. She is married to Edward Kelly. They have four children and four grandchildren.

Representative Carolyn Cheeks Kilpatrick *(Democrat, Fifteenth District, Michigan)* was first elected to the House in 1996. She sits on the House Appropriations Committee and on its Transportation and Foreign Operations Subcommittees. She came to Congress after serving 18 years in the Michigan legislature. Earlier, she taught in the Detroit public schools.

Congresswoman Kilpatrick spent her undergraduate years at Ferris State University and Western Michigan University, and earned her M.S. in education administration from the University of Michigan. A native of Detroit, she has a son and a daughter and four grandsons.

Senator Mary L. Landrieu *(Democrat, Louisiana)* was elected to the Senate in 1996—the first woman ever elected to that body from Louisiana. She is a member of the Committee on Armed Services—the first Democratic woman and only the second Louisianan ever to serve on that committee—and is the ranking Democrat on its Strategic Forces Subcommittee. She also serves on the Committee on Energy and Natural Resources and the Committee on Small Business.

Senator Landrieu takes pride in her reputation for fiscal discipline as well as in her advocacy for children and working families. She launched "Steps to Success," a public-private partnership providing volunteer mentors and professional guidance to parents with young children.

Senator Landrieu first won elective office at the age of 23, when she became the youngest woman ever elected to the Louisiana legislature. After two terms in the Louisiana House, she was elected Louisiana state treasurer.

Senator Landrieu, whose father, Moon Landrieu, was mayor of New Orleans, was born in 1955. A graduate of Louisiana State University in Baton Rouge, she is married to Frank Snellings. They have two young children.

Representative Barbara Lee *(Democrat, Ninth District, California)* was first elected to Congress in April 1998 to complete the remaining term of Representative Ron Dellums, who retired before finishing his term. Congresswoman Lee was re-elected in November 1998 to serve in the 106th Congress. She sits on the Committee on Banking and Financial Services and the Committee on International Relations.

Before coming to Congress, Representative Lee served three consecutive terms in the California Assembly and one term in the California Senate, where she chaired its Committee on Housing and Land Use.

Born in 1946 in El Paso, Texas, Congresswoman Lee moved with her family to California as a teenager. A graduate of Mills College, she also has a master's degree in public welfare from the University of California, Berkeley.

Senator Blanche L. Lincoln *(Democrat, Arkansas),* elected to the Senate in 1998, is the youngest woman ever elected to that body and only the second woman to win a Senate seat from Arkansas. She previously served two terms in the House of Representatives (1993–1997), where she championed children's and women's health issues and worked to foster rural development.

Her committee assignments in the Senate are the Agriculture Committee, the Energy and Natural Resources Committee, and the Special Committee on Aging. She is also a member of the Senate Social Security Task Force.

Senator Lincoln was born in 1960 in Helena, Arkansas. She received her bachelor's degree from Randolph-Macon Women's College. She is married to Dr. Steve Lincoln; they have twin boys.

Representative Zoe Lofgren *(Democrat, Sixteenth District, California)* was first elected to the House in 1994. She is a member of the Judiciary Committee, the Science Committee, and the Committee on Standards of Official Conduct. Before her election to Congress, she served on the Santa Clara (California) County Board of Supervisors.

Following her graduation from Stanford University, Congresswoman Lofgren worked on the Watergate hearings with then-Congressman Don Edwards (D–CA), who preceded her as the representative from the 16th District. She received her law degree from the University of Santa Clara Law School.

Congresswoman Lofgren is married to John Marshall Collins. They have two children.

Representative Nita Lowey *(Democrat, Eighteenth District, New York)* was first elected to the House in 1988. She is a member of the Appropriations Committee and serves on two of its subcommittees: the Subcommittee on Foreign Operations, Export Financing, and Related Programs and the Subcommittee on Labor, Health and Human Services, and Education.

Congresswoman Lowey is an advocate of biomedical and breast cancer research, women's preventive health programs, aid to Israel, worker retraining initiatives, tough anticrime legislation, and educational reform.

Born in 1937 in the Bronx, New York, Representative Lowey graduated from Mount Holyoke College. She is married to Stephen Lowey and has three grown children.

Representative Carolyn B. Maloney *(Democrat, Fourteenth District, New York)* was first elected to Congress in 1992. She is a member of the Banking and Financial Services Committee; the Government Reform and Oversight Committee, where she is the ranking Democrat on the Subcommittee on the Census; and the Joint Economic Committee. Congresswoman Maloney cochairs the Congressional Caucus for Women's Issues and the Census Caucus.

Representative Maloney has a strong interest in women's and children's issues. During her 10 years on the New York City Council before coming to Congress, she offered a comprehensive legislative package to increase the availability and affordability of child-care services. In Congress, she has advocated on behalf of children in the child-welfare system.

Congresswoman Maloney was born in 1948 in Greensboro, North Carolina. She is a graduate of Greensboro College. She and her husband, Clifton Maloney, have two daughters.

Representative Carolyn McCarthy *(Democrat, Fourth District, New York)* was elected to the House in 1996. She sits on the Committee on Education and the Workforce and the Committee on Small Business, where she is the ranking Democrat on the Subcommittee on Tax, Finance and Exports. Her legislative priorities include education, health care reform, reducing gun violence, and providing targeted tax cuts for working families.

Representative McCarthy, who was born in 1944, is a graduate of Glen Cove Nursing School. A lifelong resident of Mineola, New York, she became politically active after her husband was killed and her son was gravely injured by an assault weapon on a Long Island Rail Road commuter train.

Representative Karen McCarthy *(Democrat, Fifth District, Missouri)* was first elected to Congress in November 1994. She serves on the Commerce Committee and its subcommittees on Energy and Power; Telecommunications, Trade, and Consumer Protection; and Oversight and Investigations.

Before her election to Congress, Congresswoman McCarthy was in the Missouri legislature, where she chaired the Ways and Means Committee. She received her B.A. from Kansas University, her M.A. in English from the University of Missouri at Kansas City, and her M.B.A. from the University of Kansas.

Representative Cynthia McKinney *(Democrat, Fourth District, Georgia),* first elected to the House in 1992, is the first African American woman to be elected to Congress from Georgia. She sits on the Armed Services Committee and the International Relations Committee, and is the ranking Democrat on the latter's Subcommittee on International Operations and Human Rights. Her legislative priorities in the 106th Congress include women and children's issues, arms control, and ending corporate welfare.

Born in 1955 in Atlanta, Congresswoman McKinney is a graduate of the University of Southern California. Before her election to Congress, she served in the Georgia legislature. She was also a professor of political science at Agnes Scott College in Decatur, Georgia. She is presently a doctoral candidate in international relations at Tufts University. She has one child.

Representative Carrie Meek *(Democrat, Seventeenth District, Florida),* first elected to the House in 1992, is the first African American elected to Congress from Florida since Reconstruction. She is a member of the Appropriations Committee.

Congresswoman Meek came to Congress following a dozen years of service in the Florida legislature, where she served in both chambers. During her last term in the Florida Senate, she chaired the Appropriations Subcommittee on Education.

In Congress, Representative Meek has championed legislation to provide retirement security to domestic workers, including household workers, gardeners, and nannies. She also has worked to improve low-income individuals' access to such government services as housing and education.

Congresswoman Meek was born in 1926 in Tallahassee, Florida. She is a graduate of Florida A&M University and holds an M.A. from the University of Michigan. She has three children.

Senator Barbara Mikulski *(Democrat, Maryland)* was first elected to the Senate in 1986. She is the first Democratic woman elected to a Senate seat that had not previously been held by the woman's husband. A five-term member of the House when she won her Senate seat, she is also the first Democratic woman to have served in both the House and the Senate.

Senator Mikulski is the ranking Democratic member of two subcommittees: the Subcommittee on Veterans' Affairs, Housing and Urban Development, and Independent Agencies of the Appropriations Committee and the Subcommittee on Aging of the Health, Education, Labor, and Pensions Committee. A leader on women's health issues, Senator Mikulski won enactment of legislation requiring licensing of clinical laboratories to ensure proper analysis of Pap smears and access to mammograms for low-income women.

Born in Baltimore in 1936, Senator Mikulski earned her B.A. from Mount Saint Agnes College in Baltimore and her M.S.W. from the University of Maryland. She began her career in public service as a social worker in Baltimore and entered politics with her election to the Baltimore City Council.

Representative Juanita Millender-McDonald *(Democrat, Thirty-seventh District, California)* began her service in Congress in 1996, after winning a special election to fill an open seat, and was re-elected in November 1996. She sits on the Transportation and Infrastructure Committee and the Small Business Committee, where she is the ranking Democrat on the Empowerment Subcommittee. Congresswoman Millender-McDonald is vice chair of the Congressional Caucus for Women's Issues.

Before her election to the House, Congresswoman Millender-McDonald served in the California legislature, where she made education reform one of her top priorities. Earlier, she had been a member of the Carson (California) City Council. She began her professional career as a teacher.

A native of Birmingham, Alabama, Representative Millender-McDonald resides in Carson. She is married to James McDonald, Jr. They have five adult children and four grandchildren.

Representative Patsy Mink *(Democrat, Second District, Hawaii)* was first elected to Congress in 1964 and served six terms. In 1976, she made a bid for the U.S. Senate but lost in the primary. She returned to the House in 1990, when she was elected to complete the unexpired term of Daniel Akaka (D-HI), who had been appointed to the Senate.

Representative Mink is a member of the Education and the Workforce Committee—on which she has served throughout her years in Congress—and of the Government Reform Committee, where she is the ranking Democrat on the Subcommittee on Criminal Justice, Drug Policy and Human Resources. She was a principal author of Title IX, which prohibits education programs that receive federal assistance from discriminating on the basis of sex, and of the Women's Educational Equity Act (WEEA). She has fought for women's health issues and against restrictive product liability legislation.

Congresswoman Mink was born in Paia, Hawaii. She earned her B.A. at the University of Hawaii and her law degree at the University of Chicago. Before coming to Congress she served in Hawaii's House and later in its Senate. She and her husband, John Francis Mink, have one daughter.

Representative Constance Morella *(Republican, Eighth District, Maryland)* was first elected to the House in 1986. She sits on the Science Committee and chairs its Subcommittee on Technology. She is also a member of the Government Reform Committee.

Congresswoman Morella has been a leader on women's issues, championing legislation to increase research on and prevention of AIDS in women. She also has been in the forefront of the fight against domestic violence, winning enactment of several bills addressing this issue. In the 104th Congress, she served as cochair of the Congressional Caucus for Women's Issues.

Born in Somerville, Massachusetts, in 1931, Representative Morella received her A.B. from Boston University and her M.A. from American University in Washington, D.C. She served for eight years in the Maryland General Assembly. Before entering politics, she was a professor of English at Montgomery College, in Montgomery County, Maryland. Congresswoman Morella is married to Tony Morella. They have raised nine children, six of whom are her late sister's children.

Senator Patty Murray *(Democrat, Washington),* first elected to the U.S. Senate in 1992, sits on four committees: Health, Education, Labor and Pension; Budget; Veterans' Affairs; and Appropriations, where she is the ranking Democrat on the Military Construction Subcommittee.

Before coming to the U.S. Senate, Senator Murray served in the Washington State Senate, where she championed legislation to provide family leave to parents of terminally ill children. She is a strong advocate for families and children, education, abortion rights, and tax relief for the middle class.

Senator Murray, who was born in 1950, is a native of Seattle. She earned her B.A. from Washington State University. She is married to Rob Murray. They have two children.

Representative Sue Myrick *(Republican, Ninth District, North Carolina)* was first elected to the House in 1994. A member of the Rules Committee, she has championed small-business issues.

Before coming to Congress, Representative Myrick served as mayor of Charlotte, North Carolina. Born in 1941 in Tifflin, Ohio, she attended Heidelberg College. She is married and has five children and seven grandchildren.

Representative Grace Napolitano *(Democrat, Thirty-fourth District, California)* was elected to Congress in 1998. She serves on the Resources Committee and two of its subcommittees—Water and Power, and Forests and Forest Health—as well as on the Small Business Committee and its Subcommittee on Tax, Finance and Exports. With these assignments, she continues to work on two priority issue areas with which she was concerned before coming to Congress—international trade and the environment.

Congresswoman Napolitano began her political career in 1986 with her election to the Norwalk (California) City Council. She was the first Latina ever elected to that body. She subsequently served two terms as Norwalk's mayor. In 1992, she was elected to the California Assembly, where she served three terms before coming to Congress.

Congresswoman Napolitano is married to Frank Napolitano. She and her husband have five grown children and 12 grandchildren.

Representative Anne Meagher Northup *(Republican, Third District, Kentucky)* was first elected to the House in 1996. She is a member of the Appropriations Committee.

Before her election to Congress, Representative Northup served for nine years in the Kentucky House of Representatives, where she supported increased fiscal responsibility, free enterprise, and small-business concerns.

Born in 1948, Congresswoman Northup earned her B.A. in economics and business from

St. Mary's College. She and her husband, Robert Wood Northup, have six children.

Delegate Eleanor Holmes Norton *(Democrat, At Large, District of Columbia),* was first elected to Congress in 1990. The first woman elected to represent the District in the House, Delegate Norton serves on the Government Reform and Oversight Committee, where she is the ranking Democratic member of the District of Columbia Subcommittee. She also serves on the Transportation and Infrastructure Committee. Delegate Norton is an advocate for civil rights issues and for the economic and political independence of the District of Columbia.

Born in the District of Columbia in 1937, Delegate Norton is a graduate of Antioch College. She holds both an M.A. and an L.L.B. from Yale University. A professor of law at Georgetown University before her election to Congress, she also served as chair of the Equal Employment Opportunity Commission during the Carter Administration. She has two children.

Representative Nancy Pelosi *(Democrat, Eighth District, California)* was first elected to Congress in 1987. She sits on the Appropriations Committee and is the ranking Democratic member of its Subcommittee on Foreign Operations and Export Financing. She also serves on the Select Committee on Intelligence and chairs the Congressional Working Group on China.

Congresswoman Pelosi has focused much of her attention on funding for AIDS research and prevention and on increasing prenatal care for low-income families. She is also the author of legislation to preserve the supply of housing for low-income families and to establish programs to alleviate homelessness among individuals with AIDS.

Born in 1940 in Baltimore, Maryland, Representative Pelosi earned her B.A. from Trinity College in Washington, D.C. She later served as state chair of the California Democratic party. She and her husband, Paul Pelosi, have five children.

Representative Deborah Pryce *(Republican, Fifteenth District, Ohio)*, was first elected to the House in 1992. She is a member of the Rules Committee and is serving her second term as secretary of the House Republican Conference. She has a strong interest in family- and child-welfare issues.

Before her election to Congress, Representative Pryce served as a judge on the Franklin County Municipal Court. She is a graduate of Ohio State University and has a law degree from Capital University in Columbus, Ohio. Born in 1952 in Warren, Ohio, she is married and has two children.

Representative Lynn Rivers *(Democrat, Thirteenth District, Michigan)* was first elected to the House in 1994. She sits on the Budget Committee and the Science Committee.

Congresswoman Rivers began her public service as a member of the Ann Arbor school board, of which she was president for three years. Before her election to Congress, she served one term in the Michigan legislature.

Born in 1956 in Au Gres, Michigan, Congresswoman Rivers has a B.A. from the University of Michigan and a J.D. from Wayne State University Law School. She and her husband, Joe Rivers, live in Ann Arbor with their two daughters.

Representative Ileana Ros-Lehtinen *(Republican, Eighteenth District, Florida)*, who was first elected to the House in a special election in 1989, made history as the first Hispanic woman to be elected to Congress. She is a member of the Government Reform and Oversight Committee and the Committee on International Relations, where she chairs the Subcommittee on Economic Policy and Trade.

Congresswoman Ros-Lehtinen, who was born in Havana, Cuba, in 1952, obtained her A.A. from Miami-Dade Community College and her B.A. and M.S. degrees from Florida International University. Before coming to Congress, she served in both houses of the Florida legislature. She is married to Dexter Lehtinen and has two daughters.

Representative Marge Roukema *(Republican, Fifth District, New Jersey)* was first elected to the House in 1980. She sits on the Banking and Financial Services Committee, where she chairs the Subcommittee on Financial Institutions and Consumer Credit. She is also a member of the Committee on Education and the Workforce. She has been active on a variety of women's issues, including family and medical leave, welfare reform, and child-support enforcement.

Congresswoman Roukema was born in 1929 in West Orange, New Jersey. She holds a B.A. from Montclair State College in New Jersey. Before coming to Congress, she was a secondary school teacher. She and her husband, Richard W. Roukema, have two children and five grandchildren.

Representative Lucille Roybal-Allard *(Democrat, Thirty-third District, California)*, first elected to the House in 1992, is the first Mexican American woman to be elected to Congress.

In the 106th Congress, she became the first Latina ever to be appointed to the House Appropriations Committee, as well as the first woman to be elected chair of the Congressional Hispanic Caucus. She formerly served as chair of the California Democratic congressional delegation.

Congresswoman Roybal-Allard's legislative priorities include school construction and modernization, class size reduction, increasing the minimum wage, saving Social Security, and stimulating economic growth for her upwardly mobile, largely Hispanic district.

Before her election to Congress, Representative Roybal-Allard served in the California Assembly for six years. Born in Los Angeles in 1941, she received her B.S. from California State University at Los Angeles. She is married to Edward T. Allard, III, and has two grown children.

Representative Loretta Sanchez *(Democrat, Forty-sixth District, California)* was elected to the House in 1996. She is a member of the Committee on Education and the Workforce and the Committee on Armed Services.

Representative Sanchez earned a bachelor's degree in economics from Chapman University and holds an M.B.A. in finance from American University. Before coming to Congress, she was a businesswoman in Santa Ana, California, specializing in assisting public agencies with financial matters. Congresswoman Sanchez, who was born in 1960, is married to Stephen Brixey. They live in Anaheim.

Representative Janice D. Schakowsky *(Democrat, Ninth District, Illinois)* was elected to the House in 1998. She serves on the Banking and Financial Services Committee and the Government Reform and Oversight Committee. She has also been appointed a Democratic at-large whip.

Before her election to Congress, Congresswoman Schakowsky served for eight years in the Illinois General Assembly, where she chaired the Labor and Commerce Committee. She also served as a Democratic floor leader and as secretary of the Conference of Women Legislators. She is deeply involved in the fight to protect women's reproductive rights.

A graduate of the University of Illinois with a B.S. in elementary education, Congresswoman Schakowsky lives in Evanston with her husband, Robert Creamer. She has three children, one stepdaughter, and one granddaughter.

Representative Louise Slaughter *(Democrat, Twenty-eighth District, New York)* was first elected to the House in 1986. She is a member of the Rules Committee.

Congresswoman Slaughter has fought to lower air fares by encouraging competition in the airline industry. Her priorities also include providing educational opportunities to homeless children, broadening safeguards for victims of domestic violence, expanding funds for women's health research, and protecting against genetic discrimination in health insurance.

Born in Harlan County, Kentucky, in 1929, Congresswoman Slaughter received both a B.S. and an M.S. from the University of Kentucky. She entered the Monroe County (New York) legislature in 1975 and went on to serve in the New York State Assembly before running successfully for Congress. She is married to Robert Slaughter and has three grown daughters and four grandchildren.

Senator Olympia J. Snowe *(Republican, Maine)* was elected to the Senate in 1994 after serving eight terms in the House of Representatives. She sits on the Budget Committee, the Armed Services Committee, the Commerce, Science, and Transportation Committee, and the Small Business Committee. She is chair of both the Commerce Subcommittee on Oceans and Fisheries and the Armed Services Subcommittee on Seapower.

While in the House, Senator Snowe served for many years as cochair of the Congressional Caucus for Women's Issues. She focused her energies on a successful effort to establish the Office of Research on Women's Health at the National Institutes of Health, thus ensuring that women are included in medical research. She also has been a leader on international family planning issues.

Senator Snowe, who was born in Augusta, Maine, in 1947, received her B.A. from the University of Maine. She began her political career in 1973 when she was elected to the Maine legislature to fill the seat made vacant by the death of her first husband. She is now married to John R. McKernan, Jr.

Representative Debbie Stabenow *(Democrat, Eighth District, Michigan)* was first elected to the House in 1996. She sits on the Agriculture Committee and the Science Committee.

Representative Stabenow served in both houses of the Michigan legislature before coming to Congress. Born in Michigan in 1950, she was raised in Clare, Michigan, and received her bachelor's and master's degrees from Michigan State University. The mother of two children, she lives in Lansing.

Representative Ellen O. Tauscher *(Democrat, Tenth District, California)* launched her career in public service in 1996 when, as a Democrat, she won a congressional seat in a Republican district. During her first term in the House, she was selected to be vice chair of the Democratic Congressional Campaign Committee. She currently sits on the Transportation and Infrastructure Committee and the Armed Services Committee.

Before her election to Congress, she cochaired Senator Dianne Feinstein's Senate campaigns in 1992 and 1994. She also founded the ChildCare Registry and published *The ChildCare Sourcebook*. Born in New Jersey in 1951, Congresswoman Tauscher received her B.S. in early childhood education from Seton Hall University. She is married and has one daughter.

Representative Karen Thurman *(Democrat, Fifth District, Florida)* was first elected to the House in 1992. She sits on the Ways and Means Committee.

Congresswoman Thurman is a supporter of reproductive rights and is working to broaden women's issues to areas beyond health care and jobs. Before her election to Congress, Representative Thurman served on the Dunnellon (Florida) City Council and as that city's mayor from 1979 to 1981. She also served for 10 years in the Florida Senate, where she chaired the Agriculture Committee, the Professional Regulation Committee, and the Congressional Redistricting Committee.

Born in Rapid City, South Dakota, in 1951, Representative Thurman is a graduate of the University of Florida. She is married to John Thurman. They have two children.

Representative Nydia Velázquez *(Democrat, Twelfth District, New York),* first elected to Congress in 1992, is the first Puerto Rican woman to be elected to the House of Representatives. Congresswoman Velázquez is the ranking Democratic member of the Small Business Committee. She also sits on the Banking and Financial Services Committee.

Before coming to Congress, Representative Velázquez worked as a liaison between the Puerto Rican government and the Puerto Rican community in New York, where she organized efforts to increase AIDS education and to register voters. She also was the first Hispanic woman to be elected to the New York City Council, where she served from 1984 to 1986. In Congress, she is continuing her work on women's and poverty issues.

Born in Puerto Rico in 1953, Representative Velázquez received her B.A. from the University of Puerto Rico and her M.S. in political science from New York University.

Representative Maxine Waters *(Democrat, Thirty-fifth District, California)* was first elected to the House in 1990. She serves on the Judiciary Committee and on the Banking and Financial Services Committee, where she is the ranking Democrat on the Subcommittee on Domestic and International Monetary Policy. As one of the four Democratic chief deputy whips, she is part of the Democratic leadership.

Congresswoman Waters has been a leader on the issue of AIDS in the African American community. She also has been a vocal advocate of increased investment in programs and services in the nation's urban areas.

Before coming to Congress, Representative Waters served for 15 years in the California Assembly, where she was the first woman in the state's history to be elected chair of the Democratic Caucus. She was born in St. Louis, Missouri, in 1938, and holds a B.A. from California State University at Los Angeles. She is married to Sidney Williams and has two children and two grandchildren.

Representative Heather Wilson *(Republican, First District, New Mexico)* was first elected to the House in mid-1998 in a special election. She was reelected to a full term in November 1998. She is the first woman veteran ever elected to Congress, and the first woman in a half-century to represent New Mexico in Congress.

Congresswoman Wilson serves on the Commerce Committee, the Select Committee on Intelligence, and the House Republican Policy Committee. Her priorities include improving education, reducing the size of government, lowering federal taxes, and making sure that Social Security is solvent for the long term.

Congresswoman Wilson graduated in 1982 from the U.S. Air Force Academy. She won a Rhodes Scholarship to Oxford University (England), from which she received her master's and doctoral degrees. She then served as an Air Force officer until 1989. Subsequently, she was on the National Security Council staff at the White House. Before coming to Congress, she served as secretary of the New Mexico Children, Youth and Families Department. She is married to Jay Hone. They have three children.

Representative Lynn Woolsey *(Democrat, Sixth District, California),* first elected to the House in 1992, is the first former welfare mother ever elected to Congress.

Congresswoman Woolsey is a member of the Education and the Workforce Committee and the Science Committee. She has been a leader on welfare reform and children's issues.

Before her election to Congress, Representative Woolsey was a member of the Petaluma (California) City Council. She was also that city's vice mayor. In these positions, she was successful in her efforts to expand low- and moderate-income housing, and led the fight to build the first emergency family shelter for homeless families in Sonoma County.

Representative Woolsey, who was born in Seattle, Washington, in 1937, is a graduate of the University of San Francisco. She has four children.

Congressional Caucus for Women's Issues[1]

Sue W. Kelly (R-NY), cochair

Carolyn B. Maloney (D-NY), cochair

Kay Granger (R-TX), vice chair

Juanita Millender-McDonald (D-CA), vice chair

Tammy Baldwin (D-WI)

Shelley Berkley (D-NV)

Judy Biggert (R-IL)

Mary Bono (R-CA)

Corrine Brown (D-FL)

Lois Capps (D-CA)

Julia Carson (D-IN)

Helen Chenoweth-Hage (R-ID)

Donna Christian-Christensen (D-VI)

Eva Clayton (D-NC)

Barbara Cubin (R-WY)

Patricia Danner (D-MO)

Diana DeGette (D-CO)

Rosa L. DeLauro (D-CT)

Jennifer Dunn (R-WA)

Anna Eshoo (D-CA)

Tillie Fowler (R-FL)

Darlene Hooley (D-OR)

Sheila Jackson Lee (D-TX)

Eddie Bernice Johnson (D-TX)

Nancy Johnson (R-CT)

Stephanie Tubbs Jones (D-OH)

Marcy Kaptur (D-OH)

Carolyn Cheeks Kilpatrick (D-MI)

Barbara Lee (D-CA)

Zoe Lofgren (D-CA)

Nita Lowey (D-NY)

Carolyn McCarthy (D-NY)

Karen McCarthy (D-MO)

Cynthia McKinney (D-GA)

Carrie Meek (D-FL)

Patsy Mink (D-HI)

Constance Morella (R-MD)

Sue Myrick (R-NC)

Grace Napolitano (D-CA)

Eleanor Holmes Norton (D-DC)

Nancy Pelosi (D-CA)

Deborah Pryce (R-OH)

Lynn Rivers (D-MI)

Ileana Ros-Lehtinen (R-FL)

Marge Roukema (R-NJ)

Lucille Roybal-Allard (D-CA)

Loretta Sanchez (D-CA)

[1]106th Congress (as of November 15, 1999).

Janice D. Schakowsky (D–IL)

Louise Slaughter (D–NY)

Debbie Stabenow (D–MI)

Ellen O. Tauscher (D–CA)

Karen Thurman (D–FL)

Nydia Velázquez (D–NY)

Maxine Waters (D–CA)

Lynn Woolsey (D–CA)

References

THE AMERICAN WOMAN: GETTING TO THE TOP

Chapter One   Women's Leadership in American Politics: The Legacy and the Promise

Ayres, B. Drummond, Jr. "Women to the Rescue of Elizabeth Dole." *The New York Times,* July 22, 1999.

Bruni, Frank. "3 Democratic Women Lead on Gun Control." *The New York Times,* June 14, 1999.

Carroll, Susan J. *Women as Candidates in American Politics.* Bloomington: Indiana University Press, 1985.

Carroll, Susan J., Debra L. Dodson, and Ruth B. Mandel. *The Impact of Women in Public Office: An Overview.* New Brunswick, NJ: Center for American Women and Politics, Eagleton Institute of Politics, Rutgers University, 1991.

Center for American Women and Politics (CAWP) (formerly Center for the American Woman and Politics). *Not One of the Boys.* 60-min. documentary. 1984. Aired on PBS's "Frontline" in October 1984.

————. *Women in Congressional Leadership Roles.* New Brunswick, NJ: CAWP, March 1999.

————. *Women in Elective Office 1999.* New Brunswick, NJ: CAWP, August 1999.

————. *Women State Legislators: Leadership Positions and Committee Chairs 1999.* New Brunswick, NJ: CAWP, 1999.

Chafe, William H. *The American Woman: Her Changing Social, Economic, and Political Roles, 1920–1970.* New York: Oxford University Press, 1972.

Dodson, Debra L., and Susan J. Carroll. *Reshaping the Agenda: Women in State Legislatures.* New Brunswick, NJ: Center for American Women and Politics, Eagleton Institute of Politics, Rutgers University, 1991.

Dodson, Debra L., Susan J. Carroll, Ruth B. Mandel, Katherine E. Kleeman, Ronnee Schreiber, and Debra Liebowitz. *Voices, Views, Votes: The Impact of Women* in the 103rd Congress. New Brunswick, NJ: Center for American Women and Politics, Eagleton Institute of Politics, Rutgers University, 1995.

Gertzog, Irwin N. *Congressional Women: Their Recruitment, Treatment, and Behavior,* 2d ed. New York: Praeger, 1995.

Lippman, Thomas W. "State Dept. Sets Priority on Women." *The Washington Post,* March 25, 1997.

Mandel, Ruth B. *In the Running: The New Woman Candidate.* New York: Ticknor & Fields, 1981; Boston: Beacon Press, 1983.

Mandel, Ruth B., and Debra L. Dodson. "Do Women Officeholders Make a Difference?" In *The American Woman 1992–93,* edited by Paula Ries and Anne J. Stone. New York: W. W. Norton & Co., 1992.

Norris, Pippa, ed. *Women, Media, and Politics.* New York: Oxford University Press, 1997.

Rogers, Mary Beth. *Barbara Jordan: American Hero.* New York: Bantam Books, 1998.

Roosevelt, Eleanor. *The Autobiography of Eleanor Roosevelt.* New York: Harper and Row, Barnes & Noble Books edition, 1978.

Rosener, Judy B. "Ways Women Lead." *Harvard Business Review* 68 (November–December 1990): 119–25.

Rosenthal, Cindy Simon. *When Women Lead: Integrative Leadership in State Legislatures.* New York: Oxford University Press, 1998.

Witt, Linda, Karen M. Paget, and Glenna Matthews. *Running as a Woman: Gender and Power in American Politics.* New York: Free Press, 1993.

Chapter Two   Women and Leadership in Higher Education

American Council on Education (ACE). *Women Presidents in U.S. Colleges and Universities. A 1995 Higher Education Update.* Washington, DC: ACE Office of Women in Higher Education, 1995.

Association of Governing Boards (AGB). *Composition of Governing Boards 1985.* Washington, DC: AGB Special Report, 1986.

Benjamin, Ernst. "Disparities in the Salaries and Appointments of Academic Women and Men." *Academe* 85 (January–February 1999): 60–63.

Benjamin, Lois, ed. *Black Women in the Academy: Promises and Perils.* Gainesville: University Press of Florida, 1997.

Chamberlain, Mariam K., ed. *Women in Academe: Progress and Prospects.* New York: Russell Sage Foundation, 1988.

College and University Personnel Association (CUPA). *Administrative Compensation Survey. 1998–99.* Washington, DC: CUPA, 1999.

Goldberg, Carey. "M.I.T. Acknowledges Bias Against Female Professors." *The New York Times,* March 23, 1999.

Hartnett, Rodney T. *College and University Trustees: Their Background, Role, and Educational Attitudes.* Princeton: Educational Testing Service, 1969.

James, Edward T., ed. *Notable American Women, 1607–1950.* A Biographical Dictionary, Third Volume. Cambridge, MA: Balknap Press of Harvard University, 1971.

Koerner, Brendan I. "Where the Boys Aren't." *U.S. News and World Report,* February 8, 1999, 46–55.

LaNoue, George R., and Barbara A. Lee. *Academics in Court. The Consequences of Faculty Discrimination Litigation.* Ann Arbor: University of Michigan Press, 1987.

Madsden, Holly. *Composition of Governing Boards of Independent Colleges and Universities, 1997.* AGB Occasional Paper, no. 36. Washington, DC: Association of Governing Boards, 1998.

———. *Composition of Governing Boards of Public Colleges and Universities, 1997.* AGB Occasional Paper, no. 37. Washington, DC: Association of Governing Boards, 1998.

Mitchell, Patricia Turner, ed. *Cracking the Wall: Women in Higher Education Administration.* Washington, DC: College and University Personnel Administration, 1993.

National Center for Education Statistics. *Fall Staff in Postsecondary Institutions, 1995.* Washington, DC: U.S. Department of Education, Office of Educational Improvement, 1998.

Ries, Paula, and Dolores H. Thurgood. *Summary Report 1991: Doctorate Recipients from United States Universities.* Washington, DC: National Academy Press, 1993.

Rimer, Sara. "Radcliffe Women, Once Docile, Prod Harvard Sharply on Equality of Sexes." *The New York Times,* February 24, 1997.

Rolnick, Joshua. "A New Challenge for a Theoretical Physicist." *The Chronicle of Higher Education,* January 8, 1999.

Sanderson, Allen R., and Bernard Drugoni. *Summary Report 1997: Doctorate Recipients from the United States Universities.* Chicago: National Opinion Research Center, 1999.

Tinsley, Adrian, Cynthia Secor, and Sheila Kaplan, eds. *Women in Higher Education Administration.* San Francisco: Jossey-Bass, Inc., 1984.

Touchton, Judith G., Donna Shavlik, and Lynn Davis. *Women in Presidencies: A Descriptive Study of College and University Presidents.* Washington, DC: American Council on Education, 1993.

Chapter Three   Women and Leadership in Corporate America

Byrne, John A., David Leonhardt, Lori Bongiorno, and Fred Jespersen. "The Best B-Schools." *Business Week,* October 21, 1996, 110.

Bureau of Labor Statistics. Current Population Survey, March 1999. Unpublished data, Washington, DC.

Catalyst. *Census of Women Board Directors of the Fortune 1000.* New York: Catalyst, 1999a.

———. *Census of Women Corporate Officers and Top Earners.* New York: Catalyst, 1999b.

———. *Creating Women's Networks.* San Francisco: Jossey-Bass, 1999c.

———. *Women of Color in Corporate Management: A Statistical Picture.* New York: Catalyst, 1998a.

————. *Women of Color in Corporate Management: Dynamics of Career Advancement.* New York: Catalyst, 1998b.

————. *Women of Color in Corporate Management: Opportunities and Barriers.* New York: Catalyst, 1999d.

————. *Women in Corporate Leadership: Progress and Prospects.* New York: Catalyst, 1996.

Cornell University and Ray Berndtson Associates. *Database of Senior Executive Pay,* 1994. Cited in Catalyst 1999d.

Fullerton, Howard N. "Labor Force Projections to 2008: Steady Growth and Changing Composition." *Monthly Labor Review* 122, no. 11 (November 1999): 19–32.

Chapter Four   Women in Union Leadership

Aburdene, Patricia, and John Naisbitt. *Megatrends for Women.* New York: Villard Books, 1992.

Andriappan, P., and Gary N. Chaison. *The Emerging Role of Women in National Union Governance: The Results of a Canadian Study.* Paper presented at the Sixth World Congress of the International Industrial Relations Association, March 28–31, 1989.

Baden, Naomi. "Developing an Agenda: Expanding the Role of Women in Unions." *Labor Studies Journal* 10, no. 3 (winter 1986): 230–39.

Balser, Diane. *Sisterhood and Solidarity.* Boston: South End Press, 1987.

Bernard, Elaine. "Tips for Women Achieving Power and Leadership in Their Unions." Unpublished speech, September 14, 1996.

Briskin, Linda, and Patricia McDermott. *Women Challenging Unions: Feminization, Democracy and Militancy.* Toronto Press, 1993.

Bronfenbrenner, Kate. *Lifting As They Climb: The Promise and Potential of Organizing Women Workers.* Working Women's Department, AFL-CIO, March 18, 1998.

Catlett, Judith H. "After the Long Goodbyes: A Long-Term Look at the Southern School for Union Women." *Labor Studies Journal* 10, no. 3 (winter 1986): 300–11.

Chaison, Gary N., and P. Andriappan. "An Analysis of the Barriers to Women Becoming Head Union Officers." *Journal of Labor Research* 10 (1987): 149–62.

————. "A Study of Female Union Officers in Canada." Paper presented at the meeting of the Canadian Industrial Relations Association, Ottawa, Canada, 1982.

Cobble, Dorothy Sue. "Rethinking Troubled Relations between Women and Unions: Craft Unionism and Female Activism." *Feminist Studies* 26, no. 3 (fall 1990): 519–48.

Cook, Alice H. "Women and American Trade Unions." *Annals of the American Academy of Political and Social Science* 375 (January 1968): 124–32.

Eaton, Susan C. "Women in Trade Union Leadership: How More Women Can Become Leaders of Today's and Tomorrow's Unions." Unpublished paper. City University of New York, Graduate Center, 1990.

Elkiss, Helen. "Training Women for Union Office: Breaking the Glass Ceiling." *Labor Studies Journal* 19, no. 2 (summer 1994): 25–42.

Epstein, Cynthia Fuchs. "Ways Men and Women Lead." *Harvard Business Review* 69, no. 1 (January–February 1991): 150–60.

Fellner, Kim. "Comments." In *Women and Unions: Forging a Partnership,* edited by Dorothy Sue Cobble. Ithaca, NY: ILR Press, 1993.

Foner, Philip S. *Women and the American Labor Movement: From Colonial Times to the End of World War I.* New York: Free Press, 1979.

———. *Women and the American Labor Movement: From World War I to the Present.* New York: Free Press, 1980.

Freeman, Richard B., and James L. Medoff. *What Do Unions Do?* New York: Basic Books, Inc., 1984.

Gabin, Nancy. "Women and the United Auto Workers in the 1940's and 1950's." *Labor's Heritage* 1, no. 1 (January 1989): 58–68.

Gifford, C. D. *Directory of the United States Labor Organizations.* Washington, DC: Bureau of National Affairs, 1998.

Glassberg, Elyse, Naomi Baden, and Karin Gerstel. *Absent from the Agenda: A Report on the Role of Women in American Unions.* Coalition of Labor Union Women, Center for Education and Research, 1980.

Gray, Lois S. Interviews conducted by author, 1999.

———. "The Route to the Top: Female Union Leaders and Union Policy." In *Women and Unions; Forging a Partnership,* edited by Dorothy Sue Cobble. Ithaca, NY: ILR Press, 1993.

———. "Women in Union Leadership Roles." *Interface.* (Department of Professional Employees, AFL-CIO) 17, no. 3 (summer 1998): 7–9.

Harriford, Diane. "Comments." In *Women and Unions: Forging a Partnership,* edited by Dorothy Sue Cobble. Ithaca, NY: ILR Press, 1993.

Hartmann, Heidi, Roberta Spalter-Roth, and Nancy Collins. "What Do Unions Do for Women?" *Challenge* (July/August 1994): 4–11.

Heery, Edmund, and John Kelly. "Do Female Representatives Make a Difference? Women Full-Time Union Officials and Trade Union Work." *Work, Employment and Society* 2, no. 4 (December 1988): 487–505.

Hurd, Richard W. "Organizing and Representing Clerical Workers: The Harvard Model." In *Women and Unions: Forging a Partnership,* edited by Dorothy Sue Cobble. Ithaca, NY: ILR Press, 1993.

International Labour Office. *The Role of Trade Unions in Promoting Gender Equality and Protecting Vulnerable Women Workers.* First Report of the ILO-ICFTU Survey, May 1999.

Kochan, Thomas A. "How American Workers View Labor Unions." *Monthly Labor Review* 102, no. 4 (April 1979): 23–31.

Kopelov, Connie. "Labor's Herstory: The Women's Trade Union League." Paper presented at the New York State Labor History Association, November–December, 1984.

Koziara, Karen, and David A. Pierson. "Barriers to Women Becoming Union

Leaders." Proceedings of the 33rd Annual Meeting of the Industrial Relations Association, 1980.

Lunneberg, Patricia. *Women Changing Work*. New York: Bergen and Garvey, 1990.

Milkman, Ruth. "The New Gender Politics in Organized Labor." *Proceedings of the 45th Annual Meeting of the Industrial Relations Research Association,* Anaheim, CA, 1995.

Needleman, Ruth. "Comment." In *Women and Unions: Forging a Partnership,* edited by Dorothy Sue Cobble. Ithaca, NY: ILR Press, 1993a.

————."Space and Opportunities: Developing New Leaders to Meet Labor's Future." *Labor Research Review* 20, no. 1 (Spring–Summer 1993b): 5–20.

————. "Women Workers: A Force for Rebuilding Unions." *Labor Research Review* (Special Issue on Feminizing Unions) 11, no. 1 (spring 1998): 1–14.

Needleman, Ruth, and Lucretia Dewey Tanner. "Women in Unions: Current Issues." In *Working Women: Past, Present, and Future, "* edited by K. Koziara, M. H. Moscow, and L. D. Tanner. Washington, DC: Bureau of National Affairs, 1987.

O'Cleiracain, Carol. "Women and the Future of the Labor Movement." *Social Policy* 16 (winter 1986): 40–42.

Quaglieri, Philip L. "The New People of Power: The Backgrounds and Careers of Top Labor Leaders." *Journal of Labor Research* 9, no. 3 (1998): 271–84.

Roby, Pamela, and Lynet Uttal. "Putting It All Together: The Dilemmas of Rank and File Union Leaders." In *Women and Unions: Forging a Partnership,* edited by Dorothy Sue Cobble. Ithaca, NY: ILR Press, 1993.

Rosener, Judy B. "Ways Women Lead." *Harvard Business Review* 68, no. 6 (November–December 1990): 119–25.

Trebilcock, Anne. "Strategies for Strengthening Women's Participation in Trade Union Leadership." *International Labour Review* 130, no. 4 (1991): 407–26.

Wajcman, Judy. *Managing Like a Man: Women and Men in Corporate Management.* University Park, PA: Pennsylvania State University Press, 1998.

Waldman, Amy. "Labor's New Face: Women Renegotiate Their Role." *The Nation,* September 22, 1997, 11–16.

Wertheimer, Barbara Mayer. *We Were There*. New York: Pantheon Books, 1977.

Wertheimer, Barbara Mayer, and Ann Nelson. *Trade Union Women: A Study of Their Participation in New York City Locals*. New York: Praeger, 1975.

Chapter Five   Women in the Military: The Struggle to Lead

Ambrose, Stephen E. *Citizen Soldiers*. New York: Touchstone, 1997.

Bacevich, Andrew J. "Who Will Serve?" *The Wilson Quarterly* 22 (summer 1998): 81–91.

Collins, Joseph J. "The Complex Context of American Military Culture: A Practitioner's View," *The Washington Quarterly* 21, no. 4 (autumn 1998): 213–28.

Coyle, Commander Barry USN. "Women on the Front Lines." *Proceedings of the U.S. Military Institute* 115 (April 1989): 37–40.

Dane Hansen Productions. *In Service to America: A History of Women in the Military.* 60 min. documentary. Boulder, CO: Dane Hansen Productions, 1994.

Gibson, James William. *Warrior Dreams: Violence and Manhood in Post-Vietnam America.* New York: Hill and Wang, 1994.

Institute of Medicine. National Academy of Sciences. *Assessing Readiness in Military Women.* Washington, DC: National Academy Press, 1998.

Johnson, Cecil. *Women Content in the Army: REFORGER (REFWAC 77).* Alexandria, VA: U.S. Army Research Institute, 1978.

Lehman, John. "An Exchange on Civil-Military Relations." *The National Interest* 36 (summer 1994): 23–25.

Miller, Laura, and Charles C. Moskos. "Humanitarians or Warriors? Race, Gender and Combat Status in Operation Restore Hope," *Armed Forces and Society* 21 (summer 1995): 615–37.

Moskos, Charles C., Jr. "The American Combat Soldier in Vietnam," *Journal of Social Issues* 31 (1975): 25–31.

Reinisch, June M., and Stephanie A. Sanders. "A Test of Sex Differences in Aggressive Response to Hypothetical Conflict Situations," *Journal of Personality and Social Psychology* 50, no. 5 (1986): 1045–49.

Segal, David, and Mady Weschler Segal. *Peacekeepers and Their Wives: American Participation in the Multinational Force and Their Observers.* Westport, CT: Greenwood Press, 1993.

Snider, Don M. "An Uninformed Debate in Military Culture," *Orbis* 43 (winter 1999): 1–16.

United States v. *Virginia Military Institute* (518 U.S. 2).

U.S. Army Research Institute of Environmental Medicine. *Effects of a Specifically Designed Physical Conditioning Program on the Load Carriage and Lifting Performance of Female Soldiers.* Preliminary Report. Washington, DC, January 26, 1996.

U.S. Department of Defense. Defense Advisory Committee on Women in the Services (DACOWITS). "Remarks by General Henry H. Shelton." Speech presented at the Spring Conference of the Defense Advisory Committee on Women in the Services (DACOWITS) in Reston, VA, April 24, 1998.

————. Defense Manpower Data Center. *1988 Sexual Harassment Survey.* Washington, DC, 1990.

————. Defense Manpower Data Center. *1995 Sexual Harassment Survey.* Washington, DC, 1996.

————. Defense Manpower Data Center. *Surveys of Force Composition.* Unpublished data, 1997–1999.

AMERICAN WOMEN TODAY: A STATISTICAL PORTRAIT

Section 1: Demographics

Bureau of the Census. Current Population Reports, Series P20-514. *Marital Status and Living Arrangements: March 1998* (PPL-100). Washington, DC: U.S. Government Printing Office, 1999.

————. Current Population Reports, Series P-60-200. *Money Income in the United States: 1997.* Washington, DC: U.S. Government Printing Office, 1998.

————. Current Population Reports, Series P-25-1130. *Population Projections of the United States by Age, Sex, Race, and Hispanic Origin: 1995 to 2050.* Washington, DC: U.S. Government Printing Office, 1996.

————. *Historical Income Tables.* <http://www.census.gov/hhes/income/histinc/>.

————. *Statistical Abstract of the United States: 1980.* Washington, DC: U.S. Government Printing Office, 1980.

————. *Statistical Abstract of the United States: 1998.* Washington, DC: U.S. Government Printing Office, 1998.

National Center for Health Statistics. *Health, United States, 1998.* Hyattsville, MD: Public Health Service, 1998.

————. *National Vital Statistics Report* 47, no. 4 (October 7, 1998).

————. *National Vital Statistics Report* 47, no. 14 (December 23, 1998).

Section 2: Education

Bureau of the Census. Current Population Reports, Series P20-513. *Educational Attainment in the United States: March 1998 (Update)* (PPL-99). Washington, DC: U.S. Government Printing Office, 1998.

————. *Statistical Abstract of the United States: 1998.* Washington, DC: U.S. Government Printing Office, 1998.

National Center for Education Statistics. *Digest of Education Statistics, 1977–78.* Washington, DC: U.S. Government Printing Office, 1978.

————. *Digest of Education Statistics, 1980.* Washington, DC: U.S. Government Printing Office, 1980.

————. *Digest of Education Statistics, 1990.* Washington, DC: U.S. Government Printing Office, 1991.

————. *Digest of Education Statistics, 1998.* Washington, DC: U.S. Government Printing Office, 1999.

Section 3: Health

Bureau of the Census. Current Population Reports, Series P-25-1130. *Population Projections of the United States by Age, Sex, Race, and Hispanic Origin: 1995 to 2050.* Washington, DC: U.S. Government Printing Office, February 1996.

Centers for Disease Control and Prevention. *Abortion Surveillance: Preliminary Analysis—United States, 1996* 47, no. 47 (December 4, 1998).

————. *HIV/AIDS Surveillance Report* 7, no. 2 (1995).

————. *HIV/AIDS Surveillance Report* 8, no. 2 (1996).

————. *HIV/AIDS Surveillance Report* 9, no. 2 (1997).

————. *HIV/AIDS Surveillance Report* 10, no. 2 (1998).

————. *Sexually Transmitted Disease Surveillance, 1997.* Atlanta, GA: Public Health Service, 1998.

National Cancer Institute. *SEER Cancer Statistics Review, 1973–1996 Initial Content: Tables and Graphs.* Bethesda, MD: National Cancer Institute, 1999.

National Center for Health Statistics. *Fertility, Family Planning, and Women's Health: New Data from the 1995 National Survey of Family Growth.* Hyattsville, MD: Public Health Service, 1997.

———. *Health, United States, 1993.* Hyattsville, MD: Public Health Service, 1994.

———. *Health, United States, 1995.* Hyattsville, MD: Public Health Service, 1996.

———. *Health, United States, 1998.* Hyattsville, MD: Public Health Service, 1998.

———. *National Vital Statistics Report* 47, no. 9 (November 10, 1998).

Section 4: Employment

Bureau of Labor Statistics. "A Profile of Contingent Workers." *Monthly Labor Review* 119, no. 10 (October 1996): 10–21.

———. "Contingent Work: Results from the Second Survey." *Monthly Labor Review* 121, no. 11 (November 1998): 22–35.

———. Current Population Survey, March 1976. Unpublished data, Washington, DC.

———. Current Population Survey, March 1978. Unpublished data, Washington, DC.

———. Current Population Survey, March 1980. Unpublished data, Washington, DC.

———. Current Population Survey, March 1982. Unpublished data, Washington, DC.

———. Current Population Survey, March 1984. Unpublished data, Washington, DC.

———. Current Population Survey, March 1986. Unpublished data, Washington, DC.

———. Current Population Survey, March 1988. Unpublished data, Washington, DC.

———. Current Population Survey, March 1990. Unpublished data, Washington, DC.

———. Current Population Survey, March 1992. Unpublished data, Washington, DC.

———. Current Population Survey, March 1994. Unpublished data, Washington, DC.

———. Current Population Survey, February 1995. Unpublished data, Washington, DC.

———. Current Population Survey, March 1996. Unpublished data, Washington, DC.

———. Current Population Survey, February 1997. Unpublished data, Washington, DC.

———. Current Population Survey, March 1998. Unpublished data, Washington, DC.

———. Current Population Survey, 1999. Unpublished data. <http://146.4.24/cgi-bin/dsrv?ee>.

————. *Employment and Earnings* 11, no. 1. Washington, DC: U.S. Government Printing Office, January 1964.

————. *Employment and Earnings* 16, no. 1. Washington, DC: U.S. Government Printing Office, January 1969.

————. *Employment and Earnings* 21, no. 1. Washington, DC: U.S. Government Printing Office, January 1974.

————. *Employment and Earnings* 26, no. 1. Washington, DC: U.S. Government Printing Office, January 1979.

————. *Employment and Earnings* 31, no. 1. Washington, DC: U.S. Government Printing Office, January 1984.

————. *Employment and Earnings* 36, no. 1. Washington, DC: U.S. Government Printing Office, January 1989.

————. *Employment and Earnings* 38, no. 1. Washington, DC: U.S. Government Printing Office, January 1991.

————. *Employment and Earnings* 40, no. 1. Washington, DC: U.S. Government Printing Office, January 1993.

————. *Employment and Earnings* 41, no. 1. Washington, DC: U.S. Government Printing Office, January 1994.

————. *Employment and Earnings* 43, no. 1. Washington, DC: U.S. Government Printing Office, January 1996.

————. *Employment and Earnings* 44, no. 1. Washington, DC: U.S. Government Printing Office, January 1997.

————. *Employment and Earnings* 46, no. 1. Washington, DC: U.S. Government Printing Office, January 1999.

————. *Handbook of Labor Statistics.* Washington, DC: U.S. Government Printing Office, 1989.

————. "Labor Force 2006: Slowing Down and Changing Composition." *Monthly Labor Review* 120, no. 11 (November 1997): 23–39.

————. *Labor Force Statistics Derived from the Current Population Survey, 1948–87.* Washington, DC: U.S. Government Printing Office, 1988.

————. "Multiple Jobholding Up Sharply in the 1980's." *Monthly Labor Review* 113, no. 7 (July 1990): 3–10.

————. "Workers in Alternative Employment Arrangements: A Second Look." *Monthly Labor Review* 121, no. 11 (November 1998): 3–21.

Bureau of the Census. Current Population Reports, Series P20-506. *Marital Status and Living Arrangements: March 1997 (Update)* (PPL-90). Washington, DC: U.S. Government Printing Office, 1998.

————. Current Population Reports, Series P60-193. *Money Income in the United States: 1995 (With Separate Data on Valuation of Noncash Benefits).* Washington, DC: U.S. Government Printing Office, 1996.

————. Current Population Reports, Series P60-200. *Money Income in the United States: 1997 (With Separate Data on Valuation of Noncash Benefits).* Washington, DC: U.S. Government Printing Office, 1998.

————. Current Population Reports, Series P-60, no. 180. *Money Income of House-*

holds, Families, and Persons in the United States: 1991. Washington, DC: U.S. Government Printing Office, 1992.

————. Current Population Reports, Series P70-62. *Who's Minding Our Preschoolers? Fall 1994 (Update)*. Washington, DC: U.S. Government Printing Office, 1997.

Section 5: Earnings and Benefits

Bureau of Labor Statistics. *Employment and Earnings* 38, no. 1. Washington, DC: U.S. Government Printing Office, January 1991.

————. *Employment and Earnings* 40, no. 1. Washington, DC: U.S. Government Printing Office, January 1993.

————. *Employment and Earnings* 42, no. 1. Washington, DC: U.S. Government Printing Office, January 1995.

————. *Employment and Earnings* 43, no. 1. Washington, DC: U.S. Government Printing Office, January 1996.

————. *Employment and Earnings* 44, no. 1. Washington, DC: U.S. Government Printing Office, January 1997.

————. *Employment and Earnings* 46, no. 1. Washington, DC: U.S. Government Printing Office, January 1999.

————. *Handbook of Labor Statistics*. Washington, DC: U.S. Government Printing Office, 1989.

————. Current Population Survey, May 1978. Unpublished data, Washington, DC.

————. Current Population Survey, March 1998. Unpublished data, Washington, DC.

Bureau of the Census. *Historical Income Tables*. <http://www.census.gov/hhes/income/histinc/>.

————. Current Population Reports, Series P-60, no. 162. *Money Income of Households, Families, and Persons in the United States: 1987*. Washington, DC: U.S. Government Printing Office, 1988.

————. Current Population Reports, Series P-60, no. 200. *Money Income in the United States: 1997*. Washington, DC: U.S. Government Printing Office, 1998.

————. Current Population Survey, March 1998. <http://ferret.bls.census.gov/macro/031998/noncash/7_000.htm>.

————. Current Population Survey, March 1998. <http://ferret.bls.census.gov/macro/031998/noncash/8_000.htm>.

————. Current Population Survey, March 1998. <http://ferret.bls.census.gov/macro/031998/pov/new24_000.htm>.

————. Current Population Survey, March 1998. <http://www.census.gov/income/hlthins/hi01.txt>.

Section 6: Economic Security

Bureau of the Census. Current Population Survey, Series P23-190. *65+ in the United States*. Washington, DC: U.S. Government Printing Office, 1996.

———. Current Population Survey, March 1998. <http://ferret.bls.census.gov/macro/031998/perinc/12_000.htm>.

———. Current Population Survey, March 1998. <http://ferret.bls.census.gov/macro/031998/pov/new1_000.htm>.

———. *Historical Income Tables.* <http://www.census.gov/hhes/income/histinc/>.

———. Current Population Reports, Series P60-188. *Income, Poverty, and Valuation of Noncash Benefits: 1993.* Washington, DC: U.S. Government Printing Office, 1995.

———. Current Population Reports, Series P60-189. *Income, Poverty, and Valuation of Noncash Benefits: 1994.* Washington, DC: U.S. Government Printing Office, 1996.

———. Current Population Reports, Series P60-163. *Poverty in the United States: 1987.* Washington, DC: U.S. Government Printing Office, 1989.

———. Current Population Reports, Series P60-171. *Poverty in the United States: 1988 and 1989.* Washington, DC: U.S. Government Printing Office, 1991.

———. Current Population Reports, Series P60-175. *Poverty in the United States: 1990.* Washington, DC: U.S. Government Printing Office, 1991.

———. Current Population Reports, Series P60-181. *Poverty in the United States: 1991.* Washington, DC: U.S. Government Printing Office, 1992.

———. Current Population Reports, Series P60-194. *Poverty in the United States: 1995.* Washington, DC: U.S. Government Printing Office, 1996.

———. Current Population Reports, Series P60-198. *Poverty in the United States: 1996.* Washington, DC: U.S. Government Printing Office, 1997.

———. Current Population Reports, Series P60-201. *Poverty in the United States: 1997.* Washington, DC: U.S. Government Printing Office, 1998.

Bureau of the Census and Department of Housing and Urban Development. *American Housing Survey for the United States in 1997.* Washington, DC: U.S. Government Printing Office, 1999.

Bureau of Labor Statistics. Current Population Survey, March 1998. Unpublished data, Washington, DC.

Section 7: Women in the Military

Bureau of Labor Statistics. Current Population Survey, March 1998. Unpublished data, Washington, DC.

U.S. Department of Defense. Defense Manpower Data Center. Unpublished data, Arlington, VA, August 1997.

———. Defense Manpower Data Center. Unpublished data, Arlington, VA, May 31, 1999.

———. Office of the Assistant Secretary of Defense for Public Affairs. Public Affairs News Release no. 449–94, July 29, 1994.

———. Staff of the Office of the Chief of Naval Operations. Unpublished data, Arlington, VA, 1999.

———. Unpublished data provided by each service academy, June 1993.

———. Unpublished data provided by each service academy, June 1999.

U.S. Department of Transportation. Unpublished data provided by the Coast Guard Academy, New London, CT, June 1993.

———. Unpublished data provided by the Coast Guard Academy, New London, CT, June 1999.

Section 8: Elections and Officials

Administrative Office of the United States Courts. *Annual Report on the Judiciary Equal Employment Opportunity Program for the Twelve-Month Period Ended September 30, 1991.* Washington, DC: 1991.

———. Unpublished data, September 1998.

Bureau of the Census. *Historical Time Series Tables.* <http://www.census.gov/population/www/socdemo/voting.html>.

Center for American Women and Politics (CAWP) (formerly Center for the American Woman and Politics). *Statewide Elective Executive Women: 1969–1999.* New Brunswick, NJ: CAWP, February 1999.

———. *Statewide Elective Executive Women 1999.* New Brunswick, NJ: CAWP, September 1999.

———. *Women in Elective Office 1999.* New Brunswick, NJ: CAWP, August 1999.

———. *Women in State Legislatures 1999.* New Brunswick, NJ: CAWP, May 1999.

———. *Women in the U.S. Congress 1917–2001.* New Brunswick, NJ: CAWP, January 1999.

The New York Times Company. "A Look at Voting Patterns of 115 Demographic Groups in House Races." *The New York Times,* 1998. <http://www.nytimes.com/library/politics/camp/110998voter3.html>.

———. "The Vote Under a Microscope." *The New York Times,* 1997. <http://www.nytimes.com/library/politics/elect-port.html>.

Women in the 106th Congress

Amer, Mildred L. *Women in the United States Congress 1917–1998.* CRS Report 97-672 GOV. Washington, DC: Congressional Research Service, 1998.

Congress at Your Fingertips: 106th Congress, 1st Session-1999. Merrifield, VA: Capitol Advantage, 1999.

Pope, Charles. "New Congress is Older, More Politically Seasoned." *Congressional Quarterly* 57, no. 2 (January 9, 1999): 60–63.

NOTES ON THE CONTRIBUTORS

Mariam K. Chamberlain is founding president of the National Council for Research on Women. Previously, she served as program officer in education and public policy at the Ford Foundation. Dr. Chamberlain is an economist by training with a Ph.D. in economics from Harvard University. She is also the editor of *Women in Academe,* published by the Russell Sage Foundation in 1998. Compiled under her direction, this report was the culmination of a four-year study of women in higher education, carried out by a 15-member task force.

Katherine Giscombe is the director of research and advisory services for Catalyst, a national, nonprofit research and advisory organization focused on women's private-sector leadership. Dr. Giscombe directs a variety of research projects, including the landmark Women of Color project, which has examined the status, attitudes, and strategies of corporate managers who are women of color. She has authored articles for academic publications and has delivered academic presentations on a variety of topics, such as the influence of race and environment on policy implementation in human service organizations. Before joining Catalyst, Dr. Giscombe conducted market research for Fortune 500 companies. She also has served on the board of the New York Association of Black Psychologists. Dr. Giscombe received her B.A. in psychology and her doctorate in organizational psychology from the University of Michigan.

Lois Gray is the Jean McKelvey–Alice Grant Professor of Labor Management Relations Emeritus at the New York State School of Industrial and Labor Relations, where she served as associate dean. Among the innovative programs inaugurated under her leadership is Cornell's Institute for Women and Work. In 1998, Dr. Gray received the Cook Award for her contributions to women at Cornell University.

Her published works deal with women and minorities in the labor force, labor economics, labor-management relations, and union structure and government.

Ruth B. Mandel is director of the Eagleton Institute of Politics at Rutgers University, where she also holds a faculty appointment as Board of Governors Professor of Politics. As a senior scholar, Dr. Mandel writes and speaks widely about women and leadership, with a special emphasis on women candidates, women in office, women's political networks, and the gender gap. Her book, *In the Running: The New Woman Candidate,* published in 1983, describes women's experiences campaigning for political office. Since 1991, Dr. Mandel has been a member of the U.S. Holocaust Memorial Council, the governing body of the Holocaust Memorial Museum in Washington, DC. In 1993, President Clinton named her vice chairperson of the council's board. Dr. Mandel holds numerous awards for her pioneering research, education, and public-service activities focused on women's political leadership.

Lesley Primmer Persily has worked on public-policy issues affecting women since 1981. In 1995, she cofounded Women's Policy, Inc. (WPI), where she served as president until 1999. Earlier (1989–1995), Ms. Primmer Persily was executive director of the Congressional Caucus for Women's Issues. She also served as a legislative representative for Planned Parenthood Federation of America and as legislative director for Olympia Snowe when Senator Snowe was a member of the House. Ms. Primmer Persily, who has a master's degree in women's studies from the George Washington University, first came to Capitol Hill in 1981 as a WREI public policy fellow. She is currently a public policy consultant for governmental and nonprofit organizations.

Jean Stapleton, chair of WREI's board of directors, has starred in many plays, motion pictures, and television productions. She has served on the council of Actors' Equity Association. Long committed to, and active in, the women's movement, Ms. Stapleton was a commissioner for the National Women's Conference in Houston, Texas, and a leading proponent of the Equal Rights Amendment. She was deeply involved in the successful effort to have Val-Kill, Eleanor Roosevelt's home, declared a national historic site.

Sheila W. Wellington is the president of Catalyst, a national, nonprofit research and advisory organization focused on women's private-sector leadership. Ms. Wellington joined Catalyst in 1993 after six years at Yale University, where she was the first woman to serve as university secretary and vice president. Previously, she worked in the public-health arena for over 20 years, serving on the faculty of Yale Medical School and as director of two major mental health facilities. As president of Catalyst, Ms. Wellington regularly addresses national and international leaders on women's leadership issues. She is a trustee of the Nuveen Select Portfolios and a director of the Business Council of New York State, the Institute for Women's Policy Research, the Tri-State United Way, and other nonprofit institutions. A Phi Beta Kappa graduate of Wellesley College, Ms. Wellington received concurrent master's degrees in public health and urban studies from Yale, and has served on presidential, federal, and state boards and commissions.

Judith Youngman is an associate professor of political science at the U.S. Coast Guard Academy. She previously served as a visiting associate professor of social sciences at the U.S. Military Academy (1978–1981) and as a senior public-affairs executive at Pfizer Inc., Merck & Co., Inc., and Rhone-Poulenc Rorer. Dr. Youngman is the author of several books, articles, and papers in international business, military studies, and political science. She is the coauthor of *Keeping America Competitive: Employment Policy for the 21st Century,* published in 1995, and author of the forthcoming *Women in the Twenty-first Century Military.* Dr. Youngman frequently serves on policy advisory committees to the federal government and international organizations. She was a member of the Defense Advisory Committee on Women in the Services (DACOWITS) from 1995 through 1997, and served as its chair in 1997.

About the Women's Research and Education Institute (WREI)

Susan Scanlan, *president*
Anne Kuh, *accounting associate*
Lory Manning, *director, Women in the Military project*
Brigid O'Farrell, *senior fellow*
Anne J. Stone, *senior research associate*
Vanessa R. Wight, *research associate*

The Women's Research and Education Institute (WREI), established in 1977, is an independent nonprofit organization in Washington, D.C. WREI gathers, synthesizes, and analyzes policy-relevant information on issues that concern or affect women, and serves as a resource for federal and state policymakers, advocates for women, scholars, the media, and the interested public.

WREI's projects include:

- *The American Woman,* a series of books, published biennially, about the status of women. This volume is the eighth in the series.
- Congressional Fellowships on Women and Public Policy. By means of the fellowship program, which is open to graduate students with strong academic skills and a proven commitment to equity for women, WREI enhances the research capacity of congressional offices, especially with respect to the implications of federal policy for women. Now in its twentieth year, the WREI fellowship program has given more than 200 women hands-on experience in the federal legislative process.
- Women in the Military. This project monitors the status of women in the U.S. armed forces and gathers and disseminates research findings and data about military women and the issues that concern them. Biennial conferences serve as important vehicles for sharing and disseminating information. The most recent of

these have involved women in the uniformed civilian services—such as firefighting and police—as well as women in the armed forces.

- Hire A Vet, She's a Good Investment. This project aims to improve civilian career opportunities for women leaving the armed forces, both by making employers aware that women veterans represent a pool of skilled and committed workers, and by helping employers find women veterans with the right skills and experience for the job.
- Women's Health. Women's health and policies to improve it have been concerns of WREI for many years. They were the focus of the fifth edition of *The American Woman* (1994–95), as well as of *Women's Health Insurance Costs and Experiences* (1994), *The Health of Mid-Life Women in the States* (1998), and several other WREI publications.
- More information about WREI projects and publications can be found on our website at http://www.wrei.org.

BOARD OF DIRECTORS

INDEX

Page numbers in *italics* refer to figures and tables.

About the Editors

Cynthia B. Costello is an independent consultant and former research director for the Women's Research and Education Institute (WREI) where she served as senior editor for the fifth, sixth, and seventh editions of *The American Woman*. Dr. Costello's previous positions include director of research at the American Sociological Association, director of employment policy at Families USA Foundation, and director of the Committee on Women's Employment at the National Academy of Sciences. She is the author of *We're Worth It! Women and Collective Action in the Insurance Workplace* and a number of policy reports on employment, health care, and income security issues. She holds a B.A. in sociology from the University of California and both an M.S. and a Ph.D. in sociology from the University of Wisconsin. Dr. Costello lives in Bethesda, MD, with her husband, Peter Caulkins, and their son, Michael.

Anne J. Stone is senior research associate at WREI, where she has authored or co-authored policy analyses on various subjects, including women's employment and the economic situation of older women. She has worked on all seven of the previous editions of *The American Woman,* and coedited the fourth, fifth, and seventh editions. Ms. Stone lives in Washington, DC, with her husband Herbert Stone. They have two grown daughters and two granddaughters.